Barry Pilton was born in 1946
College and King's College,
Street as a journalist for the *Sunday Post*. Before becoming a free-lance writer in 1976 he trained unsuccessfully as a surveyor, a fork-lift truck driver, a furniture removal man, a cooking-oil oper-ative, and a dish-washer; on days off he travelled extensively in Europe, the Middle East, North Africa and the USA. Since 1984 he has lived in mid-Wales.

Barry Pilton's TV work includes the plays *Everyone a Winner* and *Slimming Down*, and the sitcoms *Downwardly Mobile* (co-written with Alistair Beaton) and *Shelley*. Extensive radio work ranges from Radio 3 talks to Radio 4 documentary series, sketch shows and situ-ation comedy. He is also a regular broadcaster on Radio 4's *Fourth Column*, occasional contributor to *Country Living*, and editor of the *Breconshire Naturalist* (circulation 800 and rising). He has also written *One Man and His Bog*, *One Man and His Log* and *Miles of London*.

'For those of us who never quite made it to Paris with Henry, Arthur or Max Miller, nor yet any of the Hemingways ("When I reach for my gun I hear the word culture"), this is a wonderfully entertaining account of what it was like to be there instead with Barry Pilton. His *événe-ments* of 1968 will live as long as General de Gaulle himself'
Sheridan Morley

'Piltdown Man was a fake, but Pilton Man is the genuine thing – puzzled, wistful, observant, charming, comic'
Miles Kington

AN INNOCENT ABROAD:
THE PARIS YEARS

Barry Pilton

CORGI BOOKS

AN INNOCENT ABROAD: THE PARIS YEARS
A CORGI BOOK : 0 552 99717 X

First publication in Great Britain

PRINTING HISTORY
Corgi edition published 1997

Copyright © Barry Pilton 1997

The right of Barry Pilton to be identified as the author of
this work has been asserted in accordance with sections 77 and 78
of the Copyright Designs and Patents Act 1988.

Set in 11/12¼ Monotype Bembo by
Phoenix Typesetting, Ilkley, West Yorkshire

Corgi Books are published by Transworld Publishers Ltd,
61–63 Uxbridge Road, London W5 5SA,
in Australia by Transworld Publishers (Australia) Pty Ltd,
15-25 Helles Avenue, Moorebank, NSW 2170
and in New Zealand by Transworld Publishers (NZ) Ltd,
3 William Pickering Drive, Albany, Auckland.

Reproduced, printed and bound in Great Britain by
Cox & Wyman Ltd, Reading, Berks.

For Janice

ACKNOWLEDGEMENTS

I would like to thank Alistair Beaton and Paul Ashton for their advice and assistance in keeping my life entertaining yet grammatical. And I am indebted to Sue Jones who forsook her sheep to put these pages on disc.

This book was previously broadcast on Radio 4 under the title *Chocolate Nuns and Firebombs*.

CHAPTER 1

Paris was never part of the plan. Paris was to have been but a pit-stop. As the out-of-work waiters dropped me in the dark rush-hour chaos of place de la Concorde, my mind was fixed on Germany, land of the *Gastarbeiter*. I had come from London to Paris the long way round, via Istanbul, Jerusalem and North Africa, and ever since Spain I had been in desperate need of an economic miracle. The franc was the last of seventeen currencies to trickle wantonly through my fingers, and my only hope left was to make it to the nation whose streets were, according to Sixties legend, paved with work permits.

For weeks, I had dragged my baggage north through France's ice and snow in search of the financial grail. And as the mercury fell, so morale had dropped off the dial. I continued to clutch my fraying map open at *Deutschland* – a far-off country where I had once changed trains as a boy – but disaster upon disaster slowly turned my trek into a journey of Napoleonic folly. And now, just ten months after tacking my running-away-from-home note to the family banisters, I found myself alone and cold and miserable in an unknown city. It was a wet, windswept February night, and all I had was a phone number.

The fairy-tale summer had finally ended in December. Its last rites were on a Barcelona beach, by a late-night bonfire, over a shared bucket of very salty mussels. For seven days I had tried to leave Arenys del Mar; on seven mornings I had said my farewells, and on seven nights I had said my hellos again. My grasp of

9

mañana would have qualified me for naturalization. But it was not just weak will, it was a severe attack of the metaphysics. I had lapped the Mediterranean, broadened the mind by several feet, got to know about life, got to hear about death, and yet still my adolescent existential crisis was far from resolution: where, indeed, *was* I going?

Everybody else, it seemed, was going south, or preparing to go south, or talking about going south; the rooms of the big, antiseptic *albergue de juventud* echoed daily to so many foreign pipedreams and escape plans that only a black pianist would have been needed for a *Casablanca* remake. An unlikely postwar Rick's Bar, the modern brick building was a focus for the new generation of exiles, the backpacking dispossessed, as they paused to regroup after their flight from the horrors of bourgeois capitalism; strategically placed on the main escape route from the Riviera, each winter the youth hostel found itself a refuge for the new radicals, on their way to seek a freer life of sun, sand and sex in a non-exploitative environment with potential for personal growth and hashish. The fact that I already had three continents under my belt, as well as wide experience of sun and sand, did little to diminish my envy; the sights and sounds of people leaving on a journey, especially a journey to their dreams, offer a virtual guarantee of discontent.

It certainly got right up both nostrils of the warden, a man who saw himself not as a Bogartian bar owner but as an *Obersturmführer* with a heel-clicking walk and tank accessories. Spain was at that time marching into its fourth decade of dictatorship, and in a country where Franco was alive and sick and glowering from every wall, where sober louts in uniform had not yet given way to drunken louts in T-shirts, a youth hostel was still seen as a military posting. A zealot, and a disciplinarian for whom a love of wild flowers was not – as in England – a qualification for the job, he would stride through his over-polished, hippy-packed domain like a man who had discovered the last Republican redoubt of the Civil War. Principal among his areas of jurisdiction was foreign hair, and on the day before my arrival he had called out the Emergency Hair Section of the

Guardia Civil, who – sirens wailing, no doubt – had corralled three over-hairy Germans and baton-charged them to a barber.

Yet his act of animal brutality to me on my first night was to set in motion events that, in one of this century's rare plus points for fascism, were ultimately to transform my life.

If cleanliness is next to godliness, punctuality is next to Führerliness, and hostellers, like trains, were expected to run on time. Sleep – head-hitting-pillow sleep – was scheduled at 22.00 hours. And each night as that hour approached, the warden would make his rounds, locking the gates, bolting the doors, plunging the ping-pongers into darkness in mid-smash. It was a two-storey building, impersonal and square, yet curiously generous in its proportions, reflecting that totalitarian taste in architecture which requires even a toilet to look triumphal. The dormitories were on the second floor, a series of identical eight-bunked rooms, but remarkable in that they faced each other across a corridor of such width that its only obvious use was for holding a march past.

I was the last to finish washing (and judiciously trimming those parts of my hair and beard which might be considered a threat to the State), and by the time I got back to my room my seven bunk-mates were already trussed up in their sleeping-bags.

I pottered for a moment, doing the usual household traveller's chores, scraping the mould off my soap, standing my towel on end, and then, before seeing to my bed on the remaining lower bunk, I decided to get a glass of water. I turned to go out – and found the door blocked by the warden, by his part-time understorm-trooper and by a very large Alsatian dog, straining viciously at a very short chain-link leash.

'I was just off to get a drink of water,' I said, in a tone which tried to indicate this position was open to negotiation.

His right arm hurtled out to its full length – with an abruptness which made me think Hitler had just climbed in the window behind me – and, shaking with fury, he thrust his watch under my nose.

'It is von minit passt ten and you vont a drink of vasser?' he shrieked incredulously. (He actually shrieked incredulously in a

Spanish accent, but somehow on paper this looks too much like a temperamental waiter to carry dramatic credibility.)

'No,' I replied, recognizing a rhetorical question when I heard one.

'Bed!' His rigid arm jerked round to point peremptorily at my bunk. I turned to unpack my sleeping-bag.

'Now!' he screamed, and jabbed his forefinger at the bare mattress.

'Yes, but—'

'NOW!' His right-hand man pointed his right hand at the bunk as well, and together they gave a display of synchronized jabbing.

'But . . .' It was a but too far.

I heard a 'Grr!' and then with horror I saw the Alsatian start to advance, teeth bared, into the dormitory. To my disbelief, I realized it had been unleashed. Having only my underpants on, I quickly started to back off – though, on reflection, I would have backed off equally quickly whatever outfit I had been wearing. I looked around desperately for help, but all seven sleeping-bag owners had decided that simulated sleep was the better part of valour. Meanwhile, the gap between the advancing teeth and my travelworn Y-fronts kept narrowing. But my head kept telling me the dog must be bluffing. Then the dog gave another of its Grrs and in my panic I fell backwards into an assorted debris of stale boots and rucksack parts.

The animal approached where I lay by the bed – and paused. The warden gave a brief command. I waited, stiffening, to see if I had just learnt the Spanish for 'Kill!' Deep down, though, a sense of realism told me that this was hysteria on my part, that I had been witness to a misunderstanding, and that the dog would now return to heel. It did not. Instead, in a clearly rehearsed move that was a tribute to the training and discipline of Franco's dog schools, it positioned itself parallel to the bed, raised its rear leg – and urinated comprehensively and hotly over my mattress. All I remember, as I watched, is being curiously impressed by the fact it could piss and growl at the same time. Then it lowered its leg and trotted proudly back to heel.

The two men gave a short, brutish laugh each and left. I lay there in the dark, upended, shaking with fear and anger, and listening to their steel-tipped boots recede down the echoing corridor like twin metronomes.

'Mind-blowing!' said a soft voice from the bunk above mine. And a pair of long, fit-looking legs dangled into view.

A six-foot US presence landed beside me, with none of that nation's usual clumsy scramble, and a firm handgrip raised me to my feet. By the light from the streetlamp I could make out features that called for those corny, improbable adjectives used only of cowboys in Westerns: words like rangy and craggy. I learnt later, to my disillusion, that his secret was tennis, jogging and health foods.

Together we gazed at the bed. 'Jesus!' he said. 'Sure gave that a bladder and a half!' I was only part-way through a long, resigned 'mmm' when he leant over and, with scarcely a muscle spasm, arm-wrestled the still-steaming, pee-ponging mattress dryside up. It was the start of a beautiful friendship which was to endure for over a quarter of a century.

Vernon had dropped out. But he had dropped out from Berkeley. And dropping out from Berkeley in the Sixties was not only par for the course, it was usually part of the course, and could add at least two credits towards a Master's degree. In fact, in that West Coast eye of the world's gathering student hurricane, those who stuck to their studies had to answer the charge of misjudging the cultural climate of the age. Not that Vernon was without the more traditional American eye to the main chance. A student of film (as opposed to films) and, like all cineastes, a man who noticed the camera angles in car chases, his dearest wish was to be a Hollywood luminary; to that end he never went outdoors without at least one project or concept or bankable idea upon his person – just in case he should meet the head of MGM on holiday. Even in darkest Africa, to which he was languidly *en route*, he claimed to have kept a marketable termite-free first draft of a children's soap opera in his backpack pocket. As early as the next morning's communal teeth-brushing, I could sense that life and travels with him would not be dull, but I resisted his offer to hang around – my path, I said, was onwards and homewards.

I did, though, accept an offer to say a parting 'hello' to his travelling companion. Of her, I already knew three interesting things before breakfast.

One, her origins were grand, lairdly and tartan-blooded; two, her family's emigration to the land of opportunity had been financed by the sale of the family castle; and three, Vernon had first set eyes on her in a friend's front room – when she had casually walked stark naked across it to introduce herself. (The Californian lifestyle has much to be recommended in its refreshing informality.)

That morning, however, Diana was fully clothed – a fact I blamed on Franco – when our eyes met across the crowded breakfast-room. Even at twenty-two she was an effortlessly imposing figure. Scottish ancestry and American food had produced a stunningly statuesque end result: very tall, with tumbling reddy-brown hair, she had a body worthy of a plinth, a face with immoderately bold cheek-bones, and an unexpectedly diffident, gentle smile. It was the start of a quarter of a century of unrequited lust – but much-requited friendship.

My 'hello' stretched to a coffee, and the three of us sat together along a wooden bench. Vernon narrated – and produced and directed – my shaggy Alsatian story (in which he seemed to see great potential for a cult B movie); Diana revealed that she too had dropped out – though not, I felt, from educational dissatisfaction or political disaffection so much as from a commitment to full-time hedonism; and I passed on a few handy hints about large North African insects.

As our biographies spilled out, I was struck by how strangely the two of them gelled as a couple – he, the New World rugged hustler, mean-streetwise and yearning to climb the greasy LA pole and see his name on billboards; she, the free-loving, rose-complexioned Old World beauty, from a family who had run the Empire, and whose great-aunt had thought nothing of shooting a small tiger for Sunday lunch. It was the stuff of A-movie scripts – and it captivated me. But even so, I resisted, reluctantly, her offer to hang around – my path, I said again, was onwards and . . . homewards.

'But you haven't met Walt yet!'

'. . . Walt?'

'You must meet *him*! You'll love him! Walt really *is* something else!'

The idea of someone even higher up the hierarchy of something-elseness proved enough to further delay my departure. I agreed to stay just a little longer to meet the third of the travelling trio. Unexpectedly, though, this took the rest of the day. Walt, yet another graduate from the school of drop-outs, was resident, for reasons not immediately clear to me, in a five-star hotel in Barcelona, some twenty minutes down the track. We filled a string bag with oranges and took the compulsively whistling two-coach train along the beach to town.

Walt's problem, they explained, was total poverty. All he had in the world was a Gold American Express card. And *that* was his father's. (But fortunately the signature ran in the family.) Consequently, Spain being still somewhat new to a credit-card lifestyle, poor Walt had found himself forced to hitchhike, desperate and famished, from one de luxe hotel to the next.

But Walt did not disappoint, he had not been oversold by his friends. Vernon and Diana, both in knee-holed dirty denim, strode ahead of me into the glitzy lobby with the egalitarian self-confidence which enables Americans to wander into anywhere in the world and immediately complain about the service – and there waiting for us was the exquisite sound of a flute. What seemed like an improvised twiddly bit brought it to a sudden end, and the small, intense young performer, dressed in maestro black, hurried eagerly over to greet us. 'Mozart!' he cried, and without further ado we all had a second breakfast at the expense of absent Walt senior.

Walt junior's origins needed little detective work. Thirty nervy seconds into the fruit juice, and one knew he was not from laid-back surfing stock; he had East Coast neuroses stamped all over him. He veritably twitched with nervous energy. Indeed, Walt was not made for sitting: he came from New York, the city where one is only motionless on a psychiatrist's couch or a mortuary slab. But he was much, much more than just anguished urbanite.

In its basics, his was a familiar family story: sensitive Jewish boy wishes to be world-famous musician, practical Jewish parents want for him the security of the real-estate business. Except that in his case, he had real talent. And unreal parents. Theirs was not the orthodox Jewish tradition of honest thrift and hard graft: Prohibition had given them a bootleg up. At the family home on the Hudson, on a stretch where the river used to flow dark and secret at night, there was – in the Twenties – to be found a little-used, yet unusually large, swimming-pool. Little-used because, in an operation worthy of Al Capone, and in a style worthy of *The Great Gatsby*, its contents were 90° proof. Whilst normal families have wine in the cellar, and drink it by the bottle, Walt's had whisky in the pool – and sold it by the boat. Such a background had not made the family sympathetic to the flute; indeed, although Walt was never explicit about current dynastic details, one sensed the key to the flight and the fraud lay in the likelihood that his family had a career mapped out for him at the luxury end of the knee-capping business.

The account of this unconventional musical life story left me sitting in silence. It was nice to eat in an establishment which did not signal the end of breakfast by setting dogs on you, and great to do it in such convivial company, and wonderful to be welcome . . . but . . . yet . . . as the food settled, and stories were swapped, and laughter shared, I began to realize that deep down I was feeling troubled. It had been an eventful and colourful twelve hours.

And that was the trouble.

In nineteen years in a South London suburb I had seen less of life than in the last twelve hours. It was a suburb once described by its one famous son, Kingsley Amis, as only existing 'because the train had to stop *somewhere*!' The only moment of real excitement in Norbury had been the arrival of sodium streetlamps. Even the dogs died of boredom. And now I was going back.

Walt picked up his flute and, saying the bodegas were

beckoning, he sort of jigged out into the street. 'Recital time!' he grinned. It was the slightly fazed grin of Catalan culture shock. Upon hitting town a week ago he had, in a burst of adolescent *joie de vivre*, tooted his flute as he wandered along the street. In New York, the Muggers' Association would give 2:1 against the flute ever reaching his lips. In Barcelona, the crowd which gathered were trying to put money *into* his pocket! And so now he was hoping to build up a concert circuit of bars in the Ramblas, the Catalans' Greenwich Village.

'Coming?'

It is not often one gets asked to join the world's smallest claque. I decided to put off leaving town, just for the one day.

Few cities have found the magic recipe for making a *demimonde* warm and vivid enough to live up to the expectations of literature; the standard ingredients are, of course, artists, aesthetic slums, petty criminals, *femmes de nuit* with hearts of gold, never-closing cafés and several ladlings of sleaze, but the exact proportions are a mystery to all except the likes of Rabelais and Runyon.

Nonetheless, whatever mix is needed, the Ramblas had it. As Walt and Diana and Vernon and I made our way into the old quarter, along Lorca's favourite street in all the world, we found there was scarcely a corner or a kiosk or even a cobblestone without some temptation; we could have our palms read, our portraits painted, our penises pleased (*pace* Diana); we could watch street performers – everything from canaries to fleas – and pavement artists worth an Arts Council grant; and we could still take in half a dozen murals and an alfresco mime show without stirring from a sangria. No census form could possibly have coped. Every single inhabitant seemed to be at the forefront of culture, from declamatory poets and abstract jewellers to Picasso paint-alikes and performance artists doing unusual things with body fluids – even the prostitutes were transsexual transvestites, involved in some of the most avant-garde movements in sex. Like the cave of a kinky Aladdin, the Ramblas was the sort of place where 'normal' was a dirty word.

The day confirmed my worst fears. Eight months of 'seeing

the world' had not exorcized a single wanderlust demon, not cured so much as an itchy toe. I was not ready to go back.

All that day long, and all that week, Walt busked. Buskers in Barcelona were two a peseta – they came not as single entertainers, but as battalions – and we ranged the Ramblas and beyond for music-free zones. Walt insisted on the classics, an uphill repertoire in the docks, and he frequently faced unexpected competition in the bars – rarely does a virtuoso have to compete with an off-duty circus clown who, in the middle of a slow movement, taps him on the shoulder and removes two eggs and a tangerine from his left ear. But Walt's intensity and transparent talent won over most of the audiences, and emptied much of their pockets; it certainly enabled him to turn down our offer to form a backing maracas group. Meanwhile, deep down inside me, all was discordancy.

And then, as the days passed, and we fell to chatting as travelling minstrels do, I began to realize they were not quite the free-wheeling globe-trotters of my romantic imaginings. They had not so much burnt their boats as singed them. Each had a clear European plan. After their winter travels, Vernon was intending to enrol in a European film school, Walt was hoping for acceptance at a European music academy, and Diana was planning research into her Scottish roots. They were all into serious residence. It was only I, the true Brit, who was racing aimlessly around my home continent like some displaced character from an American road movie; somehow, stopping – rather than auto-stopping – on my cultural doorstep had been too obvious to ever enter my mind. But now, slowly, I felt the first small waves of a sea change breaking over my life, and the thought of actually **living** *sur le continent*, stationary, in one place, with an address, residentwise, started to take fuzzy shape.

Then, without warning, on the seventh day of procrastination, I received a sign, a vision, a phantasmagoric revelation – and, in a Damascene Road moment lasting one and a half hours, the die was cast! (It was preceded, admittedly, by an excess of cheap red wine.) In a happy, slightly silly mood, we had set off after lunch, up through a maze of winding alleys, to see Gaudi's

Parc Guell. The Sixties like to claim Gaudi, the Catalan answer to Art Nouveau, as the world's first hallucinogenic architect; his unique and gigantic Gothic structures seem to owe more to the laws of LSD than to gravity. Of his park we knew *nada*.

As we climbed up through the tiny back streets our unsteady, and somewhat showy, progress began to attract the attention of urchin truants. Walt's rendition of a Sousa march bounced well off the plaster-patched walls and proved an infant crowd-puller, its notes echoing again and again into a gathering mist; our own messy attempts to master the mouthpieces of the wineskins appealed to the comic end of the gamin market. It was a longer haul than expected and by the time we arrived we had an entourage of over twenty . . . and the mist had thickened.

It was the children who guided us into Parc Guell.

Nothing on this earth could prepare one for Parc Guell – not even the description 'at once a funfair, a petrified forest, and the great temple of Amun at Karnak, itself drunk, and reeling in an eccentric earthquake'. And Sacheverell Sitwell was sober. On every side wild Gothic grotesqueries, even giant decorative lizards, loomed like hallucinations out of the mist, fantastic parabolic-arched doorways beckoned, vast classical columns threatened, and inset everywhere gaudy Gaudi ceramics flashed and glittered. It was as if, like Alice, one had gone through a looking-glass into another world, but a world where – in a phrase soon to become famous – the imagination had seized power.

Then, as I wandered entranced, wondering whether it was I or the world that was drunk, I heard subliminally through the mist the haunting strains of 'Danny Boy'. And, like an apparition, I saw Walt dance light-footedly into view . . . at the head of a seemingly unending line of ragamuffins, no longer jeering or joking, but leaping gently, intently, in his footsteps, as though all their life they had been waiting for the Pied Piper to come, to call. Silently, but with a shiver ruffling my neck-hairs I, and Vernon, and Diana, joined the serpent-like line, as it weaved in a magical mystery tour through the grottoes and the gardens of Gaudi's fantastical mind. Round and round we went, the Pied

Piper of Brooklyn and the baby bovver-boys of Barcelona, past the caves and the rocks and the animals, in and out and about the vast Hall of Columns, and finally through into fairy-tale land, where, exhausted, and dazzled by the glint of a million ceramics, we circled the marzipan and gingerbread House of Grimm. And then we collapsed upon the ground, and lay in silence as the drifting mist rose, revealing all Barcelona below us.

I knew it then. My future had been decided. I had heard the Voice of Gaudi. And he had said 'Never Norbury No More'. Or words to that effect. I now *knew* that I was not going back.

We built a bonfire on the beach that night. It was the last night for all of us. To give the occasion a touch of class we filled a bucket with mussels and unscrewed a bottle of fizzy white wine. Yet it was not the jolly, somewhat romantic scene of fictional farewells. We were all rather sad, deep in private reflections, as we stood in the flickering dark, gazing into the orange-box embers. A pervasive drizzle had begun to fall at dusk, and we had our anoraks zipped against an unforeseen chill; the one glow of homely warmth came from the lighted train-carriages that occasionally racketed past, spreading our shadows across the wet sands to the cold sea. Winter was coming south, a vicious, hard winter that was driving all the easy-living drifters before it.

'Will they like the flute in Africa?' asked Walt.

'Oh yes!' I replied. 'Especially if you get yourself a cobra.' Walt smiled. He smiled rarely, his brow so permanently furrowed by thoughts of his music that I half-expected his worry-lines to develop minims and crotchets.

'Is that what's called subtle English humour?' asked Vernon.

Diana squeezed my arm affectionately. 'Give him a snake-bite!' she said. We all laughed.

It was not that funny, but somehow it seemed the sort of night for feeble jokes and excess laughter.

We gave up on the mussels. Diana, who knew about such things, said they needed lemon juice.

The bottle went round one more time. Then we exchanged addresses.

In the fading firelight I hugged each of them. This time the farewells were for real. I was making an early start. I was not to know it then, but over the years, over the decades, we would meet and re-meet, in different cities and different continents, and in very different circumstances. At that moment, though, my feelings were those of someone who, floating free, has been briefly caught up in the orbit of a larger body, and then been flung out along a new, unknown course into deep space.

We kicked sand over the fire and started to walk back to the hostel.

CHAPTER 2

I bent double in agony as I struggled to reach the white aluminium chair. I did not know whether to be glad or sorry there was no-one to see me in the deserted village square. Outside the darkened café were several dozen chairs, many with their legs upturned on tables as they waited for the dawn. I gripped the cold metal rim fiercely as I gasped for breath, my empty stomach pulsating with pain. Clouds of crackling brown leaves swirled chest-high across the cobbles, and somewhere overhead a loose shutter smashed repeatedly against a wall as the savagery of the gathering mistral tested the seriousness of its hinges. As I was jerked double again, I remembered the glass of iced water I had unwisely downed in one – and the food that I had not downed all day. I tried sitting, I tried squatting, and crouching, and bending, I even tried lying, but there seemed no easy cure for stomach cramps – and the odds were on a long wait. I was soon shivering: icy wind outside, iced water inside, is not a good combination at three in the morning, in the foothills of the Spanish Pyrenees.

I had broken my own golden rule, tried to hitchhike on through the night, and this was the penalty. Sunny Nice and a hauntingly exquisite young girl were to have been the prize. Nice! Again I ran through the names of the towns to come: Nice . . . Grenoble . . . Annecy . . . Paris . . . Strasbourg. I found myself wondering if a code-breaker could unravel their common thread. It was not the most logical route to Germany, to the pot of gold at the end of the traveller's rainbow.

A row of fairy lights, still on, hung incongruously over the historic, almost medieval, square; yo-yoing frantically on their wire, like corks in invisible rapids, the coloured bulbs cast improbable, leaping glows over their ancient surroundings. Below them, the awnings thwacked noisily and tugged like frustrated spinnakers at their fastenings. And everywhere the leaves scuttled to and fro in endless tumbling flurries. Yet in the midst of all this sound and fury, the old square itself – each building seemingly the life's work of a monumental stonemason – exuded an eerie immobility. Throughout the square there was nobody to be seen, no late drunkard, no furtive trysters (they still trysted in Sixties' Spain), no upstairs light, not even a dog with a windswept tail between its legs. It was my own private showing of the storm.

I had folded myself double, like a rug, over the back of the chair. My stomach was unreachable under the tightly zipped layers of anorak – all I could do was wait for the thirty yards of ice in my intestines to melt. Again I tried to focus on the future . . . Nice, Grenoble, Annecy, Paris, Strasbourg. Germany. A tiny disintegrating green address-book, tucked tightly against my passport, held the doorkey, I hoped, to all these cities. I felt as though I were engaged in a wartime dash for freedom, and here were my safe houses. But these beds and boards were not an upshot of the usual hastily scrawled scraps of hieroglyphics, those fickle promissory notes that are the standard holiday bounty of a thirty-second conversation with a camel-driver or a ten-pint session in some dimly-lit bar. These were kosher addresses – indeed, as kosher as can be. Halfway round the Mediterranean, halfway through the summer, I had earned my keep as a kibbutznik – and on that kibbutz I had been the only Anglo-Saxon among a visiting force of some twenty French students. When a man labours six long weeks in the living hell of a banana plantation he forges profound, enduring human bonds which . . . My mind was just drifting back to the steamy heat of summer when the icy blast of winter made me moan and the mistral upended a loaded litter bin which cannoned into my legs.

The unreality of the setting – I felt I had stumbled on the

home town of the *Marie Celeste* – was strangely heightened by the great beauty and even greater detail of its architecture. And as, on the bonging stroke of four, the week's rubbish flew at knee-cap height past the village memorial's list of war dead, I began to wonder whether Buñuel was treating me to a private joke. My twenty-third hour without food or sleep easily encouraged drowsy fantasies, and I was soon half-convinced that my last driver had left me not in a village but on an elaborate film set, whose crew had gone to their beds forgetting to turn off the wind-machine.

I also began to drowsily fantasize about Nicole, now less than a day's lifts away in Nice, and last seen more than two thousand miles away in Israel. It had, in fact, been four o'clock in the morning when we first met (and, by one of those curiously symmetric quirks of fate, it had been with a violent stomach-ache that we had last parted). It was one of the few first meetings at which I had saved someone's life and I liked to think this created a favourable impression. Indeed, single-handedly I had rescued her from death by scorpion. Admittedly, there was no arm-to-arm combat – as I opened Nicole's hut door, it had simply run off into the night – but I got the clear feeling the thing was waving its pincers in surrender as it passed by. My first view of Nicole was her standing barefoot on the rough wooden floor, wearing only a nightdress and with her arms stretched taut above her head, grasping a large broom in the kill mode; this was the position which she had held for half the night, transfixed with horror by the unblinking, unrelenting stare of the scorpion as it crouched, exposed by the blanket she had folded back, on the warm whiteness of her bed. A slight, fragile figure, Nicole had been too terrified to strike lest she missed and the creature scuttled to a site unseen, there to plan a revenge attack.

She was excused that first day in the bananas. But my role was the early-morning alarm-call, or tractor-toot, for the banana gang – banana days began and ended so early because plantation humidity rose so quickly – and we continued to yawn at each other on a regular basis. Life in a plantation, however, is back-aching, fetid and sweaty, and conversation, let alone

24

communion, finds little fertile ground; garrotting the old growth (the 'grandma' shoots) was the main daily grind, and this act releases a stench so overpoweringly anti-social as to relegate skunk's piss to the status of an eau-de-Cologne. Nor was my accommodation – a derelict room in a battered stone watch-tower – ideal for off-duty entertaining. Not only did I share it with the original Ugly American, a crass, brash, beer-belching, baseball-capped, bollock-brained Bronx brat (a person whom I disliked), given to tuneless guitar-strumming thirty-three times a day between and during meals, but it was also, being a building prominent on the area's only hill, equipped with an air-conditioning system made exclusively of bazooka holes – of foreign, and recent, origin. (Kibbutz Barka'i stood on the border at the narrowest and weakest point of pre-'67 Israel, and should Arab forces have decided to invade and split the country in two, they would have come straight through my bedroom – assuming, of course, that Abe's guitar riffs failed to act as a sonic deterrent.)

So, to give our acquaintanceship that little nudge towards something deeper (or, as I saw it in those days, something dirtier), on my last weekend I had invited Nicole to the seaside for a twenty-four hour furlough.

The memory lingered on in the Pyrenean dawn. We had arrived in Natanya at dusk, but still some hours before the hostel closed. The sea at Natanya surfs in thunderously along an immense sandy beach that lies hidden from the road and prying eyes. I disingenuously proposed a frolic in the surf, or there-abouts. I had not been sure until that moment whether we shared a common grasp of the weekend's subtext, but Nicole unhesitatingly, uncomplicatedly, gave a willing smile in response. She did, though, insist on just one preliminary. A hamburger. We were, in fact, both hungry from the journey, and we soon found a little café reeking of onions. There, in earshot of the rollers breaking with noisy sexual symbolism on the beach, we munched our way through two hamburgers, onions and buns, with a side-helping of French fries, and a Jumbo strawberry milk-shake each.

Then we left all belongings behind us and, as darkness fell, I set off with Nicole of Nice towards the sound of the sea and the loss of my virginity. A new moon was coming up, offering just enough of a glow to be a useful visual aid. We made our way down a long grassy inlet, following a nearby dry stream, and then turned southwards along the huge deserted beach. I began to feel slightly queasy. A certain uneasiness gripped my throat. I blamed it on nerves, but when Nicole threw up I realized it was the onions. A few seconds later, the same pole-axing convulsions hit me and I vomited helplessly into the silvery sea. The onions gone, we then came to regret the fries, the milk-shakes and the pair of burgers. After this, we lay on the sand and writhed, we crawled behind a dune and whimpered, we quivered behind a bush and sighed – in short, we achieved all the essential sounds and movements of intercourse . . . but unfortunately we did them separately. Even the stomachs we constantly rubbed were our own. All there was to show for my first serious courtship was a humpy landscape of curious worm-casts sicked up across the moonlit shore, as if testimony to the passage of a rare crustacean.

. . . The pain in my stomach began to ease as the Spanish sun came up. An early rider took me to the border on his Harley Davidson. The mistral had by then become a zephyr. By late afternoon I was on the Riviera.

Nice was immaculate, the most chic, most opulent, most superior city I had yet seen. Had a fifty-franc note blown down any of its boulevards, the fastidious mink-coated citizenry would have put it in a litter bin. In fact, along some of its boulevards I feared my year-old beard and travel-scarred clothes might, under city ordinances, destine me for a similar fate. My little green book of addresses was leading me down ever-grander avenues, thoroughfares not merely washed twice-daily but pomaded and sprayed with a money-scented aerosol.

Worry was replacing pain as I faced up to my new future. It was with apprehension that I worked out the squiggles under N corresponded to a palatial apartment block; and it was with nervousness that I wondered whether '*Viens me voir*' might be the polite, formal French for adieu; . . . but it was with full-blown fear that I realized I would soon have to phone home and announce my lasting exile.

Nicole's mother was as surprised to meet me as I to meet her. Upon sight of her, my expectations of a little flat, a double duvet and an attendant Nicole, went into terminal, detumescent decline. A bed with scorpions, a bedroom with bazooka-holes, a beach with burger-vomit, and now an apartment with mother: I was sadly forced to accept that our coupling was probably not part of Fate's grand scheme.

Nonetheless, her mother could not have been more welcoming. A small energetic matriarch, she fussed me into the wide, high-ceilinged entrance hall and straightaway proposed mint tea. The apartment dated from the turn of the century, its long L-shaped corridor designed for a bygone age when every family had a maid to hide. Such a view soon betrayed my out-of-touch suburban origins – no sooner had I entered the lounge than a maid appeared. As I sat on the Louis-looking chaise longue and partook of the *thé au menthe* and *petits fours* I reflected that there were worse ways to start a life in exile. The rest of the family were out shopping (buying the weekly jewels, I assumed) and we chatted away happily for over an hour while I awaited formal identification. (Ideally, I would like to have been preceded by a favourable version of the Night of The Giant Scorpions story, but apparently Nicole had only mentioned horseflies and lizards.) I can, *in extremis*, give a workmanlike impression of good manners, and, as I sat picking delicacies off the inlaid mahogany side-table, I believe I was able to imply successfully that I was the direct spiritual descendant of the nineteenth-century nobleman on his Grand Tour. I was especially proud of the *bon mot*, 'I always believe the best way to approach a foreign culture is through its *pâtisserie*!!!'

Where Nicole was gentle and shy and sad, her mother was ebullient and full of enthusiasm – particularly, it seemed, for rugs. Rugs figured frequently, indeed well beyond the statistically normal, in our conversation, and until I had grasped that the family were rug and carpet importers I was baffled by her choice of small talk. Fortunately, unlike music and art, there is no cultural stigma attached to rug ignorance; I was able to play that perfect guest, the willing listener, and the last of the wintry daylight passed almost unnoticed as she treated me to an eye-opening exposition of patterns and colours and symbols. Indeed, we were on our hands and knees working through a woof when the door opened and a pile of packages appeared, obscuring all but the occasional arm and leg of her three children.

I was immediately plunged into a warm, lively world, full of family laughter. The thick, velvet curtains were pulled to and the standard lamps switched on as Nicole, more fragilely beautiful than ever now that a green mini-dress had replaced her muddy bananawear, gave me a soft, affectionate hug and introduced me to the family bosom. As an only child, I am always surprised by the flexibility and capaciousness of bosoms that belong to large families: like Nicole's mother, her teenage brother and sister seemed quite unfazed by the arrival of a foreign tramp. Such was their acceptance and unforced hospitality that I felt almost relaxed enough to try an exploratory leg-up on the chaise longue. 'Are you staying?' asked Nicole, as if the decision were mine – and gave me a warm but platonic smile, a clear post-holiday-romance smile. 'Yes, stay for Christmas!' urged her mother.

Christmas? And suddenly I remembered the bouncing fairy-lights, and I realized for the first time that they were festive, and that the parcels piled up around were to be presents . . . and that Christmas was only a few days away.

'Oh, yes, please!' I said. '*Yes, please!*'

I lay in late the following morning. It was not just from fear that the rather severe maid, clearly trained to lay out gentlemen's clothes, looked likely to give all mine to Oxfam the moment I left the room. It was also to put off the first, and most difficult, international phone call of my life. The equivalent of a filial 'Dear John', but person-to-person. Or rather, son-to-father. Or, more precisely, prodigal son to loving father. Non-returning prodigal son. Reversing the charges.

It did not help that I had never been ill-treated nor neglected nor even denied pocket-money. All I had to complain of was excessive love and care. All I had run away from was my father's belief, born of a difficult life, that job security was the cure for all ills. It was to be some years before I would come to appreciate that wanderlust and a notion one might like to be a writer do not inspire great confidence as the building-blocks of a career. With anguish, he saw me on the road to perdition – and indeed in dark hours to come I was to fear he might be right.

From the day I had vanished – a day too painful ever to be spoken of again – until that morning in Nice, I had only communicated by postcard. (I had, though, at least proved myself to be the Barbara Cartland of postcards, sometimes writing several a day, and eventually filling our G-plan sideboard with five large albums.) But slowly their postmarks had edged closer to home shores, and slowly but surely the postman had heightened hopes of the wanderer's return.

It was to dash these hopes that I called the operator. And the fateful connection was made.

'Where are you, son?'

A quiet, shy man, my father's unsuppressed joy triumphed over the crackling of the line.

'Nice.'

'He's in Nice!' I heard him cry to my mother. Yet I knew the news meant no more than a name on the map.

'. . . What's the weather like?'

I marvelled at his restraint. And, as I told him about the weather, I marvelled at mine. But the weather did not hold his interest for long.

'Have you got enough money?'

I knew the phrase so well. That instinctive, compulsive concern for my welfare could have been his epitaph.

'Yes,' I lied.

'Where are you staying?'

'With friends. Rug dealers.'

There was a pause, costing several pounds, which puzzled me. And then he said, with a touch of panic in his voice, 'What . . . pot, you mean?'

29

It was my turn to pause, and in great confusion we had to re-run the conversation several times before the phonetics finally became clear. And then we laughed, a really good, genuine laugh – but in that moment I had had a glimpse of the terrors my solo wanderings were capable of inflicting.

We started to chat, in that awkward long-distance way, about health, about his work, about my postcards, and the ice seemed broken. But in truth it was only cracked. He could only guess at my world and I had no time for his. And thus we skated around each other. And all the while he avoided asking questions, because he feared the answers.

'I'm going to spend Christmas here.'

'I see.' I could hear the disappointment, yet I could feel the stoicism.

'When . . . ?'

'I'm not coming home – not for a while, at least. I'd like you and Mum to send out a suitcase with some more clothes in. You know, clean ones!'

'But what will you do? Why? Where are you going? How will you manage?'

Full-scale alarm began to flood his defence systems, and a torrent of jerky questions poured out. I desperately tried to explain, but I myself was too unsure of the answers, too embarrassed almost by their vagueness, their naïvety, to make any convincing sense. All I could do was say I wasn't ready yet. Wasn't ready for what? I didn't know.

I do not remember whether the struggle was brief or long. All I remember is his final plea, the only plea he ever made, the only time I ever heard him fight back tears.

'Please won't you come home . . . ?'

I turned him down.

We continued to talk perfunctorily, with all the usual unexpressed fondness, for a little while longer. I knew that the phone call must have already cost more than the normal bill for a full quarter in our tidy home life.

He promised the suitcase would be sent. He told me to take

care. And we tried to say goodbye. His last words were 'You sure you're all right for money?'

My new life became more and more headily exotic with every passing day. Nicole's family proved to be not just rug dealers, they trafficked in fabrics of every kind. Nor were they French, but Moroccan. The family was, in that old-fashioned history-book phrase, the merchant class. From Fez and Tangiers and Casablanca and all oases south, they bought and brought the loveliest and most antique of weavings; their exquisite, air-conditioned gallery was a multi-coloured maze of floor-coverings and wall-hangings and ceiling-danglers, each oh so discreetly for sale in the most sanitized souk I had ever seen. The prices were also unique – in a first for alchemy, the family had taken the dazzling colours of the casbah and turned them into gold.

Those twenty-five-hour pre-Christmas days were a poor man's guide on How to Jet-Set. Each evening, another batch of *jeunesse dorée* would drop by, another convoy of high-revving coupés would race off, another target zone of nightspots would be intensively bopped. As someone whose daily budget for fine wines, gourmet meals, cabaret shows, cigars and hat-check girls was (including all other living expenses) fixed at seventy-five pence a day, my first reaction was to be deterred by Mr Micawber's cautionary sums and cry off – claiming a need to stay home and wash my hair, and iron my hair-shirt. But I was advised – and it gave me a sudden sybaritic frisson – that being outrageously pampered was part of my duties as guest. 'Jewish wealth, Arabic hospitality,' murmured Nicole's mother, in an irresistible display of *realpolitik* and charm.

She added sweetly, knowing that I also worried about my inability to afford any presents, '*You* are Nicole's Christmas present, you cheer her up.' I smiled gratefully, but a little wist-fully. Present for Nicole I might have been – and I certainly cheered her up – but I could tell that my chances of being unwrapped by her had ended with the summer. Passion had now come to seem inappropriate – if only because I now knew the secret of her sad face, its precise childlike features vividly made up and mascaraed to hide a tired pallidness.

For two years – she was now twenty-two – Nicole had lived with a lover dying of leukaemia. *Jusqu'à la fin.*

He had died in the spring, and she had gone to Israel to forget. There she had sought someone to love, but her first choice had been too busy with the bananas and too unlucky with the burgers. She had found another. And now the need was gone.

I knew no more than that, I asked no more, but at least I understood her readiness to find cause for mindless laughter, her eagerness to aimlessly dance the night away . . . and her capacity to suddenly melt, helpless, in an embrace. And so I graciously accepted the role of non-paying – and platonic – guest, and I gladly went out on the town.

It wasn't Roma, but it was certainly what I understood by *La Dolce Vita*; I had seen the film and I knew that when a lot of posh, fashionably-dressed people wander drunk around a city all night long they have achieved the ultimate in decadence. Thus it was in Nice, as we hoorayed from joint to joint down its deserted, shining black streets. After ten days of partying, discoing, night-clubbing and sitting in never-closing cocktail bars the length of the Riviera, I felt almost qualified to be the foreign correspondent of the *Tatler*. Evening after evening, I would struggle towards mastery over snails; night after night, immaculate heel-clicking waiters would mix me lethal concoctions of drinks, not one ingredient of which I had ever even sniffed on its own; early hour after early hour, pearl necklaces and loose breasts (yet more objects I was unfamiliar with) would bounce up and down around me, strobe-lit and vibrating to the beat of Petula Clark.

And yet . . . somehow I was not so much participant as spectator in this new world. Perhaps it was language, perhaps it was class, perhaps it was even puritanism. Perhaps it was shyness. Certainly I did not find it easy to dance, partly because the chest measurements of Nicole's younger brother meant that use of his jacket precluded 90 per cent of all arm movements (and certainly the interesting ones) – and partly because I had never danced before (public school having placed girls on the banned substances list). But I also came to realize that there is an innate, effortless confidence to the very rich, even in the retail trade, which no amount of evening classes can teach. So for much of the time I tried to look like a happy wallflower and pretended that alcoholism was my thing. At least vomiting seemed to be classless.

Even to a reluctant roué's palate, though, the final festive fling was a bit extra-special.

It was a wonderfully crisp, starlit night, or, as is known in young Beautiful People's circles, a racing driver's night. Around midnight, a dozen or so of us emerged from a run-of-the-mill Masked Ball and tumbled onto the sea-front. Along the Promenade des Anglais our loosely parked mean machines were gleaming in a line. The Corniche awaited. I was the fourth to pile into the back-pocket of an open-top Alfa – bad for road-holding but excellent for body-holding – and with an extrovert roar the car moved into pole position. Suddenly from nowhere up went the cry, '*Au casino!*' All the two-tone horns blasted out their approval. And Vrrrrrm! With a rousing cheer and a violent clutch-lurch we were off! Off, with our hair blowing in the night wind, our tyres screeching in the skid marks of Cary Grant and Grace Kelly, along the high, winding, much-filmed coast road to Monte Carlo.

The exhilarating sense of speed, the intoxicating smell of Chanel, a silk scarf waving in my face, a silver moon shining on the sea, and a legendary coastline . . . it was all the clichés, and yet it was *still* the journey of one's dreams. And at journey's end was a magic castle.

It was my first casino. I understood none of the games, none of the rules, nor did I want to. Instead, I just gazed, mesmerized, at the candelabra-lit splendour of the super-rich at play. I risked no money, mine or others'; my pleasure was in the peepshow, in watching Mr and Mrs Croesus's idea of a quiet night out. I had never been in the presence of such wealth before – were one loose collar-stud to have rolled my way, I could have financed a trip twice round the world. It was my very first sight of people so rich as to be bored with money, of people so world-weary that one could not tell whether they were becoming overnight millionaires or bankrupts.

And I remained, gawping at the dudes and the dukes, the diamonds and the décolletages, until the first signs of light began to glimmer outside – and Christmas Eve reached the Riviera. Then, the others having lost enough to prove they too were rich, we drove slowly, sensuously, back to Nice as the sun rose in a magnificent, misty red ball over the sea.

Christmas Eve was the big day in the Nicole household. Unlike Santa-fixated Britons, the French traditional belief is in a blow-out, and the Christmas Eve custom is to feast unfettered until midnight and then, without any pretence at Anglo-Saxon self-discipline, to rip open all the presents. Breakfast was almost over when Nicole and I returned, hot from the tiles, to eat the last cold croissant, and already the apartment showed signs of a monster meal in the making . . . and in the marinading, and the whisking, and the chopping, and the blending and the baking. Four generations, from all walks of textiles, were coming to wine and dine that night, to chew the year's fat, to toast the year's profits, and to celebrate the family being twelve months older and deeper in carpets. It was a highlight of their Franco-Arab calendar; even the gossip had to be up to scratch.

It was also a big day in the one-man Pilton household. I had a card from the railway station. My suitcase had arrived. It was a battered old beigey-brown job, and as I hauled it out of the depot I noticed it still had Bognor stickers on its side, the peeling reminders of thirteen summer holidays loyally served at the same boarding-house. Inside it were all the essentials for a new life in Germany: a sports jacket, grey flannels and a sensible pair of brogues. And tucked in one of the pockets were several five-pound notes.

The case's arrival was so well-timed, so prompt and re-assuring, I took it as a clear sign that my plans, my still fuzzy plans, had received the thumbs-up from Fate, that the non-suburban gods had given me the green light. As I unpacked its contents, my clothes still hopelessly outnumbered by the hangers, I felt I had crossed a small Rubicon tributary, and a nervous exhilaration about my future remained with me while I dressed and re-dressed for the grand Christmas dinner, the dinner of celebration.

It was a meal almost worthy of Chabrol, a dynastic set-piece with every leaf of the long dining-table laid for action, and every velvet-backed seat supporting a bourgeois bottom. This particular family occasion, though, was a murder short, and any tracking shot would have revealed little but harmony, the characters and dialogue easily qualifying for a U certificate. On my left sat a bald eighty-two-year-old, who advised me what to look for when buying my first race-horse, on my right sat a seven-and-a-half-year-old, who had a precocity which suggested she would soon be selling her used dolls at a profit, and opposite me sat a dazzling Nicole, who had freshly frizzed her hair for Noël. To this day, I remember the food of that night. It started with the most ambitious programme of *crudités*, from which many a lesser, non-French mortal would have retired burst, and then we tackled several much-decorated giant salmon, and after that we paused for a pear sorbet, *pour mieux sauter* onto the centrepiece of the night: the bird. Each course was brought in by the maid, specially dressed in lacy, nuptial white for the occasion. I can still recall leaning back, smiling at Nicole, as I awaited the climactic entrance of the traditional, much-loved Henry VIII-style turkey. Whereupon over my shoulder came a bird scarcely 4" x 4" x 3", sitting cross-legged on a plate the size of a saucer. At twenty, I had never heard of guinea-fowl and for some years I puzzled over why Riviera society should have such a high regard for pigeons. It was, nonetheless, a delicious pigeon, and came attended by all the vegetables from artichoke to zucchini. Then, unrelentingly, there followed a daunting selection of desserts, an impossible choice of cheeses, and an orchard of fruit which exhausted hyperbole. All around me, as the eating gradually slowed, the talking gathered pace, and the laughter gathered volume, until a truly Christmas spirit of well-fed, well-oiled well-being reigned over the table. The time had come for toasts – and for the only time in my life I and my future were drunk to in Bollinger. No runaway ever had a more auspicious launch. And finally, with midnight nearing, the whole extended, distended family adjourned into deep armchairs for liqueurs and exquisite, outrageously expensive Swiss chocolates.

CHAPTER 3

The cockroach fell out of my lump of day-old baguette as I raised it to my mouth. It landed briefly on the rim of my soup bowl, and then toppled back on to the deeply scored wooden table. As it paused to readjust its legs, there was a brief window of opportunity to hit it with my spoon, but I hesitated too long, being reluctant to tackle a creature allegedly immune to a thermonuclear explosion. Looking evil, the thing scuttled off down the table, ignored by the row of hunched men in overcoats slurping their soup and gnawing at their stale crusts.

'*T'en veux pas?*'

The old, grey-bearded man next to me indicated the bread I had let drop three seconds earlier. I knew its importance. A few minutes before, I had seen two residents dispute the ownership of a very similar-sized lump of baguette, and they eventually had to be separated as they rolled, kicking and punching, across the stone floor. It could have been worse, I thought gloomily. I had read my Orwell. They could have been fighting over the cockroach. I shook my head. The old man seized my bread, wiped it twice round the tidemark of the unidentified soup, and thrust it into his mouth. I prodded at my soup without enthusiasm, wary of what might emerge from the deep.

It was only the second day. The emergency money was expected to take another week.

The municipal doss-house block was functional, impersonal and dispiritingly post-war – a clinical, sterile gleam in some central planner's eye; its bare corridors reeked of anonymity and disinfectant. That said, I was greatly relieved to have a roof over my head, even if it did lack the baroque cornice-work to which I had become accustomed. Outside it was minus twenty and dropping. Grenoble was in the grip of the coldest winter in statisticians' memory. And the entry for Grenoble in my little green book now read 'Moved. Address unknown'. I was stranded. Two hundred laborious miles of blizzards and bus-fares and train-fares, and my German plans were frozen to the drawing-board. My money was gone, my seed-corn husked. And my filial UDI had been swiftly succeeded by an appeal to the parental IMF. It was my darkest, coldest hour.

As I picked my way through the cabbage, I could hear the words of the man from the Pru. He had sat on the edge of our family sofa, his patter strained to breaking point. 'But no-one cashes in a life-policy at *nineteen*!' he kept repeating, incredulously. 'No-one!' He made it sound illegal as well as immoral. 'It's for your security. A nest-egg. For when you're sixty-five.' I had then delivered the standard nineteen-year-old's two-fingered view of security, and of being sixty-five – and insisted upon the immediate surrender of my nest-egg. Which, after eighteen months, had matured to something less than embryonic. Now, as I listened to the sound of watery cabbage being hungrily belched down on every side, I began to succumb, with rising panic, to the belief that the ageing down-and-outs around me all owed their presence in the doss-house to a confident, juvenile rejection of the man from the Pru.

But it was delousing that had scratched deepest into my psyche. Admittedly, it was the affectation of the times to look like a threat to civilization as we knew it. To be derelict was hip, it was the middle-class way to open-road cred. But the key to dropping out was to have the passport for dropping in again. Having unknown council officials examine your private pores for insect life was too much like playing the game for real. Even my personal word, my public-school bond, on licelessness had not protected me from the probing rubber gloves and disinfectant douche. I had slipped off the bottom rung of society's ladder – and, to my horror, society had merely assumed that I was in my natural place, that I probably had – or was destined for – lifelong membership of the tenebrous *bas fonds*. The slippery slope down had been so short, and so slippery, that life never again seemed quite safe. And on many a glad confident morning in future years, I would suddenly feel a passing chill of inexplicable fear.

Each doss-house day was the same. We skidded onto the frozen street at 9.00, we had a buff lunch-voucher for 1.15, we huddled by the central-heating ducts at 5.30. Grenoble in winter had the granite grimness of Aberdeen, and was no city for the lingerer. The background was dominated by mountains, the foreground by block after block of grey stone, icy to the touch, and in every direction the street grid connected the wind to the Arctic – one unfavourable traffic light and a pedestrian could die of hypothermia. And I had just fifty francs left for the next ten days.

War and Peace was my salvation. In little more than pious hope, from little more than schoolboy guilt, I had transported Mr and Mrs Maude's mightily praised three-volume translation of the classic on a journey even longer than that undertaken by Napoleon's army. The exquisite hardback Oxford edition, miniature but perfectly formed, seemed made to measure for a backpack's back pockets, and for months I had carried it with me, saving it for a rainy season. Now, not merely much travelled but mildewed, it was a 1,700-page work whose time had come.

Every morning and every afternoon of every day for ten days I sat in the same window seat of the same café and tried to make *un petit chocolat* last longer than the Battle of Borodino. Tolstoy never had a more determined reader. Art cocooning me from reality, I escaped for eight hours a day into the world of nineteenth-century Tsarist Russia, while outside, in the square beyond the plate-glass, the trees filled up with snow and the statues in the swirling fountain came to bitterly regret their cavalier nudity. I let my mind go, and immersed myself in the silver samovars and gold-leaf salons of the Moscow aristocracy; pondered on the alleged mystical nature of the illiterate Russian peasantry; and watched from a safe distance as the two great armies bloodied each other in the snow. I even made my way safely through the linguistic minefield of patronymics and family names and first names and diminutives (which, unless mastered, allow Russian characters to appear and reappear in bewildering anonymity, like guests at a masked ball); I regularly referred to the pages and pages of historical footnotes; and I once took the trouble to check the length of a verst. The café could have been on Tverskoi Boulevard itself.

Yet I was still not immune to reminders of reality. On the very day when the feared Russian winter at last forced Napoleon to set off on his epic, snow-clogged retreat, I looked up from Tolstoy to discover that, so cold had become the French winter, the great fountain in the square had – in an historic first of its own – frozen solid even as it swirled and flowed. Added to my nightmare world and my escapist world was now a surrealist's world where, with every passing page, a giant snow-capped ice sculpture towered higher and higher above the café – like some priapic Jack Frost, determined that his power over the city should not go unnoticed.

Those ten trance-like days in the window seat, where I sat like an undemanding house guest, were my first, lastingly addictive taste of the civilized joys of the French café. There, I was not a malingering, long-haired layabout, nurturing his lice on free heating, but a serious-minded Man Reading Book. The white-aproned waiter who paid the twice-daily visits to my small marble table displayed an unruffled decorum that would not have been out of place in the British Museum Reading Room. I had yet to fully realize that the French sit in their cafés to eat, drink and be literate; that I was now in a country where opening a book in public is not looked upon as the intellectual equivalent of flashing. Indeed, had I chosen to make notes on my Tolstoy, I could probably have qualified for a cushion. Such a liberal attitude in so materialistic a society was disarming . . . and I found myself wondering about the tolerance extended to book readers in German beerhalls.

The ten nights, however, had no hiding place. The

dormitory of squeaking springs and racking coughs and scarcely human moans offered no asylum. It was two nights before I even slept fitfully. The shadows held yet more shadows, and creeping through them were the incontinent and insomniac.

But amidst the terminal coughers and shuffling no-hopers there were, I learnt, those who still boasted plans for their future; they were down but not, they insisted, yet out.

'I'm a ballet dancer, you know,' said the middle-aged occupant of the next mattress by way of introduction. And with a speed designed to pre-empt even a raised eyebrow, he had dived beneath the bed and emerged with a cardboard box; lighting a match, he revealed its contents to be a pair of somewhat worn ballet shoes. He was a trim, nimble man and I had noticed earlier that his clothes, although also past their best, showed unexpected signs of an iron. I admired his ageing shoes – they were presented like an exhibit for the court's attention – and, clearly gratified, he returned them to their hiding place. 'Once I get to Biarritz, I'll be able to start dancing again. Got a pal runs a club at the casino there. Jimmy's Club. Classy place!' Then, in a second fluent, evidentiary move, he passed the club's card to me; the match now out, I ran my thumb over its embossed name, and tried to sound enthusiastic in the darkness. 'I've had classical training, of course,' he continued, and, as I lay on my back trying not to wonder whether cockroaches fell from ceilings, his conversation became a biography full of dates and places and personal details . . . except the longer I listened, the more I realized that I was not hearing the story of his life, but the recital, the almost formal, much-rehearsed recital, of a man's curriculum vitae.

Night after night he told the same story. Night after night he was no nearer to Biarritz. Gradually my gullibility faded. His public plans were just private dreams. His downfall was owed to a larger Achilles' heel than the fluke weak tendon upon which his story put so much weight. But, as I drifted off to sleep to the whiff of his wine and the reprise of his promise that 'once the weather cleared, he would be off to Biarritz', I was not at all sure whether to admire his attempts at self-respect, or to be saddened by his success at self-deception.

Perhaps this was because, although twenty years his junior, I had heard a faint, unnerving echo of my own hopes of finding the promised land in Germany.

The bus was half empty, and as it climbed into the French Alps above Lake Annecy it swung around the hairpin bends with an insouciance that made possession of a return ticket seem like an act of faith. Yellow headlights blazing, it powered on up through the mist and pines like a bus possessed. Clinging on to its bench seats were the bobble-hatted brigade, all skis and multi-coloured vulgarity, full of loud holiday fun; the art of indoor yodelling was never more popular. I shared much of their excitement. I too was en route to a ski-resort, to the chic snow of Mégève, but with my drab, fusty grey anorak giving me all the glamour of a peahen I had begun to feel already cast in my forthcoming role as washer-up and waiter.

The kibbutz connection at Annecy, the latest link north, had not let me down. My father's last envelope of used readies, which arrived as I was about to start my first volume of *Anna Karenina*, had underestimated the cost of Arctic travel; by the time I made it through to Jean-Paul, another old comrade-in-bananas, it was dispiritingly clear that Germany was still a further envelope away. I was stranded yet again, but no ex-kibbutznik is without influence; after just one evening's table-tennis at the Maison de la Culture and one morning's holiday snaps by the lovely ice-fringed lake, it was announced that family had spoken unto family and thanks to the old-burgher network a nice little earner was awaiting me in the mountains.

Mégève, fashionable resort and winter playpen for the mink-booted, did not look like a real place. With its scattered, immaculate timber chalets, made from what appeared to be giant matches, it looked more like a hobby. The only serious thing in sight was Mont Blanc.

But it looked a good place to make one's fortune – or at least to transfer the wealth of the rich to waiters. As I gazed down the

Alpine valley in the dazzling afternoon sunlight, I could see a decidedly pleasant few weeks ahead – a trainee playboy's life of meal-times on the make and play-times on the *piste*. And money in my emaciated money-bag. Of the job itself, I knew little (a restaurant of the *intime* type, run by rich Parisians who were unexpectedly caught a *garçon* short, was all I had been told) and of waitering I knew even less (it having been a careers option not much discussed at my late public school). Nonetheless, I felt my future life in exile was taking on its first rosy hues.

Nothing in this Toytown-on-sleighs was more than a snowball's throw from the centre, and after only a moment's walk through the slush (the significance of the slush was not to register until the following day) I could see the timber portals of my new employers. Le Maronnier, named presumably after the ex-chestnut-tree responsible for its existence, belonged to the de luxe cabin school of architecture, and had been blended expensively into the bank of a mountain stream. A menu with tasteful copperplate script was nailed, in the style pioneered by Luther, to the large wooden door, as if intended to convey a slightly roguish sophistication. I cleared my beard of lunch and entered.

Inside, the *intime*, tasteful restaurant and bar were deserted, its dozen or so tables laid in waiting for dinner. The artificial lighting off, the premises were in semi-darkness. It was that strange hour when restaurants go into limbo, and a distinctive well-carpeted silence, permeated with faint reminders of smoke and drink, filled my mind with echoes of an abandoned theatre.

'Hallo-o-o!' I called, in a quiet, non-threatening way. There was a comprehensive red ambience to the room: the walls, the tablecloths, the velvet chairbacks, the very candles, all were in tasteful, matching reds. Even in the vermilion half-light, one could see that the thematic decor input had not been cheap. The effect hovered between cosy and oppressive; the designer had clearly wished that, should Mr Poe ever make a reservation, he would feel at home.

'Hallo-o-o-o' I called again.

Somewhere offstage, something slammed. After a faint crash of breaking crockery, a stocky man of about thirty, with close-cropped hair and a dirty apron stained with blood, stomped into the dining area. He ignored my presence, except to growl, in passing, something brief and incomprehensibly foreign, and went straight to the bar. He removed a bottle of spirits and then returned to wherever he had stomped from, his exit succeeded by the distant sound of more slamming. It was not until the following day that I realized I had met the chef and that I now knew the Russian for 'Fuck Off!'

I waited. An age passed. Then the large wooden door opened, casting a streak of warm sunlight over the scarlet surroundings, and an elegant, fully-furred couple entered the restaurant. 'Oh, how chic! A beard!' cried the woman, with a smile and tone that made clear she was addressing her new employee. I smiled back nervously, hoping she didn't want it sprayed red. The man was in his fifties, tall, with hair cover only left on the lower slopes of his skull, and he moved with an aloof, disdainful air; he had a deep tan – that short cut to looking distinguished – which seemed the work (or, I suspected, the idleness) of years. His wife was some ten years younger, still successfully blonde though less successfully *belle*, and seemed to speak and smile for both of them; only the tan appeared to be in joint names.

They gave me their coats to hang up, and then Madame offered me a glass of water, bubbles optional. They looked me over and up and down. My Englishness seemed to be judged a plus, a sort of social magnet in the Haute-Savoie; apparently my Norbury accent would add an extra cultural dimension to the food – presumably earning the establishment a star from Berlitz. My ragged appearance was also thought to have marketing possibilities. Le Maronnier, it was explained, was keen on themed soirées, on fancy-dress evenings, and had a clientèle who would apparently relish the conceptual challenge of poverty. (I considered suggesting a doss-house evening, with the main attraction *coqroach au vin*, but feared my irony would pass unnoticed.) Overall, the unspoken verdict was that my presence could help empty a few more post-*piste* pockets. Madame smiled her smile again. It was terms time.

The good news was that accommodations would be free, that

meals would be provided, that waiters' wear would be supplied, and that I started the next day. The really good news – here Monsieur gave a concurring nod – was that, in accordance with historic French restaurateur traditions, I would receive no wages – but that all the tips, all the manifold tokens of esteem and gratitude, could remain jingling in my own pockets. This, I was told, was how the owners of the Ritz had started.

The audience over, my future assured, I was led through the restaurant to my accommodations. Opening the back door, Madame pointed me to a small, slippery track which led upstream, and wished me good night.

As the door shut behind me, I peered through the fading light and could just make out a small hut at the foot of a large rocky outcrop. I struggled up to it with my suitcase. As I grew closer, I realized it was less a hut, more a garden shed – indeed, almost a privy with pretensions; stylistically unusual for local architecture, it had been constructed from a plywood tree. Reaching its threshold, I shivered. Its site almost permanently out of the sun, there was already – or still? – a smear of frost on its two window-panes.

I pushed the door open; inside there was just enough light to discern there were no lights, only a paraffin lamp. I could decipher the shape of a small table, a small chair, a couple of beds. I ran my finger along the dust on the window – and found the frost was inside as well as out. I closed the flimsy token door and crunched down on to one of the beds. It was not interior-sprung. Once again, Germany seemed a long way off. As did England – and everywhere else in the world. Henceforth, I feared, it would be tips and the generosity of strangers that shaped my life. I sighed miserably, and resolved to raise sycophancy to an art form.

'You are the English?' said a voice.

In my shock, the correct answer escaped me at first. A pair of legs in long johns then emerged from the blanket on the bed opposite.

'Er, yes – yes.'

'Alain.' He leaned across and we shook hands. He had a gentle

45

voice, and as he pumped the paraffin lamp into life its hesitant flares lit up a gentle, sensitive face.

'Dishwasher and barman to the bourgeoisie.'

It made me happy to hear irony again. Later he was to treat me to philosophy, his Sorbonne specialization.

'Don't tell me – you won a scholarship here,' he said, and smiled. He was perhaps twenty-five, yet under his light touch I sensed a sadness and a seriousness beyond his years. But for the moment I had other concerns.

'What are they like to work for, the . . .' I searched for their name.

'*Les salauds?*' The irony was more savage now. 'You don't know them?'

I shook my head.

'Hotel in Portugal, restaurant in the Alps, château in Provence, apartment in Paris – in rue Royale . . .' If he had been a spitter, he would have spat.

'I shan't be staying long. Just till I've saved up enough tips to—'

'—Tips? *Tips?*' He assumed a mocking incredulity. And then he saw my puzzlement. 'Listen!' He raised his hand for silence. 'What do you hear?'

All I could hear was the sound of the rushing mountain stream.

'. . . Nothing . . . Just water.'

'*Exactement!* Except it is not water. It is melted snow.' I still did not understand.

'There is no snow this year in the mountains. No snow – no skiers. No skiers – no tips.'

'But—'

'It is the worst winter in memory.'

'But I thought—'

'All the cold weather, it has gone somewhere else.'

'Grenoble,' I said.

The next day at lunchtime I made my début as a waiter. It was not hard. There were no customers. A couple of redundant ski-

46

instructors wandered by for a long drawn-out drink and moan and the local postman accepted *le patron*'s offer of a free coffee, but otherwise Le Maronnier remained as deserted as when I first saw it. The only waiting to be done was when I had to take Madame's pooch for a piss in the slush, a duty hidden in the small print of the previous day's conversation; as I loitered in the sun and watched another half-empty bus arrive, I could sense the target-date for my down payment on the Ritz fast receding from sight. My only hope – apart from a blizzard – was to overthrow France's historic restaurateur tradition and demand a salary.

Unfortunately, my negotiating position was, as each side knew, somewhat non-existent. Not only was I untried and untrained, I was also unlawful; if I fell from favour it was a black mark on my passport and back to Blighty. (My French prede-cessor, I now learnt, had thrown in the towel and the dicky-bow after just two weeks and fled to Paris.) Moreover, as my only lunchtime task was to wash two glasses and a cup – a task even the most militant of unions could hardly classify as more than semi-skilled – it had been a little regrettable to record a 33$\frac{1}{3}$ per cent breakage rate. I decided to hope instead for a blizzard.

The two hours of this first lunch passed uneasily. Monsieur scarcely stirred from his bar stool and his *marc*, the convivial mask of mein host constantly creased with that melancholia exclusive to the rich. Meanwhile Madame fluttered solicitously around the decor, always on the look-out for unsightly candle-wax, as she practised her range of smiles in vain anticipation of a gourmet. When together, they displayed that exaggerated public warmth which distinguishes couples who hate each other.

Ivan, however, made no pretence of not hating me. Unaware of the feudal regime of a cook or his territorial rights to the kitchen, I had innocently rummaged through the baguette-bin in search of breakfast. And been found *in flagrante delicto*. From that moment, I was a marked waiter. From then on, Ivan would snarl drunkenly at my every entrance, threatening me with the nearest vegetable to hand. An emigré from the Caucasus, as Madame glossily described him to would-be diners, he had fled his country in a car-boot owning only the clothes he crouched in, and the traumas of his past (even a Lada *front* seat for more than an hour is not a happy experience) had comprehensively removed sweetness and light from his menu of emotions. As he strutted to and fro along his cutting-boards, it was evident that Ivan had been lured to the land of individualism by the concept of 'cook as temperamental food impresario'; he had learned the language of abuse even before knowing the vocabulary of ingredients. It was Alain's theory that we were in the presence of the first KGB chef to defect to the West.

As the days wore on and morale wore down, a dispiriting routine started to shape my life. The non-events of lunch and dinner were the landmarks, the white-slave activities of dusting, boiler-duty and dog-walking were the untipped curricular extras. Apart from mid-morning asylum in a friendly corner café, where the schemes of fellow foreign workers would not have disgraced a POW meeting in Colditz, there was little to enliven the daily drudge. Even the fringe benefits of free meals were a dubious pleasure, being leftovers of unknown provenance – and served by Ivan in a manner so malevolent as to suggest investment in a KGB food-taster could be a useful precaution. Only at midnight, after the last theoretical customer had left, was there the time and the space to break free.

In the emptiness of the silent, starlit nights, I took to accompanying Alain on his long, contemplative wanders in the hills. The hut, hidden from the sun all day, mocked us with Mégève's lowest temperatures at night, and offered only the home discomforts of stiffened blankets and frosted breath. The mountains gave us clear air and the hope of clear thoughts. I felt the walking would perhaps lead me to solace and solutions; both of us were steadily succumbing to despair, and in Alain I looked for answers. But as the nights passed I realized he could not help. Alain's requirements for salvation had a metaphysical quality which transcended big tips.

'The better the view, the more I believe in heaven,' he announced one night, gazing at the mountains ranged around us in a ghostly monochrome tint.

'It's hard to understand how people can be bad when

surrounded by beauty . . .' The Sorbonne Philosophy Department had not prepared him for bad people. 'Don't you think of a mountain as a moral example?' Indeed, it had not really prepared him for any sort of people.

'It is not right, the way we live. I dream sometimes of a country where . . .' He left the sentence hanging for a moment. He had a face which whenever the world left him alone, plunged into deep, painful thought.

'. . . of a country where one can be good. Which is so much harder than *doing* good.'

After this, I was on my own. I realized that whilst I was panicking about my personal future, he was trying to sort out the future of humankind. Whereas I wanted to know about next month, Alain was enquiring into eternity (and other related matters). And so I would come back down to our two-man stalag and its freezing floorboards late in the early hours feeling a little more familiar with the dark nights of the soul but no further forward with the dark days of the pocket.

Yet it was high in those slush-capped Alps that I gained my first glimmerings of the French character. In essence, while the English idea of a hobby is mowing the lawn, the French like to spend their spare time working away on the meaning of life, usually noisily and preferably in public. I found it rather an appealing vision.

But, back at base camp, my Barcelona vision of a larger-than-life life as a fun-packed free spirit was degenerating fast. Themed soirées had begun! First Russian soirées − distinguished by a bit of balalaika tape and a bowl of bortsch − and then Spanish − a plate of paella and me on the maracas. As I grimaced my way nightly around an average audience of six, I began to empathize with the lot of a dancing bear.

A casual remark on Arab headdress triggered the final spiral from despair to disaster. Alluding one day to my past as a world traveller, and making modest mention to Madame of my mementoes, I spoke of my *àgàl* and my *keffiyeh*. Instantly, she exclaimed, 'Couscous night!' And proposed that I disport myself in my Middle Eastern spoils. I resisted vigorously. The prospect of parading up and down like a latter-day Sambo rolling the whites of his eyes for public applause would be the final humiliation. Madame persisted, with iron charm. Again and again she used her smile, an instant smile, of the packet variety that lacks the real ingredients and has a wide range of poisonous additives. I tried to argue, I tried to convey my English sensibilities, but I was talking to the deaf, and my employer. The headdress was compulsory. Saturday night was to be Arab night.

As I approached the end of that third week in waiting, despair became compounded by panic. Contrary to all known economic theory, I had nil expenditure yet my capital – my paltry capital – was *decreasing*. I was growing poorer by the day. Initially, the problem had just been breakages. In my zeal to clean the glasses thoroughly I had tended to break them into smaller, more manageable parts. Unfortunately, each time this occurred, Madame, whose inner ear was tuned to a pitch beyond human understanding and could hear breaking glass in the next canton, would loom into vision, advance across the room, and, with the pained smile of one brought close to penury, make a large note in the red column of a private accounts book. But, as time went on, in addition to breakages there were 'incidents'. Customers being few, I was naturally short of practice. During one meal, I lost control of a plate of oysters – serving them onto an area of the body which suggested I was trying to administer their aphro-disiac effects externally – and my reward was a dry-cleaning bill. Nor had the accident with the creamed leek come cheap. And the square footage which the contents of a vigorously shaken, inadequately secured sauce bottle can cover passes all under-standing. In none of these cases had my outgoings been offset by a tip. I was beginning to dread the arrival of customers for fear of what they would cost me.

The turn-out in response to the '*Nuit Arabe*' posters filled nearly half the tables. There was the odd après-skier, fresh from a liquid-mud slalom, but it was scarcely the tourist trade. Mostly it was the tourist industry, fellow snow-professionals – guides, instructors, a hotelier or two – down on their climatic luck and come to cast a critical neighbourly eye over proceedings. And then there was Jean-Marie Muller.

I knew at once that Jean-Marie Muller was important because *Monsieur le patron* made a rare excursion into speech. 'That's Jean-Marie Muller,' he said to me. 'He's important.' This was quickly confirmed as Madame marked his entry by selecting a rare sycophantic smile from her repertoire. 'That's Jean-Marie Muller,' she said to me. 'He's important.' And then, in case there was still any room for doubt, Jean-Marie Muller gave me a signed photograph. (It has the ambiguous caption 'To Barry very kindly' and is still the only signed photograph of a World Ski Champion in my possession.) Also in his party were the Director of Tourism ('he's important as well!' (*bis*)) and two pneumatic blonde ladies, status unknown, but each with a *décolletage* sufficient to provide an indoor ski slope. As further proof of the group's importance I was not allowed to serve them.

Whether the group was equally impressed by me is not known. To complete the authentic Bedouin look, Madame had prevailed upon me to wrap myself in a sheet. It was not a made-to-measure sheet and the stylistic accuracy of the three safety-pins was open to question. Furthermore, the disorderly Jordanian headdress, although *bona fide*, had come without folding instructions and showed a marked desire to spend life as a neckerchief. Nor was its pristine whiteness an exact match for the multi-occupancy grey of the sheet, which came from the shed. The other great threat to authenticity came from my Hush Puppies. They had self-evidently not seen desert service, and were considerably more chic than sheik. For ambience, Madame had somehow acquired a disc of what she called 'cat music', and as its solo ululations pierced the restaurant air she instructed me to serve 'sinuously' in order to create a casbah effect. I was not a happy waiter.

When I took the first orders to the kitchen I was quickly made aware that Ivan was not a happy cook. The artistic exile was stomping to and fro and slamming each of the cupboard doors in sequence, in a fit of *haute cuisine* temperament. The evening's menu lay in small pieces across the floor. His angry tirade of

Russian told me nothing, but I gathered from Alain, who was assisting me in mufti, that he held 'Arab stews' to be beneath his dignity, that he had not risked the Gulag for goulash, that no man destined for cordon bleudom practised his art on Third World swill, and so on and so on. It was clear that half a lifetime in the Caucasus had not predisposed him to Moslems, or to their food. He gestured contemptuously in the direction of the restaurant and its clientele. 'I peess on their couscous!' he proclaimed, taking several large swigs of vodka to give the flavour of his urine more spice. He then made an unsteady lunge at my headdress as I left to take more orders, and I realized that he held me responsible for the soirée.

As I stumbled around the tables of smirking guests, looking like the booby-prize at a drag fancy-dress ball, I too felt a surge of temperament, an urge to slam a cupboard door or two. Each time I returned to the kitchen with more orders, more *basse-cuisine* requests, my waiterly conduct grew worse – as did my reception. My one consolation was that I had resisted the management demand to smear my face with essence of charcoal and stumble around in full dago Dayglo.

Meanwhile, Madame shadowed every movement of mine, sweet-talking her celebrity catches as she sprinkled little jokes in my wake. An hour into the evening, she took me aside and informed me that my portrayal of the Maghreb character was not up to expectations.

'More into the spirit!' she kept hissing into my ear. 'More *Arabe!*' The Algerian War of Independence was not long ended – I had personally seen the remains of burnt-out tanks still disfiguring the roadsides – and the Arab spirit as perceived by the Haute-Savoie bourgeoisie did not seem an easy subject to symbolize while carrying hot plates.

I questioned her as to specifics.

'*Salaam!*' she hissed. 'Do a bit of *salaaming!*'

It was a demand too far. Even Lawrence of Arabia, with his remarkable thirst for humiliation, would have found it hard to comply. With my English reserve, I found it emotionally impossible. I hitched up my sheet and bolted for the kitchen.

Standing at the chopping-board, his vodka bottle now almost empty, Ivan was gutting the chickens and steaming the wheat flour with venom. I handed him his latest couscous commands – and he spat extensively on them.

Suddenly I was overcome with hunger and anger and exhaustion. Almost without thinking – certainly without caring – I took some cooked sausage from one of his prepared plates. It was a breach of the kitchen's holy writ, and I instantly knew it. Ivan snatched the sausage back, hurled it to the floor and ground it spitefully under his heel as he pushed me violently backwards. I fell against the boiler and banged my shoulder. In a reflex action, and consumed by a desire to do what would annoy him most, I picked up a handful of coal from the scuttle and, with pleasing accuracy, lobbed three medium-sized lumps through the air into the open stewpot where his beef was simmering.

I realized immediately this was a mistake. I realized it was a mistake even when the coal was in mid-air, and would have recalled each lump to base had it been possible.

Ivan looked on in disbelief as the boiling water hissed over on to the stove and splashed into what remained of his vodka.

He paused only to look for a weapon. It was sticking in the chicken.

Before I could speak he was advancing upon me with a meat cleaver held high in his right hand. He was drunk enough to be serious and suddenly I could see myself being bloodily slain in a primitive Caucasian food feud.

I burst through the swing doors and entered the restaurant with a formidable crash. All eating came to an immediate stop, every eye on the waiter as he hurtled into the dining-room a short axe-head in front of the chef. Terrified, I zigzagged desperately around the tables and the chairs and the astonished diners, pursued by Ivan bellowing at the top of his voice in Russian, his apron dripping with fresh chicken blood. I was almost halfway across the room when I caught my foot in my sheet, stumbled and overbalanced. As I fell forward I accidentally head-butted the world skiing champion – overturning his table and scattering his party's couscous into three laps and a vast bosom. I scrabbled helplessly among the debris, vaguely aware that my imminent beheading could be the finest hour for the Poe decor. I was only saved from disaster by Ivan's vodka content, which destabilized him as he cornered. But as I struggled back to my feet, he caught up with me. He raised his axe to take aim. I heard the sound of screaming. Then, out of nowhere, the Director of Tourism rugby-tackled him from behind and they both fell to the food-strewn floor amidst general pandemonium. I scrambled out of range, raced unseen to the exit door, and fled into the night.

It did at least give me pleasure to observe in passing that, for once, Madame seemed unable to find a suitable smile for the occasion.

Alain and I stood gazing a long time at the moonlit splendour of Mont Blanc that night. It was to be our last night together, though for several years strange, sad letters would arrive at my home address from lonely corners of the world. He had decided to leave for Africa, where the night skies were bigger and the mysteries of the soul more accessible. I had decided to leave for Paris, for my next kibbutz contact; a free lift out of Mégève, with two other waiters *manqués*, had been an offer I could not refuse. It was a city I had never visited – it was somehow too close to home to make the effort – and I had heard it was quite nice. So, with the remains of my money, I resolved to spend five days in Paris before finding another lift for the final lap to Germany.

CHAPTER 4

After five days, I decided to stay in Paris, possibly for ever. I set myself two goals: to fall in love (preferably in the spring), and to become a famous writer (preferably by summer) . . .

I had arrived in Paris with a shameful ignorance of its reputation. I was quite unschooled in the literature expended on the city. I knew nothing of the paeans it inspired in writers, and even less of the paintings it inspired in artists. I had read some Hemingway, mostly about killing in Spain, but the macho views of a man who thought adverbs and adjectives cissy had kept me from his gentler, and deeply affectionate, classic work on Paris. I had sampled some Henry Miller, mostly about fucking in Greece, but whilst it was instructive to learn that orgasms can be delayed by thinking about a loved one's funeral (a piece of advice I found somewhat too dependent on being able to organize an orgasm in the first place), his infamous accounts of Paris and its sex life had escaped me. And the cultural roll-call of the inter-war years – Joyce, Fitzgerald, Pound *et al* – rang with names whose presence in Paris I had all but forgotten. Had I known that the French capital was the world's most sought-after posting for the artist in exile (or that *La Cimitière du Père-Lachaise* was the after-life's most prestigious address for the artist in death), I would have realized that she had to be a city of extraordinary charms.

Instead, I came in innocence, I arrived without expectations . . . and I was everlastingly captivated by my first impressions.

I had never before realized that an urban landscape could be a triumph of aesthetics. Every idle moment – and I had no other sort of moment – was spent ogling the architecture. On the streets, Paris was still romantically displaying the last anachronistic trappings of an earlier era, of a bygone age about to finally go by. Everyone who ever lives a while in Paris lachrymosely laments that they saw the end of an era; in my case, however, it was true. When I arrived, the Quartier Latin was still cobbled, the pavements still had wrought-iron alfresco *pissoirs*, the backs of the ageing buses still had open-air platforms to leap on and cling to, the giant yellow capital 'M' still led you to a Metro and not a big Mac, and les Halles was still a meat market offering onion soup and tarts all night long. When I left, the twentieth century moved in.

Only one Parisian ingredient was missing from the magic of those first days: the *demi-monde* had failed to make personal contact with me. I had yet to receive an introduction to the café corners where Art and the Revolution were under twenty-four-hour discussion by the latest poets and pot-heads; I had still to locate the bohemian underworld where smoke-filled dives were echoing to sultry late-night jazz; and I had so far established no casual liaisons with Rodinesque Beaux Arts models.

Indeed, those first days of enchantment were filled with a constant struggle to put down roots and intertwine with the heart-strings of Paris.

Night was approaching when the would-be waiters dropped me in the Champs Elysées, and I had immediately set off to find the home of José Harle, my Paris connection, whose name I had in bold, confident capitals. It was the first, and the saddest, of my setbacks. In faraway Israel, he had seemed a matey, back-slapping extrovert, his anecdotes seductively hinting at a private life of raffishness, and each afternoon as we lay by the kibbutz pool his worldly chatter had been larded with invitations and promises. In cosmopolitan Paris, I found him buried deep in the most boring of *banlieues*, high in the most poky of tower-block boxes, and silent in front of the family telly; my unannounced arrival from the Alps, with luggage, cast a lasting unease over the dingy kitchen-diner and his sullenly hostile parents. Unwittingly, I had stumbled into the *petite bourgeoisie*.

Awkward and anecdoteless, José offered me dinner and the family stew was stretched to four. Too late, I realized his was the holiday invitation that ends with the holiday. His father put away my anorak and baggage with the distaste of a man who lacks confidence in the efficacy of the State delousing service; the insipid meal was eaten mostly in silence, the parents' eyes lifting from the food only to deliver an occasional incurious xenophobic stare; a tea-towel of the Eiffel Tower went over the hamster cage at 10.30 sharp. I spent the night under the dining-table in my sleeping bag. When I left the next morning, José's father said to me, with a sort of surly pride, 'No-one can say we haven't done our duty now.' José arranged to meet me later in the day, by a fountain in boulevard St Michel, to introduce me to Paris proper, to ease my path. He never showed up, and I never saw him again.

In disarray, I decamped to the youth hostel. But youth hostels in big cities are tawdry places. They are not about the glamour of travel, but the squalor of survival. They are little more than down-market stock-markets where the steerage class talk of nothing but the day's best buys. And Paris was no exception. By day, I roamed the world's most beautiful city; by night, I listened to hot tips on the cheapest chips. From Monday to Friday, I heard Paris reduced to a guided tour of freebies and scams, where the only recognized art-form was to come in under budget.

I hoped in vain for a Vernon and Diana – or, indeed, just a Diana. It being Paris, the hostel had certainly fulfilled its quota of *femmes fatales*, but nearly all seemed in single-minded pursuit of a career as au pair and bilingual mistress to the capital's *haute bourgeoisie*. Occasionally, over the brief breakfasts, I managed to exchange smiles and sugar with a sympathetic, though rather mysterious, Nordic blonde – whose shoulder-length flaxen hair and big blue eyes gave her the look of a grown-up Gretel, recently escaped from some German fairy tale – but this was the nearest to companionship that I came.

After five days the house rules moved me on again – and I was glad to go. But not to Germany any more. Now I was irrevocably under the old Paris spell. And I yearned to be permanently under an old Paris roof. I wanted to tread in historic footsteps, and gaze from historic windows, and squat on historic toilets. The great romantic appeal of Paris is poverty with style. I had the poverty. All I needed was the style.

But after the bleak tower block and the sordid youth hostel came the anonymous and amorphous campus – the *Résidence Universitaire, Pavillon C, Chambre 166, circa 1950*. Fortunately, I managed to avoid the form-filling, circumvent the bursar and skip the need to take a degree. Instead, I got the room, dirt-cheap, no questions asked, from a Mr Gupta who, for reasons that were never quite clear to me, was temporarily suspending his engineering studies to return to India. Indeed, I never *actually* met Mr Gupta, as I dealt through an Algerian intermediary I had met in the hostel games room who liked to help young foreigners in straitened financial circumstances. (I gathered his services also extended to the supply of illegal substances.)

The campus was short on aesthetic joy. *Pavillons A* to *E* were not by the same firm who had done Notre Dame. The briskly functional buildings appeared to have been dropped at random from the sky. Moreover, they had been dropped in the suburbs. I was reduced to the ultimate indignity of commuting, of taking a daily suburban train to the bohemian part of town. Artists, my soul instinctively told me, did not commute.

I soon found myself wandering the streets of the Left Bank all day, knowing no-one, and then returning to sit alone all night in the soullessness of *Chambre 166*, at the end of an empty, featureless corridor where I also knew no-one. This was an isolation difficult to remedy; I had been advised not to cultivate other tenants since, under the conditions of my lease, I did not exist. Indeed, my presence in this academic Alphaville had various disadvantages, not least of which was a requirement to impersonate the unseen Mr Gupta should I ever be approached by men in university uniform.

I had, however, gained funds for another few weeks: it had dawned upon me that writers usually pay tribute, in the early, struggling, section of their careers, to invaluable assistance from loved ones. Accordingly, I had written to every friend and acquaintance I could think of, familiarizing them with my new destiny and asking for money. I had also asked my father to send out my old Model T typewriter, adding yet further to my growing collection of immovable objects.

After ten days or so, my aimless, somewhat dismal routine was well-established. I even felt it might have the makings of a Chekhovian short story. I was, however, increasingly uncertain of my next move; I felt more like a mislaid tourist, forgotten by the tour bus, than a real resident.

The routine was unexpectedly broken one wet Wednesday evening, shortly after getting off my usual 8.07 train home. Casual water lay across the landscaped tarmac, and I was eager to get my flaccid baguette and rain-damaged Brie into the dry. I hurried into the neon-lit entrance lobby, ran up two flights of stairs ahead of the lift, panted along the corridor – and found four people in my room: a very tetchy young Dane, just back from two weeks at a family funeral and studying archaeology, and three men in university uniforms studying my belongings. I was the only one who had heard of Mr Gupta.

The rain was still falling remorselessly at 11.15 that night as I sloshed along the dark, narrow pavements of rue de Seine. Even in nearby boulevard St Germain, main highway of the Latin Quarter, the usual late-walking, loud-talking legion of prom-enaders had opted to stay put for another round of drinks. There is rarely a good time to look for a hotel. But late at night, alone, overladen and sodden, on foot, with limited money, in a foreign tongue, in a full town, the search is a lonely, dispiriting business.

It was here my resolve to be an exile began to weaken. I had tried five hotels without success, without even a smile, and the full hopelessness of my lot was seeping deep. For the first time I heard the siren-call of SW16. I dragged my suitcase into the recess of a shop doorway and slumped down on it, my type-writer case upon my knees, my rucksack clamped soddenly to my back. As I sat dripping and self-pitying, my loneliness was heightened by the coloured spotlights of a nearby art gallery shimmering in the puddles of the dark, wet street.

I remember gazing forlornly through the rain at the warm, private world of a sculptor's opening night. In a pink glow, young men my age in velvet jackets and nubile women in back-less dresses flirted and drank red wine as they insouciantly jostled around the exhibits. The exhibits, I noted with wonder, were a series of giant stone fish, symbolically harpooned on to black plinths. Rough-edged and chiselled out of granite, yet with gold-leaf defining their imaginary boned innards, these deep-sea sculptures reared upright in rows, and glinted surreally in the lights. Faintly, but tantalizingly, I could hear the hubbub of laughter and clink of glasses. Here, at hand, was the world I so sought – artistic and cosmopolitan, chic and frivolous, talented and carefree. And utterly unattainable.

It took three more hotels before I struck what might relatively be called 'lucky'. Lit by a solitary streetlamp, a narrow no-nonsense alley led to a grubby little flophouse specializing in the rough trade of travel. The building had no bath, no douche, no heat, no hope. The one vacant room was on the ground floor, on the far side of a dustbin-filled courtyard. It was basic, as was the manager. Damp and shivering, I paid a week's rent in advance.

My longing for the reassuring banalities of home life, for the security of the familiar, began to grow acute. It was a longing which the next few days did not lessen; my creativity seemed in even shorter supply than my money, and time was running out for my artistic rebirth. I did not know what to do, or how to do it. This fourth bolthole in three weeks was the loneliest yet. The hotel had all the personal touch of a railway station, and the rooms had fewer visiting rights than a prison. Even in the daytime its short-stayed inhabitants passed like strangers in the night.

Then, one sunny morning, as I made my way to a little café on the rue de Buci where I liked to sit and stare between ten and eleven, I came across two vaguely familiar female faces. Acknowledging me, the taller woman smiled. It was the shoulder-length flaxen hair which I recognized. They had seemed an improbable pair in the hostel, the inscrutable Nordic blonde and the squat gum-chewing matron.

Slim, smiling Ulrika had an impeccable Canadian accent curiously coupled with impeccable German features; noisy, worried Joan, her travelling companion, was from Pittsburgh and always carried a plastic mac.

For a moment, we stood blocking the pavement, exchanging notes on our lives. They too had fallen prey to the spell of Paris. They too were trying to go native. And then, apropos of nothing, Ulrika said, 'We've found an amazing little old hotel to live in!'

'Really?' I said.

'Full of artists!' added Joan, very enthusiastically.

'Yes, tucked down an old cobbled street!'

'And built in 1784 AD!' added Joan, even more enthusiastically.

'I think there might be a spare room going,' said Ulrika.

CHAPTER 5

The Hotel de Carcassonne stood just off a tiny square with five struggling trees, at the top of a noisy canyon of a street whose ancient buildings were cracking with decay. From the outside, one could be forgiven for not noticing the existence of the hotel. From the inside, one could be forgiven for the same mistake. Entry from the street was through a drab, *merde*-brown door, its upper half a murky, impenetrable glass diagonally criss-crossed by protective bars. It opened to reveal an inner brown door and beyond this lay a bare-walled passageway which remained in Stygian blackness if the timed light-switch could not be located. The only hint of what lay beyond this flagstoned passage was a fading fascia board above the front door, where a flaking cream paint had once tried to spell out the words Hotel de Carcassonne on a begrimed brown background.

Between the doors and the darkness, however, lay Madame.

She was not easily visible through the thick net curtains which hung on the side door to her bed sitting-room. Nonetheless, few entrants had escaped her attention since the First World War. As Madame sat, day after day, knitting and reading, surrounded by the clutter of her very ordinary furniture, the black-and-white television set almost constantly on, she might at first have been taken for the standard concierge. But the vigour with which this plump, voluble old lady inspected all newcomers, and the en-thusiasm with which she showed them the crumbling fabric of their rooms, quickly betrayed a proprietorial pride. And the gruff affection with which she referred to her motley crowd of would-be poets and painters and performers (and poseurs) let slip an almost maternal pride. Now seventy-six, and able to recount vividly the details of the day when Sarah Bernhardt's funeral mourners had clogged solid the street outside, the white-haired widow had been the owner for over half a century. Moreover, she claimed a line of forebears who, it seemed, had lurked behind the same net curtains as far back as the last Louis.

At the end of the passage, a tightly curving staircase – in yet more brown – rose up to the left. There were six floors to the main building, and usually four rooms to each floor – and a separate cooking smell to each room. Eight francs a day got you a view of the street and a right to plunge to your death from a lethal balconette; seven francs a day gave you a view of the courtyard and people undressing in the annexe; six francs a day drew you the short straw of a room with no windows or ventilation. The four-storey annexe – reached by crossing the little concrete courtyard at the end of the passage – was cheapest because its rooms were smallest: five francs a day got you a windowless cell which would have given claustrophobia to St Jerome. The daily rate was, however, academic: all the rooms were let on a monthly basis to synchronize with the changing of the sheets.

Chambre numero 5 was a seven-francer. It was located on the first floor, at the start of another dark, forbidding corridor. It was a roughly square room, about a bed and three-quarters long in each direction, and contained an almost classic definition of a 'few sticks of furniture': one small table, one small chair, a single bed and an unstable wardrobe.

But when I first saw it, on that mild February afternoon, Madame had flung the door wide open to a cry of '*Le voilà!*', as if revealing the contents of a tomb overlooked by Lord Caernarvon – and then launched pell-mell into the social and artistic history of the room, the pleasure and inspiration it had given to previous inhabitants, and the finer points of the view. Unfortunately, the breathless, tumultuous speed of her speech, in a dialect distorted by age, left me in possession of little but the occasional indefinite article.

63

But already I knew the two essentials: the room was available, and I needed a room. So, when at last her flow arrived at a natural break, I accepted the terms and agreed to the seven francs. Whereupon she immediately announced, '*Et un franc pour le chauffage!*'

Yet somehow such artfulness was endearingly forgivable. Indeed, over the months I came to look upon this as her catch-phrase, a rent-day refrain which reflected not only her shrewd business sense but also her inordinate, though misplaced, pride in the hotel's prewar heating system. I plunged into the thread-bare bowels of my money-bag and gave her a month's rent. She thanked me by drawing my attention to the police ordinances on the back of the door, gave me detailed if incomprehensible directions to the nearest municipal bathhouse, and then bustled back to her watch-post by the front door, happy to have a full hotel again.

I had reached the definitive end of my journeyings.

I lowered my rucksack one last time to the floor, laid my case upon the bed, and slowly, with deliberation, took stock of my new surroundings. It was mid-afternoon and the room was quiet. The floor was flagstoned and cold to the touch, except for a small rush mat which was rough and scratchy. In the corner was an old washbasin with a single tap, which provided slow, cold, noisy water. Underneath the only window – large, cracked and permanently rattling – was an ancient, school-style ribbed radiator, which provided slow, cold, noisy heating. The bed, placed along the wall adjoining the corridor, had a solid base and was as firm to the touch as the flagstones. The wardrobe stood by the door, above tiny pyramids of woodworm dust. The one chair was hard-backed, the one table loose-legged. The walls had once upon a time been painted, but in a colour no longer ident-ifiable. Outside the room, up half a flight of flaking plaster, there was a stand-up toilet with freshly torn quarter-pages of *Le Figaro* behind the cistern pipe. Along the dark corridor was a smell of fish cooking. From somewhere in the building came the sound of slapping and cries in Spanish.

Many, many years later, secure and comfortable, I opened a

telephone bank account which required some personal details for use as security checks. One of the questions asked for 'A Memorable Address'. Unhesitatingly, with tears of nostalgia welling in my eyes, I wrote 'Hotel de Carcassonne'.

CHAPTER 6

I was about halfway through my unpacking when there was a
knock at the door. There is a sensuous satisfaction to the rituals
of slowly unpacking in strange surroundings. The leisurely and
meticulous placing of socks in drawers is the human version of
a dog sniffing out its new territory, and is meant to be fully
savoured. I was therefore torn between irritation at this break in
my carefully ordered routine and delight at receiving a visitor so
soon and so unexpectedly.

In the corridor outside it was semi-Stygian, with shades of
brown.

'Hallo!'

I caught a potent snatch of a foreign accent which puzzled me.
As did the appearance of the speaker, whose cheap black flannels and crumpled white shirt created an oddly formal but
dilapidated look. I put him at thirty, but ageing badly and early.

'Hallo!' I replied.

He paused, looking at me for a second, though he seemed far
from nervous. I noticed that his stubble – and in the Sixties
stubble came without a designer – was already greying in parts.

'Would you like to pose for me?'

It was my turn to pause. I had not expected bohemianism to
arrive quite this precipitately. And I suddenly realized I was not
entirely certain as to the exact nature of bohemianism. I stalled.
However, at least one thing – one very surprising thing – was
now clear.

'That's a Liverpool accent, isn't it?'

He nodded, but it was a nod reserved for irrelevancies, and he continued, 'I heard you were here. Thought I'd get in first!'

'. . . First?'

'Bloody poet on the third floor! He's always after models!'

'Why's a poet need models?' I was floundering.

'Claims it gives him inspiration!' A sniff. 'Just gives him a hard-on!'

'Oh, I see.' I did not entirely see, but at least the contempt in his reply seemed to suggest I had received a serious artistic offer. Of some sort. I tried to concentrate on looking worldly-wise, but something of my confusion must have registered.

'Oh, it's not a life class!' he snorted. 'I only want your face!' I tried to give a blasé nod, hoping to convey that the whole of me was naturally at the service of art. 'Couldn't afford your body!' he added. And smiled for the first time, somewhat bitterly.

'I get paid?'

'A cup of tea?'

His room was at the far, dark end of the corridor, narrower than mine, but with sight and sound of the street. The walls, a mass of pinpricks, were covered with pencil sketches, of hands, faces, feet, and miscellaneous muscles. As he lit a tiny cooking Gaz cylinder to heat water for the tea, I did several slow circuits of his work, awkwardly aware that my judgement was probably also under surveillance. A schoolboy fear of being asked my opinion resurfaced to unsettle me. As did an adult fear of art. They were perverse fears: I thought his drawings seemed remarkably good, but some instinct cautioned me that he would decry them as rubbish. He had a single-mindedness about him that suggested a rarely satisfied perfectionist. Every aspect of his life was shabby, but shabby because subservient to his work. Not many poor, working-class Liverpudlian men beat out a path that leads to a foreign hotel-room wallpapered with their own art work.

'D'you sell any of them?'

'These? I'm not an artist. I'm a sculptor.'

'Oh.'

'Except I can't afford the sodding materials!'

As if to emphasize the point he took the two cups of boiling water to where a tea bag hung from a nail above the sink, and dunked it in them for a distressingly short time.

I took my cup and stood by the balcony window as directed. Outside, the narrow, crowded street curved away downhill in various colourful stages of dereliction, and, below, a hubbub of back street backchat was echoing up from the square, accompanied by a solo trombone. Although only ten minutes' walk from the Sorbonne, and on the fringes of the Latin Quarter, it was a neighbourhood redolent with the intimacy of a village – and with alluring hints of the debauchery of a city.

'Have you been here long?' I asked.

He glared at me, and I realized that I had neglected my profile. I focused my eyes to the front again. He said nothing for some time, sketching intently while the winter light lasted. I watched his reflection in a mirror: severely balding, with heavy-rimmed NHS specs, a bulbous nose, and a dress sense that belonged to an early 1950s bank clerk, he was a body blow to my preconceptions of Paris sculptors. It was appealingly romantic to believe that his absorbed, distant air meant he was oblivious to his appearance, but a series of self-portraits above the bed set out his ugliness with unsentimental savagery. Indeed, none of his line drawings was sentimental; few of his subjects would have won an award for sweetness and light.

'Six months. Since the start of the Beaux Arts year,' he suddenly said. So, I thought, I had been right about the quality.

Then he removed the paper from the pad, looked at it critically – and screwed it into a ball. To my dismay, he sharpened his pencil once more, but before restarting he allowed me the rest of my tea, now lukewarm as well as disgusting.

'You don't get a studio?'

'I don't get a grant! That's why I get up and clean office blocks at five o'clock every morning.'

For ten years he had been doing shitwork and shiftwork to subsidize his sculpting. For ten years he had turned down commercial art offers rather than compromise. For ten years he had ploughed a lonely, unworldly furrow, saving and penny-pinching for the dream of France's greatest art school. This information came in sudden spurts of bitterness, of resentment against those who had it easy. But it came because I asked, and my lasting impression was of his simplicity and his dedication.

My brief, revolting tea-break was over. I changed profiles, and looked out over the square, where a man with a monkey was arguing with a policeman. The extra franc for the front rooms would seem to be worth it.

I had never been a model before, but the inherent flattery of being portrayed obscured any unease about the result. There is a curious mystique to modelling: the simple act of stillness suddenly becomes a source of inspiration, an artistic debt owed by the artist. Without the model, the picture would not exist. It began to seem to me, as I stood and suffered, that the model's signature should also be on the work, as joint creator. '*By Barry and Tony*'. (He had yet to introduce himself: I got his name off the wall.) There would, of course, be some technical problems. Most of Veronese's work would need an extra yard of canvas for the names, and the list of credits on the Sistine Chapel would make it look like an early telephone directory. But the idea would be in line with the growing egalitarianism of the Sixties.

There was nothing much to do but muse idly on such fanciful notions, and I worked on these plans for over an hour while Tony screwed draft after draft into paper balls.

'It's the beard,' he kept complaining. 'You could be anybody behind that beard.'

But eventually he seemed reasonably satisfied. Outside, the first street lights were coming on. Inside, my left leg was going to sleep. Tony came over to the window, looking uncharacteristically vulnerable, to show me the finished work.

When I saw my portrait I was shocked by how wild and woolly and gaunt I looked. But I was pleased. I seemed to have a rather stronger character on paper than I remembered from real life. It was also the first time that I had been immortalized by an artist. Or indeed been in the same room as one. I had finally located the bohemian underworld.

Tony offered me the picture as a gift and I proudly accepted. I had never been on my own wall before. I got up to go.

And then he asked, 'And what do you do?'

'Oh, I'm a writer!' I replied, considerably to my surprise.

At the time, it seemed the nearest attractive identity to hand. And I did want to be one. But it seemed an embarrassingly personal thing to have said, like boasting about penis size. It felt more like a value judgement than a job description, more like an assessment of worth than a statement of fact. And, of course, it was a lie.

At least, though, I was glad I had opted for writing rather than any other art form. I doubted I had the dedication to save ten years for a block of marble.

But as I said goodbye and felt my way back along the corridor to *Chambre 5*, it occurred to me that I had maybe – accidentally – taken the first crucial step. I now felt committed, or at least obliged, to write something . . . to actually begin work on my goal of becoming a famous writer (preferably by summer).

All that remained was to unpack the typewriter.

CHAPTER 7

When I pushed open my door and saw my room again, it was like coming home. Even in the half-light of early evening, the small table, small chair, single bed and unstable wardrobe were familiar, friendly objects. The split sandals by the bed, the tar-stained anorak on the door hook, the holed sweater over the chairback, and the overused underwear in the sink, all held personal memories that helped create an atmosphere of re-assuring intimacy.

There was even a note waiting for me. It said 'Go to the window and wave if you want dinner.'

I switched on the light, the 40-watt bulb converting the natural half-light to an unnatural three-quarter light, and went over to the window. All across the fifth *arrondissement*, people were returning from a hard day's artistry and I could see the first scattered glows appearing in the rear rooms of the ancient ten-ements which formed the backdrop to my view.

Immediately ahead of me, though, was the hotel annexe, as yet in gloom. I waved vigorously, if self-consciously, feeling rather like Robinson Crusoe trying to attract room-service from a distant ship. Before long, however, Ulrika appeared at the window opposite mine and, in the first of many shouted conver-sations to echo across that courtyard, called, 'D'you want to join us for some food?'

I offered to buy some wine, promised to be two minutes, and grabbed my coat. I felt a thrill at the informality and un-predictability of life's latest tapestry. Suburbia was never like this.

As I hurried down the dark stairs, wondering whether to stretch to a 12° bottle, I nearly cannoned into a hefty, slow-moving figure on his way up. I stepped aside since he showed no signs of giving way. The time-switch was still on in the passage and he was lit from below like Citizen Kane. Over six feet and bulky, with a hint of shoulder pads, he was most noticeable for his white canvas jacket and black fedora. I was surprised to see that he was little more than thirty-five.

'Sorry!' I said.

He didn't reply. He had what writers call a beetling brow and from it he looked down at me with the cold, scientific interest of a pathologist. I sensed that he moved slowly because of his opinion of himself. His judgement of me made, he moved on, and I scampered out to find an épicerie.

Ulrika had left her door ajar, to allow the smell of spaghetti sauce out to mingle with the fierce curry coming up from the ground floor immediately below. The annexe was slightly less old and much less rambling, an hotelier's commercial after-thought, but what it lacked in mystery it made up for in pungency.

I went to knock on the door, but she had already heard my full-blooded advance up the stairs. The concept of including subtlety and restraint in my approach to women was still some ten years distant.

'Come in!'

She was dressed simply, in sweater and jeans, her long, immaculate blonde hair the centrepiece, as always, of her appearance. Her face, for one of those indefinable reasons to do with a misplaced millimetre around the mouth (or was it around the eyes?), fell just short of classical beauty. Her long-legged body was slim and slender in the favoured Sixties proportions. Yet, despite an image and an impact of a fully qualified ice-maiden, there was a surprising hesitancy and shyness in her manner.

'We thought you might like a hotel-warming!' She laughed as I looked around. 'Afraid all the seats are taken, though!'

There were no seats – apart from a loose-legged hard-backed chair on which a pile of washing was balanced. There was no space for seats. The room was the length of a bed and the width of a midget. Or, as Madame would doubtless have said, 'very cosy'. I settled down on a bolster and watched the pasta and the sauce bubbling away on the chest of drawers, the only space for her baby Gaz bottle.

'Joan's still upstairs – probably dressing for dinner!'

This time I laughed with her, though the thrust of the jest was slightly ambiguous.

I knew little of Ulrika except that, like me, she was new to Paris. She was not, however, new to Europe.

'My parents are German, but we live in Canada now. Since the war. They left Germany because they were ashamed. I left Canada because I was bored.'

Bored and beautiful – I found myself thinking that sexual history had few more potent combinations.

'It's confusing. I feel at home in Europe somehow. It's three months now, and already the thought of Canada makes me cringe.'

'So you'll stay over here?'

'I don't know. Don't really know what I want to do.'

I nodded with more than necessary vigour at hearing these words. It was a truth close to my heart: I always empathized strongly with confusion.

She thought some more. 'Could move on, I suppose. But Paris is so romantic. I'm twenty-five, and definitely due some romance!'

I did not make an immediate comment on her romantic short-fall – the one small snag to this heart-stopping, throwaway remark was that it had been addressed vaguely, wistfully, to the ether, and appeared to take no account whatsoever of my presence.

Uncertain how to segue into this line of conversation, I made my gaze wander around the tiny room, noting her few belongings. It took only a second before I spotted, just above the head of the bed, another pencil portrait by Tony. I looked at it carefully. He was good, there was no doubt about it. He had located the misplaced millimetre and slightly flattened her face, stretching the smile and capturing to perfection a more uncertain, slightly lonely young woman.

'He had a shot at me today.' I nodded at the picture. 'I look like Wild Bill Hickock! Really good, though.'

She nodded in agreement. 'He takes such pains.'

'Yes, it's real starving-artist stuff, isn't it? Lifetime of dedication to his work, and all that!'

'And no bullshit either. I offered to take my clothes off for him, 'cos he's so poor, but he said no – anatomically my most interesting part was my cheekbones!'

I found myself trembling with shock and lust and wild jealousy. The free availability of Ulrika's body to artists, however dedicated, had sent sexual shockwaves through my bourgeois nervous system. The 500-year-old European tradition of artist and model carried little weight – I was overcome with hot sweats at the casualness, the unconcernedness, with which she contemplated nudity. Her nudity.

I immediately decided to pursue my other goal, and have a love affair. I could see us looking good together in the spring. With luck, my writing would impress her into taking her clothes off. Perhaps we could pose nude *à deux* for a marble statue? Clasped in each other's arms for months on end, while Tony struggled for perfection . . . ?

'D'you think mice eat chewing-gum?'

Joan was looking disconsolately at an empty packet; her nasal query was more by way of complaint than scientific enquiry.

She came and sat heavily beside me on the bed while Ulrika, still on her feet, continued to discourage the sauce from enamelling the pan. Joan had on a shapeless, synthetic cardigan-top in bright blue, and a pair of baggy, vaguely athletic bottoms in a second, equally primal colour. Her perm had gone to seed and straggled around a curiously mottled face – possibly victim of a deficient sun-ray lamp – which sported a pair of the vibrantly-framed American glasses favoured by the Disney school of opticians. She was somewhere in her thirties and looked as though she were training for retirement in Miami.

It was her first trip to Europe, and she was constantly amazed by how different it was to Pittsburgh.

'They hadn't got that ice-cream I wanted for tonight! You know, the blueberry. Said they didn't *do* blueberry. And didn't seem to have any idea who did. To tell the honest truth, I don't think they'd heard of blueberry. They didn't even have banana. In the whole refrigeration unit, they only had eight flavours! Eight!'

'Well, I think I've got a few yoghurts tucked under the bed,' said Ulrika placatingly, and smiled at her. She flicked a small piece of spaghetti at the wall, to check if dinner were done. It clung on for about three seconds and then fell away, taking a slightly larger piece of plaster with it.

'D'you have blueberry ice-cream in England, Barry?' Joan looked at me enquiringly.

Patriotism can take unexpected forms, and, without thinking, I brazenly, and wholly dishonestly, said 'Oh yes!' – and went on to confirm its presence throughout the land. I resented Joan's interruption of our tête-à-tête, and I resented Ulrika's apparent failure to resent Joan's interruption of it. This was, of course, quite unreasonable of me, but then I was in love.

The three of us squashed up along the bed to eat dinner. I had neglected to supply a plate and I was awarded the saucepan to forage in; my fork was a folding travelling-fork and, having seen many miles of service, it was almost as flexible as the spaghetti; the wine went into two toothbrush mugs and was shared around. The meal was my first-ever social engagement in Paris.

'We had hoped there'd be four of us,' said Ulrika, lamenting the leftovers.

'Four! What were you going to do? Build an extension?'

'Oh, Dave's used to crouching! He lives in the cubby-hole under the stairs.'

'He's a writer!' said Joan, with what I thought to be an estimable reverence.

This time, though, I decided to maintain a wary reticence about my new-found profession. 'Oh, pity he couldn't come.'

'Wouldn't come,' corrected Ulrika.

'He's got a block,' said Joan. 'He doesn't go out when he's got a block.'

'Oh, I see. . . . What's he writing?'

'A modern version of Dostoevsky's *Crime and Punishment*, set in New York,' said an impressed Joan, and then added, as if it were a helpful literary footnote, 'He's *from* New York.'

'He's very serious, our Dostoevsky Dave,' said Ulrika. 'Very intellectual. Very troubled.'

'It's a *very* small room,' said Joan.

'D'you know a big guy, with a white jacket, black hat?' I asked.

'Him? He doesn't speak to women!' snorted Ulrika. 'Only young men and God.'

'Oh.' Tony's opening words clicked into place. 'Is he the poet?'

'That's what he likes you to think.'

Gradually, a picture of the hotel's residents began to build up. There was a German painter no-one had seen, who apparently lived on the top floor and only left his garret in the middle of the night; rumour had it he did big things with lots of colour. There was a gauche young Canadian, who carried a notebook everywhere and was on twenty-four-hour call for inspiration and rhymes; he lived in white-hot creativity on the floor above me. There was an Argentinian guitarist, who busked for the rent and was saving for a course in chord control; as luck would have it, he occupied the windowless room adjacent to me, which possibly explained why my room had become vacant. There were also sightings of an inscrutable middle-aged Japanese gentleman, who spoke no known language but was reputed to hum very professionally. Of the other occupants, the only details so far known were the random limbs and ligaments anonymously adorning Tony's walls.

'How did you stumble on this hotel?' I asked Ulrika.

'Oh, no stumbling!' she said. 'It was Joan's cultural planning.' I sensed an edge of ambivalence in her choice of words.

'Sorry?'

'Oh I just love culture!' said Joan. She made it sound even more desirable than blueberry ice-cream.

And then she explained how much she loved Paris. And how she loved the buildings, and how she loved the cafés, and how she loved the *quais*, and how she loved the cobbled streets (though she was not so sure about the *pissoirs*), and how she loved the cute buses, and so on, and so on. Part of me felt very superior to her wide-eyed hicksville homage – and part of me sensed they were basically my own emotions, but stripped, of course, of my deep sophistication and worldliness.

'And so I bought some stuff on Paris. You know, books, about artists, and writers, and things.'

Her phrasing induced stretch-marks in my polite smile.

'Joan loves the beauty of the English language,' said Ulrika. And the barb in her irony was fully exposed for the first time.

It was not, however, fully exposed to Joan, who merely smiled appreciatively, and continued, 'Because I always like to know where creative people get their ideas from. You know, like where they find all that inspiration.'

I nodded. It was a problem I too was worrying about.

'Which is why I like to see where famous artists lived. To sort of sniff out the vibrations.'

'I see.'

'So, when we were in the youth hostel, I looked through these books, to see who'd lived where in this beautiful town, and guess what I found out!' She looked straight at me through her rainbow-finned frames. 'You'll never guess who used to live round *here*!'

I shook my head, genuinely interested to know.

She paused, and then, deciding to go for maximum dramatic effect, said, 'I'll get the book,' and hurried off upstairs.

Ulrika got up to make the coffee.

'When I first met her in Frankfurt after Christmas,' she said, in what I took to be a subtly-worded way of squashing any notion that they might be old friends, 'it was like bumping into a tour guide! "How to Do Culture on Five Dollars a Day!"'

She did not say it nastily, but with an amused detachment.

Detachment – a rather dreamy detachment – seemed to underlie much of her character.

'So I sat back and let her organize me! And be my route-planner, and my Paris planner.'

'I'd have thought it was a bit short of mod cons for her here. No hot and cold, no bellhop, no Gideon Bible by the bed.'

'Ah, but she's suffering for art.' She smiled.

'Oh, of course.' I felt encouraged by her smile.

'And anyway she goes home in a week.' I moved closer, feeling suddenly hot again.

'Here we are!' Joan bubbled back into the room, carrying half a dozen books.

She dropped various paperbacks – an A to Z of Paris Life, a couple of Henry Millers, a Scott Fitzgerald – onto the bed. She kept in her hands a Hemingway, which she held up.

It was *A Moveable Feast*, the all-time classic account of Paris literary life.

She opened it for me at page one. 'Read the second paragraph!' she insisted.

I read it aloud.

It began, 'The Café des Amateurs was the cesspool of the rue Mouffetard, that wonderful narrow crowded market street which led into the place Contrescarpe.'

The balconettes of the Hotel de Carcassonne looked down on the rue Mouffetard, and the little square with the five struggling trees was the place Contrescarpe.

I felt a sudden overwhelming excitement.

Culture-vulture Joan from Pittsburgh had led me to the heart of the old Parisian literati. Middle-American, all-gum-chewing Joan had single-handedly located one of the last, great strongholds of the *demi-monde*. She had found me my Ramblas.

CHAPTER 8

Early the next morning, when the air was still fresh, I stepped out from the hotel and stood on the narrow pavement of rue Mouffetard, and for five minutes I just looked and listened. Horse-drawn tank wagons were no longer pumping out the previous day's sewage from the houses, disturbing Hemingway's nostrils, but otherwise the life of the street seemed unaffected by forty years of progress. In the square, people were drifting across to the *boulangerie* four doors up. Just beyond, on the corner, the owner of the *charcuterie (Maison fondée en 1748)* was washing down the elaborately coloured tiling on her shop-front. In the square's main café, a black-waistcoated waiter was unstacking his chairs for the first coffee-drinkers of the day. All around, a clean, invigorating smell of damp pavements was lingering from the municipal hose-down at dawn.

From the hotel doorway, I noticed an easel – the first easel of the day? – already in position on the square. The painter was all in black – black corduroys, black sweater, woolly black hat, wiry black beard – and he was working on a roofscape of one of the small streets which led off place de la Contrescarpe. The outline complete, he was cautiously dabbing in coloured details, occasionally muttering under his brush. In England, the scene would be cause for a wide berth, even a discreet 999 call to the nutter disposal squad, but here random passers-by, often with baguette in hand, would halt, observe carefully – and then enter into a discussion of alternative techniques. Across the still-quiet square, I caught snatches of populist advice on perspective, a sentence or two on pigments in paint, and something about the tonal qualities of grey in roof slate. At the end of five minutes, the painter had accumulated a sufficient quorum for an art seminar – and everyone trooped across the square for a coffee.

I turned away from the square, to follow rue Mouffetard downhill, to see the sights that lay beyond the gently curling bend. Too narrow to be other than a one-way street, here the locals had almost gained dominion over traffic, and I joined the early-morning jay-walkers in the middle of the road. The regulation five-and-a-half storeys of central Paris crowded in on either side, and the winter sun was as yet too low to lift a cool blanket of shadow.

Rue Mouffetard was no chocolate box. The long, slowly unfurling street was a curious mixture of the perfectly proportioned and the grossly intrusive, of the unaffectedly picturesque and the downright ugly. It was still too poor a street to lure in flash money, and few developers had yet gutted their way through the old shops. These shops, often with frontages still unlicked by postwar paint, and unfashionably true to the village tradition of selling what people actually needed, existed in a retailing time-warp. Above the shops, serried ranks of slatted shutters, occasionally hung about with washing, added extra colour to the much-patched walls of decaying plaster. In some places, the decline of the walls had become literal, and giant timbers shored up the rotting structure of still-inhabited buildings. Elsewhere, the State had done its share of damage to the street, the nineteenth century bequeathing a grim, grey-barred barracks for servicing the forces of law and order. And at one point the concrete industry of the Fifties had donated a shabby little arcade which, oblivious to all laws of perspective, gouged an unsightly hole in the long rhythmic sweep of the street.

But rue Mouffetard was more than the sum of its architecture. And more than the sum of its artists. It was a cobbled conduit to the loveliest, probably oldest, street market in all Paris. As the door numbers topped the 100 mark, the street straightened and steepened, and one's eye was suddenly drawn downwards by the line of the buildings, and one's ear was pricked upwards by the cry of the stallholders. Then the crowds thickened, the stalls multiplied, the smells solidified, and one was swept along the sweating, food-smeared cobbles into a gleaming Eldorado of fruit and fish and fowl and meat and veg and pasta and pastries and cheeses and wines and herbs and all those 1,001 other comestibles known only to the French. Down to this bargain basement came not only lovers of food but lovers of life. Artists, addicts, buskers, con men, sensation seekers and simple tourists, all ended up in the tide of flotsam, jetsam and genius that had kept rue Mouffetard afloat since long before the French Revolution.

At the heart of the market was a café. It was a no-frills affair, painted with the now familiar Mouffetard brown, and it stood on an unprepossessing corner, with a rocky strip of concrete given over to a single row of chairs and tables. From outside, the place had all the familiar signs of a transport caff, but none of the familiar smells. Instead of the cholesteric odour of greasy bacon, there was the healthy aroma of fresh baking, and through the old, embossed windows I could see a tray of home-made *brioches* and warm-looking croissants. Instead of the whiff of stewed tea, the pungency of fresh coffee eddied around the door, and through the condensation on the glass I could make out a row of aproned stallholders standing by the bar, sipping their first *petit noir* of the day.

I had so far only riffled briefly through *A Moveable Feast*, but as early as page 2 it had made clear that every writer needed a café. (Joan had promised to leave me her books when she departed this life for Pittsburgh, and I was keenly awaiting knowledge of the other prerequisites for writing.) It seemed a little premature to be choosing a café to write in when I had yet to choose a genre, or indeed a subject, but Café Mouffetard looked the sort of place that might be full of ideas. I pushed the door open, keeping my writer's pad concealed lest it look showy, and went into its inviting, homely fug.

It was a surprisingly large café, medium-barn-size almost, full of simple chairs and simple tables. It was as yet less than a quarter full of people. I sat down by the window, ordered a hot chocolate, and waited for some material to happen.

Immediately, a biggish, middle-aged woman, dressed in a man's black suit and black shoes, with a black sweater over loose, bulky breasts, and accompanied by a black Alsatian crossbreed on a black leather-thonged leash, entered and sat by the bar on a high stool. She wore a peaked cap, also in black, pierced by a giant silver pen brooch. On all eight fingers she had large knuckleduster rings. Her hair was close-cropped, her sideburns accentuated by what seemed to be charcoal. She ordered a hot milk, and began to smile methodically at each of the single women in the café.

Outside, a middle-aged Spaniard – he had a notice saying 'Espagnol' – arrived with a large rucksack. He was poorly dressed, in thin, stained slacks and a parka, but had an intelligent, sensitive face made charming by boyishly curly dark hair. A small crowd gathered. In a scene reminiscent of Barcelona, he carefully unpacked his rucksack and, over the course of five minutes, meticulously laid out some dozen different-sized wooden flutes along the kerb on a small woollen rug. Then, beside them, he placed his upturned hat, whose brim he continued to adjust for a further five minutes, apparently fine-tuning its receptivity to money. Then, like an orchestra warming up, he spent some ten minutes blowing on his hands, and adjusting his feet to the desired playing position. By this time, his only remaining audience was an elderly military-looking gentleman, with an elderly military-looking moustache and a deaf aid, who was patiently standing upright and pukka in a camel-haired overcoat. There was also a large stray dog. Then the Spaniard took the flutes one by one, in ascending order of size, and blew a single, protracted note on each, carefully testing the street's acoustics. During this test period, the military-looking gentleman left. Finally, the Spaniard chose the flute most suitable, blew on his hands once more, tweaked his hat, shuffled his feet, and began to play. Whereupon the dog savaged him. And he left, running.

The mauled flutist had not been long gone when a bearded young man in an old woolly hat and torn woolly jacket staggered into the middle of the street, holding up a Bible and a tin of what appeared to be throat lozenges. Preaching at the top of his voice he then tried to sell the tin's contents . . . lozenge by lozenge. Failure made him increasingly aggressive, and he soon began to pester every passer-by, pursuing them on rubbery legs and thrusting a lozenge and explanatory text under their nose. However, what was in the text and what was in the lozenge and, indeed, what he was actually saying, one could not tell from inside the café, and so these events unrolled with all the mystery of Noh theatre. Until, that is, a well-dressed little old lady – the classic little old lady of anecdotage – approached him, quietened him, read the message he had for the world, discussed his product – and then hit him repeatedly and violently with her shopping bag, driving him out of the market and down an alleyway.

The action outside over, I looked around the café again – and saw that the mysterious woman and dog in black were just leaving . . . in the company of a slim young blonde from the table next to me. I decided it would also be a good moment for my departure: as the writer in me walked slowly back up rue Mouffetard, I wondered whether I was in danger of receiving more inspiration than I could cope with.

CHAPTER 9

Over the next few days, I steadily pottered, trying out my new lifestyle for size; gently adding flesh to those first faint Spanish fantasies of living, stationary, in one place, with an address, residentwise, *sur le continent*.

I bought a tiny cooking Gaz cylinder, and a pan, and a second and third plate, so that I could throw dinner parties. I went shopping for tea bags and a tin of coffee and a candle, so that I could entertain women. I tore up a back issue of *Le Monde Diplomatique* and saved the pieces, so that an upset stomach could be an educational experience. I removed the bits of guy-rope from my three-quarter-person drizzle-proof tent, and rigged up a washing line. I also gained a left profile and a right profile from Tony, and sellotaped all three portraits together, like a poor man's triptych, above the cracked shaving mirror.

I learnt that rue Mouffetard had entered recorded history in 1274. (I also learnt that *mouffetard* was not folkloric slang for something like 'kip late', but meant, approximately and prosaically, 'stinking'.) I found a plaque which showed that Monsieur Diderot had drawn up his encyclopedia just around the corner. I became privy to the information that, such was the intellectual timbre of the area, the local *clochards* sleeping over the heating vents included a doctor of law and a professor, who between them spoke nine languages (though presumably in too slurred a tone to be understood). I stumbled on a zoo nearby, and made the discovery that in food-conscious France even the rheas had their carrots served *râpées*. And I learnt that when you emerged from the up escalator at place Monge, the nearest Metro, you were revivified by a lovely view of the trees and the sky above your head.

All this and much more I immediately exaggerated and romanticized in letters to England . . . or, to be painfully precise, in letters to Oxford and Cambridge. Had it not been for my adolescent idleness – a trait which, as the years rolled by, I was to publicly recharacterize as, first, 'waywardness', then 'alienation', then 'rebelliousness', and finally 'independence of spirit' – I could have been currently cloistered somewhere very hallowed in academia, in the upwardly mobile company of my school friends. Alone of my contemporaries, I had defaulted on the dreaming spires. My erstwhile mates could now talk of Wittgenstein, allude to Cervantes, disparage the *Areopagitica*, and be effortlessly polysyllabic in public. They had already gained the ineffable intellectual confidence which comes of drinking the water in Oxbridge, and were soon to be in possession of the tickets for the reserved seats on the non-stopping train to High Places.

By contrast, I (to milk the metaphor) had somehow become uncoupled in the sidings at an early age; a mysterious laziness – my only explanation was a rogue recessive gene – and a failure to realize that life was a serious business had eventually shunted me into the buffers of 'A' Level. My life and theirs, my plans and theirs, my self-esteem and theirs, my intellectual confidence and theirs, all had henceforth gone their separate ways.

Now, to redress the balance, to camouflage the gulf, to disguise the guilt, I sat in my struggling writer's room and sent to my far-off friends some of the most excessively exotic, erotically allusive and subtextually exciting change-of-address notifications in postal history. I wanted them to eat their hearts out. As they sweated and swotted for their Tripos papers, I wanted them to be daily distracted by thoughts of me living the life of Monsieur O'Reilly. As they made their conventional way up the main staircase of life, I wanted them to know I was frolicking to fame and fortune along the fire escape.

I had moved the small, much-scratched table from the far

corner to the window; it was not an inspirational view, but it reminded me – it reassured me – that I really was in Paris, and this small core of truth somehow gave licence to my air-mail flights of fancy. From innuendo and inference, my readers could reasonably assume that I lived in the likes of the Chelsea Hotel, that I dined with a sort of Algonquin set, sipped hot chocolate on Jean-Paul terms with Mr Sartre, possessed a bone structure which caused the Beaux Arts to name statues after me, and all night long was to be found crotch-deep in can-can girls.

An air-mail letter is a less revered art form than the novel, but when the act of writing is viewed from a distance (say, from a hotel annexe) the distinction is not an easy one to make. This was the second reason I had moved the table to the window. It not only enabled me to sit and look in Ulrika's direction, it also enabled her to stand and gaze in mine – and see a serious writer hard at work. I was not trying to outdo Dostoevsky Dave, but to establish a desirable identity. At the end of that very first soirée, when the last of my plastic bottle of 11.5° Beaujolais had drained from our shared toothbrush mug, and Joan had retired to mix the mud for her nightly face pack, Ulrika had spoken dreamily, wistfully, to me of a wish to express herself in poetry. I had taken this to reflect an interest in literature . . . and its practitioners.

Accordingly, whilst my first few days passed in pottering, they also passed in writing as publicly as possible about my pottering.

Of Ulrika herself, there was, unfortunately, no sign. Each day, she was out early and back late. And each day, all day, in a grotesque fluke of erotic cruelty, her drawn-back curtains exposed a perfect view of her empty, crumpled, waiting bed.

As I watched from my seat at the window, constructing convoluted sentences of sensual suggestion, I could do no more than dream of fevered couplings yet to come. But it was a view rich in wider meaning. It was a taunting, haunting glimpse of total liberty. For the first time in my life I sensed a world free of restraint and full of possibility. Behind me lay a single-sex childhood, a repressed adolescence and a brief, bewildered adulthood. My past had meant the confinements of the public school, the conventions of the parental home, the curfews of the hostel dorm, and the solitude of the open road. My body had known only onanistic nights. But now a future fit for my libido was suddenly in sight. I was a free agent, in a city of free agents. I was a wanting man in a city of willing women. I was a twenty-one-year-old in the capital city of lovers. Sex, like crime, is an act that needs Motivation, Means and Opportunity, but only now, after a protracted puberty overflowing with sexual motivation, and an adolescence whose phallic means was single-handedly tested to exhaustion, had I found the promised land of opportunity. Out there, the wide world of women was waiting. And already I had a room of my own, a tin of coffee and a candle. At last, I was free to entertain the opposite sex as and when I wished – though, admittedly, after ten p.m. they would have to crawl along the flagstoned passage on their stomachs if Madame's light was still on.

So, a week gone, my home-making done and my recceing over, I boldly resolved to profess my love – and, if possible, make passing reference to my lust – for flaxen-haired Ulrika.

However, by modern deadlines, even by old-fashioned deadlines, I was a late-qualifier at sex, and I lay awake for several long nights pondering upon the most appropriate *modus amandi*. I found myself faced with a cultural crisis, my sexual problem being that where I suffered most from stiffness was the upper lip. England's puritanism cast a cruel shadow: any declaration of passion, any admission of emotion, appeared contrary to the natural order. And the foreplay of a relationship threatened to remove all the fig-leaves of my painstakingly protected personality. A note, a walk, a meal, every romantic act seemed fraught with hazards; every opening move plunged into the black hole of counter-moves. Indeed, given my emotional maturity at the time, I am surprised that I didn't decide to just expose myself out of the window.

It was around eight o'clock one morning that the idea of flowers came to me. Of flowers discreetly placed against her closed door, and discreetly acknowledged, in the fullness of the day, with a sophisticated exchange of cross-courtyard smiles. I dressed at once and hurried to the market. A little alley, running at right-angles to the food stalls, had flowers for every emotion, and I chose six red carnations. I hurried back up the street with them wrapped in a sheet of pale pink paper.

It had been raining heavily overnight, and a cool gusty wind flicked loose water off the buildings as I approached place de la Contrescarpe. As I looked across the square, to enjoy yet again the smug pleasure of knowing its irresistible charms were now an everyday experience, a red soft-top Alfa Romeo Spider rumbled to an eye-catching ear-catching halt. Such a car had once given me an exhilarating, day-long, 100 m.p.h. lift the length of Yugoslavia, and the sound of its exhaust still thrilled me. I gazed enviously at the young driver – and Ulrika got out of the passenger seat.

She saw me and smiled, a glowing, happy smile. As she walked over to where I stood by the hotel entrance, the driver, a handsome – too handsome – Latin-looking chap in a fur-lined leather jacket, caught up with her at the kerb and put an arm languidly around her shoulders. Ulrika leaned back into his body and said contentedly, 'Good morning! This is Augustus.'

'Hallo.' We nodded at each other politely.

'You're up early!' she said. I nodded again. She smiled, a sexually teasing smile. 'Who are the flowers for, then?'

'Oh, no-one,' I replied. 'Just something to brighten up my room.'

'All of three days!' said Ulrika. And laughed happily.

We were sitting in La Chope, waiting for Joan to appear. It was an ugly, modern café, and disfigured the far side of the square – outside it was plate-glass, inside it was noisy game-machines. Augustus was at the bar, making a phone-call, and Ulrika and I were facing the breakfast of croissants and coffee he had ordered for us.

'Three days? You didn't leave his apartment for three days?' I tried not to sound incredulous. Or suicidal.

She grinned. 'There was a very good room service!' But then her normal tendency to be enigmatic was overcome by a desire to share her happiness, and she added, 'They seem to take passion very seriously, Latin Americans. Very thorough!' At this she blushed, but it was a touch of demureness which only served to make her behaviour the more powerfully – and painfully – erotic. 'Didn't you notice I was away?'

'I thought you were out with Joan.' My mind kept returning to the hours I had spent gazing at her bed, deep in private fantasies – unaware that they were being simultaneously enacted elsewhere.

She didn't seem to have heard. 'Mind you, long time to wait, twenty-five years,' she said. For a second I missed her meaning, but her flushed smile helped me grasp it was a hymen reference.

She glanced across at the bar. Augustus fluttered his hand and smiled lovingly. Even at this distance, I could see several chunky rings on his fingers. Even in the way he used the telephone, I could detect the body language of wealth. Still in his twenties, he already had a round, well-satisfied face; the incipient round-ness of his body was disguised by the quality of his tailoring. I also suspected the attentions of a manicurist and a hair-stylist.

'What does he do?'

'Architectural student. At the Sorbonne.' Ulrika must have realized this was insufficient information, since she added, 'His father's very rich. Seems to own Bolivia.'

Her choice of lover, rich and vain, appalled and puzzled me, but, before I could ask more, Augustus had finished his phone-call and rejoined us at the table. He brought with him an early morning cognac, and threw back his head as he drank it. He had great belief in his charm, and great confidence in his attractive-ness, and all the while he talked his right hand diligently caressed Ulrika's neck and hair. I wanted to look away and gaze out of the window, but unfortunately my field of vision was occupied by his red Alfa Romeo Spider.

I resisted the urge to request a refund for my flowers, and, trying hard to take Left-Bank life in my stride, I launched upon a little polite, neutral, conversation.

'Paris must be a great inspiration for an architecture student.'

'Why?'

So sharply aggressive, so inexplicably challenging, was his response, that for a moment the answer escaped me.

'Why? Well . . . because of . . . because of all the beautiful buildings.'

'Beautiful! You think they're beautiful?' This time his response had come loaded with contempt.

'I . . . er, yes. Yes, very beautiful . . .' This seemed to me so undeniably one of the self-evident truths of all time that, try as I might, no fudge appeared to be available. I struggled to understand. Was there a subtext? Did he think I was sleeping with Ulrika? '. . . Very,' I repeated weakly.

'Really?' He gave an arrogant little laugh.

'You, er . . . you don't? Find them beautiful, I mean?'

'I would destroy them! I would destroy them all!' And he glared furiously across the table.

The vehemence of this ambition, last voiced by Hitler, definitively silenced me. I felt such shock and astonishment that any conversational development of this theme was quite beyond me. What, I wondered, did he write in his essays? I tried to concentrate on a croissant to hide my bewilderment, and to escape his glare.

At which point Ulrika, aware of my confusion, added helpfully, 'Augustus is a revolutionary.'

'Oh, I see!' I said.

For an instant, I wondered if Ulrika could have become a terrorist's moll since Monday. But when I glanced up at her there was the hint of a familiar smile around her lips, as if in discreet reassurance that her private world was intact. Even so, her concept of romance remained impenetrable.

'Obviously the buildings wouldn't be the first things to destroy. We'd have to destroy the power structures first.'

'Oh,' I said.

He was my first revolutionary. It was a year before Che Guevara appeared on T-shirts, and the overthrow of civilization was something about which I as yet knew little.

'But you can't create a socialist society in buildings of bourgeois decadence!' he continued, giving the implosive 'b' of bourgeois enough venom to bounce it off all four walls. 'It pollutes the people's thought. It fucks up their cultural values.'

'*All* the buildings?' I asked tentatively, still stranded at the first base of Marxist dialectics. 'Would you destroy all the buildings?'

'What?'

'I said would you—' I think the idea at the back of my apolitical mind was to compile a list of which particular buildings he had got it in for, but I was angrily and summarily interrupted.

'The buildings aren't the point! The buildings don't matter! The shitty things are just a symbol! What matters is that the people have the means to construct an egalitarian society. Free from exploitation! And that means inspired by socialist values, socialist art, socialist architecture! And you can't do that if you live in a mausoleum of eighteenth-century fascist kitsch!'

'I see,' I said, again. During the course of his tirade it had gradually dawned upon me that this was the vigorous intellectual interchange of café society which I had so long been seeking.

Fortunately, a Continental breakfast is not long enough for the unabridged exposition of *Das Kapital*, and so I was only treated to an outline of revolutionary aesthetics and a few salient evils of capitalism. Unfortunately, my opportunities to intervene were rare. Augustus had clearly read widely about the proletariat and possessed that impregnable personal certainty which comes from the inner strength of a private income.

He was in mid-oration about the nature of the revolution, and the blood that would necessarily flow, when the sad, gaudy figure of Joan emerged into the rainswept square, struggling with her plastic mac and pulling a shiny suitcase on wheels behind her. She was departing, Pittsburgh-bound, and the Alfa was waiting to take her to Orly.

Augustus, ever the chivalrous, chauvinist Latin, got at once to his feet and, sprinkling some cash over the table, went outside to help load her luggage.

As Ulrika and I slowly followed him out, distance gave his dandyish figure an air of comic improbability; watching him, insulated from the world by his wealth, I was struck by a realization that for him politics was – like his sports car – just another plaything, yet another toy.

It was the first time that I had met anyone inhabiting a fantasy world of revolutionary violence, fed by wild delusions of apocalyptic grandeur, and his self-deception was bordering on the certifiable. Or so I wrote, in my apolitical wisdom, to my Oxbridge friends. The next time I was to see him would be fifteen months later – in the revolutionary month of *mai '68*. But then not even the footnotes of *Das Kapital* had forecast the firestorm that was to envelop the bourgeois citadel of Paris.

'Jeez, it looks so goddam beau-tiful in the rain!' squawked Joan, as she took one last, lingering look around the square.

Her dream of a lifetime was over, her brush with culture complete. She had the memories, and the photos to prove her memories; now she was going home in the fading hope of children and grandchildren with whom she could one day share them. In her spare hand she clutched a large plastic bag of small plaster busts, each a loving factory tribute to a famous artist; through the condensation of her mac pocket a dog-eared guidebook to the Joys of Versailles was still smudgily visible; and in her jacket, she said, was a hand-sculpted chocolate bar of the Moulin Rouge.

She paused again for one more final last look. But already, one sensed, the sweet ambivalence of departure was taking hold.

'I jest hope they'll believe this back in Pittsburgh!' she kept sighing, with an evident thrill at the thought of telling them.

'Come along, my darling!' instructed Augustus. 'I've rung Orly, you have to check in by eleven!'

He pushed the passenger seat forward and Joan bent gymnastically low to shoe-horn herself into the token back seat. The sight of her loose, shapeless bottom was the last view that I can remember of the woman who was the unwitting midwife to the new life that I had now begun.

Ulrika slid elegantly into the front seat, pulled solicitously back by Augustus, and sat looking as radiant and desirable as any Alfa Romeo marketing man could ever have wished. I stood on the pavement, longing to be the driver. Augustus settled in behind the wheel, producing a sporty little cap to give him a Grand Prix look, and squeezed first her knee and then her inner thigh. I stood on the pavement longing to punch the driver. With Ulrika sitting contented, Augustus adjusted the rear-view mirror for a better look at himself, and then started the engine.

Ulrika smiled at me. I smiled back and tried hard to understand. She was no gold-digger, of that I was sure, yet neither was she a political animal. And nor was she naïve enough to be fooled by a posturing playboy. Her behaviour was a mystery to me. His attraction was a mystery to me. Their whole relationship was a mystery to me. Indeed, amidst all my pain I felt curiously indignant – part of the attraction to becoming a bohemian was that I had understood it to have sex-appeal.

Augustus gave a blast on his horn (which appeared to play a Bolivian version of The Internationale), the car made one last throaty circuit of the square, and then they turned and disappeared down rue du Cardinal Lemoine, driving out of sight past Hemingway's old flat at no. 74.

As I watched them go, I had the feeling that my settling-in period was over.

The rain came in gusts again, and suddenly I was aware once more of my six red carnations. They were battered and unhappy. I hurried back across place de la Contrescarpe to the hotel. The goal of love might, it seemed, prove rather less straightforward than I had first imagined.

CHAPTER 10

And thus began the frivolous business of living.

For two days the winter rain continued to gust down, repeatedly rattling the window-frames, and for two days I moped, wondering how to turn suffering into art. Of Ulrika, there was no sign, and at night I would lie awake bathed in sweat as I imagined the room service she was receiving. My two spare plates and coloured candle remained in mint condition, conspicuous and idle on the old mantelpiece. For long periods I sat at my writer's table, prolific only in doodles, and gazed out over the courtyard.

It was as I gazed at the dustbins that I first saw him. He had on a dirty-white American detective's mac. Underneath it, his shoulders were noticeably hunched, yet he seemed little older than thirty. A thick beard hid much of the face and its expression, but he walked like a man with a troubled soul and I knew at once that he was Dostoevsky Dave. Oblivious to the rain, he wandered back into the annexe entrance and abstractedly made himself a roll-up. I watched him puff from the shadows, as if in a scene of homage to the Third Man, and became quickly convinced his angst was more intellectual than mine. But all the time I watched, something was niggling away at the back of my mind. That first glimpse of him by the dustbins had been somehow odd . . . his movements somehow strange. And then I realized what it was. He had not been putting something *in* to the dustbins. He had been trying to take something *out*.

It was not until I knew him much better that I realized he had been looking for food.

Then he started his pacing. He paced to and fro across the courtyard, like an automaton, like a ball bouncing back and forth off opposite walls. He paced for five minutes, for ten minutes, for twenty minutes, focusing intently on the wet cobbles, and occasionally engaging them in conversation. From a sitting position, I could not see all the courtyard, and I leaned across the table to gain a better view, and if possible catch a few lines of dialogue. I had my nose almost pressed against the glass when he suddenly stopped and looked up. It was a blank-eyed stare, and he probably never saw me, but I immediately felt intrusive, not to say foolish, and in an equally sudden reflex action I waved, flung up the window, and called 'Coffee?'

The question transfixed him. Furrows appeared in his forehead, and time stood still as he agonized like a man presented with a Finals paper in a particularly difficult year. I felt I had posed the most intractable issue of our times. The Coffee Question. For what seemed like minutes on end rain streamed across his upturned, troubled face as he struggled to assess all the pros and cons of my offer, the social subtexts, the question of precedent, the historical importance of hot liquids, and, presumably, whether or not he liked coffee. But at last he nodded his head.

I lit the Gaz under the small saucepan of water and wondered how best to establish his position on milk and sugar.

He gave a brusque knock and came into the room with a forced smile. I forced one back. He stood awkward and intense by the door, making no attempt to remove his sodden coat.

'You're Dave, aren't you?'

He nodded.

'. . . I'm Barry. Expect Ulrika's mentioned me.'

He nodded again.

'. . . Come and drip by the radiator!'

This time he gave a nod with smile. Close to, his manner confirmed a strange unworldliness. He seemed unused to the human race other than as an abstract concept. Yet his very lack of guile made me trust him. I suppose at this point in the narrative I should have looked into his eyes and established for the reader that he was 'direct' or 'hostile' or 'evasive', or blind. But I forgot. I don't even know what colour his eyes were. I just noticed he was very quiet. Silent, in fact.

He tried to warm himself by the radiator's half-hearted ribs. As he did so, he looked out on the unfamiliar view of his annexe with curiosity. For some time. In the end, it was I that broke the ice.

'I gather you haven't got a window,' I said.

'No.'

'Just a grille by the door.'

'Yes.'

'You must be glad of fresh air.'

'Oh, there are worse things in life than stale air!' He spat this view out with quite unexpected vigour.

I waited, hoping he might expound, offer some sort of list of these things – or indeed *anything* that might give a clue as to his thoughts. Especially on life. I was very conscious he was a fellow-writer and I was keen to nudge the conversation towards writerly things. Like where ideas came from. Ideally, I wanted to ask him about his block, but he seemed a very private man.

'Very true,' I said at last.

'It's noise I hate. Can't work with noise.'

'I know what you mean,' I said.

'The man in the next room.' He warmed angrily to his theme. 'He drives me out.'

'Oh . . . why?'

'Works nights. Fucks days.'

There was an over-emphasis on thin partitions in the cheaper rooms.

'Curry's the warning sign. If he's going to score he cooks a curry.'

Suddenly I recalled the penetrating smell of curry as I had raced up the stairs to Ulrika's on my first evening.

'Always Arab lads. Teenage Arabs. At 100 decibels a time.'

96

'I can see that would make it hard to write,' I said sympathetically.

'It's my *own* space. My private space. I need a private world. Where I can be alone, have my own thoughts.'

His words were spoken in a jarring New York accent, disconcertingly at odds with the intimacy of their meaning.

'What thoughts are those exactly?'

It was an unnecessary prompt. Used to his own company, he spoke without need of an audience, indeed almost unaware that he had one.

'Imagine a world where every action receives its just rewards! Not in the after-life. But in this life. On the same day. Imagine a God who dispensed justice on a daily basis. God the Supreme Vigilante! And everybody knew this to be true. You see, what Dostoevsky said was, "If there is no God, everything is permissible." But what of the opposite contention? What if everyone *knew* there was a God – not just believed – and *knew* that for every evil action there would be an avenging counter-action? What future for mankind then, eh?'

I nodded.

'Take a typical day in Harlem. A Mafia hood, a hit-man. Except *now* he knows that if he wastes someone, a tree will fall on him by nighttime. Or his car exhaust will poison him – because this God moves in very deliberate ways! What profit evil then, eh?'

I nodded again.

'And that's just the beginning! Because all of Harlem, all New York, has now to constantly work out what *is* right. And what is wrong. And not just black and white, and life and death, but all those greys. Whether to put Ma in a home. Whether to burn your draft card. Whether to spend your money in ritzy restaurants. Because one wrong move and God's giving you penalty points! A burst water pipe, maybe, a lost job, a major illness. Just imagine it! A whole city trying to work out – in New York's case, trying to guess! – what is the morally correct course of action! For the first time in human history.

'Would it mean the perfectibility of man? Or moral paralysis?

With everyone too fearful, too ignorant, to act? And total chaos sweeping the land?

'It's one of the last great themes of literature. It's philosophy, and drama, and religion, and thriller, all rolled into one! But trying to create a whole new moral universe in my head . . .'

He held his head between his hands and shook it despairingly. He sighed, and then became aware of my presence again.

'Tony says you're a writer too. What are you working on?'

I reached for the mugs. And the coffee. And the milk. And the sugar. And the bendy travelling-spoon. I could see it was my turn for the long, anguished pause.

Curiously, I envied Dave, even envied him his creative torment. Because everything about him said serious writer. He even had a proper writer's beard. It was dense and wiry and came in a manly dark-brown and grew in all the correct places. A year of counter-culture on the open road had inexplicably left me with a mangy, temperamental growth that blew about in the wind. I had initially tried just for a moustache, naively assuming my top lip would automatically grow a mucho macho *Viva Zapata* model, in accordance with my desired image. Instead, it had produced a droopy stringy thing, much favoured by ageing Eastern mandarins in *Aladdin* pantos. So I had then gone for the full facial option, only to discover I had two-tone hair – brunettish down the sides and ginger on the chin. The baffling genetics behind this meant that I also had a two-speed beard, which, unless constantly tended, looked the result of an erratic Fisons hair-spray. Perhaps I was a surrealist?

Dave was still patiently waiting for an answer. Beside him on the table lay my life's work. So far, I had less than a completed sentence to my name.

'Well . . .'

At this point, the water boiled to my rescue, and I busied myself with the technicalities of coffee.

I had just one straw I could clutch at. Two years earlier, amidst the cultural mayhem of Swinging London, there had arisen a glitzy new magazine. It was by bright young things, for bright young things, and about what bright young things were up to.

Mostly they were up to rather boring things in the Chelsea area. So, before fleeing the country, I had written to the editor advising him of my momentous journey and offering him exclusive coverage. For a reasonable fee. He had written back, saying, 'We wish you luck on your travels. If you see anything interesting, let us know.'

I handed Dave his coffee, after spooning out the four sugars he had requested for his energy levels, and replied, 'I'm a travel writer. Short stories, articles, you know.'

'Oh.'

I had expected rather more from him.

'Like Hemingway,' I added, 'in the early days.' I had just finished Chapter 1 of Joan's *Moveable Feast*, and every time Ernest went into a café he wrote a best-selling short story on somewhere foreign.

Dave nodded, like a man who couldn't quite place Hemingway.

He was starting to pace again. His private world was closing around him like a thickening mist. The trauma of exposing his life's great opus had, like childbirth, left him exhausted, incapable of further effort. I tried to draw him out on other, lighter subjects but to no effect. I suspected that his remarks on inconsiderately loud buggery represented the limit of his small talk.

He was ready to leave. He drained his coffee, took a last look from my window, said 'Thank you', and was gone.

And after he had gone, I still envied him. Above all, I envied him the fact that he was a driven writer; at best, I would never be more than a slightly pushed writer. He *had* to write, whereas I merely thought writing seemed quite a neat idea.

I also noticed that when Dave left, putting his mug on the table, he had placed it four-square, and smudgily damp, on a sheet of my doodles. Perhaps it was artistic paranoia on my part, but for some time afterwards I pondered as to the symbolism intended by his action.

CHAPTER 11

Although hungry from a hard night's thinking, I was glad to see the early-morning queue in the square's *boulangerie*. The warm aroma from the freshly-baked dough always made the waiting a sensuous pleasure. I stood in line by the gleaming white tiles and continued to ponder the choice between climbing an active volcano with a party of six German fascists or riding a camel across the Jordan desert to camp in Lawrence of Arabia's hideout.

'*Oui, monsieur?*'

'*Une religieuse à chocolat, s'il vous plaît, madame.*'

It was not a financially wise or protein-efficient purchase, a two-tier nun-shaped chocolate cream bun, but I had come to regard my forays into *pâtisserie* as essentially educational, a way of getting to grips with the technical vocabulary of *la langue française*. The French language is a hard task-mistress and some cakes I had had to buy four or five times before being able to order them with confidence. Indeed, I could already foresee that mastering the pronunciation of *mille-feuille* might take me weeks. I would also like to have tackled the world of *charcuterie* but my funds limited me to the linguistic basics.

Penury led to an odd diet. French cuisine made only fleeting appearances, usually in the shape of a Brie-packed baguette. Central to my survival was the elusive fifty-centime Mars Bar – a bargain confined to the farther-flung *faubourgs* – which I would occasionally garnish with chips on the walk back. Cooking meals was, I had decided, too recherché an art-form.

'*Le voilà, monsieur!*' The elderly assistant placed a package on the counter.

The other joy of a chocolate nun was watching it be expertly boxed, wrapped, and bowed in gift-ribbon. In its deft elegance this ritual exemplified both the French taste for formality and their reverence for food. I never ceased to enjoy the transformation of my modest purchases. Admittedly, I was going to rip it all open and wolf down the contents in thirty seconds flat, but, as service, it had a definite edge over the English tradition of smearing the bun in a brown paper bag and yawning.

'*Merci bien, madame.*' I made my way back down the line and out.

I was now decided. The midnight assault on an erupting Stromboli would be the first Traveller's Tale. The camel would come next. In an initial series of six. Possibly published as a paperback the following year.

A writer's first creative act is the laying-on of coffee. A few doors along, as anonymous and peeling as the hotel, stood an ancient bar. It was of the spit 'n' sawdust genre, and had no truck with shiny metal surfaces or juke boxes. At the back was a pool hall, at the front were serious drinkers in berets. In such bars had a hung-over Jean Gabin hung out when the world was still in black and white.

I ordered a *café noir* and sat by the nicotine-stained window overlooking the square. Underneath one of the bare trees, the street artist from my first morning was setting up his easel again. Tugging at his black beard, he gazed down rue Mouffetard and carefully considered his opening brush-strokes. I pulled out my own pad. I had overcome my shyness at making notes in public – especially now I had six Traveller's Tales on the stocks.

The fiery volcano shot its load into the night sky. From the deck of the ferry, the island looked like a Roman candle. Which was appropriate, because this was Italy. As I waited my turn to leap into the rowing-boat full of chickens, it erupted every fifteen minutes, with more reliability than British Rail! I was glad that I would soon be safe and sound in the island taverna, eating spaghetti as only Italian Mamas make it. Next to me I noticed a party of Germans, clad in their national uniform of lederhosen and boots. 'We are going to climb Stromboli tonight. Are you?' Recognizing a gauntlet, I said, 'Yes.'

'Hi!'

I looked up from my pad. A man about my age, in frayed jeans, a paint-speckled T-shirt and a black leather jacket was standing by my table. The door to the street clicked shut behind him. He smiled.

'Are you English?'

He looked a little rough, his dark curly hair in rampant disorder. I noted, though, that his beard was successful.

'Yes.'

'Thought so! Mind if I join you?'

He smiled again, a certain streetwise cocky charm about him. I gestured to the empty chair.

'Thanks!'

He sat down and blew on his gloveless hands, chilled by the early-morning air. 'Name's Colin, by the way.' He held out a hand.

'Barry,' I said, shaking it.

I was intrigued by his attentions. I wondered if he was a fellow-writer.

'Couldn't spare the price of a beer, could you?'

'Oh . . .'

The sight of a used bun had clearly given him a false impression of my wealth. But then I remembered my Orwell from school. And how beggars with two francs gave money to beggars with one franc. And how this was part of the bohemian value system. Which I wished to espouse. Unfortunately.

'Sure!' I ordered him a demi.

I was curious about him, but felt it pettily bourgeois to pose personal questions. By his accent – and he had good gravelly diction – he was evidently English, but something about his hair suggested Mediterranean roots.

'Been painting,' he said, gesturing to the white flecks on his chest. 'Rooms!' he added with a grin, lest there be any confusion. 'For a mate.'

'You should paint *my* room!' I said. 'Be a first for the twentieth century!'

'You live round here?'

'In the hotel next door. You?'

'Er . . . it's a bit complicated,' he replied.

A brief pause followed, and he stretched for his beer. I noticed there was a slogan across his flecked chest. It invited the exploited lower classes to do something obscured by his leather jacket. He caught my gaze.

'WRP.'

'Sorry?'

'Workers' Revolutionary Party.'

'Oh. I've been abroad.'

'I was very active in Portsmouth. You know, demos, marches. To support the dockers.'

'Right,' I said. 'Right!' And hoped that such emphasis adequately conveyed my solidarity. '. . . Are you very active over here?' I asked, slightly concerned lest, like Augustus, he too had it in for the architecture.

'Can't afford to be!' he said ruefully.

'Oh?'

'Yeah. Had a bit of trouble.'

I waited. I sensed he wanted to tell me more.

'Pigs got my passport!'

'Really!' I was impressed. 'Why?'

'Couldn't pay the hotel bill!' He laughed. 'Hotel's got all my luggage. Clothes, the lot. Step back in there and a vanload of fascists will jump me.'

I had never had a drink with a man on the run before. His insouciance made me wonder what other crimes he had to his name. There was an air of danger about him, a sense that he was a man going to the bad.

'So what'll you do?'

'I don't know yet. Trouble with sleeping rough, if the pigs

pick you up, they work you over. And with no papers . . . !' He shook his head ominously and took a long draught of beer.

I was uneasy in his presence, yet intrigued by the way he lived . . . and oddly flattered by his confidences. It made me feel less of an outsider in my new world, to be chosen as a confidant. Perhaps it was my writer's pad, but I was beginning to suspect he had seen in me a kindred spirit, another rebel living life on the margins of society.

'Couldn't crash in your place, could I?'

A lot of things became very clear very quickly.

I struggled.

'I'm afraid I'm a writer. I pace a lot.'

'Sorry?'

'At night. Thinking.'

'I'd only need a small corner.'

'It's a flagstone floor.'

'Oh, so's the pavement. Don't worry about me, I'm used to it.'

'Oh.'

'I mean, if you don't want me to—'

'—No! No, it's not that,' I lied hastily. Pathetically, I was keen not to give offence, eager not to be uncool. 'You'd be very welcome—' I was about to say 'but' when he said 'Great!'

Neatly dressed small children with leather satchels were on their way to kindergarten, greeting one another with grown-up handshakes, when I emerged from the bar. The bourgeois day was beginning.

I had seen Tony pass by earlier with his demi-baguette under his arm, looking tired and misanthropic after a night of executive toilet-scrubbing, and I felt a sudden longing for a recycled tea bag and a grudging chat. I knew that, underneath, he would be glad to see me. There were some muscles in my forearm that he had expressed an interest in.

I felt my way along the dark corridor to the door.

'Flamenco! He's learning bloody flamenco now!' was the cry of outrage that greeted me. Tony gestured helplessly at the wall he had in common with the Argentinian guitarist.

I had heard the first suspect strums a day or two before. Rumour on the corridors was that my mystery neighbour had been offered work at a club in Montmartre.

'Has he been doing a lot of *Olés*?'

'God knows what he's been doing! But if he stamps his feet once more, I'll show him another Spanish tradition. Garrotting!' Tony struck a match for the Gaz with excess vigour and the flaming end sheared into the saucepan of water.

'Perhaps you could clap out of tune and drive him mad?'

'Thought I could get him under the Police Code,' Tony jerked his head at the daunting list of ordinances on the back of the door, 'but what he's up to isn't even mentioned! I mean, what's the point of living in a fascist state if you can't arrest people for doing the flamenco at nine o'clock in the morning?'

I did not realize it at the time, but this was known as Liverpool Wit, and in later years became much sought after.

'I just wish he'd practise at night when normal people are out working,' he continued.

I ignored this jibe and fished the burnt match out of the tea water on grounds of hygiene. I could clearly hear a chord being warmed up. 'Does Madame know?'

'Yes.' Tony sighed. 'Says she used to dance it with her husband in 1914. Before he left for the trenches. Brings back very happy memories apparently, does flamenco. She'll probably give him a rent reduction!' And he snorted with laughter at the thought.

'What other type of music makes her happy?' I enquired with interest.

Tony's anger was deceptive. He was not cross with Juan because he practised his guitar. In fact, I imagined he would rather respect his dedication. What irked Tony – apart from long nights in tall office blocks – was Juan's stubborn refusal to pose for him. Even with a guitar. And Tony took refusal very personally.

As I waited for the water to boil I pulled my shirtsleeve up. Tony wanted to sketch my raised arm and clenched fist, to capture the highlighted muscles and tendons. It was not the most satisfying of postures. When I looked in the mirror I saw the unflattering sight of a rather embarrassed, failed he-man who appeared to have misplaced his Olympic torch. I averted my eyes.

It was then that I saw, in a row next to the mirror, a series of new portraits, starring a new sitter. Even though Tony belonged to the warts-and-all school of drawing, I could see he had persuaded a woman of rare good looks to be his latest tea drinker. If the original were as lovely, I was prepared to award her straight A's for eyes, nose and mouth.

Tony had followed my gaze and, unusually for him, he spoke as he sketched.

'How d'you like our new Joan?'

'New Joan?'

'Yes. *That*,' he pointed, 'is who's got Joan's old room.'

'Really?' I had noticed a degree of curtain movement across the courtyard but, being engrossed in my rejected lover phase, I had not thought to investigate. 'What do you know about her?'

'Oh, I don't ask questions,' said Tony, displaying – and enjoying – an uncharacteristic wilfulness.

'What do you know about her?' I threatened to lower my arm and unclench my fist. 'Tony!'

He looked up at me.

'Rich, beautiful and tragic.' He resumed sketching.

'You could tell all that from the bone structure, could you?'

'She talked to me a bit.'

'Go on. What's her name? Where's she from?'

'Eleanor. She's from Washington.' He paused. 'She's the daughter of the President's doctor.'

'The President's doctor?' I stared at him. 'What, the President of the United States?'

'Yeah, that one.'

His news had the desired effect and my jaw stayed open for some time.

'So what's she doing in a flea-pit at six francs a night?'

It was a while before Tony answered. He had enjoyed giving

me his news, making me tease out his information. But now he seemed genuinely reluctant to say more.

'That's the tragic bit.'

I looked at her face again. It did not seem a face familiar with tragedy.

Tony was ahead of my thoughts. He spoke embarrassedly. 'I – I tried to . . . soften her features a bit.'

I knew now that we were talking of something really serious. I decided not to ask, in case Tony did not wish to tell me. Indeed, in case I did not wish to hear.

After a moment or two he said, 'She's twenty. The man she was going to marry hit a wall at 100 miles an hour, night before the wedding. I don't think it's meant to be a secret.'

He concentrated again on his drawing. My arm started to ache, because as usual he needed five, six, seven attempts before he was even mildly satisfied. I was, however, scarcely aware of the pain. His news had opened another wound. My mind was back in Nice. I was remembering another woman whose lover had died.

It still hurt me to think how I had failed to even notice Nicole's desires, how I had failed to spot her signals, how I had failed to act with confidence and passion, how I had blown the chance of a wonderful summer love affair. But if that hurt, it hurt even more to know that crass, brash, beer-belching, baseball-capped Abe from the Bronx, my Ugly American room-mate, had been the one she turned to, no, the one she gave herself to. Why? Why? I had looked for answers every day in Nice. And halfway across France. And then, just as the humiliation was beginning to fade, the lovely Ulrika had appeared – and had fallen for the disgusting Augustus. What was I doing wrong?

'OK. You can relax!' said Tony, putting down his pencil. 'It's not great. But then neither are your muscles.'

I lowered my arm, flexing my fingers to entice the blood back.

'I've sacrificed my arm for your art. It's completely dead.'

'Leave it on the table then. I'll use it for a still life.'

He handed me my tea. It was cold. I loved these moments. I

stood by the balcony and gazed out over the square where a greengroceer was trying to remove a pineapple from a drunk. At such times the reality of my life seemed almost *too* romantic.

'How's the writing going?'

'Good. Very good.' And that wasn't a lie.

★   ★   ★

As the sky went a blood-orange, so did my feet. The razor-sharp clinker started to purée my sandals, and I limped up the 3,000 foot cone in last place. Clouds of choking dust were kicked up by the Panzer division in front, who also had the advantage of a torch. Soon I lost touch, and I found myself alone with the elements, most of which were very hot and noisy. But I kept scrabbling upwards, like a lemming crossed with a bulldog. The Second World War had, I told myself, begun with similarly unequal odds.

At the end of each carefully chiselled phrase, I cast an eye over the annexe. From the moment I had seen Eleanor's portrait I had resolved to be decisive. But each small room had its curtain pulled back, offering sad proof its occupant was elsewhere.

I had struggled almost to the top of the volcano when suddenly I glimpsed her crossing the courtyard. So, ninety seconds later, when she appeared at her window to gaze at my side of the world, I immediately invoked the Hotel de Carcassonne social protocol – and yelled 'Coffee?' at the startled woman.

One minute later, this time to *my* consternation, she was sitting on my bed. (Due, admittedly, to the widespread chair shortage.) As I looked at her, I instinctively found myself trying to make comparisons with Nicole. But at least two dress-sizes separated the nations, and where Nicole was immaculately chic, Eleanor had disorderly long hair, a big face free of make-up, and a body which had contempt for rules on posture. In fact, comparisons were pointless. For a long time after, my sub-conscious kept it a dark secret from me, but I think my coffee invitation, my rush to lust, was an attempt to exorcize my failure with bereaved women, and to prove I could detect their secret semaphore a second time round.

'You're Barry,' she said.

'You're Eleanor,' I replied.

'You're not as haggard as your portrait!'

'You're even prettier than yours,' I heard myself say, decisiveness having gone to my head.

Too late, I realized I was the one likely to blush first. I had been somehow bounced into a chat-up line, and felt instantly ashamed of my crassness. I was keen to know her, but equally keen not to be an opportunist jerk. I tried to gain control of my next remark.

'This your first time in Paris?' I enquired. I cringed again. It was not an intentional deceit, but, in my desire for laid-backness, I had unmistakably implied I was an old Paris hand, a familiar of all taxi-drivers, restaurateurs and *boîte de nuit* doormen.

'No. I've been to Europe before, with my parents.' She smiled. 'My father's got a thing about well-finished daughters. Wants to be sure they can ask for burgers in four languages!'

Even allowing for the Ivy League climbing up her family tree, she was more self-possessed than I had expected. But then I remembered how Nicole had had maturity thrust upon her. The only hint of anything amiss was the alacrity with which Eleanor had responded to my call. I suspected that she was – and here my Freudian analysis went into overdrive – over-eager for distraction, over-happy to have company.

'I've been recapping European civilization,' she went on. 'Florence, Siena, Athens, Amsterdam, Vienna. Six months of self-improvement!'

'That long! Are you improved?'

The ambiguity of my question was deliberate, an opportunity for her to talk more personally, but she either ignored it or failed to notice it.

'I could do a doctoral thesis on train timetables!'

'Right. From Julius Caesar to the present day.'

'Don't joke! You can do anything at American universities . . . I'd really like to visit Oxford. D'you know Oxford?'

'Yes. I have friends there.' I resisted the urge to add 'the bastards!' My social skills were improving.

We went on to talk of dreaming spires and punts and thatched cottages and fox-hunting and bagpipes and various other subjects on which I was an expert. In one respect only did she disconcert me. She had out-of-sync laughter. When I thought I had made a witticism, she did not react. When she did laugh at what I said, I had no idea why. I could not tell whose sense of humour was at fault. But she was good company, and enjoyed hearing all about Britain and British history. After a while, I turned the conversation to America.

'Tony says you're from Washington.'

'Yes. That's right, DC. What else did he say?' She asked casually enough, sitting calmly in her skirt and sweater, assessing my few home comforts without comment, but it was an enquiry with a single purpose.

I was uncertain whether I should feign ignorance of her dead fiancé. Perhaps my knowledge would make it harder for her to be stoically good-humoured. Or perhaps she still needed the comfort of people's sympathy. But my hesitation answered her question.

'Yeah, I guess I dumped it all on poor Tony. He was a bit unlucky. Saw me on a bad day. I have good days as well now though.' And she forced a grin. I looked at her more closely. I had not got Tony's acuity of vision, all that the face revealed to me of its past were eyes possibly more deeply-set than usual, and cheeks perhaps a touch strained. It remained, for all its suffering, an open, cheerful face. 'I'm throwing myself back into the world!'

'Into the down-market end!'

'People in cheap hotels are more friendly.' It was meant as a general observation, but then she realized the situation and added with a grin, 'You get offered free coffee!'

I risked a compliment. 'Depends who you are. The last occupant of your room only used to get a wave and a smile.'

'Was that Joan?'

'Yes. A woman from Pittsburgh with no dress sense.'

'No-one from Pittsburgh's got dress sense. There's a state law against it.'

She kept a straight face and caught me off-guard. After laughing, I asked, 'Are you staying long in Paris?'

'Oh, I don't know. I don't plan ahead these days.'

I recognized a conversational dead-end, and the talk turned to her travels, to her train journeys, to her other hotels. Her emotions, her feelings, we avoided. But the realm of 'neutral' facts kept us more than entertained, and we talked with what seemed a growing rapport until well after the winter light had faded.

Yoghurts were good value. They needed no cooking, they needed no washing-up, and some tasted quite nice. I ate my way through a six-pack while I waited up for Colin's arrival.

I had laid my sleeping bag in the nearest thing to a spare corner. I was keen not to be thought inhospitable. Nevertheless I was not displeased that it had a streak of light engine oil down one side and gave off a multicultural whiff of some seventeen countries.

The time of his arrival had been left unspecified. Colin had spoken of 'business', and 'loose ends', but had felt he would 'probably not be that late'. Under the circumstances, therefore, I had not felt it relevant to advise him that entry after ten p.m. should be conducted on all fours without audible intake of breath. As eleven p.m. came and went, I could not entirely suppress the hope that Madame had burst forth in her nightdress and accosted him with a large rolled-up newspaper, obliging him to find another man in another bar.

Colin eventually knocked on my door a little after midnight, a knock which I felt had inconsiderate elements of rat-a-tat-tat in it.

'Sorry I'm late,' he said loudly, leaning against the corridor wall at an angle which suggested several other people had bought him a beer.

At that moment, the light on the stairs was switched on from below. I moved hurriedly to usher him into my room. He resisted.

'What's the matter?' he asked. Loudly.

I grabbed for his arm. 'Sssh!' I said.

As I spoke, a beetling brow under a black fedora rose into view, and the cold eyes of the pederast poet locked onto the sight of me dragging a reluctant Colin into my bedroom. He paused fractionally at the turn in the stairs, minutely curling a lip to convey a more sympathetic interest than on our previous encounter.

Colin turned to him. 'Hallo there!' he said cheerily.

Mr Fedora slowly looked each of us up and down. 'If you boys want a nightcap,' he announced, 'I'm in number nine.' And he continued on his stately way.

'I could do with a coffee,' said Colin, as soon as he was got safely into my room. He was shivering from the cold, his clothes unchanged, his top coat still in protective custody. I noticed that there was now a tear in his leather jacket.

'How was your day?' I asked.

'So-so.' He warmed his hands on the mug for a while, and then he tired of being non-committal. 'I had some money owing me. For the decorating. But the guy realized I was illegal, and I had to fight him for it.' It was not altogether clear whether he had won, and from somewhere within came a disapproval that made me not wish to ask.

'You ought to squat,' he said, casting an eye about.

'Sorry?'

'You ought to squat. Get yourself somewhere decent. I used to have a great squat in Portsmouth.'

'Oh really?'

'Yeah, these old mansion blocks around here, they're fucking asking for it. *Wanting* a boot through the door!'

I nodded sagely. 'I guess so.'

'I got contacts in international squatting. I could have us fixed up with a group, no hassle.'

The unannounced arrival of the first person plural was a worrying development, but I kept my eyelids unbatted.

'Political activists, no crap. Because these Paris pads, they all belong to rich fucking bastards, sunning it on the Riviera for the winter. Tanning their wallets. Be months before they notice they're a flat short, so many candelabras coming out their arses!'

'Right!'

'Fascist property laws! Should be a criminal offence, having two homes. There wouldn't *be* any homeless if everybody just had one home. And they shot the bastards with two!'

His body language suggested a man who was gearing up to talk deep into the early hours, probably about life, politics, and the injustices of the system. It had been a long day and I felt weary at such a prospect, even if it was why I wanted to live in Paris in the first place. I worked hard at a few pre-emptive yawns. Fortunately, having to fight for a living wage had tired him, and he was soon ready to hit the flagstones. I outlined the basic geography of the room with a sweep of my arm; I unzipped the smell in the corner; and we both retired for the night. I took the precaution of slipping my passport under my pillow.

I woke early. Colin did not appear likely to wake for a day or two. Rather than be made bitter and twisted by his dormant presence, I went for a walk.

Paris has a walk for every mood. From place de la Contrescarpe a different mood lay in every direction. East, sloping down the hill past the Metro at place Monge, one moved towards the solid bourgeoisie, with sensible shops, and anonymity in the air. South, down rue Mouffetard, one was sucked into the market, and made part of the mayhem. North, through crooked and steep streets, one had the hint of well-heeled artiness. West lay the drab, protective walls of a lycée and the windswept monumentalism of the Panthéon, a psychological barrier separating the village life of the square from the bright lights of the Latin Quarter.

I felt in the mood for a change of scene, so I set off down rue du Cardinal-Lemoine, and aimed towards the Seine. It was another grey day with a cold, rain-flecked wind.

On such a day, at a fast walking pace, the picturesque source of the old street is soon left behind. The street widens and straightens and becomes more serious as it approaches rue des Ecoles, where all the pedestrians carry books, and is lethal to cross by the time it hits boulevard St Germain; here, the identity of that famously chic boulevard finally disintegrates, and the hip character of the Latin Quarter dribbles away in an ugly junction. Nothing offered a reason to dawdle and I pressed on to the Ile St-Louis. There I tried to sit on a parapet and watch the river go by. But it was a month too soon to sit on stone. So I wandered slowly round the Ile, that most prestigious of old addresses, where former Heads of State can be seen in corner shops, and idly checked out the names on the blue plaques. I also watched a bit of power-parking, when a pearled woman in a Lancia determinedly shunted six cars the length of a cobbled street in order to create a space outside her immaculately decaying home. And then for a while I browsed sporadically and spuriously for antiques. And after that I watched fishermen pierce maggots on the *quais*.

But most of the time, my mind was elsewhere. In the vicinity of Eleanor. As always, in the wake of a good conversation comes a cascade of thoughts to be pursued, allusions to be clarified, anecdotes to be added, and, with luck, body-parts to be felt. Our talk had left me eager for more. Eleanor was only my age, and already her view of the world had been shaped by love and sex and death; perversely, perhaps it was obscenely, I wanted to learn about, to undergo even, the maturing influence of tragedy, and suffering, and pain. And meanwhile, amidst this snowstorm of adult emotions, a small boy was wondering whether the offer of a second coffee in two days would be unduly pushy.

I was also, when my mind was free, grappling with the Colin crisis, a man whose presence on my floor constituted a serious handicap to the entertaining of ladies. But, I kept saying to myself, it was *my* floor, in *my* room. So, as my tour of the island brought Notre Dame into view for the fourth time, I decided that, come what may, when I got back, I would insist to Colin that *he* go for a walk.

Feeling decisive on all fronts, I bought two chocolate nuns.

Eleanor would appreciate a treat. And then I made my way back. The mood of this particular walk was forceful. I did not stroll the streets, and I took the stairs at a gallop. I entered my room fired up for plain speaking. Unfortunately, it was empty. Colin had gone – though whether for ever or just to a bar was not clear. I crossed to the window to call to Eleanor, but then I noticed my floor-mate had left a note in my typewriter. It read, 'Eleanor came round'. I looked across at the annexe, but there was no-one to call to.

A double whammy of frustration came over me. I sat at the table for a moody hour, considering the nuns. Then I put a fresh sheet of paper into the typewriter and prepared to gather my literary thoughts. I was about to hit the keys when the sounds of Seville rang out.

'*¡Silencio!*' I yelled at the wall. '*¡Silencio!*'

⋆   ⋆   ⋆

Alone, in triumph, I stood on the final ridge. The Germans were nowhere to be seen, lost on the slopes like the last of Rommel's army. Above me were the twinkling stars, below me were the earth's molten innards, glowing like angry tomato soup. Riveted, I sat and watched the eruptions, the trembling ground warming my bottom like a giant fan heater. This had to be the most exciting night of my life. And I stayed there till sunrise, watching the greatest firework display in all Italy.

I pushed back my typewriter. It was finished. My first-ever article was finished, all 2,500 words of it. It had taken over a week to fine-hone and French polish each of my phrases to perfection, but 'Night on a Hot Mountain' was now complete – A Boy's Own Story for the Sixties, a modern Hemingway adventure.

And yet . . . Although I gave myself starred Alphas for my Traveller's Tale – it was full of vivid imagery and alliteration, and would, I felt, bring zing to the lives of London's bright young things – its writing left me with one distinct regret. I had lavished my prose on the macho razzamatazz, on the high-octane danger, on the orgasmic eruptions, but for me the most strange memory of that most dramatic night would always be the haunting, surreal coda whose description was beyond my capabilities.

As the dawn light had drained all colour from the drama, a sepia-coloured sea far below had become slowly visible. A magical silvery light illuminated the distant water, broken only by a surreal sequence of grey volcanic humps, which stretched across the Tyrrhenian Sea like the floating spine of some giant serpent.

As the cruder technicolour of full day encroached, I took one last look around me, and then, high on the wonder of it all, turned to run down to the sea. It was a foolish impulse. For 3,000 feet there was nothing but loose scree. My momentum became utterly unstoppable, and I ran and I ran and I ran. I was within inches of manned flight when finally, grey with dust and fear, and scratched and bleeding, I hurtled like a torpedo into the giant vegetation which flourished along the fertile coastal wedge.

I picked myself up slowly, feeling barely alive, and reflecting that it had been a most remarkable night.

'Hi, there!' said a naked American.

He was standing in the small lemon grove of a little white-washed cottage by the jet-black beach and was sniffing the scented air.

'Camomile tea?' he enquired, with poker-faced camp. I nodded agreement. 'Richard, dear!' he called, and a second naked American appeared from the tiny terrace. 'Tea for three! – Sugar?'

We all swung gently in hammocks as we sipped the fragrant tea on the terrace. They spoke to me of the sunsets, of the flying fish, of the elemental quiet, and of the volcano brooding over everything. But most of all, they spoke to me of the ancient church, whose graveyard they rested in every afternoon. There, they said, one could communicate with the true heartbeat of the island.

And then a rare invitation was issued. To join them in the cemetery.

The church, shining white and as elaborate in wrought iron-work as in its doctrine, was but a short walk from the lemon grove. Only the sound of cicadas could be heard as we pulled back the gate and wandered in among the gravestones. Above us, as ever, loomed the summit of Stromboli, the cause of so many of the epitaphs at our feet.

Time passed. Then each of the Americans, still naked, swung up onto a vault, and lay back, eyes closed, to commune with the peace. It was an example too strange to be resisted. I too found myself a vault. And there, cut and bruised, I lay gently back on its cool marble, and let my mind drift off into the lemon-scented yonder . . .

The yonder had been a popular destination over the past few days.

Colin, who had indeed gone to a bar, had remained a guest for only two more nights. The Mediterranean quality to his curls proved to be Portuguese, and he calculated that the survival odds in Lisbon, where poverty comes with sun and extended families come with hospitality, were more in his favour. The small matter of his passport was resolved by Eleanor. Having accompanied him to the bar to buy him a beer, she was then familiarized with the wider canvas of his personal needs; it was one of the decade's lesser-known political ironies that President Johnson should, albeit indirectly, settle the French hotel bill of a Marxist hardman. After which, one American Express cheque the lighter, Eleanor's restless urge to keep her mind on the move surfaced once more – and she decided to recap European civi-lization in Lisbon. They left the following day.

I reread the article one more time, to check the spelling. And then I folded the sheets of paper carefully in a Par Avion en-velope and went out to buy a stamp.

CHAPTER 12

A Miro retrospective had begun. The vivid orange poster in the Laundromat gave details. Some fifteen spring exhibitions were featured in the Laundromat. The instructions on use of soap powder were partially obscured by a Rothko reproduction. Such was the calibre of flyposting, it was possible to trace the key developments of twentieth-century art during the course of the standard washing cycle.

Maybe I was guilty of sentimental francophilia, maybe I was going native, but this did seem a cultural advance on the South London launderette tradition of filling free wall space with little white cards offering massage (with discipline) and second-hand prams (three good wheels) at bargain rates.

I focussed on the opening hours of the Miro, trying to memorize the gallery name as my green cords and polo-necked pullover thumped their way round the spin dryer.

'*Vooz aymez les paynchures?*'

It was an outrageous accent, its comic grossness mangling the language with an abandon exclusive to Americans.

I turned round. Behind me was a lumberjack. Nearly six foot tall, he had on a brown-and-red check shirt, woolly and shapeless; industrial jeans, rolled up at the ankle, holed at the knee, and held in bunched place by a great black belt; and a pair of army boots. But even naked he would have been fairly startling. He had a huge, bushy beard seen only on cattle-drive cooks in Westerns, and his sandy-brown hair fell in waves down his back. He was probably in his early twenties and yet, most remarkable of all, his face was late Auden – across its reddish, weather-beaten façade an intricate network of fissures was already digging in for old age, prematurely cobwebbing his features. And, just to cap any consternation, this hairy Bigfoot had the body language of an innocent abroad.

'That depends on the paintings,' I replied in English.

As he realized his error, an endearing childlike grin appeared and the character lines around his eyes instantly took up their stations, to reveal a face seemingly shaped by a life spent smiling in wonderment.

'You could tell I wasn't French, uh?'

'I think it was your dress sense gave it away.'

And he roared with laughter. It was an unstinting, joyous laugh, and I have rarely warmed to anyone so quickly.

'I just wanted to know if you were an art-lover,' he said.

'Why?'

He held out a leaflet. He had several dozen in his hand.

'I'm having an exhibition.'

I tried very hard not to look surprised. I failed.

I looked down at his leaflet. I had a vague memory of noticing it before, stamped and taped to some lamppost – the French equivalent of a newsagent's window – but the ravages of the weather had diminished the impact of his information technology. I glanced at the text. It was handwritten. 'New American Artists. Jerry and Garry Gibson present their latest work . . .'

'A two-man exhibition. We're brothers.'

'Oh, right. What, psychedelic art, you mean?' I had begun to realize we were talking serious hippy. The Paris branch of flower power. Basic primary colours thrown about in a bucket. Naked artistes smearing themselves with emulsion and soft fruit. The spreading of intimate bodily fluids into canvas.

'No. Landscapes. Watercolour landscapes.'

'Oh. Nice.'

'We've been in a barn – near Chartres. Since last fall. Great leaves you get in France.'

This struck a deep artistic chord.

'I used to do trees at school,' I said. 'In Indian ink. No leaves, just the silhouette − in winter. On white parchment paper. Especially oak trees.' The memories came flooding back. 'I used to spend hours blacking in the details. Bifurcating branches − that's what I liked most.' It was my sole niche in the school hall of artistic fame. My bare tree had been the only one of my creations to receive a favourable word in four years of art lessons. Even the year spent on the papier-mâché dinosaur had ended in ignominy when its stomach had refused to leave the ground.

'Oh you *must* come then, man!'

'I will,' I said. 'I'm free this month.'

I carefully folded his leaflet. The exhibition was to run for a week, in a small gallery nearby.

'Come to the opening night, if you want. It's on Friday.'

'That OK?' I asked casually, trying to disguise my chuffedness.

'Yeah, sure. It'll be formal, though − with trousers!' A big grin. 'Bit of bread and cheese. Free glass of wine.'

'Oh good,' I said. 'A change of diet.'

He placed half a dozen leaflets beside the tokens machine and gave me a peace sign as he turned to leave.

'See you Friday then,' I said.

'Oh, by the way,' he called from the door, 'I'm Jerry.'

It had been an encounter that cheered me greatly. My clothes stopped spinning and I waited for the vacuum lock to release them.

Public washing of clothes had only recently entered my lifestyle. I had previously been content to leave them suppurating in the sink, slowly staining Madame's porcelain a darker shade of grey. But during an hour spent rippling my chest muscles at Tony in the cause of art, he had sniffed several times, and finally muttered, 'TO.'

'What's that?'

'Torso Odour,' he had replied tersely and continued sketching.

Afterwards, a few sniffs of my own in the privacy of my wardrobe revealed there to be several other areas of O. I was now hoping that the Laundromat would produce a quantum leap in human relationships.

Back out on rue Mouffetard with my washing, I stood for a moment and enjoyed the afternoon sun. A jacket was almost redundant. Nature was staging a dummy run for the spring. There was a blue sky, and shadows in the street. Paris's most famous season was, at last, in the offing.

Twenty yards away, Dave was coming up from the market carrying a cabbage. The seasons were irrelevant to his life and, as always, he was wearing his shabby white 'tec's mac. Eczema had now begun to take hold on his face, adding physical ill-health to the ravage of his soul. But he seemed to regard it with fatalistic acceptance, almost as a necessary penance for an unknown wrong.

'Behind the fish stall, this one!' was his near-triumphant greeting. 'Must have rolled over thirty yards.'

I nodded appreciatively. It looked a first-class cabbage.

'And the greengrocer hadn't noticed?'

'Oh, I showed it to her. Asked her. I wouldn't steal it.' That was true. He was punctilious about his second-hand food. 'Been bruised by bouncing, she said. Told me to keep it.'

Damaged eatables were his staple diet. Each day, after the market, Dave would hunt for discarded fruit and runaway vegetables. But he would always seek out the owner. He scavenged with honour. God had no come-back on him.

He munched on a leaf as we walked back to the hotel. Neither of us was sure how quickly bruising set in with cabbages.

The sound of people was in the air. The outdoor life of Paris was re-emerging. I felt a tremor of keen pleasure, and was in the mood for talking, but we walked in silence. Dave's presence predisposed one to silence. One feared to be trivial. Like many silent people, he seemed to conceal a life of great weight and mystery.

After a while, the silence became unnatural.

'Why did you choose Paris to come to?' I asked, partly out of politeness, but partly from a genuine curiosity.

He was a long time replying. I sensed this was from

disapproval of politeness, the more so since the eventual reply was given with such certitude.

'Because I speak no French.'

'. . . I don't understand.'

This time he took even longer to reply. I began to feel I was being vetted as to whether I was worthy of the answer.

'If I don't understand the world around me, it is easier to create my own.'

'I see.' At least, I thought I saw.

We had arrived at the hotel. He pushed the anonymous brown door open and we headed down the corridor. I considered inviting him for coffee again, but this time I was too scared of the long pauses.

I was also keen to continue the account of my camel journey. It was more than a week since I had sent off Traveller's Tale no. 1, and I wanted to hit the editor with nos. 2–6 in quick succession. I had got to the bit where me and the bedouin were seventeen hours into the desert and my bottom was beginning to bleed from bouncing on the hump.

I was exceptionally lucky. The Sixties really were the final golden age of travel, a brief and unique period when any Western kid could play at being an explorer. The first half of the century had been a traveller's nightmare: war, depression, and more war, followed by austerity and a shortage of cars to give lifts. The Seventies took away the thrill by introducing mass tourism, the Eighties took away the possibility by introducing mass fighting, and the Nineties took away the point by spreading environmental destruction. But in those halcyon Sixties days, £250 gave eight months of ersatz adventure; the chance of hospitality granted only to a youngster far from home; and a belief that the future could be postponed. It also provided sights and sounds and stories to last a lifetime. Some of the stories I could not yet interpret, some had as yet no perspective, and some were simply too painful to tell.

The rest I was going to sell. And so become famous.

'*Bonjour, Monsieur Pilton.*'

I was too weighed down with washing to make the 180-

degree turn in time. We faced each other in the open doorway of my room, the little white-haired old landlady and I. It was that time of the month.

'*Bonjour, madame.*'

Up until this moment, I had been the model tenant. I had received no police visits, vomited down no stairs, hosted no barn dances, cooked no fish.

'*Comment allez-vous, monsieur?*'

But now was the day of the Changing of the Sheets. And the laying-on of notes. I had survived once, courtesy of the Oxbridge begging bowl, but as a charitable cause the Third World had the public relations edge. Donations had ceased.

'*Je vais très bien, madame . . .*'

Independence was still a pen-dream. The slow reading-rate of Fleet Street had disrupted my cash projections. The Royal Mail response time was holding up my cheques.

'*. . . et vous?*'

Royalties on my forthcoming paperback were two years distant. So far only one magazine knew of the purple beauty of my explorer's prose.

'*Bien, merci, monsieur.*'

And I had just over 100 francs in the world.

'*Vous avez votre loyer?*'

And she wanted 248 of them.

The doyenne of rent-collectors smiled expectantly . . . And I went into fiction overdrive. In French, in English, in Euro-mime. I spoke of first novels; I spoke of publishers' advances waiting for the Biro to dry; I spoke of large pockets of money delayed by fog in the Channel; I hinted at radio contracts, television serials, Hollywood films of me and my rucksack; I implied the Royal Geographical Society were poised to drop by in person; and for artistic atmos and *vérité* I gestured constantly at my typewriter which was waiting, keys akimbo, for my creative input to start pulsing again. I think I even suggested that one day her hotel might be made an historical *monument d'État,* with a blue plaque over my sink. And then I ran dry.

Madame twinkled at me. I doubt she believed a word. She

had heard fifty years of artists' lies. Half a century of tenants' dreams. But, then again, she was a patron of artists. A long-time collector of their fantasies. She sighed sadly. *'La littérature, c'est toujours la tragédie.'* And she wagged a warning finger, and said, *'Quinze jours. Pas plus.'* And bustled off.

I closed my door. The clean sheets sat folded on the chair. For seven francs a day, the linen change was self-service. As I tugged the previous month's sheets off the bed, it crossed my mind that my chaste existence was not without its plus points. Had my linen been dyed with virgin's blood, Madame might have been a little less sympathetic.

For the next three days, I worked urgently at my camel's tale. It was full of best-selling ingredients. It began at dawn in an oasis with six hours of negotiation for a bedouin and a camel; it ended under the stars at a desert legionnaires' camp by a sandstone fort. It had danger: I was warned my bedouin would slice me into giblets; it had primitive life styles: lunch was flour and water baked into bread in a sand-hole; it had epic beauty: we rode across Lawrence of Arabia desert under the light of a full moon. And of course there was the heroism of the bloodied bottom: I made much of that. Indeed, each morning, after checking for mail and money, I became almost dewy-eyed for the manly simplicities of sun, sand and camels.

The end of the third day came and, with what I smugly regarded as professional deadlining, I managed to finish my final paragraph before dinner. I had the warm glow of a man who has earned his pickled gherkin and Brie roll. I was just grinding my typewriter rubber through the last misspelling of bedouin when I became conscious of a shaft of light across the courtyard. I looked up – in time to see Ulrika draw her curtain shut.

All manner of thoughts raced through my mind – most of them questions without answers. Why was she back? How long was she back for? Where was Augustus? Had she seen me? Did she want to see me?

Cool, mature men wait for the right moment to act. I immediately got up and rushed out of the room.

As I hurried down the stairs I had no plan, no ready-made dialogue. Whatever her state of mind, I would just drop by, pretend to be an innocent visitor. We could talk about the weather. Or we could drink a coffee. Or she could cry on my shoulder. Or I could ask her what she saw in Augustus.

As I crossed the courtyard, I glanced up at her room. Ulrika was standing close to the lighted window. I could see her shape plainly through the thin curtains, her figure silhouetted by the bedside lamp. And as I looked up, she pulled her sweater off over her head. I stopped abruptly, eager to see more, and suddenly weak with excitement. She unhooked her bra. For a brief moment I could discern the outline of her breasts – and then she moved away from the window. I felt as though an electrical charge had gone through my body.

I carried on across the courtyard, my thoughts in turmoil. I think I planned to knock on her door, announce myself, and hope that – in the unbothered way which would-be nude models have – she casually answered the door topless. That I think was my intention, and certainly it was my hope. But as I entered the annexe I did not switch on the stairwell lights. I made my way very quietly up the stairs to her door, raised my hand . . . and did not knock. Instead, trembling almost uncontrollably, I bent down, and looked through the keyhole.

The room was so narrow that it was almost inevitable she be in my range of vision. And she was. She was standing next to the window, by her wash-basin, quite naked. Almost physically sick with emotion, I watched her every move, feverishly trying to suppress any sound of my breathing. Guilt or shame did not enter my thoughts. This, at twenty-one, was the first naked woman I had ever seen. She stood almost sideways on, but at just enough of an angle to display her body to me as she gently ran her wet pink flannel over herself. I watched, my hand inside my trousers, as she slowly soaped first her breasts and then her pubic hair. As she did so, she started to hum. And it was only when I heard her humming, so innocently, so unselfconsciously, that I felt unease at my actions, ashamed of my secret presence.

The shame was not however sufficient to stop me, though my fear nearly was.

I stayed there immobile – one eye closed, the watching eye slightly back from the keyhole for safety – and was kept compulsively in position by the desire that she would turn, so that I would have seen all her body, that I would have watched her touch every part of herself.

The lights clicked on, and the full length of the stairs was lit up.

I jerked upright in panic. Someone had entered the annexe. I spun round and started to walk down the stairs with as much naturalness as I could convey. And then a door slammed shut on the floor below. A smell of curry wafted up, and I realized it was the last Arab of the day. To my enormous relief, I was safe from discovery. I was free to start watching again.

Except that I no longer wanted to. Somewhere in that brief moment of alarm I had lost the nerve, the impulse, even the desire, to creep back up, to continue spying. The reality of my actions had registered.

I carried on down.

As I left the annexe, guilt began to gather. In the open courtyard I was hit by a flood of shame – and a sense of how pathetic, how desperate I must appear. Climbing the stairs to my room, I did not feel like the hero on the camel, or the brave man up Stromboli.

Once back, I could not face sitting alone in my room. It was time for an anonymous, crowded café. I tidied my papers and put on my freshly laundered cords. But even now, I could not resist a glance in the direction of Ulrika's room, just to see if she was still there. She was. At least, her light was still on. My desire for her company, her conversation, her account of the past weeks of her life, would not easily go away.

Before leaving, I even briefly considered asking her to come out, to join me for coffee, but I was glad I did not have the chutzpah. Some period of penance seemed appropriate. In any case, I suspected she might be around for some time. Millionaire Playboy-lover's pad had presumably stretched to a shower – her return, therefore, could hardly be prompted by desire for a wash . . .

Friday evening was always an exciting time in rue Mouffetard, full of *flâneurs* and good-natured shouting. But it was especially nice to be strolling purposefully. The gallery was about halfway down, on a corner opposite the 1950s 'tribute to concrete' arcade. It had only recently abandoned life as a bicycle shop, and for nearly a fortnight the main exhibits had been a step-ladder, a paint pot, and a recumbent workman.

Now, tonight, it was alive with arty-party people, and the animated buzz of cultural chat was audible from the street. I paused on the pavement opposite and watched the mingling through the gallery windows. It was a moment to savour, because gouged on my mind was the last time I had watched such a gathering. I had been lying in a flooded doorway at midnight, cold, lonely, homeless and close to defeat. Watching the glitter from the gutter, as the banner headline in my night-mares put it. Admittedly, this night's occasion had few backless dresses and no giant sculpted fish on plinths, but that was a hard-ship I could live with. This time I was part of the glitter. I was on the inside track of art. All I needed were a few well-chosen watercolour words.

I crossed the street and pressed a path into the crowded ex-bike shop, where the cheap plonk was flowing like wine. Lingering in the smoky air was the smell of emulsion (white). There was little twee artificiality; for many of the buffs around me, it seemed probable that every night was first night. The vogue appeared to be for arguing rather than art-loving, but I could see few familiar faces, so I decided to look at the pictures. There were forty-two paintings in all, and as I elbowed my way round the walls, trying to guess what my opinions were, I found my expectations constantly confounded. All were rural scenes, but whereas I had expected large and lavish, what I got was small and sensitive; a view of life in secondary colours, not primary. And above everything else, gentle. Peace and harmony was clearly big near Chartres. I could not speak for the quality of the paintings, but the character of the painter shone through. And that was oddest of all. The exhibition could have been – indeed, appeared to be – by one painter. I could not tell the brothers' paintings apart, except by their signatures. An in-depth inspection of pigment revealed that JG was a bit more partial to blue, especially in the sky area, but when it came to fields and woods, attribution was a toss-up. I was starting – in the absence of a conversational entrée – to go round for a second time, when I at last caught sight of Jerry.

Or rather, sound of Jerry. He was standing near the trestle-table, whose baguettes were under serious siege, and laughing helplessly while a woman in a low-cut dress tried to spring-clean his beard. All the manuals on etiquette advise against crusty bread for bearded men, but he was one of nature's born rebels. The woman, European-looking yet indefinably foreign, then took advantage of a missing button to slip her hand inside his shirt and do something more than domestic with his chest hairs. He tried to twist free, but this only made him giggle the more.

As I got nearer, I was able to see the concessions he had made to the formality of the evening: a change of lumberjack shirt (different reds, different browns) and replacement of the twine in his army boots by yellow laces.

I smiled at him, but the return smile somehow lacked the personal warmth I had anticipated. Nor did he say anything.

'See! I wore trousers! As instructed.' I grinned. But our little private joke only produced another vague smile. His companion, surprisingly his senior by some years, set to work on another button.

I waved at the paintings on the wall. 'They're very good!' I said, observing the first rule of first nights.

'Thank you,' he replied.

I struggled on. 'You've certainly got a good turn-out!'

At last he grinned at me, and I felt we were making contact again. 'Yes,' he sighed, 'Jerry sure invites everyone he bumps into!'

'. . . Sorry?'

He took a long drag on his roll-up. 'I said,' and he had to shout over the hubbub, 'Jerry invites everyone he bumps into.'

The clinking cascade in my brain was the sound of pennies dropping. 'You're Garry?'

He nodded. 'Yes, that's me.' He looked down to introduce his hair-assistant, whose fingers were advancing on his nipple. 'And this is . . .' He tried to think. 'This is . . .' He drew a blank.

'Helba,' the woman said.

Garry nodded. 'She's Estonian . . .' he added. '. . . And I'm estonied!' At which, he collapsed in helpless giggles. I realized this was not likely to develop into the most fruitful of conversations, although I was now able to identify what had displaced the odour of emulsion.

'Have you seen Jerry?'

Garry waved his arm vaguely at a far corner, inadvertently giving Helba access to his armpit.

I edged through the crush. At the end of the trestle, I caught a glimpse of Dave, who was trying hard to layer an assortment of Brie, Camembert and Edam into a single loaf. I considered calling out, if only to show that I knew somebody, but then thought better of distracting him from his largest square meal of the winter.

The proportion of gate-crashers was hard to assess. Half the *quartier* was bohemian fringe anyway, so their presence and their judgement would not be unwelcome. I noticed one or two interesting faces that I had seen before, probably in cafés, but the interestingness of my own face appeared not to have registered with anyone. A bulky figure set on refilling his glass barged rudely against me. I gave a small barge back — and then saw the black fedora. It swivelled round. The pederast poet gazed down upon me, a red button-hole adding to my irritation.

'Hallo!' he said with Olympian condescension. 'Come to look at these little daubs?'

'Yes,' I replied. 'I'm a friend of the artist.'

'Oh! Done by artists, are they?' He had clearly been taken to see a film of Oscar Wilde at an impressionable age. 'And do you have an opinion of them?'

'I like the pastoral tone.'

'Yes,' he drawled. 'Big feature of landscapes, the pastoral tone.'

I tried to think of a crushing reply, and failed.

'And where's your friend in leather? Not lost him, I hope?'

'He's travelling,' I answered curtly, cross at the man's power to needle, and moved on in search of Jerry, the identical twin.

I found him in a corner, watching a man who was on all fours, snuffling.

'*Ah, whee! whee!*' I heard Jerry cry, in his French version of yes. 'I've got it!' He jigged excitedly. 'It's a pig!' (In fact, though I did not know it then, he was wrong. It was actually *un sanglier* – a wild boar). Jerry gave the thumbs-up sign to the performer on the floor, whose next trick was to stand, spread his hands out on each side of his head, and paw the ground. He and Jerry stared at each other intently, the language barrier palpable. Then, as the former pig fired a pretend rifle-shot into the air, Jerry spotted me, grinned hugely and gave me a great hug, much the sort of reception I had tried to elicit from the complete stranger by the trestles. At the same moment, I recognized the animal impersonator. It was the artist in the square, the man with the black beard who painted rue Mouffetard in the early morning.

'*Ger-ard* – Barry,' said Jerry.

With no hint of embarrassment, Gerard broke off being a wild animal and shook me vigorously by the hand. It was a rock-solid handshake, and his deep-set brown eyes focused unblinkingly on mine. '*Bonsoir, Barry. Ça va?*' He gave out an intensity and a sincerity that challenged one to be fiercely frank in return.

'*Ger-ard* was trying to explain to me about a painting he's working on . . . at least, I think it's a painting,' said Jerry. Jerry's working French was sub-rudimentary and Gerard spoke less English than any Frenchman I ever met.

'*Il est doué, non?*' said Gerard to me, nodding at Jerry's/Garry's paintings.

'He says you're talented,' I told Jerry. Jerry was hopelessly embarrassed, reacting with the social skills of a small boy. For a

130

moment, I thought I might be called upon to translate 'Aw, shucks!'

'What did you mean,' I asked, 'you "think" it's a painting he's talking about?'

'Well . . . apparently it's a hundred foot long,' replied Jerry, having the grace to look dubious.

'He'd need a bloody big easel!'

'Yes, and . . .' Jerry hesitated. 'I thought he said it'd got pterodactyls in it.'

'It's what . . . !'

'He speaks very fast,' muttered Jerry.

I turned to Gerard to sort out the confusion.

But Gerard was about to leave. Although his attention span for art was long, his attention span for people was short. I suspected he was one of the few who had come exclusively to view the paintings. And now he was eager to be off.

'*Salut!*' Again the fierce handshake, again the penetrating eyes. And then he was away, energetically parting the crowd. Although little more than 5' 5" without his beret, he had a dynamism that gave him stature. Even so, his departure was slow because on all sides he was greeted by cries of acknowledgement and had to handshake his way to the door.

'See!' I said to Jerry. 'Stuff landscapes! That's what happens when you do street scenes!'

'Jeez, is that what he does?'

'Didn't you know?'

'I'd never met him before. Thought he worked in a zoo.'

And so the mystery of the mime remained.

The gallery was now at full throttle, and as we watched the milling of the would-be buyers, I became quite envious of the power of the artist. Of the pleasure of becoming a cynosure for the night.

'So, how do you reckon it's going?' I asked.

'Well, one's gone already!'

'Really?'

'Yeah! Bloody art-thieves!' And he collapsed in laughter.

It was absolutely genuine laughter. He was immune to power-

trips and vanity. Indeed, if he had liked the thief he would probably have helped him carry the painting out.

'You had many exhibitions?'

'Nope. World-first! For both of us.'

'How long have you been painting?'

'Five or six years. Started as therapy. When our brother died.
If we can ever make any money out of it, it'll be even better
therapy!' His allusion to the death was very simply made, not
out of false sentiment, nor melodrama, nor to provoke questions.
I felt it was somehow done to bear witness to his dead brother,
to not lock his existence out of their continuing lives. I had the
desire to ask questions, but they seemed to flow from a pruri-
ence which would have reflected poorly on me. 'I'd better
mingle. Get my red dots at the ready!'

'Well, someone ought to. I don't think Garry's paying much
attention to red dots!'

'Oh. The Estonian woman still there, then?'

'Yes. What is she, a watercolour groupie?'

'Fellow artist, I gather. Someone said she's a political exile.
Official asylum, the works.'

'How exotic! I wonder what she's guilty of? Capitalist sex
acts?'

'Jerry!' came a call from the crowd.

'Listen,' he said, 'we're going to be in Paris a while. Let's have
a drink some time. You local?'

'*Mais oui!* Just up the road. Hotel de Carcassonne.'

He was impressed. 'A hotel?'

'Not so as you'd notice.'

'Oh, I'd notice! After a winter in a barn, I'd notice!' The
latticework around his eyes assembled for a grin, and then, like
a large puppy dog, he romped into the crowd.

I had wanted to talk to him about the twin thing, but I reckoned that after a lifetime of being one, he might have tired of
the topic. I really did want to tell him, though, that I thought it
most unsporting for them to wear the same clothes. Give or take
some twine.

★   ★   ★

132

It was gone ten when I woke the next morning. I had a bad head which I blamed on the emulsion. Fresh air was called for. I decided to test my French in the baker's, and then try and see if I could casually bump into Gerard in the square. I was, you understand, in no way a groupie, but the possibility of being hailed personally and given a public handshake by one of the area's leading street-artists was a quite irresistible turn-on.

On the way out, I glanced through Madame's glass window as usual. On the far side, in a tiny ante-room, were the pigeon-holes where the post was left. Retrieving post without attracting Madame's attention was a military operation much discussed by tenants in arrears. On this morning, I had a foolscap brown envelope awaiting me. And I knew at once this was the letter which contained my fate. I decided that courage was the order of the day; now was not the moment to admit the possibility of rejection.

I strode breezily in, called a loud *Bonjour* to Madame seated in her chair – and tore open the letter.

It was not a rejection. It was not an acceptance. It was a communication from a firm of accountants advising me that the magazine had gone into liquidation six months prior.

CHAPTER 13

The Alliance Française was not a pretty building. A quart of concrete poured into a pint-pot of space, with a featureless façade and a regiment of drab, square windows, it bulged unappealingly on a corner of boulevard Raspail in the *sixième*, where boulevarding was only for masochists. Now a dual carriageway, with a central mud-flat fought over by jousting parkers, this bvd was but a series of high-revving sprints from one red light to the next. It was an improbable setting for the study of aesthetics.

The Alliance Française was a language school, but French being more than just a language, the school was more than just a Berlitz. Indeed, by the fifth and final grade, one was affiliated to the Sorbonne, and the course then resonated to the *gloire*-laden nomenclature '*Langue et Civilization*'. The purpose of my visit, though, was neither language nor culture. It was lucre. For trailing in the course's wake came perks. The simple act of *enregistrement* (which, at forty-five francs, constituted my personal bankruptcy) gave access to files on all the essentials of life: jobs, rooms, and au pairships.

As I entered the cramped forecourt, its proportions made the poorer by high railings and three trees mutilated into bonsai status, I was unexpectedly demoralized by the multilingual babel of the bystanders. Admittedly, to be new in any institution brings its share of terrors and stirs up the age-old insecurity of being an outsider. But my unease was more paranoid. The others were all me. Their life was my life. And I resented the individuality

134

of my experiences as a foreigner here being replicated on a vast scale. I felt my uniqueness was being dissolved. And more personal still, the presence of so many foreigners touched on a raw psychological nerve – in my Parisian *demi-monde*, my little French Bohemia, I was rubbing shoulders with, and sharing coffee with, and living cheek by jowl with . . . fellow expatriates. Socially, the natives inhabited an invisible parallel world. So far, the only French people to impinge on my world were Gerard, with whom I had shared a handshake and a pig impersonation, and the orgasmic but unseen curry-cook across the courtyard. It was hardly integration.

This sense of failure had been enhanced by finishing Hemingway, by learning of his Paris life. The starry nature of his social circle left me not just frustrated but disillusioned. It taught me that in the world of literature there were travellers and 'travellers'. The innocent reader of travel-writing imagines his or her hero to be cast adrift in an unknown, hostile world, which he then proceeds to conquer (or, at least, survive in, to comic effect). But, in truth, the successful travel-writer frequently comes armed with introductions, is connected by birth to the ambassador, and has presents to deliver to the prima ballerina in town; if he is Hemingway, he mysteriously knows Ezra Pound, and Scott Fitzgerald, and James Joyce, and Gertrude Stein; and if his background is coyly veiled, this is merely the proof that he springs from a long line of literati loins. Such writers know their time in the garret is a *rite de passage*, and not a sentence without end. Had there been a careers advisory officer in the hotel, he would have steered me to a more secure area of literature. It was around this period of disillusion that I decided to start on the Henry Miller that Joan had left me.

As I pushed my way through the main doors of the Alliance, I was assailed by the immutable acoustics of education: the on-going echo of voices and feet. I was tempted to flee as my public school past rose up my gorge, but the lure of an easy franc focused my mind. Inside, the building appeared to belong to an earlier century than outside; an almost venerable staircase with wrought-iron rails had a crack at sweeping grandly upwards, and a marble bust was on hand to signify something lofty about scholarship. As I tried to get my bearings, a distant rumble became a surge and the moderately young of fifty nations stampeded past me to practise that day's verbs on the wider world. Pressed up against the balustrade, smiling apologetically for my presence, I could feel my hard-won alternativeness draining from my lifestyle.

The assessment exam was held in an old-fashioned classroom, designed for old-fashioned teaching methods, and ruled by old-fashioned attitudes which were to cause the collapse of the French state the following year. Unaware of these dangerous shortcomings, I sat down at a wooden desk with several Japanese, a couple of Africans and a statutory American, and scribbled away for twenty minutes. A thin professor of about forty, in a surprisingly nifty grey suit and pince-nez, checked through our work and called us up one by one.

He looked at me approvingly. '*Où est-ce que vous avez appris votre français?*' he enquired.

'*Au volant d'un Land Rover, monsieur,*' I replied. '*En traversant le Sahara.*' I had long wanted somebody to ask me that.

When I left England, my French had been more or less nil. As with most children, my French lessons had dribbled away into the sand of apathy. More unusually, they had been revived in the sands of adventure.

The previous autumn I had been travelling north in Algeria, high on a lonely road in the Atlas mountains, when I came upon an endless winding trail of brilliantly bedecked nomads who, with their camels and mules and dogs and entire worldly belongings, were slowly descending to the Sahara for the long hard winter.

It was an annual migration, a journey that had taken place since the beginning of recorded time. A primitive shudder went through me. From the very oldest to the very youngest, the whole community was on the move, on foot; only the unmarried women, fearsomely veiled, were permitted to ride on camel-back, thus advertising their status, and protecting their value. As the human chain wound down the 10,000-foot mountain range, it was a scene of awesome, almost biblical, force.

In that moment, I decided to cross the Sahara, to experience the world they were travelling into. I turned south the following day.

But my haste, and the limited literary facilities of (French-speaking) sub-Saharan Africa, left me ill-prepared for the duller moments of the journey. At the end of that week, I found myself standing in a sandstorm outside an oasis, waiting for a thousand-mile lift with just two copies of *Paris Match*, a month-old edition of *Le Figaro*, and a pocket Larousse dictionary (with an index on irregular verbs).

After twenty-four hours, no vehicle had gone by, but I could quote verbatim from an article on ice-hockey. Early on the second day, my luck changed and a Land Rover loomed slowly out of the sand-clouds, and stopped. Unfortunately, it had no driver. It was on the back of an enormous lorry, roped up, and packed around by twenty tons of cement sacks – access was possible but powdery, and only via the window. However, the alternative was to decline the offer and die. And thus I became perhaps the only person in history to have crossed the Sahara desert alone at the wheel of a Land Rover . . . without ever starting the engine.

It was a long, long journey. The mechanic, the cook and the driver from Mali kept going all day and most of the night, every day and every night. (They had once done Algiers-Mecca in four days.) I sat alone in the cockpit, and when the desert got boring I read the dictionary. I looked up every word in every article. I looked up words which weren't in any article. And then I started to go through the words which began with the *lettre A* . . .

Our destination was Tamanrasset, the ancient oasis at the heart of the Sahara, set in the spectacular mountains of the Hoggar and home to the legendary men in black, the Tuaregs. To reach it, one had to cross the Great Erg, and hundreds of miles of stony plateau. The non-existent road passed by vast abandoned Foreign Legion forts, and made chilling diversions round nuclear testing sites; it edged down cliff faces, and ground through sand-dunes and revved across long-dry river beds. By the time the lorry steered triumphantly between the crenellated sandstone ramparts of Tamanrasset and down the Beau Geste boulevard of palm trees I was on the letter P for the second time.

'*Le Quatrième*,' said the smart-suited professor. 'Your vocabulary is good, but you have no grasp of grammar. Next!'

I was rather upset not to make the fifth grade. It was not the prestige I was after, but COPAR, the university restaurant card. People into *langue et civilization* could eat a four-course meal for 1F 40 in special restaurants. But now, to move up that culinary notch, I would have to attend classes and take a further exam.

Once enrolled, I went to see to the serious business: the 'small ads' room. A jobcentre-cum-accommodation bureau, its purpose was essentially to assist Parisians who wished to exploit foreigners. Rows of cards on boards filled the walls, and behind a *guichet* was a middle-aged woman whose job was to be unhelpful and bad-tempered when supplying further details.

Along with a small huddled mass, I looked down the pink cards, the employment offers. In England before my days in exile, I had been an estate agent (failed to sell a house) and a factory store-keeper (asked to leave). Neither of these positions had prepared me to be a baby-sitter or a nude female model ('*il s'agit de l'Académie*'). Apart from a television company in search of an *androgyne* (18–24), the only other options were waiters (*pourboires seulement*) or washers-up. I had been emotionally scarred by both professions, and the thought of working somewhere with customers was enough to make me drop plates. My survival hanging in the balance, I stood and dithered. Just as I was wondering about nappy-changing, the grumpy *guichet* lady elbowed her way past and pinned up a new card, from someone wanting private English lessons.

CHAPTER 14

A faint green blur had appeared overnight on the trees in place de la Contrescarpe. A warm afternoon sun was working hard at extra chlorophyll deliveries and I knew, as soon as I set off from the hotel, that at last the seasons had changed. Already, half the world was in its shirt-sleeves and the forty-minute walk that lay ahead promised to be urban heaven. I was fast-forwarding the route in my mind when, out of nowhere, an image from my schooldays leapt into frame and I was back in the form-room of my favourite English master, Mr 'Jags' Jagger. It was the last period of the day and the angled rays of the sun were spotlighting the chalk dust adrift in the air as, without preamble, he handed out maps to the class and told us to write a twenty-minute essay capturing the atmosphere of 'Paris in the spring'.

It was a literary task that had me floundering. Happiness and *joie de vivre* seemed moods inaccessible to description; the souf-flés of writing, they collapsed at the touch of a pen. I resorted to constant exclamation marks, fatuous light-headedness, and a traffic warden's adherence to the street-map. *I sauntered along Montmartre! I promenaded the length of Montparnasse! I skipped through the Bois du Boulogne! I strode joyfully up the Champs-Elysées!* The emotions defeated me. At fifteen, I could not convey, I could scarcely conceive, what it was like to be alive in Paris in the spring.

Today it was fact. And at odds with the fiction. I had always imagined the romantic essence of life in Paris came from being footloose and fancy-free. Yet this afternoon, uniquely, I had a

139

place to go and a time to be there, and the effect was liberating. Merely by having to meet a Monsieur Bareste at 2.30 p.m. in the Champs-Elysées, I felt I had qualified as a bit player in Paris life. I was no longer a fulltime lounger, and it put a spring in my step.

Fate could not have decreed a finer journey. My appointment took me from the heart of the Left Bank to the heart of the Right Bank, required me to wander through four *arrondissements*, and gave me a panoramic view of the Seine. I was never to tire of this journey, although I was to make it hundreds of times.

As always, however, it began in the sepulchral shade of the Panthéon, whose vast dome kept the sun at bay half the day. A state mausoleum will never be a fun place, but in the late Sixties it was lonelier and bleaker than at any time in its history. The huge edifice, misled by the example of its famous residents, had itself begun to crumble away and slowly turn to dust. And so glory had ceded to safety. The display of great national bones was closed to the public, and the grand place du Panthéon had become an unfulfilled, coach-free zone. The one constant visitor was the wind, forced into life by the monumental obstructions of the architect, and left to howl at the shades of the French dead. Day or night, I seldom dawdled here.

The Panthéon behind me, I gave boulevard St Michel a rare miss, and curved round by the railings of the Jardins du Luxembourg, to carry out a quick check on the quality of its green blurs. All were doing well; spring was widespread. Indeed, opposite on rue de Vaugirard, the pavement cafés had cast off their protective glass walls, and *citrons pressés* were the fashionable order of the day. I turned down by the Théâtre de L'Odéon where, on the posh, sunny side of the square, a lobster display was tempting seafood lovers – and lovers in general – to an alfresco lunch. Being more in the shrimp bracket, I carried on across boulevard St Germain and forked out on a baguette from the Buci market.

Three mouthfuls later, and less than fifty yards down rue de Seine, I was stopped by *gendarmes*. Aware of the status of French cuisine, for a split second I thought it was the food police. But, uncharacteristically perhaps, eating on the move in France does not constitute a breakdown in public morals – even the most chic can be seen dribbling a *gaufre* – and I was simply the subject of the ubiquitous and infamous identity check. I handed the armed officers a rather bent, mildewy passport and awaited trouble. Trouble came there none. Spring had refreshed those professions other seasons cannot reach. Not only was it a bruise-less interview, courteous and correct, but my inquisitors even wished me '*Bon Appetit!*' as we parted.

Nonetheless, this was a disconcerting encounter, like a lone raven arriving to portend a shipwreck. I had just one week left on my visa. From the following Wednesday, I would be an illegal alien, and any baguette in my possession would probably be thrust up my bottom.

The Pont des Arts takes pedestrians from the Beaux Arts to the Louvre and gives them an inspirational view of the river as a small extra. This being a quintessentially French landscape, I had not expected to find my way blocked by a group of track-suited Japanese performing what appeared to be slow motion hari-kiri. At that age, I was not au fait with t'ai chi, and its silent pre-Jane Fonda movements did not immediately come across as ancient spiritual concepts of co-ordination and balance. Suspecting it to be an avant-garde circus act, I stood and watched for a full five minutes, increasingly puzzled why no-one came round with a hat.

It was by then 2.15. I pressed on into the forecourt of the Louvre, and slowly crunched past the Rodins on their plinths. Even statues got to kiss, I noticed ruefully. And then it was the Tuileries. I never warmed to the Tuileries, except in winter when frost added bite to their dull formality. It was a domestic world of stunted trees and small children, and bored nannies and irritable au pairs. The unfathomable French love of gravel had dominion here, and a distasteful dust hovered at dog level, most of which were Pekineses.

I had a couple of minutes to spare and, buoyed by the day's spirit of adventure, decided to go for broke with a raspberry-jam crêpe. The old wooden café in the trees, from where the sweet smell of roasted chestnuts would drift on dark winter afternoons, now had the look of a crèche with pram-parking problems, and so once again I ate on the hoof. Wiping the last scarlet stain from my chin, I hurried up the slope from the Tuileries and was just noticing how the giant obelisk in the square phallicly bisected the Arc de Triomphe when a violent pain seared my stomach and bent me nearly double. The pain was gone almost as suddenly as it came, but for a second or two its severity frightened me. And then, faced with the challenge of the traffic, and the 3:1 odds against reaching the far side of place de la Concorde unsplatted, the incident was forgotten.

'Ledoyen,' he had said on the phone. 'Bottom of the Champs-Elysées. You can ask anyone.' I did, and you could.

'A restaurant' was all he had said. Some restaurant! Set in mini-parkland, opposite the Elysée Palace, approached by a discreet, curving drive, bearing the date 1792 on the pillared entrance, and with more doormen to park your car than most restaurants have waiters, I was impressed. I was so impressed I was terrified.

I had spent an hour on my appearance, but my best fineries, the brogues, flannels and sports jacket sent out by my father, managed to look – in the Parisian context – like cast-offs from a failed costume drama. To have dragged them the length of snowbound France was madness, a pilgrimage worthy of a flagellant order. Unfortunately, my alternative fashion choices were holed sweaters, broken-backed sandals, and bald cords with Laundromat-resistant stains.

I strolled with worldly casualness up to the entrance, past a small coterie of chauffeurs comparing their engine sizes, and in through the glass doors. The reception area would not have disgraced a five-star hotel, the fitments splashed in gold, the carpets heavy in plush hush, and the air flown in specially from Switzerland. Luncheon was winding down, and around the foyer was a light sprinkling of departing guests; now was the endgame of the meal, and men with big cigars were giving each other significant handshakes, and immaculate young women were calmly awaiting the post-prandial adultery in a cool, darkened room.

I approached the staff, acutely conscious that I was the only tieless man within a hundred yards.

'I have an appointment with Monsieur Bareste.'

Instant attention.

'Ah, oui. Monsieur Pilton.'

A discreet phone call.

'He is coming, sir.' A charming smile, a gesture to an elegant seat.

I would have preferred to stand, but was anxious to be as uncontroversial as possible. I made my way to the seat.

'Monsieur Pilton!'

The cry came from behind, and from above my head. A wide staircase swept from the foyer to the first floor, and I turned to see the smiling face of a man in his sixties, impeccably clad in a dinner-jacket. He continued to descend as I hurried over, and he met me halfway down the stairs, his hand outstretched in greeting.

'You are very prompt,' he said in English.

'It seemed a good idea!' I tried to laugh. It appeared to go down well.

'Please. Come with me.' He spread his arm in a fatherly gesture as he turned, and we climbed the stairs side by side.

He was quite a bulky man, but moved with seamless delicacy. He had a weather-beaten, almost bald head which made a large face look extra-large. Moreover, it was a boxer's sort of face, most curiously at odds with his diffident charm.

'Would you like some coffee? Or some English tea perhaps?'

'. . . er . . .'

I believe he recognized a hesitation born of nerves. 'It will be no trouble.' A tiny pause, a slight smile. 'I am the *maitre d'*.'

He ushered me imperceptibly into a grand side dining-room, filled with flowers, where *commis*-waiters were brushing the last signs of guests from the heavy white tablecloths; as we entered they discreetly vanished, to re-emerge later with tea.

'Please . . .' Again, an infinitely courteous gesture, this time to indicate where I might choose to sit. There was nothing superficial to his impeccable manners, nor was there any grandness to his paternalism; despite his considerable status, the impact of his presence came from an unaffected simplicity.

'We see many English people here,' he said, pursuing his concern to put me at my ease.

'Like prime ministers and kings?' I asked jocularly.

'Sometimes,' he replied. And smiled broadly at my misfired joke. 'So, you see, I need to practise my English!'

This was scarcely true. His English was all but faultless. I looked at him across the damask, uncertain whether I should try my hand at some complimentary remark, provide some token of English *politesse*.

'The Alliance Française tells me your price is five francs an hour,' he said.

This was the hurdle I had feared. The Alliance had been telling employers the same wage rate since the end of World War One. It was the *guichet* lady's idea of revenge on youth. This meant the first task of every student at a job interview was to demand a pay rise. I prepared to plug myself shamelessly.

'Of course,' he went on, 'that is far too little. Shall we say fifteen?'

We said fifteen.

'And three times a week?'

We said three times a week. I was on a roll. It was the interview of my dreams. All we had not said anything about was the actual lessons. '. . . What aspects of English would you want me to cover? The grammar? The literature?'

'The menus.'

'The menus?'

He handed me a glossy white card with five exotic courses in italics. I recognized the foreign land of guinea-fowl and truffles.

'The customers are always asking me questions. About the recipes. About the sauces. About how the vegetables are prepared. *Vous comprenez?*'

It was some months since I had had a vegetable, but I was familiar with most shapes and designs. So I nodded. 'Oh yes,' I said, 'I understand. I used to be a waiter myself.' And added sagely, 'What you're after is the technical vocabulary.'

He looked pleased. 'The "technical vocabulary". Yes, that's what I want. You know about food then, Monsieur Pilton?'

'Oh yes . . . yes, I know about food.' It was a reply founded more on Jesuitry than cookery – a philosophical awareness of the existence of food was hardly an answer to the job spec – and I felt a little guilty. But then my hunger for forty-five francs a week overcame existential niceties and I moved brazenly from the truth tangential to the lie direct. 'The menus would be no problem, Monsieur Bareste,' I said reassuringly.

'*Ah bien*,' he said, '*très bien.*'

My linguistic skills sold, I glanced down at the five courses again. 'Is there anything else?'

'My Breughels.'

'I'm sorry?'

'My beloved Breughels. Are you fond of Breughels, Monsieur Pilton?'

Only a sixth sense kept me off the subject of Jewish rolls.

'Oh. What . . . Pieter van . . . ?'

'Pieter the Elder, Pieter the Younger, and, of course, Jan, the son. So much talent, in one family.' He sighed with pleasure, a private reverie briefly drifting across his features. 'What do you think of their work?'

All I could remember of it was a lot of crowded ice, peasants in need of back operations, and a definite whiff of hell. But I felt this was not the time to express a preference for the pre-Raphaelites.

'Oh, tremendous,' I replied. 'It gives one a real sense of the Middle Ages in the Low Countries.'

'Yes, and such pretty paintings.' Another dreamy sigh. 'Such beautiful detail.'

'Oh, the detail's great!' When I had made my introductory phone call, I had imagined rather dull, but manageable, afternoons wrestling with recondite tenses of the verb 'to be'. Probably in the adolescent company of a rich retard. Conversations about the finer points of fine art had not figured on the blackboard of my mind. 'Are you a collector?' I enquired, struggling towards the safer ground of biographical fact.

'Only prints, *hélas*! And the photographs that I cut from the catalogues. Your Sotheby's always send me their catalogues. Full of such lovely pictures!'

'Yes, Sotheby's are very good.' Somehow, I overshot the tone. In aiming at a nodding acquaintance with civilization, I seemed to have offered a ringing testimonial to their personal handling of my Old Masters. Fortunately, Monsieur Bareste did not notice.

'I love to read what they write about the paintings,' he continued, 'to learn what the experts think. But such long words! *oo la la!*' He shook his hands as if he had burnt his fingers.

'Long words?' At last I could see where the conversation was going. 'You would like to have them translated?'

'Just the difficult ones. The . . . "technical vocabulary".' He smiled, pleased with his new phrase. 'You could do that for me?'

'Certainly. No problem,' I replied, again with more confidence than I felt. Although vocabulary was my strongest suit, I was worried his art experts might make excessive use of words from the P to Z end of the dictionary. It also struck me that, even with artistic knowledge of trees in winter, the more esoteric aspects of chiaroscuro might leave me in difficulties.

At that moment, a silver tea-service rolled silently up to the table. A subservient *commis*-waiter did the honours and the conversation shifted to the safety of sliced lemons and milk.

Then, since the hour was not fully up, we went cursorily through one or two menus. I corrected his pronunciation of asparagus; I interfered with the occasional preposition; and I debriefed him on the bloody preparation of steak tartare. On our way back down the stairs, I turned to him and said, sincerely, 'Your English is very good.'

Monsieur Bareste smiled benignly. 'That is because you are a very good teacher.' It was outrageous charm. I could see exactly how he had become one of the top head waiters in Paris.

I stood for a moment on the Champs-Elysées, and, as I watched the late afternoon road-race, I pondered on life. In one brief hour, I had become an expert on French *haute cuisine* and medieval Dutch art. And found not so much a pupil as a patron.

It was while savouring this sudden change in fortunes that I became aware my surroundings were somewhat familiar. And then I realized that I was standing on the precise spot where I had been dropped that first dark wet lonely night in February. The symmetry of events seemed choreographed by Fate.

CHAPTER 15

'*Le chèvre, s'il vous plaît.*'

I jabbed a finger at random. There were at least a score of goat cheeses under the glass.

'*Lequel, monsieur?*'

I jabbed again. I felt a fraud. How could I possibly know the difference between twenty different goat cheeses, let alone the hundreds of other cheeses on display?

'*Celui-ci?*'

The aproned assistant picked up a large round cheese from the Ardèche. I nodded. He looked unhappy.

'*Vous n'allez pas aimer ça.*'

'*Non?*'

'***Non!***'

The elderly man shook his head firmly. I would definitely not enjoy that goat's work. I shrugged my shoulders, like a dog baring its neck in surrender. He replaced the Ardèche cheese and held up one from the Auvergne. I nodded meekly in agreement. Behind me was a small queue of serious shoppers, almost filling the tiny cheese shop, and I did not want them to hear the foolish questions I wished to ask. I took the Auvergnat, soft and moist to the touch, and stepped from the dark, penetratingly pungent world of cheese into the bright sunlight.

Water was trickling down the cobbles as the fresh slabs of ice by the fishmonger's stall gave in to the sun. I turned downhill, to stroll through the rest of the market. I was in the mood for window-shopping, but for that one needs the protection of windows; in the open air of Mouffetard, shopping was a fierce eye-contact sport. To make one's way past the racks of lamb and the trestles of fruit was to run the gauntlet of a thousand special offers. To say no meant yes, and to hesitate was to capitulate. I kept moving on, even past the hand-whorled chocolates, and eventually found myself at the very end of the market.

I rarely made it this far. It was a cul-de-sac of relative calm, where one was certainly safe from the hard sell. On one side stood the twelfth-century Eglise St Medard, and on the other was a fading advertisement for *Tripes (à la mode de Caen)*. I had not expected to find a large crowd blocking the road, all of whom were gazing upwards.

The centre of attention was a long ladder, unsafely positioned against an ancient and exotic delicatessen called Facchetti. The shop was Italian, or possibly Corsican; it exhaled rich Mediterranean food smells into the street, and looked almost as long-established as the church. I joined the growing group and looked up. Across the third and fourth storeys was an extensive and very detailed fresco; made a long time ago from white plaster, now much discoloured, and embossed on a brown background, it depicted medieval hunting scenes (thus providing the possibility of an erudite pun on venerable and venery). Scattered through the woodland foliage, which even adorned the top floor mansard surrounds, were *les animaux de la chasse*: deer, wild boar, and exotic birds.

The first floor, however, was the cause of the excitement. Here, where the ladder ended, five large new hunting tableaux were being precariously painted on to smooth fresh plaster. It was art and a high-wire act in one. And clinging to the top of the ladder was a familiar figure in black.

Gerard was currently working on ducks, fine white pot-ready ducks. He gripped a palette in one hand, a long brush in the other, and leant his lower body against the ladder for support. Occasionally, he would lean recklessly back to gain perspective. I watched for ten, fifteen minutes, partly from enjoyment of the spectacle, partly from pleasure at the painting, partly from the hope he might see me and wave. His concentration was eventually broken when the sun went behind a cloud and he turned to check on the weather. I waved, vigorously.

'*Salut!*' he cried.

'*Salut!*' I cried back.

'*C'est beau, non?*'

'*Ah, oui, c'est beau!*' And that was the extent of my reflected glory.

I stayed a few ducks longer. All five tableaux were already sketched in rough. Gerard was now putting fowl on bones. But I could see enough to reassure Jerry that he had not been mad – although he was wrong about the pterodactyls. The smart money was on peacocks.

Gerard had always reminded me of somebody, but, until today, I could not think who. It was as I watched him at work from below that I realized I could put a name to the image. Although short, Gerard had a muscular chest and disproportionately wide shoulders. He worked furiously, in intensive, jerky bursts. He was Snow White's eighth Dwarf. Arty.

'Hallo!' said a familiar heart-stopping voice in my ear. 'Friend of yours?'

It was Ulrika.

'Yes,' I said. Only to somewhat spoil the casual effect by adding, 'Famous local artist.'

I could tell blood was rushing about my body. Where it was going to, I was not sure. I just hoped it was not stopping anywhere public and causing embarrassing pink patches.

Ulrika and I had not exchanged much more than a court-yardly wave since her return. There was no estrangement, but I had somehow felt morally disqualified from approaching her, and she had presumably had her own preoccupations. A chance encounter on a sunny day was a perfect place to pick up from.

She was dressed for summer, a simple T-shirt casually outlining the breasts whose shape I had forbidden knowledge of. A fraying raffia bag slung over her shoulder contained a slim volume of poetry and a packet of Gitanes.

'Coffee?' I asked.

'Alcohol.'

We started off up the hill.

'*Salut!*' I called back to Gerard, hoping to prise his eyes from his wildfowl. To my great pleasure, he turned just in time to register that I was in the company of a beautiful woman.

As we strolled up the cobbles, more heads were turned. Ulrika had acquired large round smoky sunglasses to add to her beauty. With her eyes hidden, her thoughts inaccessible, the distant, quietly ironic, smile that hovered round her mouth had gained a challenging potency. All her wry detachment was made mysterious and sexually charged. Yet she remained innately shy, given to an almost childlike '*Zut alors!*' when embarrassed by stallholders' attentions.

We sat at a corner table in Café Mouffetard. It had become my favourite café. Outside, the life of the market would teem by; inside, the shaven-headed waiter was a Genet lookalike, half the customers seemed worthy of Ionesco, and on wet days the multi-fluted Spaniard laid on a serenade. As Ulrika and I waited for our drinks, I realized that our last meeting had also been in a café, to the joyless sound of pinballs.

I wanted to know what had happened with Augustus, but I didn't know how to ask the question. I wanted to know why *anything* had happened with Augustus, but I didn't know if I would understand the answer. I decided I would nudge the conversation in his direction at an appropriately mellow moment.

'How's your writing going?' Ulrika asked.

The prospect of mellow moments receded.

'Oh . . . I . . . my shift-key's broken.' I did briefly consider telling the truth. But rapidly concluded there was more product satisfaction in lies.

'What's a shift-key?'

'Oh, it's . . . it's technical. Gives you typewriter block!'

The sad truth was that, since receipt of the accountants' letter, my creative impulses had also gone into liquidation.

'Have you managed to sell anything?' The knife was twisted by the genuine sweetness of the enquiries.

'Possibly. I'm waiting to hear.'

'Oh, good luck!'

'Thank you.'

And to think *I* felt the right to demand honesty from *her*!

Her vodka and lemon arrived. She had a more expensive taste in drink than I remembered.

'Are you back for . . .' I had intended to say 'for good', but somehow that sounded insensitive.

'Until the next time!' She was smiling at me, quite relaxed.

'It's over, then?' It was obvious it was over, but I wanted details.

'Oh yes!' She gave a broad grin. If Ulrika was heart-broken, she was hiding the pieces extremely well.

A pause began to spread. It felt clumsy, nosy, to ask more; by silence, I hoped to leave my questions hanging persistently in the air.

'Oh yes,' she repeated. 'I don't think I'll be a welcome house-guest there again.' I looked at her encouragingly. 'Bit expensive, my stay.' Her irony had never been stronger.

'Expensive?' It was a perfectly posed question. She was now leading the conversation, I was following.

'Lot of . . . wear and tear caused by my presence.' She appeared to muse for a moment, and then laughed and said, 'I nearly had a holiday in Greece. On a yacht!'

'But?'

'But he took his girlfriend instead!'

I was suddenly disappointed in her. I had not thought power games part of her make-up. Yet I also sensed she was choosing to be provocative in some way.

'Still, he sent me a postcard. Said he realized he took the wrong one.'

'She was on the scene first?'

'Oh yes. She was a fixture.'

'She must have been pretty mad at you?'

There was a pause, whose meaning I could not read.

'. . . Only when I refused to sleep with her.'

If hearts do miss beats, mine missed a symphony's worth. She smiled, a smile that looked innocent, but could not be innocent because she had so masterfully teased me to wild sexual frenzy. 'Why didn't you sleep with her?' I asked as casually as possible, attempting a worldly amoral sophistication.

Ulrika said simply, 'I don't fancy women.'

'So it was a *ménage à trois?*' I was desperate for nitty-gritty.

'I suppose so. She'd come and go. She had a luxury pad of her own. And a Daddy like Augustus's.'

'Oh? What country did he own?'

'Let's just say he wasn't short of racehorses. And neither was she.'

'Is that why you lost out then? Money?'

This sounded unkinder than was meant. Perhaps some raw edge of jealousy had distorted my language. Ulrika looked at me more seriously. I think at that moment she regretted her light-hearted tone, her natural tendency to the spare and enigmatic.

'I didn't lose out. I walked out,' she answered, and then felt obliged to explain. 'He used to keep tropical fish, Augustus. He had a big tank in the lounge. It was because of scuba-diving that he was so keen on his yacht. And holidays in Greece. Well, this Greek trip was to be for the three of us. Except when I said I wasn't going to go as Marianne's bunk-mate as well, she threw a tantrum. A spoilt rich girl's sort of tantrum, screaming and shouting. Finally she ordered Augustus to bar me from coming.

'He refused. And she electrocuted his fish. One hundred thousand francs worth of koi carp floating the wrong way up when she'd finished. And so I left. Didn't think it was my sort of lifestyle.' It was an understatement that failed to disguise the clear disgust she had felt.

It was also the longest speech I had heard Ulrika give. I wanted to ask exactly how this bisexual heiress had electrocuted the fish but was restrained by a feeling this might not be the central focus of the story. Besides, I had another question.

'Why did you stay with him in the first place?'

This was what I had always wanted to know, except that to ask now came across not as a burning personal resentment but the reasonable enquiry of a third party.

'Sex.' A long pause. 'Can't stay a virgin for ever.'

'But he was an arrogant, vain, nasty, superficial . . .' I decided to cut back on the adjectives and get to the point, 'idiot.'

'Oh certainly,' she agreed. 'But not in bed.'

'Oh.' I was lost for a supplementary.

'I wanted sex. He was all-confident. The sex was great.'

I could not think of anything to say. I did not know it then, but I had stumbled across one of the enduring mysteries of the human condition.

Later that day, as we were strolling back up rue Mouffetard, an afterthought struck me. 'That postcard you got. They're not still together, are they, Augustus and Marianne?'

'Oh yes,' she replied. 'The fish were insured.'

We parted on good terms, perhaps the best terms we had known. She had confided in me a great deal, her sexual needs had been aired, and I had even observed civilized norms. I was not without hope that we had a future.

Nonetheless, by the time I entered the cool solitude of my room I was quietly paranoid that she had so readily located those nether regions of Paris, its private parts, whose sexual where-abouts constantly eluded me. I was now some way into Henry Miller on the subject, and scarcely a day went by without the entire clientele of a café dropping their knickers for him. I flopped onto the bed to let my head clear from the wine. But my troubled libido would not rest. I picked up *Quiet Days in Clichy* from a pile of old socks on the floor and began working conscientiously through its pages.

It was not just the frequency of his sexual encounters which amazed me. It was his description of a world in which sex was everywhere, lurking, waving, waiting, leaping upon him. As one pair of legs closed, another opened. In his world, his Paris, sex was so constant and unremitting one could actually tire of it! There were parts of his city where, to get home at night without sex, was like 'running the gauntlet'. And once home, no room, not even the bath, was free from marauding house guests wanting to fornicate in experimental positions.

But most amazing of all was his ability to recognize instantly any woman in the mood for a thirty-second relationship. Or, as he more immortally put it, 'those happy-go-lucky souls who fuck on sight'. I could not distinguish such women from those training for nunship. To me, such female moods were as un-detectable as an over-active liver. Yet no sooner had Henry said hallo to a woman than she unzipped his flies. Even at bus stops.

In fact, Miller's Paris was proving no easier to find than Hemingway's. Admittedly, Clichy was a different *arrondissement*, and perhaps morals were slightly looser there. And, of course, it was always possible that he was lying. Some people will do that to sell books. But Ulrika wasn't lying. Ulrika had located this world of deliciously louche goings-on (the fish excluded, *bien sûr*). Ulrika had found the free-loving free-thinkers.

I was stretched out on the bed, becoming over-excited at the thought of her world, and her burgeoning sexuality, and our growing rapport, when there was a soft tap at the door. It was nearly ten o'clock and the room had slipped into darkness. I scrambled to my feet and hastily adjusted my clothing. 'Coming!' I called, lest she leave.

I pulled open the door, and there, carrying a bottle of red wine and a bed-roll, was Jerry.

'Hi!' he said in Californian. 'Couldn't put me up on your floor tonight, could you?'

CHAPTER 16

Jerry stayed for about ten days, on his first visit. The paintings had not sold in great numbers. The art world had not announced the arrival of a Franco-American landscape movement. And the identical-twin genre had not captured the public imagination. Consequently, the cash from the watercolours had done little more than top up the pockets of the gallery owner. The lease on the barn was let go, and Jerry and Garry decided to focus their brushes on scenes from the city. Garry had a friend of a friend who had a spare mattress; Jerry had met a man in a launderette.

Jerry was the ideal sub-tenant: good company, he knew when you wanted no company. He also took an innocent infectious joy in the world. Often in the early mornings we would walk the deserted streets together and he would take pleasure in the smallest details: the texture of decaying plaster in a side alley, the shadow of a chimney pot, the posture of a sleeping cat. Once he even stopped to admire the ex-workings of a vandalized phone box; for several days its mangled innards rested in our room, his *objet trouvé* of the week.

This childlike quality was no jejune affectation. To my knowledge, he never wore flowers in his hair or tattooed LOVE on his head or claimed to be holier than the other 99 per cent of the population. His outlandish appearance no doubt sprang from the iconoclastic dress code of the times, but his sweet nature was home-grown, his values his own. Jerry may have been a West Coast hippy, but he was not another freeloader on the Berkeley bandwagon to nirvana. He believed in the Fall.

Several times in his company I was taken unwell. I was never the most genteel of eaters – I usually ate like a POW in receipt of a Red Cross parcel – and it was not unknown for me to have a touch of indigestion. But of late there had been more than one reprise of the raspberry-crêpe incident, when a red-hot toasting fork was jabbed into my solar plexus. I normally shrugged the pain off, for it was as brief as it was vicious, and somehow, being internal and invisible, it lacked lasting reality. However, I was walking up rue du Pot-de-Fer, after a double helping of Mars bars and chips, when my intestines exploded. I doubled up and slumped against a brick wall. My insides felt as though they were being kicked by a red-hot boot. Then, finding it a struggle to breathe, I let my body slide to the ground in case I was about to die. While I lay and prayed for the pain to pass, Jerry stood protectively by and uttered soothing noises and directed pedestrians around me.

When eventually I was resurrected and we had made it back to my room, he looked at me rather paternally, asked a few pertinent questions, felt the location of the pain – and announced that I had an ulcer. I was appalled, less by the diagnosis (which I didn't believe) than by the social stigma. Who had ever heard of a Bohemian with a stress-related illness? An ulcer was a lifestyle disorder brought on by contact with a suit. Gentle, alternative types, who had renounced the evils of competitive capitalist society, were supposed to live in harmony with the bloody world. Whilst naturally I accepted that I might occasionally fall ill, I had rather hoped it to be something like a venereal disease, so that I could gain sexual credibility within the community.

'Believe me, I know. It's an ulcer,' said Jerry. 'I've had several. My stomach used to be like fish-net stockings.'

The analogy seemed a bit medically suspect, but otherwise he displayed an alarming certainty, and a strange earnestness.

'How did *you* get ulcers?' I asked, a little incredulously. (And as I asked, I recalled his personal supply of brown rice, which I had put down to California's dietary fascism.)

'Family life!' It ought to have been a throwaway line, but he did not smile.

'You were married? I didn't know that!'

'No, no. My family back home. Where I was raised, as a child.'

'That gave you ulcers?'

He thought a while about how to answer the question.

'We all used to eat together as a family. Togetherness was father's big thing. There were four of us brothers and him. Ma died when I was ten. Accident in the pick-up.' Jerry was speaking slowly, almost in a monotone. 'And our father was pretty strict. You get like that in Arizona. He had rules for everything. Especially meal-times . . . We used to sit in this—this long, narrow kitchen to eat. And he would sit at the head of the table. My two older brothers, Marty and Greg, would sit closest to him. And he would wear steel-tipped boots. None of us was ever allowed to speak during the meal, except to ask someone to pass the food, or to ask permission to pour the water, or say please and thank you. Or grace!' He broke off, and I realized he was fighting back tears. 'And the slightest mistake, food eaten too quickly, food eaten too slowly, or head up too high, or too much noise with your knife and fork . . . well, then—' Jerry raised his left foot on to the seat of the chair, and pulled up his trouser leg. His shin was covered in scars, and there were a dozen places where the hair no longer grew. 'And Pa would lash out with the full force of his boot. We all sat in constant fear. Because we had no way of telling when his boot was going to smash into one of us. And we never knew who he'd choose. Or why. Eventually there was no reason. It could be the creaking of a floorboard. And suddenly his boot would lam into you. And all the time your stomach would be one giant knot as you tried to eat. With perfect manners!' There was a very long pause. I thought he had finished. But then he spoke again, this time in a quieter voice. 'It was much worse for the other two. They had to sit right next to him. At close range. They took the full force.

And Marty, he was just one year older than me, he was the quietest of us all. And he found it hardest to hang in there. Before some meals, we'd hear him crying. None of us realized it then, but . . . but he had developed a huge duodenal ulcer. And one night, as he was trying to force some stew down, it simply burst. Burst from terror, I reckon. And he screamed, and fell on the floor. And two days later he was dead.'

There was never a longer silence in that room. In the end it was Jerry who broke it. 'So that's how I know about ulcers. And you've got one.'

It would have been an extremely insensitive person who disagreed.

'So what do you suggest?'

The latticework grin began to reappear.

'I have got just the little old lady for you!'

An hour later, in the second jaunt of the day, Jerry and I were outside a small shop at the unfashionable end of boulevard St Germain. I had often passed by here but never noticed the place before. It had a window so cluttered that initially one was hard put to tell what sort of shop it could be. I focused on a packet of *pissenlit* herbal tea – which at first suggested a discreet sex shop for urolagniacs with botanical tastes – and then, as I worked my eye along the molasses and metzos and soya-milk cans and sticks of yarrow I slowly came to the conclusion that the only thematic link was health foods.

The layout was dourly, defiantly old-fashioned, the products so uncalorific in content that righteousness was clearly the substitute for attractive design. Eat healthy, be deadly, was the uplifting message to the passing world. Such earnestness was reminiscent of how *Health and Efficiency* magazine had achieved the impossible and made nudity boring. Admittedly, the relentlessly glamorous health-food evangelists of later years gave charisma a bad name, and might have benefited from a length of celery blocking their perfect bowel movements, but right now, when I needed comfort in an intestinal crisis, I was not keen on a diet organized by the Wee Free of food.

'Come on! Think macrobiotic!' urged Jerry, and pushed open

the door, setting off a Swiss cow bell, which had no doubt once pealed across organic Alpine meadows.

Over the flagstoned floor, and around the sacks of sorghum, and jumbo oats and millet cakes (I had brought my dictionary), came a trim old lady at a young woman's speed of knots. If, as Jerry said, she were eighty-plus, she was undeniably a fine advert for life without chemicals. Her hair was still a healthy brown in its bun, she wore no glasses, carried no stick, and had a tongue in peak physical condition. She recognized Jerry at once, and gave him a smile worthy of a long-lost bulk buyer.

Jerry had already spent much of the walk trying to persuade me how the right diet made for a happy hippy. With the fervour of a born-again eater, he had movingly testified to the non-violent qualities of the vegetable kingdom and spoken up vigorously for pumpkin seeds. To clinch his case, he had even offered to show me the superiority of his stools. I was still unconvinced.

Jerry, oblivious to the finer points of French formality, did the introductions by pointing his finger at me and saying in a loud voice, '*Mallard!*' He then rubbed my stomach vigorously with his hand, in a motion which prefigured the later models of Magimix.

I hesitated. I had a horror of the hip. I could see that a macrobiotic lifestyle was consonant with the age, but I felt uncomfortably self-parodic. However, I also felt uncomfortably ulcerous. And I wished to avoid the social embarrassment of a city-slicker's stomach. I nodded acquiescence.

Without further ado, the old lady led me to the latest shipment of brown rice. She was somewhat fierce in her sales technique; had she discovered God rather than food, she would have been a Methodist lay preacher. Obviously driven by a desire to save sinning stomachs from burning in hell, she started to trowel out sufficient brown rice for a medium-size health farm. Jerry stood on hand, smiling and urging her on.

After the brown rice, she became very insistent on herbal teas. I was shown a chart which made clear she could cater for arthritis, asthma, bronchitis, poor muscle tone, rheumatism and varicose veins. And if, through some unforeseen visitation, I was to go down with cystitis, she could provide the necessary couch grass and marshmallow infusions. We settled on fennel tea, which could also be useful in times of psoriasis.

I drew the line at lentils. A man must have some self-respect. We did briefly get into peas and beans. Yellow peas, green peas, chick peas, split peas, whole peas; red beans, brown beans, green beans, dried beans, spotted beans. But beans was Jerry's bag, I let him choose.

And then eggs. There was a wide selection of eggs, each with the personal life history of the hen. None of Madame's accredited hens had led other than a perfect pastoral existence, with good views and interior-sprung hay at night. We took lots of eggs – it was twenty years before we learnt that hens laid cholesterol.

And then we were done. The golden rule was to be gentle with my stomach. To give it soft, soothing foods. And never stand downwind of a butcher's.

That night was Macrobiotic Night in my room, a soirée for men in beards. Jerry showed me how to make a simple food-faddist's meal. He boiled some rice, burnt some onions, added some accredited eggs, fried the lot, and then mixed it all about. (In sunflower oil, of course.) We ate straight from the pan, and it slipped past the danger zone without even a tremor.

I had never been much of a chef, but I knew cooking when I saw it. I was deeply impressed. As a result, for the rest of my time in Paris, I had rice, eggs and onions – mixed all about – almost once a day.

To Jerry, I owe the lasting gift of my good health.

After ten days, he got the chance to graduate to a mattress in a nearby basement. His life seemed to proceed through chance meetings, casual acquaintanceships and off-the-cuff suggestions, as if he were the ball in a game of social bagatelle. But he did not appear to care beyond the next day's living and this haphazard existence suited him well.

By the time he left we were good friends and keen to stay in touch. As we were shaking hands at my door and joking about this and that, he suddenly turned serious.

'Barry,' he said, 'if a man in a suit ever comes asking for me, you've never seen me. Never heard of me. OK?'

'In a suit?' I said, puzzled by such specificness. 'Who is he?'

'I can't tell you that,' he replied. 'But he'll have a suit on all right.' A wry smile crossed his face. 'They always do.'

And then he left.

CHAPTER 17

It was a glorious Sunday morning, with a perfect blue sky and soft warm air. I had just returned from a most pleasurable fifteen-minute conversation in the stand-up toilet when Tony burst into my room and cried, 'Quick! Quick! Come and see what's happening!' and rushed back to his room in high excitement.

The toilet was half a floor up, in an extension that jutted out from the main building to provide space for the staircase. This toilet contained an open window – open in the sense of there being no window, just a large square hole because that's how the French are about these things. The window/hole was approximately four feet above the floor, and so provided an excellent view of the world in general, and the annexe in particular. Conversely, anyone in the annexe had an excellent view of their neighbours straining to crap. Being English, I had in the early days made extensive use of the ground-floor facilities. But I had recently discovered in my Henry Miller, now nearly finished, an account of a very similar toilet, in which he would stay for hours, trousers and boxer shorts around his ankles, conducting conversations with all and sundry as they passed by; apparently the erotic charge of being naked from the waist down served to give spice to remarks about the weather. For both parties. In his case, he had the added aphrodisiac of overlooking a whole street.

Spurred on by literary heritage, I had taken to using the upstairs toilet in the hope of engaging interesting onlookers, and more specifically Ulrika, in stimulating chit-chat. (I was, however, very strict about always having a physiological need to visit the toilet: I had no wish to become a pervert.) And on this morning, the glorious Sunday weather had caused almost every resident to fling up their window and bask in the sunshine. The quality and quantity of conversation had been so great that I had hardly found the time to evacuate my bowels. Most gratifying of all, Ulrika and I had agreed to give the park a whirl in the afternoon.

When I entered Tony's room he was leaning perilously out over its balconette railings, the full-length windows wide open. He was looking towards the square.

'What is it?' I asked, straining to see over his head. As I spoke, a rendition of *Rhapsody in Blue* drifted into earshot. The evocative chords perfectly captured the mood of the day. The performance was being given on piano and, most surprising and heart-warming of all, it was live.

I looked in the direction where Tony's body was pointing. In the middle of place de la Contrescarpe, in the shade of the trees, stood an old upright joanna. And pounding away at its keys was a young man in full evening dress. A small crowd had already started to gather and the cafés were fast filling up.

'How did it get there?'

'God knows! Fell off a lorry?'

We stood on the pocket balcony together and lapped up the sound. The spectacle even caused Parisian drivers to slow down. For five spellbinding minutes the lone performer gave Gershwin his all. Then the rhapsody soared to its emotional finale and suddenly it was over. With an outrageous theatrical flourish, the young man slammed down the piano lid, stood on his stool, and bowed low to all corners of the square. Applause and cheers echoed through the trees. Tony shouted 'Bravo!' and I clapped wildly. We would have stomped our feet, but his balcony would almost certainly have descended to the stalls. For the first time I noticed a young woman wearing a very low-cut, shiny green evening dress – and holding an upside-down top hat. She was dexterously working the crowds. She passed below us and in a moment of weakness I threw down a large amount of the next month's rent. She dipped in a brief, breast-revealing curtsy, and as I grinned back I caught sight of Madame almost directly beneath me on the pavement. The old lady was perched improbably on a dining-room chair and clutching her knitting like a benign Mme Defarge. As the collection of coins rolled around her feet she gazed up and gave me a wonderfully enigmatic look which managed to be both reproachful and approving.

A waiter with a silver tray came onto the square and placed a glass and a complimentary bottle of red wine on the piano. After a short interval to wipe away sweat, the pianist held up his hands for silence, announced something we could not hear, adjusted his bow tie, and started to play again. It was *Ragtime*. It was boppy and bouncy and just what the crowd wanted. Feet were beginning to tap and one of the cafés was clapping along to the rhythm when my arm was grasped by Tony.

'Oh-oh!' he said ominously. 'Look!'

Below us the familiar sight of a kepi was making its way through the bystanders. With no sign of a bop in his body, the gendarme advanced upon the square. The pianist, unaware of his approach, continued to jangle his way through Joplin. The crowd, realizing the military two-step was about to mix it with jazz, seemed to freeze collectively. But then as a uniformed arm fell onto the piano player's shoulder, catcalls filled the square. The pianist tried to shrug off his grip, but the gendarme only became more insistent. A struggle developed, interspersed with snatches of Joplin. Each time the pianist reached the keys, a roar went up.

Stalemate arrived at, the pianist got off his stool and the two men eyeballed each other fruitlessly, and then started to argue. Somehow, evening dress gave the pianist a moral headstart, even if one were sympathetic to the eighteenth-century penal code on seditious ivory-tinkling. To his support, almost immediately, stormed his accompanist in green, this time herself accompanied by a round of applause. She too had an unsuccessful go at eyeballing. Then the dispute raged on, two against one. The beleaguered gendarme, possibly fearing he was losing the argument of case law and precedent, moved into a defensive position and rested his bottom on the piano lid. Resumption of play started to look unlikely.

At which point, quite unexpectedly, into the fray strode Gerard. A clear favourite with the crowd, who constantly called out, '*Allez-y, mon brave!*' he had obviously deputed himself to represent the forces of reason. In his shaggy black jumper and black cords, and sucking reasonably on his pipe, he looked every bit the emissary of the common man as he set out steadfastly through the trees, on his way to talk homely good sense. Unfortunately, by the time he reached the middle of the square he had already lost his temper. For a brief moment, his body language struggled to say, 'Come on, *mon vieux*, be a sport! What about a *coup de rouge* and a bit of a blind eye, eh?' but then, his artistic temperament faced with an unyielding bottom, he launched into furious Gallic gestures, many involving digit fingers and the gendarme's nose.

Events now began to unroll rather rapidly.

The young lady in the evening dress, seeing the men locked in sterile masculine abuse at the piano, decided on a decoy strategy and advanced to the edge of the square – where she started to remove the evening dress. There was widespread support for this development, and a big cheer went up. The gendarme, suddenly aware that another affront to public order was about to occur, rushed over to restrain her, but by the time he arrived there was only a pair of small lacy pants left to restrain. And meanwhile, back at the piano, her partner had lifted the lid and begun to re-render *Ragtime*. The gendarme spun round, and then round again, clearly uncertain which was the graver of the two criminal acts in progress. To help him decide, the woman stepped back, removed the last of her underwear – tossing it into the top hat (where it nestled, I fondly hoped, amongst my very own coins) – and ran a provocative lap of dishonour round the square.

Then, naked except for a pair of green high heels, she took a series of tumultuous curtain calls, and it became evident the concert had escalated into cabaret. I glanced briefly down at

Madame and saw that she was helpless with laughter. The perspiring gendarme made several despairing grabs at the nude malefactor, but by now audience participation was seriously thwarting him. And the Joplin played on.

It was turning into a wonderful Sunday, a celebration of all the simple, impromptu pleasures of life.

And then the sirens sounded. Seconds later, two grey paddy wagons swept into the square. The thickly grilled rear doors burst open and twenty armed men poured out. All had been hand-picked and specially trained to overpower a jazz pianist and a naked girl.

It was the perfect setting for a riot. The police banged on their riot shields in hope and expectation. They raised their baton arms and looked for heads to crack. They even formed a phalanx, ready and baiting. But though the jeers of the crowd came thick and fast and angry, no actual missiles were thrown, no blows of bravado offered. Acts of violence seemed a step too far. It was a sunny Sunday morning, just a little too early for drink to have emboldened the crowd, and not at all a day to spend in jail. And so there was a stand-off in the square. It would be a year before the cobbles flew in earnest.

With professional roughness, the two miscreant performers were bundled up and into the van. A municipal lorry arrived and loaded up the offending piano. Police outriders began to circle the square in twos. And then, after much ritual shaking of fists and booing – to which Madame added her catcalls – it was over. Gerard, the people's tribune, objected as long and hard as he could, but even he remained just clear-headed enough to remain the right side of insurrection.

As the excitement started to die away, he retreated to the side-lines and watched the scene in a mixture of sorrow and disgust. He had his back to me, some thirty yards away, and I realized that, by chance, standing next to him in the thinning crowd was Ulrika. I saw his head turn, I felt him register her presence, and I knew he had recognized her. He had recognized her because, thanks to my desire to impress, I had been the one who had introduced them. He spoke. She smiled. And in that tiniest of exchanges, that smallest of glances, I saw the iron doors of finality slam shut on all my lovelorn hopes.

Tony had gone in now, but I stayed out on the balcony watching them, watching destiny at work. He was the picture-postcard painter, she was the dreamy art-lover; French heart-throb and German beauty, it was Yin and Yang. They chatted for a few moments more, and then he, the hero of the hour, took her arm with a lover's panache and they strolled off across the square together, and out of sight. Today, I realized, I would not be going to the park to play.

I turned down Tony's offer of tea. I was not in the mood for a shared tea bag. I went back to my room but could not bear to stay in it. It looked suddenly dingy in the summer brightness. I picked up my Miller, so that while I moped I could at least appear to have a purpose. Outside in the square, Sunday life was back to normal. I found a free table in the sun and opened the book at random. I felt numb. I could not believe how fast I had gone from high to low. Was it because I was upset by the loss of Ulrika herself, or by the loss of my last, best hope? All around me people were happy, a sure recipe for aggravated depression. I gazed unseeingly at the print and then, without warning, my eye snagged on the opening line of a paragraph. I read it carefully twice. It said simply: 'It was a period when cunt was in the air.'

How the hell could he tell?

I ordered a *citron pressé*. They lasted forever and kept waiters at bay. And what did the bastard mean? Today was a heady, balmy, shirt-sleeve and sandal sort of day. Was cunt in the air now? Did other people know about it? Could I be immune to it? And what if cunt wasn't in the air and I molested someone in error?

I was about to shut the book when a shadow fell across it. A fedora-shaped shadow.

'Hallo!' said an insidious, sarcastic drawl. 'Room for a couple more? It's such a tight fit today.'

My Wildean neighbour had with him the young Canadian from the floor above. They had been spending time together lately, though whether the only mutual interest was their poetry had yet to be established.

I glanced round the café. It was unfortunately true, the place was close to heaving. Outdoors on the square at the weekend was now a prime location.

'Yes, sure.' I considered saying that I was about to leave anyway, but I had a lot of lemon to get through, and it would not have been convincing.

'So kind.'

Mr W. Molmar (officially we were unintroduced, but his pigeon-hole was above mine and he had regular air-mail letters from Buffalo, sent by a pair of Molmars) lowered his frame into the chair next to mine. Even in the afternoon heat, he did not remove his white jacket, for fear of appearing normal.

He beamed. 'What an encouraging day for culture! A police force actually prepared to do something about third-rate musicians!'

I hid my annoyance. I should have said something rude to him, but he intimidated me. It was not just his bulk. His persona was built on provocation, and I was no match. 'Perhaps we should train musicians to do something about third-rate policemen,' I replied.

'Oh, I like policemen. A good baton charge is my idea of poetry in motion! Don't you agree?' He addressed the question to his acolyte.

Pete – a disappointing name for an acolyte – agreed. 'Yeah! That's right!' Pete from Canada was about twenty-one and a bit boondocksy. I remembered that, on my first night, Joan had said he always carried a pad. He was carrying a pad now. Presumably in case an ode came by.

I said nothing on the matter of batons. I recognized bait, and I was not biting.

Mr Molmar flourished an arm at a waiter, and ordered a carafe of red wine. I wondered at his other airs. In the hotel, he moved with disdain, that the world might know he was slumming. But he had been there three years. And to be pushing thirty-five made him a suspiciously late slummer.

'So, how's the art-loving going?' he asked. He turned to Pete. 'Our friend's an art-lover.'

169

'Oh, great,' said Pete.

'It's going fine,' I replied as non-committally as possible.

Mr Molmar persisted. 'I see you're collecting artists rather than paintings.' He had unfortunately come across Jerry outside the toilet one night. 'D'you find that cheaper?' He smiled.

I smiled back. And then, irritatingly, felt the need to explain myself. 'Jerry's between barns. He needed a free floor for a while.'

'I'm sure he's very grateful. Patrons must be hard to come by these days. If one's struggling with one's little watercolours.'

I could feel him trying to suck me into an argument, and I never liked to argue; lacking a degree, I always preferred to take the Fifth Amendment.

'But then,' he continued, 'according to Madame, you're a bit of an artist yourself, I understand. A writer, she says.'

Oh, shit! I fumbled the pass. 'No, not really!' I said. Damn Madame, I thought! 'Just a student, basically. With a bit of private teaching on the side.' And damn him, too! The man's compulsive, corrosive cynicism was forcing me to run for truth.

'He's being modest,' Mr Molmar archly confided in Pete. 'Apparently he's got publishers after him. And TV people.'

'Wow! Great!' said Pete. Again.

Mr Molmar treated me to another smile, his most lethal weapon. I tried to out-smile him back. Bit by bit, though, I was being driven on to the defensive. 'No, no! I just mentioned a possible newspaper article. You know how Madame likes to exaggerate. I gather you're a poet. What sort of poetry d'you write?'

He paused. His eyes were shaded by the fedora, and I could not judge the import, or indeed the impact, of my question. He briefly toyed with my book, and then asked, 'Have you heard of Byron?'

'Yes. We did him at school.'

'He is for adults as well,' he responded, with definite astringency. He hesitated, then, his usual gravitas slightly compromised by a rushed delivery, he said, 'I'm reworking *Don Juan*.'

'Why?'

'It's an update,' said Pete helpfully, and got a glare for his trouble. Clearly his mouth was not the orifice of greatest interest to Mr Molmar.

'Because, dear boy, *Don Juan* is one of the finest creations in comic verse. A d'Artagnan with balls *and* brains. Who shows man how to live his life. With flair! And panache! And passion!' He waved his arms, nearly spilling my lemon. 'Byron was a shooting star across the sky of nineteenth-century Europe. The last great iconoclast! A man forever fighting, fornicating . . .' He struggled unsuccessfully for a final 'f'. 'And that's what I am going to give this drab little century of ours – a *new Don Juan*! A full-blooded hero, with full-blooded emotions! Someone to defecate on conformity and fucking bourgeois sanctimony!'

'Sounds interesting,' I said. I had been somewhat distracted by the embarrassing stares of people at the nearby tables, who were not used to the declamatory form of drinking.

'Interesting!' he sneered. 'You think it sounds interesting?'

'Well—'

'—What an anaemic little word!'

'Well, what word would you prefer?' I asked with scrupulous politeness, but at some level maliciously aware the politeness was the most incendiary response.

'I'd prefer an emotional response, a gut response, something with feelings.'

'Oh, I see.'

He reacted with forceful contempt. 'You have heard of feelings? You do know about feelings?'

'Well, I think they're best restrained,' I said with quiet but offensive gentility.

'So typically fucking English!' he snapped. He himself was some murky mix of transatlantic and mid-European, and any retaliatory ethnic shaft would have been hard to target, but suddenly I was more interested in conforming to his prejudices. I *wanted* to act out the racial stereotyping. I had found a way under his skin.

'What exactly do you mean?' I enquired politely, 'when you use the phrase "typically English"?'

He glared at me. 'Emotionally stunted. Pathologically repressed. And as sexually explicit as an hermaphrodite earthworm.'

'Oh, I see,' I said again. 'But I do think there's a lot to be said for the stiff upper lip.'

Our opposing positions were perversely skewed. I had found myself defending what I did not believe in. I desperately wanted to be stuffed full of this unEnglish passion and emotion. By presenting myself to him as irredeemably anal, I was committing a despairing act of masochism.

'Surely to give way to emotion is to give way to weakness?' I smiled helpfully. Mr Molmar leant back and rolled his eyes to the heavens and then to Pete. Pete then tried a bit of eye-rolling for himself. 'That is,' I continued, 'one of the great lessons one learns at public school.'

'Oh! The English public school!' he cried, as if all were explained. 'Of course! So I suppose you believe that civilization is about punctuality and manners? And not—'

'—Well, politeness,' I observed, 'certainly played a very important part in creating the Empire. Sorry, did I interrupt you?'

He took a deep breath, his imperviousness to irony fuelling a growing anger. 'Civilization is about great men saying "Fuck it!"' he roared. 'It's about making your own rules! It's about leaving your mark! It's about creating great art!'

'Like poetry,' said Pete.

'Shut up!' said Mr Molmar, who had been on a roll. He was now becoming very agitated. 'But then I imagine you think art is just late nights in a hotel attic. Well, let me tell you – art is about daring! Daring to think the unthinkable, say the unsayable, do the undoable!'

As I recall it, I was trying at this moment to look like an unconvinced small-town bank manager. It must have worked, because he suddenly seized my book, and poked me in the face with it. 'What the fuck is someone like you reading Henry

Miller for? Wouldn't you be better off sticking to the *Reader's Digest*?' Similar thoughts had indeed crossed my own mind.

I tried the imperturbable English approach one more time. 'I think one needs to be in touch with a wide range of contemporary—'

'—Not you! You don't! Books like this are wasted on you!' And with cold malice he thrust the book into the inside pocket of his jacket, confiscating it.

I stared at him, scarcely able to believe what had just happened.

'Well, Mr Stiff Upper Lip?' He melodramatically downed the last of his wine. 'Show us how bourgeois manners help you now!' He chucked some coins on the passing tray of a waiter – and stood up to go. I could not think what to do. 'Oh dear!' he said. 'Please and thank you not working?'

I felt overwhelmingly helpless and foolish, hoist by a petard which wasn't even my own. I also wanted to kill him, but knew this would damage my argument. And, I realized, I suddenly wanted to cry. But not fresh tears. The whole pointless, self-destructive exercise had not been about Mr W. Molmar. It had been about Ulrika, and who was taking her to the park. And as a result I was being offered hand-to-hand combat with Don Juan the Second.

I tried to smile patronizingly at Mr Molmar, and keep my role intact. 'Come along! Don't be a silly chap! Give it back.'

'No,' he said. 'I won't. You'll have to fight me for it!' And he waited, daring me to hit him, taunting me to resort to a hot-blooded, emotional gesture.

I refused. I sat trying to look unconcerned, and above the fray, but I knew I had lost. I had been beaten by my absurd posturing. And his. Mr Molmar and Pete turned, and walked off across the square, smirking. The reality of it all took a while to sink in. A man had just stolen my book in the most public way possible, and I had done nothing about it.

My *citron pressé* was now reduced to sugar and water, and had gone gently lukewarm in the Sunday afternoon sun.

CHAPTER 18

The hour of cuisine and culture among the candelabras was now well established, and had become a gentle and civilized ritual, full of reassuring pleasures.

Three times a week, I would leave the 5th *arrondissement* as an illegal drop-out, and arrive in the 8th *arrondissement* as a respected professor. Of late, it was even possible to make the journey and never once be out of sight of blossom. It was a rendezvous that kept me not merely solvent but sane. Ledoyen, laid back amongst its elegant shrubbery, was a form of haven, a place for an alter ego to be briefly nurtured.

My transformation into bourgeois man was not total. The absence of a tie in my ensemble had resulted in a management request that I enter via the back stairs, lest the more sensitive of their truffle-eaters should collapse *en masse* in the foyer. It was nothing personal. On one occasion a very distinguished publisher turned up similarly *déshabillé* and he had to be fed in an alcove, screened by emergency palms in wheeled flower-pots.

This was the sort of diplomatic incident at which Monsieur Josef Bareste excelled. A lifetime of double bookings, delicate stomachs and dissatisfied drunks had made him a nonpareil at guest pacification. His most celebrated achievement had been to master an out-of-control *banane flambé* by severing the customer's burning tie with a carving knife – to a round of applause and a large tip. If Michelin ever instituted a 'smile' symbol for outstanding charm, he would be the bench-mark. His most appreciative audience was probably the older woman, tending toward widowhood, and usually English; only the month before, he had won a heart when he removed a gravy droplet with a gallant Gallic kiss to the back of the hand. But had he flung a bowl of bouillabaisse over these lonely, overpowdered women, they would still have emerged from the experience twittering with pleasure at the grace of his apologies.

It was not a Parisian charm, it was a peasant charm. My puzzlement at his build and his features was well-founded. He was born in the Alpes Maritimes, the austere and beautiful hills above the Riviera; he and his older brother had been raised in a small place called Escragnolles, 3,000 feet above sea level. From this rural fastness, his route into the restaurant business had not been a conventional one. He had begun his working life as a butcher in Clermont-Ferrand during the Occupation. The first professional application of his charm had been in the black market, outwitting the Nazis with his beefsteaks. For a man who possessed no detectable signs of ambition, his postwar rise was impressive. Now at the top of the serving tree, he had scattered his peasant benignity amongst some of the classiest eateries that Paris had to offer.

That such autobiographical details emerged from our English lessons was evidence of the extreme flexibility of the syllabus – and our growing rapport. To my relief, the seminars on cookery and history dwindled to little more than a canter through menus and sales particulars – and I would occasionally correct a word. A few days later we would canter through the same menu and the same sales particulars . . . and I would correct the same word. (Although his English was almost faultless, his faults were almost irremovable; he would sigh and smile like an incorrigible naughty boy when a mistake was spotted.) And then it would be Breughel time – as satisfying as any hour spent down the road in the Louvre. We did translate the occasional text, but at heart Monsieur Bareste was happiest when poring over his prints, and pointing out to me details of the geese and the windmills and the village idiot and the freshly baked bread. At these moments I realized he had no need of lessons; it was only his modesty that made him deprecate his English. The true reason for my presence was to make him feel at ease when he spoke a foreign language among strangers.

Our conversations continued until the very end of my time in Paris. The afternoons became like a paid visit to a favourite uncle, and I grew extremely fond of him.

Before long, he was recommending my services to the rest of the restaurant. This began to prove a seriously mixed blessing. First through my metaphorical portals was a young Breton, a *commis*-waiter, memorable only for the medieval splendour of his name: Yannick le Moine. His father was a self-made millionaire, owner of prestige hotels throughout Brittany, and Yannick, rough-edged and provincial, had been sent to the capital to learn the ropes of his future empire. Young Yannick was stocky, spotty, likeable – and impervious to all known educational processes. Even his written French was worse than mine. For weeks there were bleak and bruising battles over the ground rules of English grammar. And then Yannick came up with a proposal of entrepreneurial brilliance: that he continue to pay me on condition that neither of us turned up and I didn't snitch to his father. At last, the perfect working relationship.

I was now close to a living (and eating, and drinking) wage and feeling rather buoyant again. It was at this point the head barman informed me that he wished to have classes.

He was in his early twenties, a tall, fit-looking young man, with a certain showiness when near bottles. Like many Paris barmen, he had that unsettling mix of deference and arrogance. He enjoyed looking sharp, and told me he had been head-hunted because of his flair for cocktails. I put him down as single-mindedly ambitious, eager for the status symbols of life. His English was a bit better than basic – he could hold his own in bar platitudes – and I thought him likely to be a quick learner. I added Jean-Jacques to my client list (of two).

In the early afternoons, deep in subdued lighting, in the highly polished precincts of the bar, with a silver bowl of ice and a bottle of Jack Daniels between us, a hint of cigar in the air around us, the learning of English took on a faint unreality. It was not the ambience for irregular verbs. Soft leather was the fabric for intimate tête-à-têtes. I found structured teaching elusive. And always, the lesson over, Jean-Jacques would pay me from a bulging, clinking purse of tips, which gave the act the taint of winnings, and made my hour seem slightly unworthy and insubstantial.

So, to give body to my lessons, I started to bring *The Times*, intending that together we could read and parse the events of the world. Jean-Jacques then asked if he could bring in some of his own magazines for help with translation.

I was a little surprised when he brought in a gun magazine, but the French are fond of their hunting. On a good weekend, they will shoot anything from rare eagles to large, threatening butterflies. Over the next few lessons, however, he turned up with an increasingly wide range of 'sporting' magazines, and I found myself wading through bullet trajectories and comparative splat statistics. And then, the following week, he produced an altogether more specialist journal – with features on machine-guns and fragmentation grenades. I felt myself at the extremity of my language skills. I also began to wonder what sort of bar he hoped to graduate to. Up until now, I had not thought to ask the reason for his love of languages.

'I want to be a mercenary.'

The conversation lulled.

'. . . A . . . mercenary?' I waited for him to correct me. But he just nodded, and turned over a page. 'Oh,' I said. I thought some more. I was still not up to speed. 'Why do you need English?'

'You get more money if you speak a second language.'

'Oh, of course!' I had not thought about the career structure. But just to be absolutely sure I had grasped the situation, I recapped. 'You want to be a *bilingual* mercenary, then?'

'Yes, that's right.'

'Uh-huh . . .' I paused. I had a go at a second 'Uh-huh . . .' My well-meaning liberalism was having trouble getting its *Weltanschauung* round this one. '. . . And then do what, exactly?' I eventually asked.

'What do you think?' he replied, a touch exasperated at my questions.

'. . . Kill people?' I ventured.

'Right!' he said.

'Oh.'

'Communists,' he added, by way of clarification. 'I only want to kill communists.'

'Oh right. I see.' I was fast running out of neutral observations, but was not entirely sure if it was safe to disagree. Perhaps he kept a bazooka behind the bar in case a Marxist tried to order a drink. For some reason, I found myself wondering what he would need in the way of references. Did he have to supply the names and addresses of previous communists he had killed? I was suddenly very full of questions. As far as I knew, he was the first professional killer I had met socially.

'I've got a friend who's one,' he said, as if in answer. 'In the Congo.'

'Who's what? A bilingual mercenary?'

'Yes. He's on 1,200 francs a week!'

'Oh. Was he a barman too?' I don't know why I asked this. I wanted to ask exactly how his friend killed people bilingually. Did he charge them with a bayonet, shouting '*A mort, salaud!*' and 'Die, you bastard!' in alternate breaths? But Jean-Jacques was looking at me expectantly, and I suddenly realized he was expecting me to be impressed by such earnings. I could not think what to say. In the end I said, 'Is that piece rate?'

My attempt at levity failed. Jean-Jacques had thought I said 'peace rate' and looked at me as though I were very stupid. I didn't try to explain. Puns are the last frontier for a language student. 'Is he killing many communists, your friend?' I eventually asked.

'Oh yes. Every day,' he said happily.

'And you want to go to the Congo too?'

'I don't mind. I'm happy to go anywhere. So long as I can kill communists, I don't care.'

I hoped it was abroad. If he ever visited the Mouffetard area I could foresee a rather high death rate.

I asked him how he would enrol. He said it was easy. He made it sound so easy that I started to wonder if there was a code to the coloured cards in the Alliance Française. I asked how long he'd had this ambition. He said since school. I thought of asking if it was a rough sort of school, but I noticed I was becoming very tense, and had developed poor posture.

I leant back in the opulent, squishy leather and took a long time putting pieces of ice into my whisky – a drink which, incidentally, I hated. I knew what I should be asking him. The correct line of questioning was *why* he wanted to kill communists. Had they ever done anything to his sister? But he spoke as though it were an article of faith, a self-evident truth, a simple statement of what every normal well-adjusted barman wanted to do, and I could imagine no fruitful discussion. Far from a meeting of minds, I could see a blowing-out of brains. It was the openness, the certainty that his views would be shared that was most unsettling. But then perhaps the clientele of Ledoyen did share his views.

'We will translate about the grenades next time, then?' he asked.

'Er, yes. Yes, if you like.'

'Right. They are a very useful weapon, Mr Pilton.'

'Are they? That's good to know.'

As I got up to leave, I could see looming the sharp, pointy horns of a moral dilemma, the nature of which we used to discuss in the sixth form. Should I continue to teach English to Jean-Jacques, so that he could qualify as a highly-paid mass murderer (even if considerably selective)? Or should I forego thirty francs a week and miss out on luxuries like soap? I found it to be a finely balanced set of arguments. As a holding operation, though, I advised him that his English needed a great deal more time and work before he would be ready to kill people.

When I stepped outside, the bright sunlight was doubly dazzling after the deep shade of the bar, and I was assailed by that sudden strangeness of reality that surges upon one when emerging from a cinema, after having seen a particularly disturbing film. It took me a while to readjust. As I walked through the tranquil forecourt of the Louvre, the late afternoon sun was staining its stonework a deep pink, a colour I had last seen at the rose-red city of Petra. It somehow made my hour with a psychopath seem an experience of my imaginings, and left me even more uncertain what I should do.

CHAPTER 19

Jerry now had a girlfriend. I knew this from Garry, whom I had once again mistakenly accosted, this time in the street. But here, unstoned and sexually unmolested, Garry had responded with an unfazed affability, presumably born of a lifetime's mistaken greetings. By the end of our walk, he even claimed a hazy recollection of our first meeting. He was much the older of the twins, his hour's head start from the womb having given him a noticeably more mature understanding of the world. Only by their demeanour could I ever tell the brothers apart; Garry was prone to a passing seriousness, had even been known to worry, and the skin on his face accommodated these moods with a leaner layout. His eyes also twinkled a little less.

Underneath Jerry's wild-guy look, I had always suspected him to be the sort of man whom women would want to take home to protect and cosset. What I had not expected was that such a woman would be French. I, of course, knew nothing about Frenchwomen (or, indeed, cossetting) but I had assumed his hairiness, his poverty, his token mangled French, confined his appeal to the American market. Nonetheless, Garry, whose sex appeal extended as far as Estonia, assured me that his brother was experiencing a gentle togetherness with a young PE mistress called Marie-Françoise, who was not merely French but a Parisienne. This seemed to me a romantic coupling unequalled in implausibility since Tarzan met Jane, and I rather hoped for an introduction.

I did not have long to wait. A couple of days later, Jerry

reappeared in my life. He looked hungry, so I bought him an ice-cream, and we sat in the square.

He had been sketching stone urns in a park, and had a pad full of tinted rococo doodles. 'Capturing the bird-shit's the hard part,' he said.

'I'd use a camera if I were you.' I tried to look earnest. 'Never fails, and you don't have to keep soaking it in water.' Since deciding to change his genre from rural to urban, Jerry had had an inspiration shortfall. I think he was trying to work himself up to streetscapes via parks. Certainly, the Muse had only been visiting on her afternoons off, and I doubted he was selling much.

Indeed, I was unsure how he was surviving. As far as I knew, he had no other source of income, and no capital except a sack or two of rice. He had become a sort of peripatetic house guest, moving from friendly floor to friendly floor.

He finished his ice-cream well ahead of me. 'So dairy products are OK for a sensitive stomach, then?' I asked with a smile.

'Oh yes!' he said emphatically. 'So long as the cow has pure thoughts. That's what counts!'

A *clochard* lying nearby on a warm-air vent started to sing to us, waving a well-sucked bottle in our direction, and we decided to go for a stroll. I sensed Jerry had come with a purpose, but his conversation showed no sign of it as yet. We wandered down to the *quais*, where in summer even Parisians move at half-speed. We did a gentle circuit and came to rest by an ancient tree overhanging the water; here we leant our backs and watched the river flow by, washing against the most romantic picnic-site in all the world. A few yards away, an old lady's pooch stood barking at a clutch of young lovers, with the hysterical vigour of a Moral Rearmament dog rep.

'I saw Garry,' I remarked. 'He says you have a companion.'

'Marie-Françoise?'

'You have more than one?' I was only teasing, but he affected to look enigmatic. 'She's a PE mistress, right?'

'Well, yes . . . though I could think of better descriptions. She's not the dumb-bell sort. Or the dumb sort either.'

'I hope that means she speaks English! The thought of you trying to manage *l'amour* by sign language . . . !'

'Oh, I don't think it's *l'amour*,' he said cautiously. 'What's French for affection?'

'*L'affection!*'

'Ah.' He pondered. '*Je vooz affecte!*'

We went into giggles. It was Jerry's first – and probably last – intentional joke in French. 'She teaches dance and movement, mainly. Sort of gymnastics with music, I think.'

'Oh? Where's that?'

'A *lycée*. Not very far away.'

I sighed ruefully. 'You've found a Parisienne – *danseuse*. Garry's found an Estonian artist. D'you think being a twin's a turn-on?'

'The Estonian? She's long gone.'

'Oh. Was she a one-night stand?'

'First-night stand, I think. Likes to fuck artists, Garry reckoned.'

'Did he mention how she feels about writers?' I nearly said ex-writers.

Jerry just grinned.

'How did you meet her, this Marie-Françoise?'

'I bumped into her. Literally. Coming out of the Cinemathèque one night.' The thought of bumping into a giant ragamuffin like Jerry late at night was a little alarming. For her to have survived that was a very good sign. 'I'd just seen some 1922 silent film, all about the Mexican Revolution. With two horses, and one bandito!' (The Cinemathèque in rue d'Ulm was legendary for its catholic range of films.) 'And there she was, coming round the corner, on her way home from evening classes. Boomph!' His open palms re-enacted the collision of predestined bodies.

'Ah well, at least she'll think you're an intellectual, Jerry. A man who spends his last francs on culture!'

'No, she thought I was a drunk. Who can't walk around corners.'

'What's she studying at evening class?'

'No, no, she gives them. Twice a week. Course in yoga.'

'Yoga?'

'Yes. Mass nude yoga, apparently. About four stations down from place Monge. Gobelins . . . ? Or is it Tolbiac? Anyway, near place d'Italie. That's why she doesn't get back till after ten.'

The detailed station-by-station Metro information had not benefited from the closest of attention. My mind had stopped operating at the words 'mass nude yoga'. I tried to wind back the conversation casually. 'Mass nude yoga, you said?'

'Yeah,' responded Jerry with the blasé tone of a Californian who was used to more exciting things happening at his local Pentecostal church. 'Apparently it's all the rage these days.'

'Is it?' My mind homed in on the school caretaker, innocently doing his rounds, jangling his keys, opening and closing his doors as usual, and then, without warning, being exposed to the serried ranks of massed buttocks, bared in a transcendentally enlightening posture. 'How many stations did you say?' I had often thought of doing evening classes.

'Oh, you'll have to ask her yourself. I was wondering, maybe we could come round to your place, and . . .'

'Yes. Yes, we must have dinner together. I suppose she's used to eggs, rice and onions?'

Jerry smiled, but it was an uncharacteristically hesitant smile, as if something else were on his mind.

'She lives at home, you see. With her parents—'

'—Still? How old is she?'

'Er, twenty-one–twenty-two, I think. And I'm not the son-in-law material they had in mind.' I could see their point of view. Apart from banjo-playing moonshine-makers in the Appalachians, few parents would have welcomed the genetic possibilities he appeared to represent. 'In fact, I've been banned from their apartment.' He paused, and I waited to be entertained by some comic epic of an ashen-faced mother advancing on him with a broom while simultaneously struggling to make the sign of a cross. 'And where I'm dossing at the moment,' he resumed uneasily, 'well, it's got problems – and it's not exactly a cockroach-free zone . . . and I was wondering whether we could, if you didn't object . . . sleep at your place? Just for one night?'

'Oh! Yes, sure.' I realized at last what the visit and two hours of walk and chat had been leading up to. I was his only friend with a candle and a tin of coffee.

Marie-Françoise was a surprise, though perhaps only to people with fevered, maladjusted imaginations. She was quiet and petite. She wore a neat, indeed conventional, navy-blue pleated skirt and pullover. And even as she came through the door, I could see that she had lots and lots of inner calm.

'*Bonsoir!*'

She presented me with a bottle of wine, and I made a hash of the cheek-kissing. She was freshly showered after her yogic exertions and smelt blossomy. I showed her to the chair, and Jerry and I tried to make ourselves comfortable elsewhere. There followed a potentially tricky hiatus, pregnant with subtext. The lateness of the hour meant each of us had already eaten; social protocol, however, seemed to suggest that for a complete stranger to arrive in her host's only room and proceed straight to fornication was somewhat ungrateful, if not indecorous. There was therefore a window of untimely opportunity for polite conversation, set against the subtextual backdrop that two of the three small-talkers were lusting at the leash for each other's body. Even the mattress – self-sacrificingly removed from its bed-base – lay ready and crudely waiting.

The wine was opened and I asked Marie-Françoise about her hobbies. Archaeology and rock-climbing were not, un-fortunately, interests we shared; they did, however, leave me in little doubt that she was a woman with hinterland, much of it mysterious and fertile. I was also in little doubt as to her quiet strength of character. Her body, which spent its spare time being so active, assumed in repose a profound stillness (which I at-tributed to either Buddhism or deep breathing) and this gave her an innate authority. Yet she was tender; a sixth sense suggested that Jerry had mentioned me in despatches since, on the flim-siest of acquaintance with my character facets, she responded to me with touching warmth, a fact which further swung my hormones in her favour.

'While crossing the Sahara . . . ! *Mon Dieu*, what a wonderful way to learn your French!'

'It's still not as good as your English.'

'Ah, but I only had to cross a boulevard or two!'

I turned to the linguistically limited Jerry. 'What's your excuse then?'

'It's the American mouth,' said Marie-Françoise unexpectedly. 'Anything designed to fit a hamburger could never manage the delicacy of ze French vowel!'

Mr Monoglot grinned delightedly. He and de Gaulle had always been at one on the cultural crimes of America, and it took more than Anglo-French mockery to provoke his patriotism. 'Ah, yes, but then *you* couldn't sing Country and Western,' he said to her. 'You couldn't fit the gravel down your throat.'

'What is "country and western"?'

'It's the nearest we Americans get to Baudelaire!' And he rocked happily to and fro. Straight faces were not in his make-up.

Watching them at play, one could see that Marie-Françoise was genuinely fond of Jerry, able to recognize and value his rare good nature. Whenever he was being his expansive puppyish self, she would look on quietly, and an amused, tolerant smile would occupy her lips. I doubt he knew it, but she was there to protect him from the world. They made an improbable couple, in both temperament and size; in a standing cuddle, her head and its dark-brown plaits would tuck neatly below his chin, albeit obscured by the undergrowth of his beard.

Jerry was sitting cross-legged on the mattress, like an Indian guru, and as the conversation drifted rudderlessly on, to such matters as French driving habits and Marie-Françoise's version of the Cinemathèque encounter, I became aware that he was laying tobacco papers across his knee – and rolling a long joint.

This was 1967. I had never had a joint. I had only ever had four-and-a-half normal cigarettes and that was in May 1959. I had never touched, or sniffed, or injected, any drug, hard, soft or medium. I also avoided strong liquor wherever possible. I was haunted by fear that I was a weak, addictive personality; this made me susceptible to government pronouncements that cannabis led inexorably to madness and life as a werewolf.

As Jerry continued to lick and roll, I worked hard at insouciance. I wondered if Marie-Françoise had yet noticed what he was doing. I was also worried that his West Coast ways might fatally jeopardize their relationship. Would she walk out when she realized? And what should I say when the joint was offered to me? What was the best way to refuse him? Panic began to take hold.

Jerry completed his five-inch work of art, lit it, smoked it, inhaled it . . . and passed it to Marie-Françoise who did the same. I was utterly thrown. I was bewildered, I was shocked, I was even disapproving, but as I watched her calmly, naturally, professionally draw deep on the high-quality Thai Weed I was also – I had to admit it – turned on by her. And then, of course, her behaviour began to make sense. This was the woman who did mass nude yoga. A deviant. Up until then, I had failed to find the right moment to casually ask her for details about the bare-assed half-lotus hour. But I realized that now, her senses inflamed by marijuana, she would be highly receptive to such enquiries. I watched and waited as she slowly allowed the smoke to descend ritually into her lungs, while holding the joint with exquisite delicacy.

She closed her eyes sensually for a second or two, and then unhurriedly extended her arm to pass the joint to me. 'I gather you do mass nude yoga,' I said.

For the briefest of moments she looked surprised by the remark, or possibly by the manner in which it was blurted out, and then she replied, 'Yes, that's right. Thirty of us. Spiritual high spot of the week!' Spiritual? '. . . Oh!' I said, which was the best reply I could manage – I was struggling to take the joint from her, and had realized I did not know how to hold it. And then on taking it, I realized that I was suddenly, accidentally, committed to smoking it. Would I go mad? And how soon? Would unsightly lupine hair grow on my chest? Would I wake up a junkie? 'Are you interested in yoga, then?' Marie-Françoise looked encouragingly at me and smiled. I swallowed. 'Oh, er, yes, very.' With forefinger and thumb? Or between two fingers? I was starting to go sweaty. Were they watching me? Would they see my fumblings? 'Are you a beginner?' I was panicked by her question, and said, 'No!' and then remembered I meant yes. I tried to avoid her gentle dark eyes and concentrate on the joint. Smoke was curling up around my nose and face. 'Would you like to come to a session?' Me? Oh God! I only meant it to be a fantasy. Vivid images of a schoolroom with over two dozen naked mobile women – including serene Marie-Françoise – swirled into my brain, and my body started to go hot and cold – from nerves as much as from sex. She was awaiting my answer but my mind was jammed, and the joint was unstoppably on its way to my mouth. I had lost the power to pause or to think, and I blurted out 'Yes!' just as it hit my lips. Trying to arrest my trembling, I clamped my mouth on to the joint, took a deep suck – and coughed uncontrollably.

The other two looked on in undisguised surprise. Marie-Françoise came across to where I was perched uncomfortably on my bed-base, and banged me on the back until I stopped choking. I had another, more circumspect, suck – and tried to send the smoke down a different set of internal passages. Then I passed on the joint to Jerry, nervously aware that it would now continue its remorseless ritual round. Yet, although my throat was burning, my stomach was heaving and my head seemed loose, only one thought was racing round and round my mind: What if I got an erection? I could see writ large the Bateman cartoon all over again: 'THE MAN WHO HAD AN ERECTION AT YOGA!!!' I could visualize the classroom now. Thirty highly spiritual yogists and a pervert with a hard-on in the lotus position. I knew of the cobra position, the cat position, the pylon position, and the shoulder-stand, and in none of these could you easily disguise a determinedly erect penis. Indeed, in some of the more advanced positions you could probably snap it off.

The joint came round again. I really did not want another puff, but these were the years before Nancy Reagan had explained how to 'just say No'. I took a further painful gulp of smoke. I felt my whole body had gone puce, and my gaucherie seemed of international proportions. But not as big as my erection would be. Oh, how I longed for the cool of Marie-Françoise, the sang-froid of Ulrika, the sweet matter-of-factness of Nicole. I wanted to be able to take naked bodies in my stride. I did not want my life distorted by frustration. I did not want to be prey to the masturbatory fantasies of a monk. Sex on Mondays, shopping on Tuesdays, teaching on Wednesdays, sex on Thursdays, cinema on Fridays: that should be the gentle rhythm of living. Not hot sweats at the thought of an evening class, not weak knees at the mention of a life class, not dry saliva at the sight of a keyhole.

The joint came round again, and again. Conversation seemed to have ceased. My head seemed to have shrunk. I was unused to smoke of any kind, except in fireplaces, and I found inhalation as inaccessible an art as penetration. Jerry, however, was well on his way to nirvana. He just sat there nodding happily, like a hairy gnome in a rocking chair. Marie-Françoise only moved when she puffed, and she sat as if to attention, her eyelids almost closed, her face taken over by a beatific beam. In any quiz question, I would be the odd one out.

And as the joint ended, I also felt surplus to requirements. The evening was moving naturally to its climax: theirs. I got up, a little wobbly. The bedding had been put on the mattress; the sleeping bag lay ready for me on the bed-base. It was the sexual equivalent of Captain Oates going out into the snow.

The candle had guttered to a halt, and the room was now lit by a near-full moon. As the first buttons were undone, I reached over to close the curtains – but Marie-Françoise put a soft, restraining hand on my arm.

'*Elle est belle, la lune, ce soir.*'

We undressed in its light, each silhouetted in a cool, pale glow. I knew the unwritten British code of conduct – the discreet averting of eyes, the excessive interest in floorboards – but it was not easy. As I struggled modestly into my striped jim-jams (the prewar tastes of a loving mother) and as Jerry revealed an early khaki prototype of Bermuda shorts, Marie-Françoise slowly and tidily removed every last item of her clothing and then wandered full-frontally nude across the moonlit room. To join Jerry in my bed.

As they embraced under my blankets, and kissed tenderly on my mattress, I fought to make myself comfortable. The coiled springs in the bed-base were only one bound short of being free, and every time I moved they bored into my back like hyperactive corkscrews. The base itself was old and worn, and without the weight of the mattress it took on the intransigence of corrugated iron. And all within the sound of sex.

In the past I had merely suffered the pains of jealousy from a distance: from across a sea, from across a city, from across a courtyard. Now, fornication was just across the floor. The sounds, the sighs, the groans, the cries, every known intimacy was within sight, within touch, within smell. Surely, as sex grew ever closer, it must one day include me?

After a while, the now-familiar smell of Thai Weed drifted by. I looked over at the mattress beside me. Jerry was lying on his back, drawing contentedly on a second joint, and Marie-Françoise was stretched languidly on top of him. A smoke-ring floated up into the rays of the moon, and as Jerry held the joint out for me, Marie-Françoise gently raised her upper body on her hands, arched above him, and lowered her nipple into his mouth.

I took the joint, but instead of savouring the delicious sensuality of the moment, I was tormented by my exclusion from it. As I struggled with the smoke, I could not suppress the growing certainty that they were making love in order to humiliate me. That every kiss, every caress, was to taunt me. They knew I was unable to find someone to love, and they were mocking me. They knew I was ignorant of sex, so unworldly I could not even hold a joint, and they were laughing at me. I wanted to leave the room, run from the hotel, but I could not move. The bed-springs had broken free, and were skewering into my flesh. My body was impaled on points of steel and the more I twisted the more I was trapped. I begged for help, for affection, but no-one answered. And then the bed started to laugh at me . . .

Bang! . . . Bang! Bang! . . . Bang! Bang! Bang!

The bangs grew louder, and more insistent. At first, I thought they were in my head, but then as I slowly roused myself, and blinked at the new day, I realized the noise was coming from elsewhere. I raised myself stiffly on one elbow, aching in every subdivision of my body, and tried to organize my thoughts. Jerry and Marie-Françoise were lying naked on the blankets, and just coming to. My watch said ten past seven.

Bang! Bang! Bang! . . . BANG! BANG! BANG!

Jerry stirred. 'There's someone at the door,' he muttered, and slipped back into a coma.

Immediately my thoughts went to the Police Code. There were hundreds of regulations on the door, and last night had seen some pretty comprehensive violating. My mind raced through some of the possibles. Drugs. Perverted sex. Overcrowding. And most probably orgasms exceeding the decibel limit after 10 p.m. Any one of those would have been worth a fully armed van-load of the Riot Squad. But then my brain began to kick in, and I wondered how anybody could know. Madame! Maybe it was Madame at the door. But it was not the knock of Madame. And anyway, Madame did not knock.

BANG! BANG! BANG!

With great difficulty, I struggled out of bed. The evening before, I had only put on jim-jam bottoms and in the sexual trauma of the night they had become dislodged. I reached into my sleeping-bag to find them.

At that precise moment, the door was flung back and a total stranger burst in. He was about forty-five, seriously bourgeois . . . and wearing a suit. I do not know who was the more surprised.

He looked at my bollocks, he looked at Jerry and his bollocks, and he looked at the naked Marie-Françoise. And we all looked at him. There was a moment's silence.

'*Papa!*' said Marie-Françoise.

Jerry's mouth definitely opened as well, but I don't think speech was on his mind. My hope that the man had found the wrong room now evaporated.

Papa was beside himself with fury. And, in retrospect, with the maturity of years, I can see his point. The squalid little room – for so it looked that morning – still stank of drugs, and his daughter was naked on an old mattress in the company of two naked, bearded men, neither of them French. (Her father was not to know that my sexual problems ruled me out of the running on this one.)

A terrible tirade filled the air. He called his daughter a whore and a tart and a slut, he summoned up God to do terrible things to her, and then my French lost track as his abuse moved into whole sentences. I think the issue of not darkening his door came up several times. He was also very offensive about my room. The row had started at such a high pitch that there was really very little emotional distance for it to travel without constant explosions.

Jerry then made the mistake of intervening. I think he saw himself as a sort of Californian Voltaire, awash with faith in the powers of reason. '*Mer-sewer!*' he said politely, and then started to address, as I understood it, the ethical basis of premarital relationships in the late twentieth century. Touchingly oblivious to his nudity, he had got as far as '*la sex-yoo-alli-tay modern*' when Marie-Françoise's Papa called him a cunt. And a dirty, diseased druggie.

Marie-Françoise, who had remained commendably calm, and a tribute to her twice-weekly evening classes, then moved in to defend Jerry. With the quiet firmness that wilts mountains, she positioned herself between them, and prepared for pacification. But her father had done. He had spoken his mind. He had flown the flag for family values, even if his family was now one short. As full of surprises as ever, he turned and went, though not as dramatically as he had come.

Jerry, however, his optimism in human rationality still gloriously undimmed, called after him, '*Mer-sewer! Mer-sewer!*' and frantically started to dress. He located his shorts, struggled into his trousers, and then began to rummage desperately through his pockets. 'Money!' he shouted to me. 'Money!'

'What for?'

'To buy him a coffee!'

Marie-Françoise and I looked at each other in astonishment, but before we could speak he had scrabbled some coins together and rushed out of the open door, half-dressed and trailing debris. Like so many gentle people, he believed all minds could meet. I, on the other hand, was of the opinion that their conversation could be attended by stretchers and sirens. I felt my worldliness was called for. I raced after him, in an informal mixture of pyjamas and anorak. As I tumbled down the stairs I could hear echoing up from the passageway below, '*Je vooz expleek! Je vooz expleek!*'

I reached the hotel entrance a few seconds behind him.

Jerry was by now halfway across the square, his progress marked by dazed pedestrians. A light rain was falling and he was pelting barefoot through the puddles, naked from the waist up and his hair flying *à la* Botticelli, whilst waving a pair of army boots in the air and yelling. '*Vooz voolez un café?*' Only ten yards ahead of him was the Frenchman, glancing nervously backwards and starting to run, if only to escape from the American accent. As all the square stopped and watched, Jerry began closing on him, and was within three yards when they disappeared from sight down rue du Cardinal-Lemoine. I now knew what Shakespeare meant by 'Exit pursued by a bear'.

I pondered matters for a moment. A small crowd was starting to admire my pyjamas. On balance, I felt joining the chase would be inadvisable, and I returned to my drug den.

The door was still open. I had expected a severely shaken Marie-Françoise, but I found her seated contemplatively, and still very nude, upon the floor, in what I assumed to be the post-abuse position. Her eyes were closed and she did not react to my return. I tidied around her, and emptied the cups of their ash, and replaced the used mattress on the bed. Then I dressed for normal life. Still Jerry had not returned. It was presumably not easy to find a café that would serve them.

Then Marie-Françoise stood up, calm and relaxed. She smiled at me. 'I am sorry for what happened.'

'It's not your fault.' I smiled back.

For a brief moment she embraced me, and I stood rigid with nerves wondering where I could allow my fingers to touch, and then she too got dressed. I realized all my fears about erections were justified.

It was a good half hour before Jerry returned. He had now got his boots on. He stroked Marie-Françoise's hair and put one of my many eggs into a saucepan of lightly-salted water.

'Well?' I said.

'It's what I thought.' He smiled. 'He's a reasonable man.'

Even his daughter looked surprised.

'You had coffee?' I asked incredulously.

'Yes. Two. He bought the second.' And he gave me back some coins. He looked around at the tidied room. He went over to his lumberjack shirt, now neatly folded on the chair.

'Well?' said Marie-Françoise. 'What did you talk about?'

'This and that.' He grinned.

'Stop it!' she said.

'You know what really worried him? What he was most upset about?'

'No.'

'Very French,' said Jerry sadly. 'Very typically French.'

'What was?' we demanded.

'Career prospects. He was worried about my career prospects.'

'Jesus! What did you tell him?' I asked.

'Told him I was a very famous painter back home, in the Bay area. Much sought-after. Highly regarded for my landscapes.' He smiled. 'After that he was fine. Even said he'd buy a picture. As an investment, of course.'

We both looked at him, very suspiciously. He nodded vigorously, to confirm what he was saying. I had never known Jerry to lie, but I was never to know if what he said that morning was true.

'Well,' I said at last, 'at least I've met your man in a suit.'

Jerry looked at me, alarmed.

'No, you haven't, Barry,' he said. 'I don't think *he'd* ever buy me a coffee.'

And there was suddenly fear in his voice.

CHAPTER 20

I had answered another advert. I was still on the horns of my barman dilemma. I was hoping to earn enough money to be able to afford to make an ethical decision. With Dr Poli I struck gold.

He was no ordinary doctor. He was the youngest doctor ever to qualify in France. Not that he considered himself French. He was from Corsica. He was also a black belt in judo and ran five miles before breakfast every morning. And in his spare time Dr Poli also managed to be good looking.

At government request, he was shortly to chair an international medical conference. Accordingly, he had decided that, in the intervening two or three weeks, it would be groovy to learn English.

When I first turned up at his elegantly swish office (swish in my world meant white Venetian blinds) he only spoke standard broken English. He had, however, worked out his own learning programme, and handed me two dozen back numbers of the *New Yorker*. 'Shall we read these?' he said.

Accordingly, every morning after breakfast, I took the Metro to the 13th *arrondissement*, sat in a black swivel chair for two hours, answered all enquiries, and at the end of a week his English was better than mine.

'Maoism,' he said on the second Monday. 'I'd like to learn about Maoism,' and he gave me the latest edition of *Time* magazine, with a picture of Mao Tse-Tung on the cover. One of Dr Poli's hobbies, it turned out, was world revolution. Fortunately, I too was interested in politics, being able to identify with the downtrodden masses, and our lessons went from strength to strength.

On the third Monday he asked if I would like to translate the international conference. Officially. In writing.

'But it's medical,' I said, astonished.

'So? I'll give you a medical dictionary.'

'But what's it about?'

'Analysis and Comparison of Accidents on Building Sites in Western Europe.' You could have heard a nail drop in the silence. 'The first ever,' he added, not immune to ego.

'But isn't it a bit specialist?' I asked, moving from astonished to dumbfounded.

'So? I'll give you a specialist dictionary.'

He then mentioned a very large sum of money. A wave of positive thinking started to spread through me. But I still wanted reassurance. 'What would I have to do?'

'Well, first you'd have to be vetted by the Minister.'

'The who?'

Two days later I found myself in a very expensive restaurant with a borrowed tie and a member of the Government. His exact status I was never to determine, but he arrived and left in the sort of chauffeured black Citroen that has precedence over traffic lights.

Vetting is a curious business. It is more intangible than an interview, more subjective than an exam. Knowledge did not appear to be an issue, and it was hard to know what to try to do well. Mysterious qualities of character like 'bottom' and 'tone' were presumably emanating etherwards. I remember being aware that table manners might be a litmus test and I steered clear of oysters and all foods hazardous to discreet digestion. I had expected silky diplomacy from my elderly, balding interlocutor, but he was a convivial, though soberly suited, host who laughed with gusto if I chanced upon a joke. Rather bizarrely, the only snatch of conversation where judgement appeared to tip in my favour concerned my most unlovely feature.

'What a rare beard Mr Pilton has,' said the Minister to the doctor.

Dr Poli nodded. 'Unique.'

'Unique to the west,' corrected the minister. 'But familiar to Ho Chi Minh.'

'Indeed,' said the doctor.

The Minister addressed me directly. 'Knitted by his silk-worms, no doubt.'

'I don't know. It comes in the night.'

He smiled. 'Like the Vietcong!' And he gazed approvingly at my ethnic achievement.

The five-course lunch was the only time I ever had contact with the Fifth Republic. To have my wine poured by a man who was probably on surname terms with de Gaulle made me more than a little nervous, especially since, still being an illegal alien, I was only a loose word away from deportation. But at twenty-one, to try for gravitas is to try for phoniness; I suspected that the enthusiasm of youth was the virtue he wished to give a star to. So I made much of my status as a student – glossing over the unclimbed rung between me and the Sorbonne – and marked out the territory of an impoverished scholar. Old men have sons, after all, and when those sons are far from home, they love them by proxy.

Whatever the reason, whatever the test, I got the vote. Over the coffee and the brandies the Minister let it be known, in that oblique, offhand way of men enjoying the power they dispense, that he 'couldn't see there was a problem'. And I was duly appointed Official Translator.

From our reserved table by the window there was an un-impeded view of a small sunny square full of trees and summer flowers. It was a hot day, and over lunch I had gazed at the scene with uneasy emotions. The prospect of summer in the city had recently begun to set my heart sinking. The scuffed dust of gravel, the shuttered rows of shops, this had for me an unbearable melancholia. But now, added to the sight of sun was the sound of money, and I tentatively began to allow my mind to go south.

Ten days later a thick wad of transcripts arrived at the hotel.

I took them next door to the café where time stood still, ordered a large beer, and started to read page one. A beer later

I was still on page one. Other than *le* and *de* I had not discovered a single word I recognized. So polysyllabic were the nouns that pronunciation could easily ruin your glottis. My socio–medico–linguistic fears were realized: accidents on building sites did terrible damage to the French language. Every sentence appeared to have been dropped on its syntax from a great height. I ordered another beer. I had bitten off more than I could construe.

I sat in a quiet sweat, flicking pages over at random in search of any vaguely familiar words, when Gerard went past the window. He was the Frenchest thing I knew and I waved urgently at him to come in.

Of late we waved often. He was now a frequent visitor to the hotel, and Ulrika spent almost as many nights at his studio as in her room. They had become an item. Most evenings they would stroll the streets together, his arm firmly clamped to her shoulder, her face a near-permanent grin of happiness, and stop on every corner to chat to his *copains*.

'*Salut!*' He bustled in as dynamically as ever, his stubby black pipe in his hand.

'*Salut!*' I ordered him a *pastis*. I hoped he would be good value.

He gestured at the piles of paper. '*C'est quoi, ça?*'

I explained about the conference.

'*Ah! Tu es traducteur, toi?*'

I nodded. He looked down at the transcripts. He looked at them for some time. He shuffled through several pages. And then he raised his head, and said, 'It ees French, ees it?'

'Oh, shit!' I said. 'That bad?'

He blew air out of his teeth to indicate the severity of the problem. I was trying to translate French which even the French didn't know.

I had not long ago bumped into a French-Canadian, approaching thirty, who was in the final year of his seven-year translator's course. His English had been immaculate and I had asked him what he still needed to learn. 'This month,' he had replied, 'we are doing blast furnaces.' He knew over a hundred English words which related to the technology of blast furnaces. I knew 'blast' and 'furnace'. At the time, I had laughed.

That evening, as I sat alone in my room and tried to make sense of the categories of death among German building workers, I saw Ulrika lying on her bed, writing. Our windows were open, and I called across to her. We gossiped a while, complained about the oppressive heat, and then I asked her what she was writing.

'Poetry,' she replied, a little coyly. Ever since I had known her, she had spoken of poetic 'stirrings'; what she had always lacked, she said, were really powerful ideas.

'You're writing poetry?' I tried not to sound dismissive. Or jealous.

'Well, poems, anyway.'

'Big ones or little ones?'

She put two fingers very close together and laughed gaily.

'What about?'

'Oh, life!' she said, flippantly. And then added, more seriously, 'and love.' She did not elaborate. 'What about you? What are you writing about?'

'Multiple fractures of the vertebra.'

The next morning, two overweight medical dictionaries were delivered. I returned to the café with them, and spread myself across a table. I hoped to avoid panic by being public.

The content of the dictionaries was not laid out in the usual manner. Each page was divided in four columns, and each word was translated in French, English, German and Italian. And as I ran my eye across the four columns, the true extent of my predicament sank in – I could not recognize the English! The column for English was filled with words I had never seen before. When a navvie twisted his ankle on a broken brick, the resulting injury was often twenty-two letters long. When he tripped over a loose plank, dropped his scaffolding, and fell into a pit of wet concrete, he was just a mass of hyphens. I could see no way to render his condition readable. I was starting to feel the primordial clammy fear of exam failure rise from the deep of my bowels.

I was also starting to regard my tour of the cellar as premature.

A guided tour of the cellar was Madame's ultimate accolade. It was for those tenants whose luggage she was prepared to store during the summer. And it was a rare glimpse of the crumbling medieval brickwork that lay hidden beneath the building. Madame was inordinately proud of her ancient shadowy cellar; indeed, she spoke of it in terms that I had last heard used during a school trip to the catacombs in Rome. Above all, she was proud of its unique dryness ('*son sêcheur formidable*') which, she claimed, was the definitive tribute to her central heating system. Here, she had assured me, my luggage could rest in safety for a thousand years. But now, it seemed even one short summer would be more than I required.

It was Tony who saw the solution to the translation. This came as a surprise, for he was stronger on pictures than on words. I had waylaid him with a drink as well, desperate to buy in all grey cells available. Indeed, various regulars of the café had offered their services, only to wrinkle their brows and add a few *zut alors!* to my troubles.

But Tony just looked at me and said, 'You can't understand the French version, right?'

I nodded.

'And the French can't understand the French version either, right?'

I nodded again.

'So who's to know if the English version doesn't make any sense?'

I stared at him.

'This is incomprehensible French jargon. So it's your job to turn it into incomprehensible English jargon!'

And that's what I did. I just ran my finger across each of the columns, replacing one set of medical polysyllables with another. Indeed, frequently they were the same set of polysyllables – in all four languages. I had no idea what any of it meant. I simply sent it off to the government and awaited developments.

The money arrived by return of post.

The following day I left town.

INTERMISSION

I spent the summer in Morocco. I had learnt nothing of prudence and I returned penniless. I was lucky to return at all. Indeed I was lucky to have even got there.

The supposed joy of travel is the unexpected. Just one day after leaving Paris, I was travelling south from Bordeaux in perfect weather. I was being driven at high speed along the straight flat tree-shaded roads of Les Landes. My driver was an immaculate executive who wore white gloves to hold the steering wheel. A Mozart symphony was playing on a tape. It was hitchhiking of a high order, and I lay back with my eyes closed, warm fresh air billowing rhythmically through the sun-roof.

The music was interrupted by an urgent government announcement. And I realized that I was not listening to a tape. The radio news was all the more dramatic for being in a foreign language. 'Israeli troops,' intoned the French newsreader with a chilling gravity, 'have now reached the Suez Canal.'

While I had been hitting the road, the Six Day War had begun; Sinai had fallen; and a Third World War had become a distinct possibility. All in twenty-four hours. I, meanwhile, was innocently en route for the Arab world . . .

After such an unconventional start, the holiday itself was almost normal. I denounced the British government upon demand, and apart from some ritual stone-throwing in Fez was never held personally responsible for the Israeli invasion. Over the next few weeks I travelled to just about every bit of Morocco which had found time to build roads. I met a small Danish blonde who wanted a protector, and for a while we hitched in harness. At Tinerhir we were even guests of a vainglorious mayor who took us on a tour of his oasis in a 1930s fire engine – the official ceremonial vehicle – and we were saluted from every palm tree by a subjugated local populace. But in Casablanca, Inger's mint tea was drugged in a casbah café and, though I managed to save her from the white slave trade by high-speed panic and a lot of shouting, she decided to take a bus to Copenhagen. (I myself refused offers for my body in Tangiers, Meknes and Marrakesh, but always from fat old men chewing something nasty.) My social high spot was an invitation to a wild-boar hunt – which proved nutritionally similar to a wild-goose chase. My social low spot was an emergency three-hour bowel evacuation on the desert verge of the P31 to Zagora. I also experienced a small earthquake in the High Atlas region.

My return journey produced, if anything, a closer shave than the Six Day War. I was picked up outside Taroudannt on a scalding day by a Frenchman in a suit and tie, quite the neatest ensemble I had seen in over two months. A resident in Morocco, he was driving a pint-sized Fiat to Spain. Although the climb to over 10,000 feet in the Italian equivalent of a highly revved lawn-mower did have drawbacks, a lift of such length – on roads with no traffic – came as a rare treat. My driver was, however, short on the good-humoured curiosity typical of a lift-giver; this I put down to the fact he had set off that morning at dawn, crossed the Atlas Mountains . . . and then discovered he had left his pass-port at home. Twice in one day he had now driven past the sign saying 'Bends for 103 kilometres'.

It was late afternoon when we arrived at the customs post in the border town of Ceuta, one of the last Spanish enclaves left in North Africa. The Customs Officers seized on me with delight, like an offering from the Narcotics Bureau. (Or a tip-off from the father of Marie-Françoise.) Their training courses obviously used an identikit photo of the prototype crazed druggie, and I was it. They emptied my rucksack, my jacket, my trouser pockets, my water bottle; in fact, they emptied everything except my bowels, and there was an uncomfortable moment while they considered that as well. And all the time, to my great surprise, my nice bourgeois Frenchman insisted upon waiting for me; indeed, the officials even gave him a chair and apologized to him for the inconvenience.

The sun had started to lose its heat by the time we crossed into Ceuta. He drove very slowly, as if looking for something. After a couple of hundred yards we picked up a shifty-looking local. We squeezed him into the back pouch of the car and, following his directions, made our way to a derelict building site. The car then pulled off the road, jolted across the rubble and came carefully to a halt far from public view.

We all got out and the Frenchman opened the tiny bonnet. As I stood and watched, he pulled out the dip-stick, and gingerly wiped off the oil. He then pressed a catch and the dip-stick clicked open, to reveal a hollowed-out compartment running its whole length. Hollowed out and stuffed with money. My nice bourgeois Frenchman was a currency smuggler – and I had been the stool-pigeon.

But then, as he removed the notes, there was a terrible smell of singeing, and they started to disintegrate in his fingers, and float in crispy fragments up into the air. In panic, the two men leapt and bobbed and grasped at the browning particles which were drifting like a dirty snowstorm across the wasteland. But the damage was done. The day's double dose of mountains had fried his engine oil, blown his deal, and cost over £20,000. My holiday had ended with the ultimate accident on a building site.

The nice Frenchman abandoned me in Ceuta. He went off to spend his remaining *pesetas* on prostitutes.

I hit the road again, with just enough legal currency left for the journey back to Paris.

CHAPTER 21

September was under way when I took up residence once more at the Hotel de Carcassonne. Madame was effusive in her greetings, and appeared genuinely puzzled as to why my suitcase and its contents emerged from the cellar with a musty grey coating of mould.

Crossing the flaking brown portals again was scarcely a conventional homecoming, yet home is where I felt I had come. In a few full months, Paris had given me deeper roots than a lifetime in Norbury. Perhaps it was just a good place to hide, perhaps I had found where the lost tribes of Pilton hung out, perhaps I was attracted to the exotica of other, more vivid, lives, but, whatever, here I had learnt the comforting lure of community. Life in a hotel is the original soap opera, and in almost half the rooms I was following a storyline. Only Ulrika had been written out; and she was living just a brushstroke away in Gerard's studio.

And then in the courtyard I met Dave. He had not made it out of Paris for the summer. He and God had been having a difficult time. Throughout the hot, dead month of August, as Dave struggled to put on paper his morally watertight world, so his torment by eczema had worsened, and now his body had succumbed to divine retributive blotches. At least, this was Dave's Job-like view of his suffering. For him, the Old Testament God of thunderbolts and boils had given way to a more modern, medically sophisticated deity who wreaked dermatitis upon the world.

'You've lost weight,' I said. He looked gaunt.

'I know. Market's been a problem. Keeps shutting for holidays!'

'Couldn't you stock up?'

'Save food? My food's usually off when I get it!' In anybody else, this would have been self-pity; in his case, it was just the wry truth. 'The weekend before last, all I could find to eat was a carrot. And one end of that was rotten!' He almost laughed. 'Quite a test, that weekend was.' It was a very typical choice of word, 'test'. I think his stoical passivity came from a belief that he had no moral right to pursue happiness, despite the American Declaration of Independence.

'It's shortage of veg, that's what's spoiling your complexion. Lack of vitamin—' I struggled with science. '—oh, I don't know, A to K, probably!'

'Perhaps.' He showed little interest.

I remembered Marat, and his skin problems. According to the version of the French revolution that I had seen at the Cinemathèque, he had to write his death lists while sitting in a hip-bath filled with soothing oils. Had he been more comfortable, world history might have been different. I wondered about the role of eczema in literature. It had the promising ring of a PhD.

'How far have you got? With the book?'

He thought briefly. 'About six hundred pages.'

The figure astonished me. I had imagined a couple of anguished chapters, rewritten weekly, torn up monthly. He had no typewriter, so his creativity was silent. The figure also shamed me. I, of course, had a typewriter, but my creativity was silent as well.

'See you.' Dave's fleeting interest in conversation was over.

As he shambled off into the shadowy stairwell of the annexe, my cosy, self-comforting, self-deluding vision of my life began to fracture. I had always envied him his certainty – I envied everybody their certainty – but never before had the absence of any interior world of my own seemed so stark. His vigour, his purpose, his intensity, had pressed hard on my panic buttons. I too had begun the year with resolution. I well remembered my 'aims': to fall in love in spring, to be a writer by summer. Except that they were not aims, they were just the foolish fairy-wishes of a hopeless dreamer. I had no inner drive, no belief in myself. I was going nowhere. In all these rooms, I was the only one whose life had no storyline.

I tried to suppress pervading panic, but a memory from my childhood – a memory that I had tried to blank out for nearly ten years – had just hit me with a terrible force. It had been the end of the first year at my new, high-flying school, the school which held out such hope for my parents. I had begun the year very well – brightness and precociousness prevailing – but I finished the year very badly. On the final day of term, the form master – a genial ex-paratrooper who prided himself on his twin gifts for killing and character assessment – addressed us all on the class achievements. And then he paused, and said, with untypical gravity, 'On one boy's report I have written something he may not understand. I have put "in danger of becoming a drifter".' I wondered idly who this might be. 'Let me explain what I mean,' he went on, 'so that this boy can understand what I am warning him about.' At this point in his critical advice on life I became bored and gazed out across the extensive playing fields. The next thing I remember was the final bell.

Now, a decade later, standing alone in the dusty sun by the rubbish bins of a down-at-heel foreign flophouse, I found myself overwhelmed by the fear that I was fulfilling my destiny, that I was genetically programmed to drift, probably for ever. From exam failure to job failure to writer failure, all the pieces of my life's brief jigsaw now made sad sense of this childhood prophecy. I also remembered the shock I had felt in Arenys del Mar when I realized that Vernon and Diana and Walt each had a game plan for their life. As had Tony, as had Gerard, as – even – had Jerry. But my drifting was not just a failure of planning. It was not merely a dreamy inability to understand the mechanics of life. It had its roots in terror. So great were my insecurities, so deep my feelings of inferiority, that I was never able to believe that anyone, and certainly not me, could influence life. I had

207

never grasped that the direction of my life was in my own hands. I felt sure that life must be ruled by powers of which I knew nothing. Indeed, I somehow never even saw myself as part of life.

And now autumn was on its way. I had no plan for autumn. No aims. No opus in mind, no gym mistress in sight. No thoughts except survival.

My 'homecoming', my return to *chambre 5*, had, in those few moments, ceased to be a joyous, positive occasion, and become a sad squalid sign of inadequacy and defeat. As I went upstairs to my mildewed Y-fronts and bag of brown rice, I felt bleak and lonely and without a future. With the true melodrama of a twenty-one-year-old, I thought only of the broken-down ballet dancer and the cockroach . . . and the old men fighting over a crust of bread.

CHAPTER 22

All the talk was of a new bar. Mouff Cinq. It was to be on the far side of the square, an above-ground dive at number five. Small, intimate, and arty, was the rumour. The windows had been whitewashed for several weeks and from inside came the sound of competitive hammering. It was to be a venue with cachet, a new experience for the area. And to achieve that end, there would – according to Gerard – be a free glass of wine available every night to all customers who were bona fide artists. Already, the area's extensive network of alcoholics was laying greater stress on the role of art in their lives.

The advent of such a bar, targeting the louche and the chic, was, in retrospect, no act of commercial whimsy. It was born from the ripple effect of the art gallery, and it arose to serve a new breed of thirsts. Mouff Cinq self-consciously broke away from the worker-drinker tradition of the *quartier*, and was pointed upmarket in pursuit of bell-bottom pockets. As the day of opening approached, its leaflets suggested a sort of indoor Club Med for people who had heard of Warhol.

The grand opening was scheduled for a Saturday, and I was hoping to go with Sherry Bolton. Sherry Bolton did not yet know this.

It was Sherry's face which now gazed at me from Ulrika's window. She was from Alaska, a fact that, for some reason, inordinately impressed me. The additional fact that she was culturally indistinguishable from anyone from California somehow failed to take the edge off my enthusiasm. Although quiet and slightly built, she had travelled – usually alone – throughout Europe and the Near East for over a year; without irony, she was able to refer to Hotel de Carcassonne as 'the better type of hotel'.

I was intrigued by her, because her public face was demure and conventional. She had a preference for slightly bourgeois clothes, and often wore a tartan skirt, held in place by a safety pin. Unusually for those iconoclastic times, she wore make-up, with modesty and taste. Underneath her dark, compact curls she had a pretty, nicely-rounded face which broke frequently into a keen-to-please smile. Although she would not qualify for a free glass of wine, I felt her presence at Mouff Cinq would be quietly reassuring, and – just possibly – sexually rewarding.

'I'm sorry,' she said. 'I'm doing something else.'

But she gave me a keen-to-please smile, and added, 'Some other time, perhaps.' I was always a sucker for that phrase. If well delivered, it could keep me hanging about for up to five years.

The big opening night arrived. In Paris, night life is *night* life, not the anaemic, perfunctory, gosh-I'm-tired, is-it-ten-o'clock-already, can-I-have-the-bill-please, English night out. By local tradition, an evening builds, rather than sags. Accordingly, I let darkness do some gentle falling before I left for the bar, hoping to hit the moment of optimum entry.

It was close to nine when I stepped outside. I was dressed in a very optimistic approximation of arty-casualwear (mildew had reduced my repertoire) and had washed and strained my beard. The usual knots of night folk were gathering and, as I strolled across the square, the familiar Saturday-night buzz was in the air. Except that night it seemed louder and more excited than usual.

It was. A crowd had formed on the other side of the square, and was blocking rue du Cardinal-Lemoine. Traffic was starting to tail back. And horns were beginning to honk. I quickly moved closer, sensing that most delicious production of Paris street theatre: the public argument. I was correct. It was that much-loved old favourite, 'the car altercation', which regularly enlivened a Saturday night out in the Latin Quarter. This, of course, was the Sixties, that golden period in Paris traffic history when the car still ruled and the only recognized sanctuary for pedestrians and cyclists was indoors, ideally on an upper floor. Apoplectic motorists were always a good crowd-puller, and I squeezed into pole position on the kerb.

In the narrow one-way street, a large Citroen was halted, the entrance to its garage blocked by a parked car. The angry driver had completed the statutory three minutes on the horn, and was now circling the offending vehicle, like a prize-fighter trying to get a hold. He tugged at the doors, he kicked at the wheels, he pushed at the bumpers. All to no avail. The crowd murmured sympathetically.

The driver returned to his Citroen, unlocked the boot – and came back with a large axe.

A gasp ran through the crowd, appreciating the surprise element and the imaginative use of props. He strode over to the front of the empty car, raised his axe, and prepared to smash the windscreen. He was a burly, middle-aged man and clearly capable of chopping parked cars into component parts. His arms were at full stretch and he was just about to swing, when a dissenting voice rang out, '*Mais non, monsieur!*'

The Citroen owner turned, visibly taken aback. '*Comment?*'

The objector stepped out from the crowd. 'That's not right!' he said. 'It's not your property.'

'It's my bloody garage! And he's blocking it!'

The man stood his ground. 'That's not a valid reason. Not for violence.'

'He's right,' said a second voice in the crowd.

'*Merde alors!* There's a bloody No Parking sign!' the owner expostulated, pointing at it with his axe. 'Illuminated!' He turned angrily to the second speaker. 'What do you think that's for?'

'That's fair!' said a third voice. 'The driver had fair warning when he parked.'

'Not of an axe attack, he didn't!' said the first man. 'You don't deserve to have your car destroyed because of a mistake.'

'It's not a mistake,' said a fourth person, stepping up to the other side of the car. 'It's wilful selfishness!'

'Exactly!' said the Citroen owner, raising his axe again. 'And they do it every week. Which is why I bought a bloody axe.'

The first woman speaker of the evening intervened. 'But it's not for you to decide punishment. It's for the State.'

'Exactly,' agreed the first man. 'That's why we have laws.'

'Hear, hear!' cried several people approvingly.

'We've got a law about fucking parking! And this is the result!' snapped the Citroen owner, forced to lower his axe for fear of injuring someone as the debate spread.

'Hear, hear!' cried several other people.

'That is not a point about morality. That's a point about administration. Enforcement,' said yet another voice.

The audience was starting to divide into pro and anti, and two groups were now forming, one on each side of the car.

'What if one used an axe to enforce every law? What then?'

'It'd put a stop to illegal parking!'

'No, it wouldn't. It would just mean everyone'd carry an axe!'

'Rationality can only go so far. You need force to back it up.'

'That's a counsel of despair. You can't found civilization on despair.'

'You tell me a civilization which isn't underpinned by force. That's what the State is, legalized force.'

'Not in a democracy. The State functions by consent in a democracy.'

'That's what the State wants you to believe. So you'll obey the forces of reaction.'

Every so often, the Citroen owner would raise his axe as he sensed the argument swinging his way, but then there would be a further point, and counterpoint, and he would wearily lower it again. Now and then he would try to interject a point of his own, usually about being a taxpayer, but the mood of the debate was not sympathetic to the role of the individual in society, feeling it insufficiently relevant to the issues under discussion.

In the end the police came. While the crowd struggled to reach a moral consensus, they opened the parked car with a skeleton key and drove it away.

When people ask me what the French are really like, I tell them the story of the axeman and the parked car.

The alfresco hors d'oeuvre to the evening over (well, to be exact, still continuing) I turned back to the square, where I ran into Gerard and Ulrika, who had also been intellectually diverted on their way to Mouff Cinq. With them was Philippe, a lugubrious local I had seen in many a bar. He was long and stringy, like his hair, and had a straggling moustache which he was forever wiping dry of *marc*, the cheap brandy he drank in bulk. Despite the booze, he spoke machine-gun French and took no prisoners; with slurred slang and dense dialect, Philippe was one of the few whose speech I never came close to deciphering. Although always polite and courteous, every detail of his existence was a mystery to me. All I knew was that, though only in his mid-twenties, he was dying fast of drink. A new bar was a highlight in his remaining life.

As we walked in high spirits towards Mouff Cinq, I suddenly felt very English. Profound national truths are a dodgy area, veering between the Scylla of banality and the Charybdis of racism, but I couldn't help concluding that the French take real life in their stride, while the English step round it. It was not just the public baring of parking passions. We had to pass the square's *clochards*, dirty, smelly, winy people, and yet Gerard and Philippe were stopping, chatting, offering a pinch of tobacco, unfazed by their degradation. It seemed to me that whether it be mad axemen or drunks or adulterers, the French had an acceptance, albeit often a callous acceptance, of the warty side of life. But it was also a maturer understanding, a broader view, of the human condition. I put it down to the peasant gene. The paucity of peasants in Paris was a statistical anomaly I had yet to reconcile.

Mouff Cinq was already packed when we arrived. Every seat was taken, each standing room was stood in. The rumour was two-thirds right: small, intimate and sweaty. The premises were uncompromisingly narrow. Down the left-hand side were long wooden tables at right angles to the wall, with high-backed pews for seating; down the right-hand side was the bar; in the middle was a scrum.

Fortunately, we had Gerard on our team and, like a man with experience of parting the Red Sea, he arrived at the bar ahead of us – where, naturally, he knew the barman and *le patron*. Without hesitating, he held up four artist fingers and ordered the free *vin rouge*.

'*Quatre artistes?*' queried the despairing barman, who clearly had yet to find a normal, paying customer.

'*Mais oui!*' said Gerard ardently, and pointed to each of us in turn. '*Ulrika, elle est poète.*' (She blushed and said, '*Zut alors!*') '*Barry, il est écrivain.*' (I blushed and said nothing.) '*Et Philippe joue de la guitare!*' (Philippe nodded vigorously and said something incomprehensible.)

Le patron sighed wearily and gave the OK. One could tell he already regretted not having gone for the Green Shield Stamp option instead.

In the mêlée we were soon parted from each other. I looked around for familiar faces. I had already seen one and it came with a fedora. I was therefore keen to be otherwise engaged. I had encountered Mr Molmar several more times, usually on the stairs, and I always made a point of asking politely, 'Have you finished with my book yet?' So far this had not yielded success. And I feared Byron being brought into the conversation again.

None of my kindred spirits had managed to turn up. Jerry and Garry were back in their rented barn for the winter. Tony was at that moment dragging an industrial cleaner along some corridor. And Dave probably regarded the evening's frivolity as likely to turn him into a pillar of salt.

'Hallo!' A hand gently touched my arm. 'Don't I recognize you?'

I certainly recognized her. Close-up – and close-up was the only position available – her face was a little older than I had realized. Thirty, or even thirty-five. She was taller than I had thought, although admittedly I had not seen her entirely upright before. It was, however, the unconventionality of her looks and the curious angularity of her face which I had not forgotten. Amazonian or androgynous, I could not decide, yet she was intriguing, even alluring. She had beseeching brown eyes set above boldly prominent cheekbones. But it was the type of prominence that becomes a hostage to old age, and already there was a faint hint of sunken cheeks, an early warning of haggardness. Literature speaks highly of such bones, however, relating them to strong character, and I was aware of a directness to her casual question.

'Yes,' I replied. 'You're . . .' But her name had faded.

'Helba.'

'Yes. Yes, you're from Estonia,' I said, slightly over-eager to show that I had remembered.

'Do you know Estonia?'

'No. Not at all. Couldn't even find it on a map!' That sounded gratuitously offensive and, as usual, I was wanting a retake of my words.

'It's not on the map. Not any more.'

'Oh, no . . . no, of course not!' How could I have forgotten about the bloody Russians?

'You're English?'

'Yes. That's right. Born in London. Well, Croydon General. Towards Surrey. . . . You can't go back, then? Home, I mean?'

'No.' She did not seem surprised that I knew. 'Not without a war.'

'No, right! Be a bit drastic that!' I floundered.

'But I'm happy here for the moment . . . Far from home. On my own.'

She smiled at me, cryptically.

I jumped into the silence. 'You're a painter, I understand.'

'Gouache. I do gouache.'

I did not know about gouache. But I nodded.

'And you?' she asked. My heart, as was now its custom, missed a beat at this question. 'What is your name?'

'Oh! Oh right. Barry.'

'Barry,' she repeated, and she smiled again. A direct, into-the-eyes smile. At that moment, someone squashed past us to the bar, and I was pushed tightly up against her. She was wearing a simple pink cotton dress and the softness of the contact left me almost certain she had on little, if anything, else. When the crush eased, she made no immediate effort to move back. Indeed, so unconcerned did she seem about the proximity of our bodies that, in order to reciprocate such insouciant intimacy, I became frozen in a most implausible position. Only on the pretext of sipping my wine was I able to resume normal standing.

'Do you know Garry well?' I asked, knowing that she didn't, but needing to say something.

'No,' she replied. 'Are you on your own?'

'No, I'm with—oh, you mean—what, here in Paris?'

'Where else?' She seemed slightly impatient at my confusion.

'Oh, yes, yes I am.'

She looked at me again, very directly, and this time, it seemed, expectantly.

'I know his brother Jerry very well,' I said. 'We're very good friends.' My black introspective days had at least given me an insight into what I was now doing: I was gaining my identity from my friends. 'He stays with me a lot.' I talked to her about him some more but she did not look too interested, and so I tried to engage her by indiscreetly recounting the warnings of the mystery man in the suit.

'Secret police,' she said matter-of-factly when I had finished.

I laughed. 'Not in the West.'

'Everywhere.' Her glass was empty and she took a swig from mine. As she handed it back she squeezed my fingers gently and very slowly. Even I knew this was more than simple thanks . . . and, from nowhere, a panic swept over me. My first sighting of Garry under siege flashed through my mind.

I tried to stay calm. 'So. How did you end up in France?' I asked earnestly.

This did not seem the remark she had anticipated.

Indeed I am not sure she had expected conversation at all. She gave me a mysterious smile.

'Dramatically. In the middle of the night!' She said it almost coquettishly.

'Go on,' I prompted.

She shrugged. 'I was on a cultural delegation. In Grenoble. And I decided to run for it.'

'Run where?'

'I didn't know!' She gazed into my eyes, playfully helpless. She had my attention, and she surely knew it. 'It was the last night. My last chance for freedom! So before going to bed, I said to our minders, our two KGB men, that I wanted some fresh air. A walk round the block. It was bitterly, bitterly cold outside—'

'—It can be in Grenoble!' I remarked, in an attempt at geographical empathy.

'—and I took a gamble they wouldn't want to come with me. "Where could I get to?" I said to them. "Here? At this time of night?" I was lucky. They were lazy, and in the warm. So they let me out to go round the block, on my own. For five minutes.' She held up four fingers and a thumb, and I was startled by how delicate they were. 'I just had on a thin coat. No money. No passport. Nothing. And I walked down this deserted street until I reached the corner, and I turned out of sight . . . and then I ran, and ran, and ran . . . Looking for freedom!'

The thought amused her, and she fell silent and took another long swig of my wine.

This was an exile beyond my imaginings, and a danger far outside my experience. It also suggested a courage born of deepest desperation. I could only guess at the desolation of abandoning all family, all friends, possibly for ever.

'What happened then?' I asked.

Before she could reply, a late surge of artists came into the bar, and we were once more squashed against each other. Her face was very close to mine. I was conscious of how wonderfully soft her body felt and I tried not to respond in any way. I sensed I was slipping out of my depth, into uncharted emotions, and unfathomable needs.

'I kept on running till I saw a big road. It was lit up and I could see a garage. And I realized it was the auto-route to Paris. I rushed in and leapt on this poor garage man! "I want asylum" I kept shouting at him. "Asylum! Asylum!"'

She said it with a funny accent, and laughed. Her eyes remained on me as she laughed, and, almost out of politeness, I grinned back in sympathy. In the dim, fuggy light of Mouff Cinq, this became an act of tender complicity, and she took my hand in hers.

'I spoke almost no French but, somehow, I made this man understand. He hid me in his storeroom, with his mops. And said "ssh!" and left me alone in the dark. I was very frightened because I couldn't tell if I should trust him. And then after, I don't know, five, ten minutes, he came rushing back in, crying "*Vite! Vite!*" And he dragged me to a car which was filling up with petrol. It was a young woman driver, and he knew her. And I will never forget, she said, "*Paris! Je vais à Paris!*"

'And I lay across the back seat, and they covered me with a rug. And she drove all night long, and brought me to Paris. In the morning I asked the government for asylum.'

It was a story of rare drama, and all my instincts told me it was true. Her attitude to the story I was less sure of. Did she tell it from pride or from despair? Did she seek my admiration or my sympathy?

'And so,' she concluded, 'here I am! All alone in Paris!'

She joined her hands around my neck, and looked at me very pointedly in the eyes, her eyebrows minutely raised in explicit invitation. The enigmatic expectancy of her earlier look was no longer in doubt. She pressed her body very hard against mine, with a directness that made my throat go dry. I felt myself become aroused, and at the same moment I felt myself become transfixed with terror.

I had stumbled into the big league, and I was still a pre-qualifier. I had imagined candles and an hour per button. I had envisaged a reasonable opportunity to consult a manual. I had planned on spring romance, not autumn; a contemporary, not a mother. Now, most cruelly, my sexual bluff was called.

Helba's arms were still around my neck, her leg was still jammed between my loins, and her waiting, lustful gaze was still upon me.

'Are they political gouaches?' I asked.

A look of mystification came into her eyes. I tried to counter it with a look of innocence, a child-like, monk-like ob-

218

liviousness to the desires raging within her. I tried a little humour. 'Were you a danger to the State?' I enquired.

And I kept my body as still as stone.

She said nothing. She struggled to understand, and she just kept looking at me, torn between pleading and pride. I could see I was hurting her, humiliating her, by my brute impassivity. But an inaccessible blankness was now my only refuge. We remained locked in her uncomprehending clinch for what seemed a life sentence. And then, without speaking, but keeping her pained brown eyes upon me, she disentangled herself, backed off, and was swallowed up by the noisy crowd.

I struggled to the bar, and paid for a drink. I tried hard to justify myself, to persuade myself that I had not fled from sex, but triumphed over trauma; that I would have had a night of neuroses, not of passion; that I had escaped the long-term clutches of an unhinged predator; that I had avoided an emotional entanglement which would have made mincemeat of my psyche. After three drinks I was more or less convinced this was true.

On the fourth drink, Gerard and Ulrika joined me at the bar – Philippe was no longer in sight – and pronounced the place a success. Ulrika asked if I was enjoying myself and I lied. I was beginning to really dislike the French habit of not going to bed at ten o'clock. Gerard was in ruminant mood, though, and I was able to take a free ride on his discourse. Ever since I had known him, he had been the fiercest critic of his painting, questioning technique, questioning colour, questioning style. But since the summer, since the arrival of Ulrika in his life, he had begun to harbour doubts as to the very genre of his work. He had begun to wonder whether it was '*sérieux*' to be a street artist. He was almost a local mascot, and after an evening of strangers' hand-shakes and back-slaps, he would start to worry about prostituting his talent, and fret about being folkloric. This always led him to muse on the meaning of art, and the extrovert dynamo of the day was revealed by night to be a quieter, more complex soul.

Neither Ulrika nor I was equipped to quell such angst, and only after midnight did the conviviality of Châteauneuf du Pape restore his usual spirits. Eventually mine began to revive as well, and the memory of my brush with a disturbed alien faded by the glass. I was once again enjoying the evening when a taxi drew up outside. To my puzzlement, Philippe got out of it.

He had a brief dispute with *le patron*, arguing the doomed case that he was technically entitled to a free *coup de vin* for each fresh visit, and then he rejoined us.

'Where did you get to?' asked Gerard, also puzzled.

Philippe, his face as dolorous as ever, replied at some length in rapid-fire French, from which I gained no clues. But more than once, he threw me a strange, baffled look. When he had finished, Gerard grinned delightedly at his tale, and said to me, '*Philippe va vachement bien ce soir, non?*' They had all assumed my French was up to the challenge of Philippe; I gave that vague, polite smile characteristic of the monolingual and the deaf.

Then Philippe addressed a question specifically to me. I was forced to turn to Gerard for assistance. But he looked bemused by the question, and it was Ulrika who spoke up. 'He says why didn't you want her?'

I felt myself redden. 'He's been talking to Helba?'

'He's just been to bed with her.'

'He's not?'

'Yes. Said she was sensational.'

'She was?'

Ulrika nodded. I felt dizzy.

She looked at me. 'Was that the tall woman in pink, with the interesting face?'

'Er . . . er, yes. What else did Philippe say?'

'. . . That she told him she doesn't understand the English. Thinks they're very odd.'

'Odd?' I did not know what more Philippe had said, but both he and Gerard were looking at me slightly perplexed, as if they had been given news of a mystery illness.

'Yes.' Ulrika was more sympathetic, but clearly was struggling with the raw data. 'Why *didn't* you want to go to bed with her, Barry?'

'Well, you see . . . I didn't know . . . I was . . . I thought . . . that she might be disturbed,' I lied.

'Disturbed?'

'Well, with problems. A bit loopy.'

'*Qu'est-ce qu'il dit?*' asked Philippe.

Ulrika explained in French. Philippe looked mystified. As did Gerard. Ulrika tried to put a kindly gloss on it, but she too found my viewpoint puzzling. And then Philippe spoke again, but briefly, and with a challenging shrug of the shoulders. I looked to Ulrika for the translation.

Ulrika hesitated, and seemed unhappy to be the messenger. 'Philippe says he doesn't understand you either. He says all Helba was after was a friendly fuck.'

The phrase rang in my head. And I remembered Henry Miller's 'happy-go-lucky souls who fuck on sight'. The very souls I yearned for. Whom I hadn't believed in.

'Oh,' was all I could reply.

'You are strange,' Ulrika said to me, with a sweet sadness. 'All the time I've known you, you've never been interested in sex.'

When I left Mouff Cinq in the early hours, I wanted a can to kick along the gutter. I was in that lonesome, destructive mood where men kick things for no reason in empty city streets.

It seemed callow youth would never end. I could conceive of no circumstance where lust might triumph. My personality was a tailor-made chastity belt. I had no alibis left.

My only consolation was Mouff Cinq. It had a fug and a crowd and a feel. It was, despite all, a place to be cheered on lonely nights. Often in the winter months to come, I would forsake my horse-hair mattress and pad the hundred yards or so in slippers, hopeful of finding a familiar face still laughing and drinking at one in the morning. Already, the night's full house and half-full pavement showed the shrewdness of appealing to artistic wannabes, even if they just want to be hangers-on. The evenings were not to grow much darker before *le patron* found himself able to dispense with the offer of free drinks.

Yet Mouff Cinq was a straw in the wind, and the wind was

to prove a searing, all-consuming hurricane. Few of the drinkers could have guessed then that their little bar was the harbinger of a commercialism which, a quarter of a century on, would have destroyed every last charm of a once simple street. In the 1920s, Hemingway was able to write that there were no restaurants in the area; but by the 1990s, every second building would be a restaurant: from Lebanese and Greek to fast-food and 'Kiss Burgers', every palate would be catered for. The waiters would even shout their wares in the road. And to boost their trade would come natty new street signs; and postcard shops; and *'gamins de Mouffetard'* children's wear; and local jewellery at five francs; and guided tours. And by then it was no longer a *quartier* for living in.

Thus, on this dramatic night, while I faced my personal trauma of sempiternal celibacy, the community itself was on the verge of deep soul-searching. Indeed, even as I pushed the night buzzer to release the brown and grimy hotel door, the first seismic changes were not far distant.

CHAPTER 23

I slipped inside the musty corridor and felt for the timed light-switch. Many were the late nights I had fumbled through this routine, and while fantasizing on the company of one-off inamoratas, I used to rehearse in my mind how I would explain to them the romantic prerequisite of the on-all-fours crawling position. Madame's moral strictures were, I had long learnt, more bark than bite, their enforcement prone to more hot air than her heating. But, of late, there had been a second silhouette in the small dining-room. A nephew. A man less steeped in the ways of the wayward, less overawed by the ambitions of the arty, less tolerant of arrears. I was still a fistful of francs short of my autumn owings, and his attitude to latitude had not a hint of the house style. I had met his sort in Maupassant, and I suspected that, on restless nights, he would descend the stairs to sit alone and count his change. Madame was now seventy-seven. He was as yet only the power beside the throne, but there was much unease as to where he might step next. I trod warily as I passed his lair.

Back inside my room, I put on the saucepan for coffee, and sat on the end of my bed. It was the time of the night to be maudlin. I wondered what it would be like to be sixty, and live in such a room. I wondered what it would be like to be sixty, and die in such a room. I wondered if it were inevitable. I managed to wonder all this before the water had even come to the boil.

I was just getting up from the bed to make the coffee when

there was a gentle tap at the door. And a woman's voice called softly, 'Barry?'

This was a first for the female sex. I looked at my watch. It was 2.20 in the morning. At least I could rule out door-to-door selling.

I opened up. Standing there in a vestigial nightie, a coat wrapped loosely round her shoulders, was Sherry.

'Hallo!' I said.

It had been one long, bewildering night of surprises, but this was the biggest. By far. Even allowing for the wine lake befuddling my brain, this was a clear category 'A' fantasy made flesh. The *femme fatale* from next door.

'Hi,' she replied, and smiled nervously. Gone was my mood of self-pity, going were my detumescent fears of failure. This was safe homely sex. Her air of polite domesticity soothed where Helba's passionate presence had panicked; this felt not so much a seduction as an Avon lady calling for servicing.

'I hope you don't mind my coming round so late. But I saw your light was on . . .'

'That's all right. Any time.' (This was my idea of smoothness.) I waved her into my room. 'Coffee?' I was not clear on the ground rules, but I felt certain formalities should probably be observed.

'Oh, please!'

I gestured to the bed, and she sat down.

'Did you have a good evening?' she asked.

Her capacity for social correctness impressed me.

'Er, yes . . . yes, OK.' It was only equalled by my capacity for lying.

'Is it going to be a nice place, this Mouff—?'

'—Cinq. Yes, I think so.' She had a strange, almost choreographed calm; I had observed it before, and could not decide its significance. 'Certainly crowded tonight.' She kept a slight smile on her face, a psychological security blanket, which was, I felt, suppressing some inner confusion; I was, however, glad for such signs of insecurity, relieved that she too felt vulnerable. 'Full of

arty types.' I sloshed water round an extra cup. The next in-
itiative seemed to lie with me. 'I take it this isn't a purely social
visit,' I said, trying not to gawp too soon at how far up her thighs
the nightie had risen.

'No, it isn't.' She smiled nervously. 'I feel a little foolish,' she
admitted.

'Please don't!' I said, trying to fill the words with all the
warmth and maturity I could muster.

'You see, an ex-lover of mine has turned up, and I'm worried
he may get violent.'

'I'm sorry?'

I felt a very urgent need to recap, indeed to rerun the whole
scene. 'What d'you mean "turned up"? Where?'

I also wanted to check the exact meaning of 'ex-lover' and
'violent', but before I could do so, she said, 'In my room.'

'In your room? What, now?'

'Yes.'

'So a fuck's out of the question?' is what Miller would have
said, but I was preoccupied by more mundane matters. Like
'how violent?' and 'what did she want?'

'Does he know you're here?' I asked, moving unheroically
out of the sight-line from her window.

'He knows I've gone to see somebody.'

'Oh. And what do you want me to do? Hit him?' I threw that
in for light relief.

'No,' she laughed. I was glad to see she was able to laugh. 'No,
you'd come off worst.'

'Oh, thank you.'

'No, he's rather big.'

'Oh.' Nearly six long hours ago, the evening had begun with
near-violence; for it to end with a threatened punch-up would
seem an appropriate symmetry. 'I take it you've tried asking him
to leave?'

'He's just come from Munich. Hitched all the way. He can't
go back tonight.'

'He's German?'

'Yes.'

I handed her a coffee. I was beginning to see her problem. 'Why might he get violent? Are you a very annoying person?'

She just gave me a grin. And then she sighed. I knew she was going to tell me a story. Or at least assemble the relevant nuggets into some sort of explanation.

'He's very young, he's only twenty.'

'How old are you?'

'Twenty-seven.' This was older than I had thought, but I showed no reaction. 'I met him travelling, in Turkey. He was very self-confident . . . somebody who was always certain about things. Which is kind of reassuring. And so we teamed up for a while.'

'Teamed up?'

'Just to make the travelling easier. Usual thing. But then he wanted us to be lovers. And I suppose because he was so insistent it was a good idea, and he seemed so sure of himself – which is usually a plus – I agreed. Or gave in. It's as good a use as any for a sleeping bag!'

She had a matter-of-factness to her sexuality – and in her tight nipple-enhancing nightie she was very sexual – which I found most unthreatening. There was no towering, out-of-control passion to her, and, in a perverse way, I found that rather erotic.

'And what went wrong?'

'Well, nothing, until the end of the trip. I saw it just as a holiday fling. And he didn't. Doesn't. Can't. Won't.'

'So he's come all the way from Munich to do what?'

'Declare undying love.'

'Oh. Bit dramatic!'

'He's heavily into drama. If he can't get his own way. Shouting and crying and threatening. It's the flip side of being cocky at that age. He's just too young, you see. Twenty. He can't handle it. I shouldn't have ignored the age gap.'

'I'm twenty-one,' I said hopefully, with a smile. It was somehow very easy to make such a remark to her. I imagined she weighed up her sexual responses on a calibrated scale. If the pro-sex arguments outweighed the anti-sex arguments she would coolly say yes, and shake hands on an orgasm.

'I think thirty is the ball-park figure,' she replied, but sweetly.

'What's he threatening to do?'

'Well, his first idea was to drag me to Munich by my hair.'

'It'd certainly solve your problem. He'd stop loving you if you were bald.' For some reason – possibly terror – flippancy was the only gear I could engage.

'He doesn't seriously mean any harm. Really. But he loses control. That's what scares me. That he'll lash out.'

I had by now realized that Sherry had not come to ask me to intervene, to act the muscle-bound marriage counsellor; she was simply after refuge, to be safe from him for the night. I also had the feeling that, with wine, the ball-park figure of thirty might be negotiable.

'I and my room are at your service,' I said with mock gallantry. 'And so are all the facilities!'

'You don't mind company, then?' she replied, with what I felt was a touching modesty.

'I've had refugees from the storm before!'

'Oh, that's very sweet of you.' And she got up, her nightdress riding ever higher, and crossed the room to kiss me gently on the cheek. I squeezed her hand. 'I'll just go and send him over then,' she said. 'His name's Jürgen. Good night.'

Jürgen was definitely big. His foam bed-roll stretched almost seven feet across my floor. He did not, however, sleep. He just lay there saying his life was over. In a thick accent.

He had been enticed out of Sherry's room with unexpectedly little difficulty. Perhaps he feared a public spectacle. Perhaps he recognized a lost cause. Perhaps Sherry had said her new lover in no. 5 would kill him if he didn't go. Whatever his reasons, he shambled into my room a broken reed.

It is often hard to appreciate that large, bulky people have soft, intimate emotions. Delicacy of body equals delicacy of mind, that is the cruel conventional connection. Jürgen was probably fourteen stone, with a trim, gingery-brown moustache and short hair, and would have made somebody a nice bodyguard.

'She'll always be my sweetheart,' came his sad voice from the floor.

'Yes, I know,' I said.

'I'd have died for her, I would.'

'Yes, I'm sure,' I said.

'My heart has been broken into a thousand pieces.'

'Yes, I realize,' I said.

'She's the most beautiful woman I've ever met.'

'Yes, I can believe that,' I said.

'And she's got such a sweet, gentle nature.'

'Yes, I've noticed,' I said.

It was now 3.30.

'I'd have died for her, I would.'

'Yes,' I said.

'She'll always be my sweetheart.'

'Yes,' I said.

'Even though she has broken my heart into a thousand pieces.'

I turned over, buried my head in my pillow.

'I could never love anybody else. I'm finished with women.'

'Mmm,' I said.

'I shall just go away. Somewhere abroad. Become anonymous.'

'Mmm,' I said.

'Lose myself in some cause. Serve some higher purpose.'

'Mmm,' I said. 'Good night.'

'Perhaps I'll become a freedom-fighter . . . join a liberation movement . . . do something heroic. Then she'd love me. What do you think?'

'I'd avoid the Congo,' I said.

The head barman had gone. Or, to be more exact, vanished. One stifling summer night, topped up with tips, he had apparently disappeared, leaving a leaflet attached to the bar by a silver corkscrew. According to Monsieur Bareste, this method of resignation had created somewhat of a stir. Especially as the leaflet was a much-photocopied recruitment tract for hired killers, and contained several grainy photographs of current garrotting techniques. He had written across the top in ink, 'I have gone to fight for the cause of Western civilization.'

'Why should he write it in English?' Monsieur Bareste had asked, much puzzled by the whole affair. I said I had no idea. But privately I suspected that he was letting me know that his grasp of the pres. perf. tense was now sufficient to improve his financial fire-power. Deep among dead bodies in Central Africa, his take-home pay was being boosted by his knowledge of English compound conjunctions.

My moral dilemma was thus dehorned, but in its place came poverty. For Yannick le Moine had also gone – back home to Brittany, to help run his family's tourist hotels on the strength of 'please' and 'thank you'. Unexpectedly, the autumn crop of waiters had produced no new lovers of learning. And all the Alliance had to offer was more washing-up. My portfolio was reduced to dear Monsieur Bareste.

His beloved only daughter Claude ('she is very cross when I call her little Claudette') was now engaged. Her life and her prospects and her beauty had edged out Breughel as the favourite topic of conversation. I found myself slipping into international newsagents to flick through *Woman's Own* and enlarge my vocabulary on bridalwear. Monsieur Bareste had had his daughter late in life, and was as proud and as loving and as claustrophobically besotted as it is possible for a father to be. As my knowledge of the family grew, I began to feel like a young aged retainer, and saw myself in almost Tolstoyan terms, as the down-at-heel tutor who shuffles round the estate in Russian literature. It was a status enhanced by the touching promise of an invitation to the wedding.

But to talk to him of wedding bells three times a week was not enough to make all my ends meet. I was still paying my rent in arrears, not in advance, and the prospect of poverty and dark autumn evenings was not a happy combination.

In the days after Jürgen, Sherry came regularly to tap on my door, but at more normal times, in more normal clothing. Our acquaintanceship had quantum-leapt to good friendship in those intense early hours; Sherry had of necessity offered up confidences usually reserved for nearest and dearest. But at each visit I continued to be surprised, shamed even, by her openness. It was not an expansive, extrovert openness, but a simple readiness to respond to questions, a flat emotional honesty upon demand. I hoped this to be a portent of intimacy. It was years before I recognized it as the legacy of therapy.

I had always found her calmness suspect. And then, one afternoon, as she sat by the rain-streaked window, dispassionately discussing yet another past affair found wanting, I suddenly glimpsed the truth: in some way, at some time, her sense of self had been broken in pieces . . . and painstakingly put together again. Hers was a fragile maturity, guarding against a Humpty Dumpty fall. The prosaicness of her passion, which I found so appealing, was self-protective. The neatness of the clothes, the precision of the lipstick, were there as external proofs of a soul under control.

Even unshockability was part of her methodical calm. Indeed, she used often to say, 'I'm unshockable.' I doubted this were true. It is not even a desirable characteristic since it seems a boast of emotional inadequacy. But Sherry appeared to see it as a totem of emotional toughness, the sign of a woman with no neuroses running rampant. At the same time, however, she was constantly seeking, in that pseudo-philosophical West Coast way, a user-friendly value system to comprehensively buttress her existence (the sort of zeitgeist package which – like EST – comes handily with initials to help the marketing). Despite her apparent rationalism, she nurtured a hidden need to be guided through life by the magic formulae of some Philosopher's Stone, Inc.

Yet though I might have mocked her remedies, I admired her courage. She was a bruised twenty-seven, but still stoical and smiling.

Then, after lunch one day, I was lying on my bed reading the immaculately written *Le Monde Diplomatique*. It was a journal I bought every week, not for its high-powered politics, but for the heady intellectual pleasure of surfing through the sub-clauses. The weather had grown gloomily grey and, although barely two o'clock, I had switched on the light.

A few moments later, her familiar tap sounded at the door.

She came in, I made coffee, we chatted.

As always, she was trim and desirable. That afternoon, she was wearing a patterned red blouse over a pair of pale grey, neatly creased woollen slacks. I remember the creases because she did not sit down, but stood resting against the table, clasping her coffee mug with both hands. After a while, I noticed she was not drinking the coffee, apart from a few token sips, and her conversation was down to ritual politeness. In unfamiliar company she would sometimes give a small smile with a little back-up laugh when spoken to, and I would know she was nervous. I knew she was nervous now.

'Another German lover turned up?' I asked teasingly.

'Why d'you say that?'

'Just testing my powers of observation!' I liked to josh in the general area of lovers; it kept the issue of younger men alive, and with it my chances for the succession. I gave her a reassuring smile. 'I thought you seemed a bit . . . preoccupied.'

'Oh, it's nothing.' So there was something. 'Just medical.' She fell silent and glanced for some time at a headline about an uprising in Chad. 'D'you have insurance?'

'Medical insurance? Don't think so. I used to when I was travelling. In case I got a lift from an Italian. But not any more. You haven't either?'

She shook her head. 'No. Nothing.'

'I suppose if I got ill, I'd try and make a run for England.' This was not very helpful advice for an American, and I wished I had shown more tact. I wondered what might be wrong with her. She looked healthy enough. I hesitated to ask, for fear it be serious and reveal my words of compassion as inadequate. 'Are you in pain?'

She nodded. 'Now and then.' She was so sparing, so un-typically sparing, with information that I decided not to press her. I could not tell if she wanted me to press her. That I suppose was what she meant about being twenty-one.

231

'Would you like to have this after me?' I tapped *Le Monde Diplomatique*, now lying on the table beside her. Her grasp of French was quite good, though I cringed, as always, at the American accent. Some latent Old World snobbery predisposed me against Americans speaking French and made me want to issue public apologies whenever I heard them.

'Do you know where ovaries are?'

I stared at her. '. . . Ovaries?'

'I've been getting this stabbing pain. And I think it's ovaries. But I'm not sure exactly where they are.'

I don't know why she asked me. I had yet to find the vagina. All my knowledge of ovaries came from a wall chart in Form Science 3C, eight years ago.

I was, however, very reluctant to admit ignorance.

Although I knew that she must be suffering, and although I knew I could not help, I was nonetheless unwilling to forego the rare opportunity to join in a search for ovaries. Especially hers. 'Well, I know roughly,' I replied. 'How exact do you want to be?'

Sherry had moved and was standing by the chimney–breast. She looked frightened and suddenly very vulnerable. She still managed a smile though, and my heart went out to her.

'Well,' she said, and her hands moved down her body, 'the pain comes here.' And she lightly placed her fingers three or four inches below the waistline of her trousers. She glanced at me for confirmation.

I moved doctorly close and looked. 'I think that's kidneys,' I said, unsure whether this was good news or bad news.

'Kidneys?'

'Yes. Ovaries are . . .' Eager to assist, and trying not to tremble, I moved my hand the few inches that separated us, and pressed it fair and square in the loin department. Her woollen trousers were excitingly soft to the touch, and stretched tight against her body. '. . . round about, er, here.' I had never felt ovaries before. Officially or unofficially. So, in the ostensible interest of medical science, I made a tour of the area. Somewhat to my disbelief, Sherry remained impassive throughout my examination, trustingly, poignantly grateful for the care and attention. I felt fraudulent, and guilty, and ecstatically excited.

'Isn't that my liver?' she asked, after a while.

'Is it?' I said – feeling not so much foolish but grateful for the further licence to explore. I gently moved my hand lower round her loins on a second lap, occasionally able to detect the springiness of pubic hair beneath her underwear. My emotions were in total flux. I genuinely wanted to be able to reassure her . . . but I wanted to do it slowly.

I asked her various questions about the nature of the pain, and how it came and went. I found her quiet patience, her trust in me, both moving and shaming. She continued to stand motionless, fearful of some dread illness, hopeful for some words of comfort.

I fondled her relevant parts one last time. I felt the offer of an internal examination would be pushing my luck. I squeezed her hand. 'Nothing to worry about,' I said, with all the throwaway confidence of a senior gynaecologist, 'I reckon your ovaries are well out of the danger zone.'

I had fortuitously remembered my groin strain from the school long jump. And the gyp it had given me. It therefore seemed a pulled muscle was by far the likeliest candidate. With rest and relaxation the likeliest cure. I imparted this information as soothingly and professionally as I was able.

Sherry looked at me full of relief and gratitude. I was just sorry there was no room for doubt about the location of testicles.

'I was so worried,' she murmured. 'You get like that on your own.'

'I know,' I said, piling on the empathy.

'Thank you so much.' She laid her hand gently on my arm.

It seemed the consultation had come to an end. I was uncertain how to prolong it. Sherry said she wanted to rest – and I could hardly disagree with my own diagnosis. And so she went, a much happier woman than when she had arrived. She left behind a much happier – indeed exhilarated – younger man.

Once a day, I would wearily check out the Alliance bulletin board. But now I was suddenly in the mood for the walk, ready to face down the overcast skies and swirling wind. I poured away her coffee, put on my anorak, and strode out across the Jardins du Luxembourg.

The journey and the job search took just under an hour. When I returned there was a single red rose on the table.

CHAPTER 24

Puddles were forming in the gravel of place des Vosges. The most harmoniously proportioned *place* in Paris was fringed by watery mist. It had been raining all day and the turning leaves were hanging sodden and lifeless on the trees, as if finally convinced their number was up for another year. Only the very old, with dogs and umbrellas, were venturing from the shelter of the square's cloisters. I had worn the wrong shoes to the interview, and water was working up my legs by osmosis as I splashed across the square on my way home.

I had sweet-talked myself into another professorial sinecure. From now on, I would be spending four hours a week in the fashionable *4ème*; in the wood-panelled splendour of a galleried apartment with panoramic views of the city; in the company of the elegant thirty-something wife of the much–lauded architect currently designing the first major church to be built in France since the war. In other words, in clover. I therefore did not care if I got wet.

I could have taken the Metro, but my body was not in the mood for sitting. I ploughed through the Marais and on across the islands. Lights were everywhere coming on early. It was not long before the evening rush hour, and there was a bad-tempered urgency in the air. As I jostled up past the Faculté des Sciences I briefly had the sensation of being a commuter returning home to a family and a fire. For a moment, Paris seemed just another over-stressed city. I stopped off – only people with routines 'stop off', I thought to myself – at the boulangerie on the square, and bought the last *éclair à café* of the day.

I did not bother to put on the light in the passageway. I squelched steadily up the stairs, and was halfway through the éclair, struggling as usual with the waywardness of cream, when I saw a large shadowy bundle ahead of me.

'Hallo!' it said.

Squatting on a duffel bag in the corridor was a decidedly over-weight and very young-looking English girl.

'Hallo,' I replied, stepping over her to reach my door.

'Do you live here?' she asked.

'Yes,' I said, a little reluctant to encourage her conversation. I had had my fill of strays over the past few months.

'Do you know where Tony is?'

As she spoke, I recognized her accent as Liverpudlian. I turned round in the doorway, slightly regretting my brusqueness. 'At the end of the corridor. No. 7.'

'Yes, I know,' she said, 'but he's out.'

'Oh.' I switched on the light in my room, and this gave me a better view of her. She was not so much overweight as square. Her body was square, her face was square, and even her legs seemed to have right angles. This had not restrained her desire to dress as a pioneer of the Swinging Sixties. 'I've no idea where he might be. I'm sorry.'

She looked rather downcast by this news. 'Art class, perhaps,' I suggested.

'I do art,' she said, with a spurt of enthusiasm.

I wondered what she meant. I was also trying to work out how old she was. Her unconventional shape made this difficult, but I put her at little more than early teens. She was very be-draggled and, although there was an innate perkiness to her, she seemed oddly nonplussed by the situation.

'Is he expecting you?' I asked.

'No,' she said. 'But I'm family.' And then added, 'I've run away from home.'

She was towelling her hair when I returned with a selection of rolls from the café. (The interest she had expressed in a 'bit

236

of nosh' had already seen the demolition of the coffee éclair.)
Her hair was short and spiky, and even after drying it had
retained an air of truculence. I noted it was not just a towel she
was short of. She appeared to have run away with none of the
advance planning which had distinguished my own departure.
Her duffel bag offered only the limited options of dungarees or
a micro-skirt. In my brief absence, she had decided – somewhat
to my regret – that fashion-conscious Paris called for the micro-
skirt.

'What relation are you to Tony, then?' He had never
mentioned her.

'Cousin.' She set to work on the biggest baguette.

'Oh.' I wondered how close they were. 'First or second?' I
enquired.

'Dunno.'

I let the conversation lapse while she ate. It had apparently
been eighteen hours since she had last eaten, so her conspicuous
consumption had a reasonable defence. But her hunger did not
blunt her curiosity, and she chewed on the move, eager to
examine her new surroundings. Quite untouched by normal
adult proprieties, she even poked about in my wardrobe. And
she craned her neck every which way to take in the rain-soaked
cityscape outside. Her enthusiasm revived the memory of my
own initial reactions.

'First time in Paris?'

'First time anywhere!'

She was of an age for family rows. She certainly had the
temperament, an upfront adolescent gutsiness. Earlier, when
referring to her sleepless night on the run, she had joked about
her fear that 'they might catch her'. But when I had, not un-
reasonably, assumed this to mean parents in hot pursuit, she had
just laughed, and said, 'Oh, *they* couldn't give a toss!' Leaving
the clear inference that darker forces were after her. And then
she had asked for a jam buttie.

'Shall we go out later?' She turned from the pencil studies of
my anatomy which were now on three walls.

'If you like,' I replied.

237

'I've got money. I brought my Post Office book.' She reminded me of a Cockney sparrow. Except, of course, that she was large and from Liverpool.

We waited in vain for Tony's return: I left a note advising him of the unexpected developments in his life. It was eight o'clock and dark when we left the hotel. The rain had stopped but the night still felt wet. We headed towards boulevard St Michel and the Latin Quarter heartland. My slight reluctance to go out – which she had rightly detected – was not financial, but aesthetic. Whilst Parisian women are mouth-wateringly chic and fashionable, there is a conservatism about their fashion, a conformity to their chic, which the Englishwoman of the Carnaby Street era quite failed to share. Paula had on a flat Northern cap, a fluorescent-yellow heavy-duty mac which would not have been out of place on the Mumbles lifeboat (provided she were to remove the silver-glitter stars), a tight silver T-shirt, a pair of black leather calf-length boots, fishnet stockings and her crotch-revealing black micro-skirt. She was also, as I had come to realize when we walked side by side down well-lit boulevards, only just over five foot tall, which gave her the overall appearance of a rather camp tank. (Aged, I had now discovered, fifteen.)

We strolled along past the Sorbonne. The pavements were becoming busy again, the glassed extensions of the glitzy cafés filling up fast. The night's courting couples and the evening's onlookers were back on station after the rain. Paula looked exhilarated, a cocky stride coming over her short, fat legs as we made our way through the in-crowds.

'This is where the action is!' I told her.

''s fucking great!' she said. She slipped her arm through mine so that there be no doubt we were a couple. 'Thanks for being so nice.'

'That's OK.'

'I had an affair go wrong.'

'Oh. Right.' I had been expecting some sort of confessional moment, some opportunity to provide a broad shoulder, but her tenor was so adult that I felt the junior partner. 'And you're running away to forget?'

'Fuck that! I'm running away to escape!' She looked at me as though I were a soppy schoolgirl.

'Escape?' So there *were* dark forces in pursuit. I remembered Jürgen, and I wondered uneasily about her taste in men. 'There's no chance he'll find you, is there?'

'Oh, it's not him I'm worried about,' she said scornfully. 'It's his wife.'

A gaggle of young girls out on the town came towards us, giggling at the sight of her outfit, which was shining like a bad-taste beacon in the night. They nudged each other when they drew level, and smirked.

'Fuck you!' said Paula, and gave them a V-sign as they passed.

'He's married?' I said, simultaneously trying to downplay my astonishment on several fronts. And then added, somewhat redundantly, 'With a wife?'

'Yeah,' she said coolly.

I did not know what to make of her. She sounded a tough cookie, she seemed an oddball, and yet she engagingly lacked guile. Years later, I would come to look upon her as the praetorian guard of punk. 'How old is he, your boyfriend?'

'Thirty-two.'

'Thirty-two?'

'She's been to the cops, you see. Wants me prosecuted. Wants us both prosecuted. You know, that under-age sex crap. That's why I did a runner.'

'Oh.' Rue de la Huchette was passing in a daze, its seventeenth-century charms unremarked upon.

'I'm safe here, aren't I? I mean, they can't deport me, can they?'

'I don't know.' Under-age sex was not my field of expertise. 'I wouldn't have thought so. More likely to get the *Légion d'honneur* for it over here.'

'The what?'

239

'It's a medal. Does anyone know you're here? Apart from me?'

'No. No-one.' It had begun to dawn on me that everybody I ever came across was on the run from something. Bereavement, police, lovers, fathers, the Eastern bloc . . . was nobody in Paris through choice? 'My parents won't even have noticed I'm missing yet!' As she spoke, she started to unwrap pink bubble gum. For the first time, I thought seriously about giving Interpol a ring.

'What about your school?' The word felt wimpishly bourgeois in my mouth. 'Does your school know what's happened?'

'Oh yes. The school knows. First place she went, the cow.'

'And what did they do?'

'They sacked him.'

'Sacked who?'

'My bloke. He was the art teacher.'

'Oh. Oh, I see.' I was becoming reluctant to ask any more questions. She had relayed this *News of the World* saga with a disturbing casualness, her dispassion making it sound an everyday story of teenage folk. There was no embarrassment, no sense of regret, no thrill of the forbidden. It left me once again feeling a novitiate in the ways of the world. Yet she was both worldly and unworldly: worldly in the experiences she had had, and unworldly in her inability to foresee their impact. Was she streetwise or vulnerable, malicious or innocent, resilient or damaged?

'Can we sit in a café? And watch people? Like in the films?'

'Yes, sure.' I was more than a little relieved. Being on parade with the cutting edge of fashion does nothing for an Englishman's morale.

We settled on a large café in boulevard St Germain, just opposite the Odéon, with plenty of bustle to watch. I ordered a hot chocolate and Paula asked for a large beer. When the waiter brought the drinks he winked at me. I was uncertain why.

Paula gazed about her with near rapture. It was not a particularly grand café, but big and popular. The small round tables with lattice-backed chairs were set in closely spaced rows along its glassed front, and there was a constant roar of sound. The waiters, as so often in Paris, took pride in being waiters, and they rushed about at flamboyant speed, their black bow ties giving a *fin de siècle* feel to their ministrations. The customers themselves were trendy and voluble, and Gitane plumes curled from every hand, the national smell of France filling the *salle* air.

Paula sat back contentedly, and pulled out a cigarette-rolling machine. As yet she showed no sign of keeling over from her long day's night without sleep. I wondered what constituted normality in her life.

'So, you do art too. Is that Tony's influence?' I asked.

'Yes, I think so. He used to do drawings of me. In a tutu!'

'Thank God he's never asked *me* to wear one!'

Paula laughed. It was the first time I had heard her laugh. 'I want to be an actress now, though.'

I hoped she had not set her heart on romantic leads. 'Theatre?'

'No. Films. I love films. I'd like to go to Hollywood. Who's your favourite actress?'

'Ingrid Bergman.' I didn't have a favourite actress, I rarely had 'favourite' anythings, but this seemed too fastidious to explain. I felt obliged to return the question and she said James Dean.

'I had to leave my posters behind,' she added, her regret revealing a sudden glimpse of a still-young child.

'Looks as if you had to leave a lot behind.'

'Yes, I guess so. It's not the first time I've run away,' she added.

'No?'

'No. Tried it several times. I first ran away when I was eight. Only got two blocks away then, though.'

'What were you running away from then?' The thought of what she might have been up to in kindergarten beggared belief.

'Oh, it was a protest, that one. About sandwiches. My mum and dad wanted me to go to bed without any supper. So I thought sod that!'

'Did it work?'

'No. I got locked in the box-room for two days. And they

got rid of my rabbit. Humphrey,' she said ruefully. 'I missed him for years.'

I was curious about her current feelings. 'And d'you miss your art teacher?'

'Oh, I didn't love him or anything.' She was almost contemptuous of the idea, with that cruelty which is the preserve of adolescence.

'Did he love you?' I asked.

'I shouldn't think so. I mean, he said he did, but men have got to say that, haven't they?' I felt unexpectedly threatened by her cynicism. What hope if the opposition knew the game plan so young? 'He was good fun, though.'

She was on her second beer now. I ordered a Benedictine to look sophisticated. Green was a colour which always surprised people.

'He used to give these parties. When his wife was away.' She stopped to watch a steak and *frites* go by.

'Parties?' I prompted.

'Yeah, went on all night. Really weird people used to come. He had this house, with a big garden. And a barbecue.' I wondered what Paula classified as weird. Three-piece suits? 'And everyone always ended up with their clothes off!'

For several seconds I was at a complete loss for words. Then I managed to say, 'Oh'. Her capacity to astonish was unending. I struggled for words. My concern to appear blasé about sex fought its familiar losing battle with my desire to gain information on it. Eventually I said, 'Including you? I mean, you stripped off as well?'

Paula's interest was by now focused on another roll-up, and she carefully tweaked several stray tobacco hairs back into line before responding to my enquiry. 'Oh, they did that for me,' she said, almost abstractedly. And then added, 'I always used to say to them, leave my boots on. You can take everything else off me, but I want to keep my boots on.'

'Right!' I said, and I waited for further revelations. They did not come. Instead of fleshing out details of her all-night open-air orgies, she just ran her tongue slowly along the gummed edge

242

of her Rizla, and looked as though the subject produced, if anything, ennui. Nonetheless, it was a silence that I felt impelled to break, and finally I asked, as casually as possible, 'What happened next? At these parties?'

She lit her flimsy cigarette, and inhaled with calm expertise. 'Oh, the usual,' she replied. And then she yawned, and yawned again. The need for sleep was beginning to overwhelm her. I could see she was about to flake. 'Can we go now?' she asked.

I nodded with new-found reluctance and waved for the bill.

Paula gazed around the café, as if committing it to memory. She was not a discreet gazer – nor indeed a subtle yawner – and her eyes wandered brazenly from table to table, from group to group. It was clearly a world to her liking, and her look lingered on the hairy student intellectuals and the icily chic young girls with immaculate *maquillage*. The sophisticates of café society were a new range of exotica for her, and I watched as she observed how they talked, how they gestured, how they laughed, how they touched.

I left a biggish tip. We had only been smallish drinkers, but my coward's rule of thumb was to tip well where one wished to return often.

We squeezed our way between the packed tables. Paula was just ahead of me, her phosphorescent coat over her arm, her upper thighs wobbling at the world. We paused in the doorway, to zip up against the squally night. I was mentally preparing myself for the eye-swivelling double-takes of the return journey when Paula turned and smiled broadly at a girl entering the café.

'Not someone you know, surely?' I asked, more than a little surprised.

'Oh no!' she replied. 'She just looked nice.' And then she added, 'I've had enough of men. I think it's about time I tried women.'

And she slipped her arm through mine again, and we stepped out into the rain.

We did not see Tony that evening. By the time we returned he had gone on his nightly cleaning rounds. He had, however, slipped his key under my door. Around midnight I escorted an exhausted Paula down the corridor to his room, where she collapsed onto the bed with a mighty yawn. I too was feeling somewhat enervated by the evening's events and was back asleep in my own room within minutes.

The next morning, shortly before eight, an unshaven Tony appeared at my door, looking rather tired and a little fed-up.

'She's dead to the world! What did you do, drug her?'

I laughed and said, 'Yes. I gave her two beers for her life story. Blew both our minds!'

He sighed. 'You'd better fill me in before she wakes up. Couldn't give me a coffee, could you?'

'I think you might like it strong and black,' I said, winding him up.

'So might you,' he replied, somewhat mysteriously.

The occasion seemed to demand fresh air, and so I proposed class coffee, with croissants, and we went out to Café Mouffetard for breakfast. On the way, I brought him up to date with Paula's life story.

'Bloody hell!' was his main response. Several times. I found the shared sense of disbelief curiously gratifying. Although I knew much of Tony's views on art, his attitudes to life were more opaque (apart from his objection to the socio-economic structure of international capitalism) and his personal traumas were financial and aesthetic, not emotional. His private world was uncluttered by the detritus of humans, and he rarely spoke of anything approximating to an inner self. I found it hard to see him as a son or a father or a husband.

'So,' I concluded. 'I think she might be in need of cousinal guidance.'

'Oh, really!' He paused while our drinks were placed on the table, and gazed blankly at the market outside. 'Never been thought of as a role model before!'

'Has she always been a handful?'

'How would I know? I haven't seen her since she was eleven!'

'Eleven? But I thought . . . aren't you some kind of soul mate?' Tony shook his head.

'What about the drawings you did of her?'

'What drawings?'

'She used to pose for you. In a tutu. Said it changed her life.'

Tony thought back for a moment. 'That's right. She was a fairy. In a school play. Aged about nine, for God's sake!'

'Probably the year she lost her virginity!'

'Not to me!' said Tony hurriedly. He sighed. 'Jesus! See what you mean about impressionable!' He fell silent.

'What are you going to do?'

'I don't know.' He struggled to get butter into his crumbling croissant. 'Obviously can't send her back. Not to a school without an art teacher.'

There was more silence. I wondered how many such conversations took place in this café. Ever since my first visit, its tables had seemed a refuge for the anguished, the eccentric and the badly dressed, all making heavy weather of life, sex and death.

'How much money's she got?'

'Can you use an English Post Office book in France?' I asked rhetorically.

'Of course not!'

'Then she's got nothing. Just the clothes she stands up in. And personally I wouldn't advise her to do that.'

'Jesus!' said Tony again. '. . . I'll have a word with Fran.' Fran was his girlfriend, who lived by nude modelling and selling *International Herald Tribune*s. 'She's got a sofa. And she ran away from home herself. They might hit it off.'

'Not too well, I hope,' I said, and grinned.

Tony seemed not to register the remark. Instead, he said, 'She's not the only one who might be needing a sofa.'

At first, I thought he was referring to himself. 'Why?' And then, with a terrible sense of foreboding, I remembered his earlier cryptic remark. 'What do you mean?'

'We're being upgraded.'

'Upgraded?' For a moment I was puzzled.

'Showers. Wallpaper. A nice lick of non-brown paint. . . . Even talk of carpets!'

I stared at him. '. . . The nephew?'

'The nephew. Very keen on the twentieth century apparently.'

'I've noticed.' I began to feel sick. 'Has he expressed his views on anything else?'

'Like rent?'

'Like rent.'

'Yes. Yes, he has. He favours the word "double".'

CHAPTER 25

I had started to walk the streets at night. Evening after evening, the solitude of my room would lay siege to my soul. I would delay, I would resist, but as the time drifted past nine I would be drawn ineluctably to the bright lights, the loud crowds. I would stand on street corners; and stroll with the flow; and cling to gathering throngs. In the anonymity of the night, I would become a compulsive and lonely voyeur of the happiness of others.

Time after time, I hurried past the dark windswept wastelands of the Panthéon, hoping for a fairy-tale happenstance on the busy boulevards beyond. And time after time, I wandered slowly back in the early empty hours, self-pityingly desolate.

Time itself was running out. The rumours were confirmed. My bohemian Shangri-la would soon fall to the decorators. And with it would go my romantically seedy image, my trappings of louche decay. And with it also would go me. For the figures were inflexible, as was the nephew. At the end of the year, the rent would rise beyond my wherewithals. There were simply not enough chic wives of church architects to keep me in the new era of soft furnishings. I now needed another bolt-hole.

I had put out the word, let my need for a garret be known on the grapevine, but as autumn moved greyly into winter there was not even the whisper of a vacant cupboard.

I tried my friends, I tried the Alliance, I tried the lamposts. I drew nothing but blanks. There were lodgings to be had through the Alliance, but they came in exchange for domestic servitude, and to be Mr Mop in Something-sur-Seine was a degree of degradation too far. I had made some friends – what I thought of as 'normal' friends, 'square' friends – on the benches of the fourth grade, but they mostly moved in suburb circles; for them, Paris was 'the year out', the planned-for risqué blip in the bourgeois onward march. They had no hot line to digs for the near down-and-out.

My new dread of homelessness merged darkly with my old fear of sexlessness. My personality spiralled paranoidly downward.

Sherry had found a new lover, an engineer from Lyons, whose age was in the right ballpark area. 'It makes all the difference,' she kept averring, 'when a man's of similar age.' The red rose, a sweet and lovely gesture that I long cherished, proved in the end to be a fatal emotional impasse. It was not just a token of gratitude, it was a fragile declaration of trust – trust in my self-less concern, faith in my disinterested compassion. I found myself in the classic sexual armlock. I could only retain her respect and her friendship by preserving the illusion that my actions were free from lust. And all the while, a French engineer, like a French artist before him, tested the springs of the bed across the courtyard.

Even Paula, plump, bouncy Paula, now in the loose moral guardianship of Fran, added to my bafflement, widened my perspective of sexual failure. How could she, so young, so curiously shaped, so ignorant of eroticism, effortlessly fulfil my most orgiastic fantasies? Even allowing for the air in Liverpool, how had her hormones given her a six-year head start? Were my pheromones malfunctioning? Should I be using Brylcreem?

But her presence in Paris had triggered even deeper, darker worries. Paula was running away, but she knew she was running away, and she knew what she was running from. What was I running from? For months I had told myself and the world that I had a purpose, that Paris was in the scheme of things, that I was here because I chose to be. But all that was left of this grand design was the gloss of learning French. In truth, I was the victim of my own PR. While Paula was running from the Liverpool sex police, I was in hiding from my future.

It was 9.30 on a Saturday night and I was bogging down in another dark night of the adolescent soul. The last of the university bookshops that cascade onto the pavements of boulevard St Michel were pulling down their shutters as I anguished my way through the browsers. The fact that I was on the home patch of the world's leading existentialists somehow failed to help contextualize my crisis of being. I was deep into home truths.

My one true achievement had, I always believed, been travel. My journeys had been a bold, clear stroke on a clean canvas. A positive act. Yet the more travellers I came across, and the more I knew them, the more I came to understand that they were travelling to escape. To travel offers the illusion of untrammelled free will, the immediate application of a decision, the instant implementation of a choice. It offers physical evidence of being in control of one's destiny. Only gradually had I come to realize that travel also offers refuge from the more complex, more painful actions of shaping a life, of earning a living; that it provides endless procrastination, instant gratification; that it keeps the real problems of existence at bay. So strong are the sensory pleasures, the aesthetic joys, of the external world, that the intangible, muddied, long-term rewards of building one's own world fall far short on pzazz.

I turned down rue de Seine towards the river, oblivious of my surroundings. Every day the failures of England came closer, like a ball on a chain, and soon they would be the failures of France. Was my only hope to keep running? I remembered Marrakesh from the summer. People who run and run and run end up in places like Marrakesh. Lying in the heat and the flies. I had come across a heroin addict there, just a few years older than me. In order to survive he sold what I thought, at first, were paintings: red abstracts on a white background. Except that the red was blood. Each time he had his daily fix, he would lay the parchment paper beneath his arm, and the spurting blood would spray across it in strange patterns. He sold these abstract pictures to the tourists as 'drug art'. It was considered chic and retailed quite well. He charged extra if the tourists wanted to watch him at work.

I had drifted away from the crowds now and I doubled back through rue Mazarine and its little galleries, and came out on place Saint-André-des-Arts. I found myself by the fountain where, on my first day in Paris, I had waited for hours in vain for José. I crossed bvd St Michel and went down the narrow rue Saint-Séverin, a cobbled alley packed with ethnic snacks, where at night access was given exclusively to pedestrians. I wandered through the crowds in a forlorn ritual. As the days and weeks went by unchanged, my despair was slowly turning into blind anger. I was feeling angry at the world that night, and when I heard a car rumble up the cobbles behind me I was in no mood to give way.

I knew my rights, I knew the law. All I had not considered was the zeal of the Parisian motorist. The car revved its engine and I ignored it, determined to exercise my will-power upon one small part of the world. The car hooted, and my anger at my whole life boiled up in resentment. On this simple, black-and-white issue of pedestrian supremacy I was not going to surrender, and I continued on my stubborn way along the cobbles.

Suddenly, I heard the car accelerate. Before I could turn, before I could even move, I was hit from behind. As I fell backwards across the bonnet, the car roared down the street. I clung on for some fifty yards, and then the car braked violently to a halt – throwing me into the gutter. I crumpled in a heap. With jeers from the passengers, the car sped out of sight up rue St Jacques.

As I lay on the ground, the inevitable crowd began to gather. I felt stupid, humiliated, hating to be the centre of attention. I struggled to my feet, shaken and shocked. I had landed on my arm, and it was starting to throb, as was my knee which I felt was bleeding. I shrugged off all offers of help, eager only to make myself scarce. I set off alone up the wide, impersonal rue St Jacques.

I was limping, and my hand was now aching badly. The pain

grew worse as I staggered round the dark mass of the Panthéon. I was aware my anorak was torn, my trousers were dirty, and my palms were grazed and smarting. I feared my wrist might be broken. Yet all I wanted was to get back to my room, like a wounded beast to its lair. I was beginning to shake and tremble all over. I avoided passing Mouff Cinq, and managed to turn unobserved into the hotel passageway. I leant against the passage wall in the dark as pain and anger and frustration swept over me.

And then suddenly I did not want to be alone. I wanted a friendly face. I wanted comfort. I made my way through to the courtyard, and looked up. Sherry's light was still on. Hardly knowing what I was doing, I stumbled up her stairs, and tapped on her door.

'Sherry!' I whispered.

Sherry opened the door, still dressed. She looked at me, astonished.

'What's happened?'

I did not speak. I tried, but I could not speak, I could not explain. It seemed my whole life had led to this moment, to this débâcle, this humiliation. I stepped inside her door and, suddenly, uncontrollably, burst into tears.

CHAPTER 26

December was a bitter, frosty month. Urine hissed on ice in the *pissoirs* and the gravel in the parks crunched without dust. The sky stayed blue and the buildings cast biting black shadows. On the *quais* the lovers wore scarves.

Shortly after six one evening, I slipped into Mouff Cinq and ordered a small carafe of *vin rouge* to cheer me against the chill of my room. I was on my way back from a session of highly irregular subjunctives, and there was a pleasing calm to the café at this time of day. It would be several more years before American advertising men introduced the 'happy hour' to Europe and made it a time of hell. I settled down in a window seat, grateful for the subdued lighting and gently massaged by the soft tones of trad jazz. With me was my Alliance textbook, full of wordy gobbets by the French literary great; the qualifying hurdle for *langue, civilization* and subsidized dinners was only a few days off. I was just laying the book open at Balzac when I glimpsed Ulrika through the window.

She saw me and came in.

'Philippe's looking for you,' she said, slipping along the bench to sit by my side.

'Philippe? What's he want?'

'I don't know, he didn't say. Seemed important.'

I was puzzled. He and I shook hands ritually a couple of times a week, if we could reach through the crush, but that was the extent of our camaraderie. Since the night of Helba, the eccentricity of my celibacy had caused him to keep a circumspect distance. Helba herself had not been seen again, but my sexist Sixties assessment of her as a sort of artists' groupie had yet again shown my shaky grasp of women. She had since mounted an exhibition in the heart of Left Bank galleryland – and her gouaches had been the success of the season; Helba was, according to the clippings, 'unique in her vision' and 'passionate in her use of colour'. It was I who had missed the chance to be an inspirational groupie.

'Have you time for a drink?'

Ulrika nodded. 'Please.'

'*Un autre verre, s'il vous plaît!*' I called to Pierre, the rather camp young lad who had survived as barman since that first hectic night. 'You're looking well,' I said to her. She had on tight blue denim jeans that seemed to add three inches to her legs.

'Goodness!' she replied. 'You've been to charm school!' and she gave me a lovely mocking grin. I greatly missed her sympathetic presence in the hotel. Sherry was a good friend, but any opportunity to be kindred spirits had been on hold since the mature twenty-eight-year-old had swept her along the path to bliss.

'How's Gerard? I haven't seen him about lately.'

'He hasn't been about lately.'

'Oh? Why? He's not ill, is he?'

She hesitated. 'Suppose it depends what you call a life crisis.'

I looked at Ulrika, trying to judge the gravity of her remark. 'A life crisis? What, about you and him?'

'About me?' She laughed lightly, and, I thought, a touch bitterly. 'Oh, more serious than that!' She poured herself a full glass of wine. 'About painting!' And then she added, 'He thinks his entire life's work is *merde*.'

'He often thinks that,' I said.

'He doesn't usually slash his canvases with a knife.'

'Ah.' I was taken aback, although I tried to disguise it. In a way, his action was a logical consequence of dedication, and he was a passionate man, but such violence seemed akin to despair. 'Had he been drinking?'

'Of course. He's French! No, his opinion's just the same

253

stone-cold sober. He despises his work. Tourist junk, that's all he keeps on saying. Tourist junk.'

'Guess that makes me a tourist then. I've always really liked his paintings.'

'Me too. You know that. But he won't listen to what other people say.'

I did, just for a moment, allow myself to think the unthinkable. To remember that Ulrika and I were unsophisticated, starry-eyed visitors to Paris, ignorant of art and suckers for beauty. We had always revelled in its postcard romanticism. So maybe we were only one step up the evolutionary scale from coach parties? Perhaps Gerard was right? 'What sort of painting does he want to do instead?' I asked.

'He doesn't know. He doesn't even know what colours to mix at the moment!'

It shocked me that he, of all people, could suffer such a depth of crisis. Once again I thought back, with embarrassment, to the triviality of my approach to writing. And then I thought of Ulrika.

'Is it making you unhappy, all this?' I was able to ask such questions now without any sense of an ulterior motive; there was a post-lust solidity to our friendship which made me feel almost mature.

'Only for him,' she replied. 'I hate to see him so down. But me, I'm fine.' She took a sip of wine, and then casually said, 'I did have another offer, though.'

I was immediately awash with jealousy. 'Really? Who from?'

'Friend of yours.' And the old enigmatic smile reappeared.

'Of mine?' I could not imagine who she meant, and shook my head.

'I was in La Chope last week. And I had a drink with Tony, and his cousin was there – you know, the one with enough puppy fat for a St Bernard . . . ?'

'Paula,' I said, as she struggled for the name. And then, suddenly, I glimpsed her drift. 'Not Paula?'

Ulrika nodded.

'She made a pass at you?'

'That's right.'

'Well? What happened?'

'I turned her down.'

'I guessed that! But what happened?'

'Tony had left, late for something as usual, and I was just sitting beside her, chatting, about Paris and what fun it was, and then this hand appeared on my leg! In the middle of the café, in broad daylight!' Ulrika rocked with laughter.

'She wasn't just being friendly?'

'She was being bloody friendly! I had a short skirt on, and her hand was halfway up my knickers! That's the last time I tell anyone how free and easy Paris is!'

'She's obviously settling in well.' Ulrika just smiled. I was about to ask details of her anti-lesbian procedures when I caught sight of Philippe on the far pavement. He had just emerged from the grocer's with his vestigial evening shopping. I banged on the window and before I could hear more of Liverpudlian Sapphism he was on his way in.

'*M'sieursdames*,' he said to the ether of the almost empty bar. '*Salut, Ulrika! Salut, Barry!*' A lot of kissing and shaking went on and then he joined us at the table, his painfully thin body and black leather jacket giving him the look of a squashed biker. After rapidly downing his first *marc*, he leant forward, wiped his droopy moustache, and rattled a long sentence at me, in which I was able to trap the words '*nouvelle*' and '*encore*'. I looked to Ulrika, acutely aware that whilst I could have managed a high-quality natter with Balzac, I was still not up to the *langue de* Philippe. And I doubted a term at the Sorbonne would help.

'He says have you had news of a room yet?'

I shook my head, adding '*Non*,' for the record, with a rather showy accent.

Philippe spoke again, only more so. Ulrika translated. 'Because he knows of one coming up soon.'

I was both touched and delighted. The grapevine had worked. 'Where? *Où? Combien?*'

The two of them went into a protracted huddle, Ulrika

listening secretarially to the details. On emerging, she said, 'Well, it's good news and bad news.'

'Go on.'

'It's off Montparnasse. Opposite La Coupole.'

'La Coupole?' I was impressed. For generations of fashionable Parisians, La Coupole was the hottest café in town. Everyone from Jean-Paul Sartre to Jean-Paul Belmondo had held court there at some time or other. And though Montparnasse was perhaps past its Thirties heyday, it was still an address of class and charisma.

'It's a *chambre de bonne* and it's six francs a day.'

'Six?' I found it hard to believe. That was a rent reduction. '*Et un franc pour le chauffage* presumably?'

'No. No extras.'

'Really! The heating's included?'

'No. There's no heating. That's why it's six francs.'

'Oh.' I was still quite impressed. Maids' rooms were the ones with mansard windows, picturesquely perched at the very top of old-fashioned apartment buildings. I rather fancied a view of Paris.

'And there's no running water.'

'Ah.' I was becoming less impressed.

'There is a cold-water tap at the end of the corridor. But you mustn't use it after ten p.m.,' she added apologetically.

'Oh.'

'And apparently the room's quite small.' She paused.

'How small is quite?'

'About the size of my old room.'

'I see.'

'But with a low sloping ceiling.'

'Oh,' I said again, beginning to have negative feelings. But then I remembered I was not in a position to have negative feelings. I was only weeks away from having no ceiling at all. '*Merci bien*,' I said to Philippe. 'I definitely want it. When can I see it?'

'Ah, that's the bad news,' said Ulrika. And smiled.

This disconcerted me. 'Let me guess,' I said. 'I've got to share it. With five fat lesbian maids.'

'No, no. Just you.' She hesitated awkwardly. 'But it's being rented by a friend of Philippe. François. And he's not well.'

Philippe appeared to understand, and nodded sadly.

'So?'

'So . . . it's got to be fumigated first.'

'Fumigated?'

'And then sealed for a short while.'

'Why's it got to be fumigated?'

'It's the law. The council does it.'

'Yes, but why?'

'For public health reasons.'

'Ulrika. What the fuck has this friend got?'

'Oh. Tuberculosis. He's giving up the tenancy to go somewhere warmer . . .' She looked enquiringly at Philippe. '. . . *Algérie?*'

Philippe nodded his head again sadly. '*Pour mourir.*'

For the first time I had understood something he said.

Shortly before Christmas, I paid a visit to my prospective landlords, to establish my credentials as a solid bourgeois tenant. This was, of course, a betrayal of my social and political integrity, but, on the other hand, the French middle class did regard financial rectitude as the single most orgasmic virtue – and I was a pragmatic revolutionary. Accordingly, I had decided the public-school card was the open sesame to the conservative heartlands, and once again wore the fading fineries that my father had sent.

The *chambre de bonne* was, as expected, in a rather splendid turn-of-the-century apartment block, and its owners lived three floors below, in spacious, high-ceilinged, well-heated elegance. Somewhat contrary to my expectations, however, they were an elderly brother and sister, both bilingual, and unpompously friendly; moreover, my ingratiating impersonation of a spruce, sports-jacketed chappie was somewhat doomed as the sister proved to be blind. I also discovered it was an interesting blindness, caused by swimming in an unknown African lake when on safari in her twenties. Further hints of unconventionality were provided by the prolific foreign statuary which loomed out of every available alcove; the lounge even had signed portraits of French film stars. Over afternoon tea, the old couple proved to be more cultured, more travelled, and more sophisticated than anybody I had so far met in Paris. The view of the world from my Mouffetard redoubt took several direct hits.

My tenancy was settled without great ado, without any flurry of references. It was simply agreed that I move in at the start of the year. By the time I had drunk my camomile tea and got back in the lift, the next phase of my life was resolved. The only hiccup outstanding was that the room remained as yet too fatally contagious to be seen.

As the last weeks of the year slipped away, and small impromptu festivities enlivened the dying days, I grew sadder and sadder at leaving the hotel, and the street it stood on. Although its future was flock wallpaper and the decorative trappings of a sanitized brothel, its past still packed a nostalgic punch. Adding to the poignancy of departure was the knowledge that there were to be survivors of the *ancien régime*. The puritan fastness of the annexe was not amenable to the modernist movement, and both Dave and Sherry were staying on, their rents unchanged. In the main building, an embattled Tony, reluctant to surrender his view of the square, had calculated that he could survive till the spring. On almost every corridor, the claims of Art and Mammon were being finely juggled.

These last turbulent weeks also saw the arrival of a highly pregnant anniversary. One full year had now passed since the days of Nice. Since the night-clubbing and the jet-setting . . . since the fast cars and the casino . . . since the mammoth meal and the final fond farewells. I found myself wondering how some future balance sheet of life would tot up these twelve traumatic months. Would it show a hidden value to this time – an arcane learning curve perhaps, or a deep-down maturing which would one day lead me to emerge, chrysalis-like, a better, happier, more sexy person? Or was the past year just a worthless journey leading nowhere? So far, all that I could detect was one small fact of symbolic symmetry: then I had a maid, now I had a maid's room.

When Christmas Eve arrived, my second Christmas Eve in France, there was no grand blow-out, no family feast to attend, no champagne toast to drink. So instead, out of a perverse sentimentality, I chose to go to Midnight Mass at Notre Dame. I was a devout atheist, an ecumenical hater of religions, a repressed pisser in communion wine. But Notre Dame was an heroic old building, the most romantic landmark on the Seine, and in the past my enjoyment of it had always been sullied by the unending regiments of photo-snappers, clumping multilingually through its giant portals. Therefore the rare prospect of seeing the ancient nave packed by worshippers and throbbing full-throatedly with Latin refrains gave an emotional tug on my secular heart-strings; I was in the mood to be subsumed by spectacle and ceremony and ritual drama.

What I actually got was an incense-laden variant on the January Sales. Although I arrived well before the ecclesiastical curtain-up, queues ten yards long were piling through the cathedral doors. Where I had expected reverence and tranquillity, there was pushing and shoving. The Parisian matron was out in force, her burly fur-clad figure leading the charge to the prized pews. I had stumbled on the religious hot ticket of the festive season, and my ignorance of Catholic doctrine left me at a disadvantage. In particular, the use of the elbow when approaching the altar caused me constant distress, and once I was even jabbed in the groin by one of the more determined devout. As the scheduled hour of Christ's arrival neared, the scrum of heavyweight believers forced me out of the central nave and shunted me down the transept, where I came to rest crushed behind a pillar with a view of armpits and low-quality toupees. Despite the cold stone and the cold night, it was stiflingly hot. And very smelly. I speak here of personal smells. The proportion of the faithful with serious body odour was way beyond statistical probability, and made a cogent argument in favour of humanism. Whether the tenets of Catholicism lead inexorably to poor hygiene, or whether dirty people are more likely to be attracted to the Church, is of course a question for the theologians, but it made it difficult for me to concentrate on the baby Jesus. Especially as I could neither see the choir nor hear the preacher. Unable to move, struggling to breathe properly, and surrounded by the constant threat of violence, I did not find the spiritual uplift of Midnight Mass was altogether able to match the previous two thousand years' billing.

Nonetheless, it was a novel way to spend Christmas, and I did not entirely regret it. Indeed, by default, it was almost the holiday highlight, since this was a fractured time socially. Ulrika was away with Gerard, Tony was spending a few days with Fran, fending off Paula no doubt, and Sherry had gone home to Lyons with her engineer lover. Christmas Day itself proved a pleasant enough, communal sort of affair – less a lunch, more a buffet. By loose arrangement, a few stray bodies in the hotel dropped by, and a couple of fellow students turned up. One person brought a chicken, another came with cakes, a third supplied some wine; even Dave – running the risk of personal happiness – managed to appear, carrying an armful of second-hand apples. And thus the festive season drifted past in a vague, unfocused way, a limbo land between lodgings. I visited old acquaintances, hung around old haunts, and began to wander down rue Mouffetard as though it were already Memory Lane.

And then, on the last Friday of the year – I do not know quite how this came about – I found myself on a date with a Dutch au pair. A chance meeting in Mouff Cinq one evening had led to talk of onion soup. In the Sixties, onion soup was the most romantic meal in Paris. Cheap and shareable, it was always eaten in the early hours, a bonding experience at the end of a stroll through the mayhem of the Paris meat market, the produce-packed les Halles. Kiki – a nickname of impenetrable origins – was new in town, and this was a tour she much wished to take. She was nineteen and a little gawky – as with so many Dutch women, she had a slightly unnatural tallness, as if raised by intensive cultivation like the tulips – but her frizzed hair looked exciting and I knew that the farther north one went, the freer the love became.

It was shortly after midnight when we slipped out of the bar and set off through the quiet back streets to cross the river.

Just when the city is considering sleep, les Halles, a cathedral of iron, the belly of Paris, comes alive. Within its vast maw of echoing girders, a phalanx of trucks nightly unload the foodstuffs that feed the six million appetites of Paris. From all over France, every specialist taste of the nation slowly winds its way to the arc-lit caverns at the heart of the capital. Or used to. Because, like Covent Garden, les Halles is now no more. Les Halles has been rationalized to the suburbs, defeated by Pompidou. But for over half the twentieth century, in the dead of the weekday night, the grinding of gears, the cry of the porters, the frenzy of the buyers, the smell of the produce, all made this improbable place a Mecca for the adventurous tourist, the insomniac party-goer, the slumming smart set, the onion-soup lover.

My troubled nights had brought me here before and so, with Kiki close behind me, shy and a little giggly, I was able to flesh out the role of a man-about-town. Together we dodged the lorries and the trolleys and the forklift trucks, and she wandered like an awestruck alien amongst the mammoth stacks of farm-fresh vegetables, gleaming unreally in the bright white light. This was a man's world, almost a time-warp land of sweat and swearing, and as I led Kiki slowly round the mounds of market goodies, I was not displeased by the ribald, good-natured banter that pursued her, for it made her cling just that little bit closer.

After half an hour spent admiring cabbages and swedes, and the subtler reaches of figs and artichokes and kiwi fruit, we were occasionally walking hand in hand. I decided, with slight dis-ingenuousness, to climax our tour with a visit to the pavilion where they stored the meat. Outside, in the night, clouds of icy mist billowed from the rear doors of giant refrigerated lorries which jammed the street, generators vibrating with noise, while their frozen cargoes were unloaded. Inside, in the cavernous hall, row upon row of huge carcasses hung down on hooks from re-inforced steel rails, whole sides of cow corpses blocking the view like bloodstained washing on a busy Monday. It felt more like an abattoir than a market, more the result of Al Capone than a friendly family butcher. We were gingerly picking our way through the rigid bodies when one carcass suddenly swung from side to side. There was a deafening 'Moo', a rattle of hooks – and a big porter in bloodied overalls grabbed Kiki from behind. She screamed, and hurtled into my arms. And the porter continued on his way, laughing. It was a familiar turn for tourists; as I hugged Kiki, I reflected that its effect was . . . not unexpected.

Over the legendary onion soup, I tried to do some gazing into eyes. We had enjoyed ourselves, and the packed café – everybody from toffs in DJs to slobs in Levis and porters in blood-gunged overalls – was warm and friendly. Kiki had a bubbliness and a wide-eyed innocence which was endearing, yet made her frustratingly inaccessible. Physically, she was open, unresisting and cuddly, yet intellectually, I could not contact her wavelength. Perhaps this did not matter. It was a bad time of night for active brains, and our chat drifted into cosy silences as we struggled with the long strands of melted cheese. We had been gone for over three hours, much of the time on foot, and we were both ready for bed. Whether it was the same bed, I had still to establish.

Paris was silent and deserted as we walked back through the early hours. An occasional pedestrian hurrying home, an occasional taxi slowly cruising, these were the only signs of life in the dark streets. The Right Bank was living up to its reputation for dull rectitude. But then as we reached the Seine, Kiki suddenly squeezed my arm, and pointed ahead.

At the end of an otherwise deserted bridge, a group of people were gathered. My first thought was drunks, but these people were in a straight line. And they were all leaning over the parapet. Staring down. There were only men in the group, and as we drew closer I could see they were all standing perfectly still – in silence.

I looked at my watch. It was a quarter to three. And the only people visible in Paris were standing in a line, leaning over a bridge, in total silence.

Kiki and I hurried to join them. We stood at the end of the line, and we too leaned over the parapet.

The cobbled *quais* were directly below, in deep shadow. Parked on them was a solitary saloon car, facing the bridge. A street lamp from the embankment shone down through the windscreen. Inside, unaware of the watching world above, and naked from the waist down, were a courting couple – *in flagrante delicto*, and fully illuminated.

Kiki and I burst out laughing. The absurdity of the scene belonged to cinema, not life.

The two nearest men rounded on us furiously. 'Shut up!' they hissed, and pressed fingers to lips. 'You disturb them, and *you*'ll take their place! We'll watch *you* instead!' Then, after more threatening gestures, they turned back to their entertainment.

Kiki and I looked at each other, torn between fear and a desire to giggle helplessly. I counted. There were eleven voyeurs in all.

We continued over the bridge in silence. As we reached the Left Bank, I realized our paths diverged. I paused. In that pause, Kiki kissed me on the cheek, said, 'I had a lovely time,' and set off alone for her au pair's bed.

I stood still for a moment, a familiar sense of failure seeping over me. And I looked back at the bridge, and the middle-aged men, and I wondered how many years it would be before I joined them on the parapet.

It was a few minutes past three when I returned to my room. Out of habit, I glanced across the courtyard. To my surprise, Sherry's light was on. She was not due back from Lyons until after the New Year. Her curtains were not yet closed and, as I looked out, the brightness from my window caught her attention. She waved – and then beckoned me over. She was, I could see, still dressed.

I was yawning as I crossed the courtyard, but my curiosity was gaining ground on my sleepiness. Her door was open and she was sitting on her bed when I entered. I saw that under her eyes were the pallid, discoloured signs of tears.

'Not a good holiday?' I asked.

'I've had better.' She graced the cliché with a stoical grin.

'Michel?'

263

'Yes, Michel.'

'What happened?'

'He's being called up.'

'Called up?' At first, I did not understand her.

'Conscription.'

'Oh. You'll miss him.' Even then, her meaning had not fully reached me. Slowly, however, the implications sank in. '. . . But . . . but conscription is for eighteen-year-olds . . . ?'

'Precisely.'

'He's only eighteen?'

She nodded. Too late, I realized that my tone of disbelief was tantamount to ridicule of her. 'He said he had something to tell me over Christmas.' She allowed bitterness into her voice. 'Well, that was it.'

I thought back. 'So when you first met him—'

'—He lied.'

'All that time?'

Sherry nodded again, wryly. 'So much for being able to tell about age!' She sighed. 'It seems you do get mature eighteen-year-olds. Even if they are liars!'

I sat on the bed beside her. I too felt the aftershock of Michel's confession. Months had passed since Sherry's arrival in the hotel. Months during which we had been friends, and I had wanted us to be lovers.

And during those lonely months, all that I, a twenty-one-year-old, had needed to do was to show a little simple self-confidence. Or learn how to lie well.

CHAPTER 27

The lift ended at the fifth floor. There was carpet on the walk up to the sixth floor. On the seventh floor there were just bare boards. A dingy, narrow passage, unpainted and lit by an occasional bare bulb, crept along under the roof; had it been under the ground, it would, one felt, have been supported by pit-props.

The smell of disinfectant began towards the end of the passage. It expunged the stale, faintly foreign, odour of food which clung to the walls, and as I approached the door, almost the last in a sad line of sad, anonymous doors, the suppressed memories of childhood clinics drifted across my mind. I thought it was perhaps proof of a cleaner – until I turned the key in the door, and smelt my new home.

The room was L-shaped, maybe nine foot by seven along its more extensive sides, and smelt like a toilet which had overdosed on bleach. (Would that the toilet had smelt the same.) The floors had been scrubbed, the walls had been scrubbed, the ceiling had been scrubbed, and it seemed the very air itself had had its molecules subjected to a wire brush. I knew nothing of the epidemiology of TB, but it was clearly thought of as a determined germ, likely to defend its territory with a last stand worthy of Custer.

The air was acrid. I held my breath and took a hurried two paces across the room to the skylight, which I forced wide open. Clinging to its rim, I gulped down deep mouthfuls of rooftop Paris air, and tried not to feel negative about my new tenancy. But I had the hypochondriac's view of fatal diseases. Until I had seen the resident bacillus on a microscope slide with a stake through its heart, I doubted I would ever sleep easy. And the choking, pungent reality of the tiny room left me unsure whether to be more concerned by the disease or the cure.

In between thrusting my head out of the skylight for essential doses of oxygen, I took stock of my new lodgings. A quick blink was sufficient. Facing the door was a rail for clothes and a bucket for water; on the right of the door was the roof sloping down to the floor, and a mattress lying beneath it; behind the door, in the only space remaining, was a tiny table and chair. The other fixtures and fittings were a light bulb, a dust-pan and a glass. And that was the sum total of my new world. 'Think garret!' I kept saying to myself, 'Think garret!' as if it were the artist's mantra for salvation. At least the skylight was a nice touch. And it had a panoramic view – though only, unfortunately, of the sky.

It was all a far cry from the front door. Or, rather, the double front doors, where the varnished wood, the highly polished brass handles, the diamond-patterned marble entrance hall and the subdued lighting gave no hint of the decontamination chamber in the attic. Indeed, so imposingly grand was the bourgeois frontage – the small-paned French windows on every floor, the wrought-iron railings on every balcony, the substantial stonework on every inch – that I felt like a threat to public order even when walking down the street. In fact, rue de Cicé was a street seldom visited by strangers since it consisted of only two buildings, nos. 2 and 4; across the road, instead of odd numbers, there had been ten centuries of temples and priories and monasteries and nunneries, with a reworked doctrine to fit each rebuilt edifice. Although very close to Montparnasse, the small street was almost a secret, currently separated from the bright lights and existentialist sinners by the Catholic bulk of the nineteenth-century Eglise de Notre-Dame des Champs and its clock tower. And for much of every day, a sobering religious shadow was cast over no. 4 rue de Cicé.

I dragged my luggage into the room, where it appeared to occupy 150 per cent of the available space, and decided to vacate the premises for a few hours, to allow the outside air to miscegenate with the forces of fumigation. Besides, I too felt the need to interact with the outside world. Or just escape. I now lived the briefest of strolls from boulevard Raspail; in the time it takes to read one of Proust's more periphrastic sentences I could reach my wooden bench-desk at the Alliance. I sensed the axis of my social life was likely to shift.

The new term had yet to begin. But by the coffee machine I found half a dozen Grade-4 Italians, a group whose innate anarchy regularly enlivened the lessons, and with whom I had occasionally spent sunny Sundays picnicking in the Bois de Boulogne. All were southern Italian – Sicilian and Neapolitan – and, true to the perverse rules of poverty, had a reckless generosity. On learning of my improbable new start to life and the year, they insisted that wine should be poured down throats to mark the event; and that the pleasures of Montparnasse should be invoked. I did not resist. Today was a day to relish plush surroundings and ignore the future.

Eventually, with evening upon us, we ended up at Le Dôme. Le Dôme had long been on my hit-list of cultural cafés still to be sat in. Le Dôme had fame and history and artistic legends and a very high quality of drunk, often capable of slurring in blank verse. Even so, with the seven of us squashed round two small tables in almost caricature Latin chaos, we were soon the jolliest group in the bar, adding to the gaiety of nations in at least four languages (thanks to my belief that Spanish was Italian). Every second customer had the body language of an off-duty celebrity, but for a gaggle of Italians in full flow the centre of attention is always themselves, and they provided an object lesson in unabashed animation. They were also great touchers.

I envied people who could touch. I watched them all evening in Le Dôme, Evelina, Riccardo, Fabrizio, *et al*, and they touched with innocence and spontaneity. When I touched people it took hours of advance planning: where to touch, when to touch, how long to touch for, its relation to dialogue, its coordination with eye contact, the pressure per square inch, altogether it was a manoeuvre of military subtlety. And yet, despite such attention to detail, the result was, at best, a puzzling cross between a slap and a grope. Which left me the equally intractable problem of how to get my hand off again. Were Italians taught touching at school? Or were the English a gene short?

It was around one in the morning when we finally spilled onto the pavement of Montparnasse . . . and out of what I realized was now, technically, my local – could I but afford it. Riccardo, the most gregarious of the group, looked upon the night as still young, and proposed that we adjourn *chez moi* with some vino, and wet the room's bottom, so to speak. Unwilling though I was for near-strangers to witness my straitened circumstances, I was even less willing to return to my sad, possibly poisonous, cell on my own. Distraction was what I craved. And so, waving a bottle of cheap red wine, we all went back for a nightcap.

As we walked along the wide, well-lit pavements of boulevard du Montparnasse, its four traffic-lanes at last becoming empty, I realized that already I was missing the narrow, crooked alleys that used to lead me home to place de la Contrescarpe. A sense of anonymity grew as I reached my mansion block. And as I led the way up the bald staircase, along the blank passage, past the stained hand-basin and the single, dripping tap, I knew that never in a hundred years could colour and character enrich my new world.

It was eight hours since I had fled my room. Suddenly rather sober, I opened my door with caution, like a canary sent to test for gas, and sniffed. The dark room was icy. I shivered at its dank chill. And behind me someone went 'Brrr!' in Italian. But the invading night air had conquered, had purged the atmosphere; the only reminder of the room's tubercular past was a hint of over-zealousness with carbolic. For the first time in my tenancy, I felt it safe to inhale.

I clambered over my luggage and closed the skylight. The others, laughing a little tentatively at the squalor, piled in behind, Evelina perching on the suitcase, Carla squatting over the ruck-sack, Marco wobbling astride the typewriter, and the rest standing – or, indeed, crouching – in a huddle. Riccardo forced the cork down the bottle, and the cheap plonk was passed with exaggerated brio from mouth to mouth in a house-warming toast. With foresight, I would have booked the lift for the ceremony, since its official capacity was greater; there is, after all, only so much jubilation one can have in a clothes cupboard.

And so it quickly proved. The high spirits ran out with the wine. After five minutes of small talk and smaller jokes, and failed attempts to find interesting little features to the room, my guests started to yawn. They each complained of unexpected tiredness, and then, after some quality touching, they left me. The day's displacement activity was finally over.

Alone again, I surveyed the squalid scene. Once, in Marrakesh, I had been offered a windowless room six by six by six, with dirty rush mats on the floor, and cockroaches on the ceiling; it was the only time on my travels that I ever rejected a room, unable to face the degradation it represented. And that had been for just one night. Here, my stay had no known end.

I laid my sleeping bag over the bedding for warmth, squeezed onto the mattress below the sloping ceiling, and turned out the light.

I woke early the next day: 0600 hours to be precise, at the first stroke. Whether I was actually woken by the clang of the clock-tower chimes – hidden from view some ten yards beyond my bed – or by the crash of my head on the ceiling when I leapt upright, is a matter for medical debate. As I fell back concussed onto the pillow, and lay vibrating to the sound of the succeeding clangs, my principal concern was the frequency with which L'Eglise de Notre-Dame des Champs celebrated the passing of time. The answer became apparent at 0615.

Unable to sleep, I tried to potter. There was no space. Unable to potter, I tried to unpack. I took things out, and there was even less space. Unable to unpack, I tried to wash. I collected cold water in the bucket and poured it into the jug and splashed it onto my face. Unable to wash, I went back to bed.

At 0815, I decided to go out for coffee. As I stepped from the lift, the concierge emerged from her door, as if alerted by supernatural forces. We had been introduced by my landlord on the first visit. She was a single woman somewhere in her late forties, that difficult French age when one is on the cusp of Mlle and Mme. (To call such a woman Mademoiselle risks implying she is left on the shelf; to call her Madame risks implying she is too old a bag to receive any offers.) I was by now well aware of the mythic powers of the Paris concierge, especially one whose *logement* faces full frontally on to the entrance doors – a strategic emplacement equal to the Guns of Navarone, with the added tactical advantage of net curtains. I was, therefore, in no doubt as to the need for unctuousness and some old-fashioned English charm.

I gave her a broad smile, the one reserved for aunts. '*Bonjour* . . .' and I hesitated fractionally, '*mademoiselle*.'

'*Monsieur*,' she replied, with cold courtesy. I smiled again, wondering whether I should compliment her on something. Her dress was on the scale between neat and frumpy, her hair carefully bunned. As I searched for an opening, she said frostily, 'There have been complaints.'

'Complaints?' I stared at her, astonished. 'Complaints, *madame*?' I repeated, inadvertently transforming her marital status in my bewilderment.

'Six, *monsieur*,' she replied, pointing to a pile of letters in my landlord's pigeon-hole. 'From *chambres* two, three, four, five, six and seven.' Even the non-complainant in *chambre* one afforded little satisfaction as that was me. 'I will also be speaking to your landlord myself. *Naturellement*.' She turned to go.

'But why? What have I done?'

It was her turn to stare, astonished. 'Wild all-night parties, *monsieur*,' she replied, and vanished into her ground-floor watch-tower.

As I trudged out across the marble entrance hall, I reflected that my tenancy was but twenty-four hours old.

CHAPTER 28

My *dictées* had passed muster. As had my loose acquaintanceship with French literature, and my ability to translate the likes of 'if I were to have been born, it was possible I might have come' at speed. The men with pince-nez were satisfied. I and the Sorbonne were to be affiliated. And the French state was to subsidize my dinner.

As I sat in the classroom (or, as we in the fifth grade say, 'lecture room') and listened to the roll call of those destined for '*langue et civilization*', I felt unexpectedly cheered. Although I had always said that an entrée to university restaurants was my educational goal, the word Sorbonne had a glamour, a cachet, a rare academic resonance; it was a word that oozed with learning and scholarship and history; it was also a word I could bandy about in air-mail letters, were I ever to write to my high-flying Oxbridge friends again. Yet, officially proud though I was, I knew I could make few claims for blood, sweat and genius: fluency in French was but the predictable consequence of residence in France. It was not the occasion to puff the intellectual chest excessively.

The real pleasure came from mastering the language, from grasping its structure and its cadences. Had I finished up in Germany, I would have been glottally challenged. Here, in France, my temperament seemed suited to the rising rhythm of the sentences. I was the sort of person who took satisfaction in the delicate layers of the still-extant subjunctive. And now, with my fifth-grade fluency, I was starting to appreciate those myriad interstices of foreign life: the overheard snatches of conversation, the punning adverts, the ritualized street-cries; I even enjoyed unravelling the abuse of drunks.

But also I was much taken by a nation whose press would print learned disquisitions on the state of the language. Indeed, *Le Monde*'s weekly 'Defence of the French Language' read like a rallying call to arms. Consistently to devote a third of a page to tracing the history of a grammatical infelicity or logging the mystery fall from grace of an adjective, was the undeniable hall-mark of civilization, and was to become the fount of my lifelong love affair with linguistic pedantry.

As the professor's recital of winning names, prefaced respect-fully with *monsieur* and *mademoiselle*, came to an end at Yonkmann, I hurried out of the door. I was eager to collect my COPAR card, the hard evidence of my new status, and took the stairs two at a time. I had just spiralled past the unamused bust of the founder on the landing and was halfway down the final flight of steps when I saw, about to come up, a shortish girl with dark-brown hair and olive skin.

Our eyes met. She did not look away . . . and for once neither did I.

Her nationality was hard to decide. There was a Mediterranean feel to her looks, but no Mediterranean style to her movements. Her brunette hair almost reached her shoulders, and she had dark, serious eyes. Her shortness made her seem a touch plump, and created the impression of a bosom rather than individual breasts. She had on a purplish cardigan over a slightly lacy white blouse and heavy woollen skirt, and looked un-fashionable to the point of homeliness. This was an image reinforced by very sensible shoes, in which she moved like a rambler. It was her expression of wide-eyed innocence, simul-taneously brave yet lost, that appealed to me so strongly. Such unworldliness, and such an absence of chic, made her seem safe . . . and cuddly.

We drew level, and the thought of a smile was in both our minds, yet it never quite happened. But each of us had regis-tered the other's presence, and we both knew it. Indeed, I could not remember when I last gave a stranger so direct a look. It was to be a long time before I fully understood the reason why. In that brief moment, I had been confident. In that brief moment, I had achievements to my name. In that moment, I had a sense of identity.

I had only gone a few paces further when I regretted my inaction. And I turned back to look at her. And I found her looking back to me. But in the melée of the changing classes it was too late. The moment had gone.

It took an hour of unsmiling bureaucracy to obtain my card. My daily existence was unnaturally free of rules and regulations, and such simple acts as form-filling unnerved my bowels and fed my paranoid fear of a life back in society. But there was one unexpected pleasure: a passport-sized photo was *obligatoire*. Thanks to murky Gothic lighting and an abundance of facial hair there was no hint of my weak profile and my wimpy grin. Instead, the unblinking gaze of a nineteenth-century sea captain focused on a distant horizon, moral certainties etched in all visible skin. Through the wonders of modern photography, I had become a man with ramrods up his back. After supplying the photograph and some biographical background, I was given a personal number – surely even Kafka was never no. 1,125,634? – and required to nominate a university restaurant for my future eating. I nominated a restaurant just off rue Mouffetard. This was scarcely convenient, but since my mind kept drifting back to place de la Contrescarpe I decided that my stomach might as well go with it; the prospect of rounding off each meal with a liberal portion of friends seemed the perfectly balanced diet. That this decision would also change the course of my entire life was not, as yet, apparent.

It was early afternoon when I took my new textbooks back to rue de Cicé. I was now nearly two weeks into my tenancy but, other than the complaints of bacchanalia, there had been not a single sign of human life-forms to be witnessed anywhere on the seventh floor. (Under advisement from my landlords, I had dutifully shovelled large portions of humble pie beneath the doors of my neighbours; and controlled my breathing during the period of darkness; and obeyed the misspelt notice warning against after-hours use of the water tap.) This eerie absence of the other tenants was not, though, the consequence of a second rampant bacillus, but of a malaise to the body politic. Here, in a mansion block, I had found the true nether world of Paris, the authentic Orwellian underclass. No longer were my neighbours artists who burned their candles at both ends. Instead, they were immigrant workers, on eighteen-hour days, who couldn't afford a candle in the first place. Behind the blank doors lay the Third World, exhausted and asleep. And when the demon clock struck six with the full force of the *1812 Overture*, my fellow-tenants were already at work in the sewers and the dust-carts and the washing-up bowls.

Perhaps my apologies had pacified the neighbours, but they had cut the merest ice with the concierge. Not that she was malevolent. Her life was a constant search for the opportunity to be righteous. And I was clearly an ideal target.

If righteousness has a body language it is found in trimness, and my abiding memory of her is 'trim': trim in build, trim in clothes, trim in walk, trim in handbag; she was a woman without excess or excrescence, a woman whose soul was not only pure, but dry-cleaned and neatly folded. With lazy judgement, I had initially packaged her as the stereotypical spinster, repository of those thwarted urges so well documented by literature. But, on closer acquaintance with her personality, I had come to realize that her real desire in life was not to be a wife, but a widow. Only through a dead husband could she achieve the levels of martyred yet noble suffering that would grant her a moral head-start in perpetuity.

I walked into the empty entrance hall, shaking off the scatter-gun drops of a sporadic sleet, and made for the lift. I did not reach it. With the speed of a presidential guard dog, she was through the net curtains, across the marble floor, and positioned squarely in front of me, resplendent in outrage.

'*Bonjour, madame—oiselle.*' (I badly needed guidance on this matter.)

'*Bonjour, monsieur.*' She took several calming breaths. 'There has been an unpleasant incident.'

'Oh? I'm sorry to hear that.' I realized that I was required to show more concern. 'What, exactly?'

'A tramp!'

'. . . A tramp?'

'A tramp covered in fleas, *monsieur.*'

'Oh.'

'In this very building!' She pointed to a spot near the opposite wall, where the *scandale de* tramp had taken place, and trembled with indignation.

'That's shocking!' I said, wondering what I was supposed to do about it.

'I had to order him to leave!' She paused accusingly. 'And he did not want to go.'

'Did you call the police?' I tried to sound sympathetic. 'You should call the police.'

'He said he was a friend of yours.'

I stopped trying to edge towards the lift.

My tenancy was already hanging by a thread. Visiting tramps were not a plus point. For a second, I considered denial, but rejected it. What I needed was a plausible explanation. I could think of none. I quickly switched to a look of compassion, while my mind raced wildly, trying to narrow down the field of suspects. 'With fleas, you said?'

There were, I immediately realized, better questions. Dividing my derelict friends into flea-ed and flea-less was scarcely a public relations coup.

'Infested! He was scratching everywhere.' Her hands twitched distastefully around her body, deeply reluctant to indicate specific locations.

In some recess of my brain, her movements triggered a familiar series of images. And I began to fear her imagination was not fevered. That perhaps the melodrama of menopause was not to blame. 'This man . . . what was he wearing?'

'A raincoat. A filthy white raincoat.'

*   *   *

Next to the forbidding bulk of the church was a children's playground. This was an age before the advent of the 'adventure' playground, and there were no designer piles of old logs, no used tyres arranged challengingly by social workers. Behind neat railings, freshly painted by the parish, were swings and a slide and a sandpit; today, the skies grey, a patchy film of wet snow smearing the city, the playground was silent and deserted. Almost. In the far corner, alone on a see-saw, sat a distinctive bearded figure, hunched against the cold, and bouncing lightly.

'Didn't think you did visits!' I said jokingly, secretly flattered that he had made the twenty-minute journey from Mouffetard. By some instinct, I felt free to make the first personal remark in nine months' acquaintanceship.

He let the see-saw ground gently. 'It's not really a visit. . . . Which is yours?' Dave gazed up at the mansion block behind me with a sort of detached curiosity. I pointed to the roof space which I called home.

'A garret?'

I nodded.

He scratched forcefully and painfully at his chest, his knuckles red-raw with dry and dying skin. 'I've come to say goodbye.'

'Goodbye?'

'I'm going back to New York. The book's finished.'

I felt an awful sadness. We were not close friends, not really even friends, but we had shared a lifestyle, we had unique memories in common, and I knew I would feel the lonelier for his absence. In any group, one should always be the first to leave, never the one who stays behind, crippled by nostalgia.

'Congratulations! Must have been a long haul.'

He considered. 'Seventeen months.' He scratched again at his sores, with the unrelenting vigour of sandpaper.

As I absorbed his news, my foot resting on a toddler's swing, and flurries of snow tumbling in my eyelashes like wet French kisses, I was not immune to the surrealism of the scene. And yet, such was Dave's monk-like innocence and obsession with God, it seemed that only a symmetry ordained by Fate could

276

have ended his tale in the playground of a Catholic church. The scene would also have been of interest to the Vice Squad ('child molesters by the sandpit again, *Monsieur l'inspecteur*'), and so I persuaded him to adjourn to Le Dôme, for a final farewell drink.

'So, did you create a new moral universe?' I asked over the coffee.

'Hard to say,' he replied, as forthcoming as ever. 'I tried.'

I had hoped that by constructing his fictional world of just deserts, his ethically self-correcting society, he might feel happier. He merely looked more haggard. 'Perhaps New Yorkers are too hopeless a case. Perhaps you should have set the book somewhere like Wyoming,' I said half-jokingly.

'God would never bother about Wyoming.'

So Dave did have a sense of humour. That in itself was a small miracle, as the magnum opus had destroyed his health, and nearly derailed his mind. As he sat back, derelict and scabrous, I was relieved to be in the de luxe surroundings of Le Dôme. It was, paradoxically, its very fame as a watering-hole for the arty, that made it possible for him to sit unnoticed, uncommented upon. In a cheap bar *ordinaire*, he would have received the concierge treatment.

My mind was much exercised by the concierge. I could tell that she had trained as an informer under the Germans, and I feared my every character flaw was being transcribed in a big black book, and relayed nightly to my landlords. Though constitutionally but a humble employee, she had the power of life and tenancy over me, and a scratching tramp was a deadly weapon.

'I was morally in the wrong,' said Dave, furrowing his brow, and sucking the table's spare sugar lumps for nutrition.

'You?'

'I alarmed her. I shouldn't have done that.'

'You could have hit her with a baseball bat, I wouldn't have held it against you.'

Dave was no longer listening. 'Recompense. That's what's wanted.'

'Recompense?'

He nodded, the usual look of abstraction creeping across his face.

'For *her*?'

'Yes. What would make her happy?'

'D'you remember what made Salome happy?'

He ignored me, and pondered. 'Needs to be an act of kindness. Something unexpected.'

An hour later, he and I were to be seen walking back from the market with a reduced-price bunch of gladioli.

On entering the apartment block, we made a show of responsibly banging the snow off our shoes. (In Dave's case, the flapping sole of his boot meant that slivers of ice had to be prised from between his toes.) I was by now aware that all details of entry were subject to the secret scrutiny of Mademoiselle, a woman whose 360° vision preceded the modern surveillance camera by more than two decades.

We advanced upon her net curtains, a concierge-friendly smile on our lips, a dozen scarlet blooms in our hands. As we approached, I suddenly realized that these were the actions required by Dave of his characters. This was the righting of wrongs, the pre-empting of retribution, that kept his God happy, and at bay, in his book. As I prepared to present the gladioli, I realized I was life imitating art.

Mademoiselle only half-opened her door, deeply suspicious at the sight of tramps in tandem. '*Messieurs?*'

I held out the flowers.

'*On veut faire des excuses, mademoiselle.*' I was the spokesman for this ceremony, Dave still not having sullied his thought processes with an understanding of French.

Mademoiselle looked at the flowers, her distrust far from allayed.

I pointed to Dave, apologetically. '*Mon ami n'est pas méchant.*' And then, with the specialist linguistics gained from a knowledge of medical dictionaries, I added proudly, '*Il a l'eczema.*'

Dave smiled at her. It did not somehow seem the moment to explain that he was also a tormented creative artist.

Mademoiselle appeared uncertain what to say. I gave the scarlet gladioli another push in her direction, and offered a big smile of my own.

She looked from one to the other, and then to the flowers. Hesitantly, she too began to smile, and delicately took the bouquet from my hands. '*Merci, messieurs. Merci bien.*' She inclined her head in gratitude. '*C'est très gentil.*' And with a further courteous gesture, she retreated indoors with her gift, her recompense.

She never forgave me. She never forgot the humiliation of being obliged to smile at me, to be friendly, to show appreciation. I was never to see Dave again, to tell him how his grand philosophy for universal happiness worked out in practice, but, for the remainder of my tenancy, the concierge was to acknowledge my presence with a forced smile of limitless suppressed hatred.

CHAPTER 29

The shape of the middle-aged man on horseback was definitely familiar, even in the murky light. I peered more closely.

'It's Napoleon,' commented my new pupil as he guided me down the long hallway, its gloom made vaguely grand by the sepulchral wallpaper. Though little more than my age, he walked with the cautious, delicate tread of an invalid. Pausing a few yards on, by a large waist-high urn, he pointed up at a second huge and grimy oil painting, this time of man and cannon. 'That's Napoleon as well.'

Opening a door, he ushered me into a grand but fusty old salon, as little touched by the twentieth century as was the hall. He gestured to a damassin-covered sofa and I sank politely into its gold-patterned depths. Facing me above a marble fireplace I saw the largest oil painting yet, depicting an endless procession of men struggling through snow – and led by a heroic figure with his sword raised. 'Napoleon on his way to Moscow,' said my young host before I could ask.

The Alliance advert had immediately caught my eye. 'Writer,' it had read, 'seeks English lessons from literary-minded student.' Not since Dr Johnson advertised for a diarist had there been such an appropriate dovetailing of skills. Moreover, the card was freshly tin-tacked, making me a clear front runner. And, as my client base was currently at zero, apart from dear, perennial Monsieur Bareste, there was an added edge to my cultural enthusiasm. I had quickly scrawled down the details and turned to make a fast exit to the phone booth.

A sturdy bottom and a loose purple cardigan immediately caught my eye. She of the olive skin and sensible walking shoes was studying the 'au pair' board. I felt my hands go sweaty, my mind recalling the eye contact which had made my recent descent of the main staircase so memorable. And then I felt my personality drain away, rendered null by the thought of speech. Her back was to me, making the casual-smile option a technically fraught procedure. But if I tapped her on the shoulder what should I say? 'Hi, I recognized your bottom'? I thought of standing around, looking elaborately casual, while I waited for her to turn, but she was taking copious notes. And what if she failed to recognize me? Like a New Man ahead of his time, I was fearful that her definition of pestering might be speech outside marriage. In a funk, a familiar funk, I decided to phone first (after all, it was, I said to myself, the financial equivalent of a 999 call) and then to return and 'bump' into her as she finished. I made my call. I returned. She was finished. She had left.

'There are eight portraits of Napoleon in all,' his unsettling monotone continued.

I felt tempted to enquire if there was one in the toilet. This was not entirely fanciful. Not since Nicole, and the rug dealers of Nice, had I been in an apartment on such an heroic scale and the toilet seemed likely to have a surface area sufficient to re-enact several of the Emperor's favourite battles. 'My grandfather, he has a very high opinion of Napoleon,' added the young novelist.

'It shows,' I said.

He sat down in a high-backed chair beside me, its seat upholstered in the sort of silver stripes which indicate ownership by a good class of backside. The tall shutters were only half-open, and we were seated in a diagonal streak of late-afternoon light, dark shadow lying like a dust-sheet over the corners of the room. His face bore several days' stubble, but it was skimpy, and the skin underneath was pasty. It might have been thought a harmless, if sickly, pallor, but he wore a collarless white shirt, its front stud missing, with slippers and grey slacks, and the effect created was curiously institutional, as if his appearance was decided by an unseen matron. His movements were oddly slow, almost post-operatively slow, and with his awkward politeness, his unpredictable pauses, he stirred memories of some of cinema's great psychotics.

'Are you likely to be deported?'

I found myself staring at him, a guilty smile locking onto my lips. 'Deported? . . . No, I don't think so.' His question had caught me off guard; my passport still lacked the vital stamp of the State, and I tried never to come within handcuffing distance of people in uniform. 'Why?'

'My last one was deported.'

'Your last English professor?' (My status had mysteriously increased in response to the size of the room.) He nodded. 'What was it he did?'

He gave a shrug. 'Who knows?'

A silence fell. This did not feel a propitious start to an introductory chat. In a loose attempt at professionalism, I asked, 'What sort of subject matter did he cover?'

He gazed vaguely into the middle distance, an area where he seemed to keep most of his thoughts. After a while he said, 'I went to England once.' A pause. 'Wolverhampton.'

'Did you like it?'

'I had a pen-friend there.'

'Oh. I see.'

'He kept pigeons. Do you keep pigeons?'

I shook my head.

'He had twenty-three. In a shed specially for pigeons, at the end of the garden. Like a pigeon hotel. His family, they feed them, they clean them, they . . .' He cradled his hands and looked at me expectantly.

'Cuddle?'

'They cuddle them.' He ruminated on these facts, with more than a hint of puzzlement. 'And then they take them in a big basket on a bus. Up to the top of the hills. And then they let them go. . . . And then,' he flapped his hands, 'they fly back home. It is very English, I think.' He seemed both impressed and bewildered. 'In France we open the basket and we shoot them.'

He delivered his avian experience of English folk almost as a set piece, a gobbet of undigested speech, as though the more traditional two-way structure of conversation was too emotionally challenging. In dialogue, his words came regularly to a halt. I tried to kick-start the silences with questions, but his answers were a mismatch, as if our minds were out of synch. I asked what attracted him to the English language, and he gave an account of a childhood Spanish maid whose volubility caused her to spit, often onto food.

Slowly it emerged that Henri – the formality of introduction was a vague afterthought – lived alone with his uncle and his grandfather. Both were retired gentlemen, presumably on the far side of sixty. No mention of closer family was made. I would have put money on his being an only child, or if he had sisters, I was sure they would have died at birth. Henri seemed to belong to an age when consumption stalked the boudoirs.

I wondered about his claim to be a writer. I remembered my own claim. Perhaps he too lived in a fantasy world. Of his work, he said nothing. I raised the question of literature, and mentioned that I read books, but we had no authors in common after about 1750, and the conversation languished once more. He remained unforthcoming about his own prose. It was, of course, possible that he wrote poetry. He had sufficient personality problems to be a love poet, or at least a specialist in rhyming angst. But his silence left me doubtful.

Suspicious, I probed. 'What sort of writing do you do?'

'I've just finished my first novel,' he replied. I considered there to be a strong taste of juvenilia in his statement, and sceptically awaited more details. 'It's being published by Gallimard in the spring.'

All of Henri's failings immediately fell into place. His social inadequacies, his emotional stuntedness, his reclusive domestic arrangements, these were the hallmarks of Proustian genius. Although I had never actually read Proust, I was aware that he rarely went out, even to the shops, and was prone to moping. He was also keen on artificial lighting, had a complexion normally found in mortuaries, and spent an unusual amount of time with his mother. (For mother read uncle/grandfather.) Although not familiar with the frequency of Marcel's shaving, or indeed the style of oil paintings in the Proust apartment, I realized the well-springs of inspiration were unmistakably similar.

To have one's first novel published – especially by Gallimard – was a remarkable achievement, and I could now see that I was dealing with an original, and interestingly eccentric, talent. As a fellow-toiler in the vineyard of words, I was keen to slap on the empathy. I was also intrigued as to what a book such as his might be about.

'I don't know . . .' offered Henri. '. . . Life?'

And that was the extent of the insight I gained. On art as on life, he stayed shtumm. He did, however, invite me to the book launch, and so I assumed that I was henceforth employed.

The rest of the fifteen-franc conversation dribbled away with the light. The hour up, we made an appointment for the same time the following week.

As Henri opened the salon door to guide me back to the lift, I heard raised voices at the end of the corridor. I looked round just in time to see the shadowy figures of two old men disappear from sight. Months of language lessons were to pass before I heard them again, in circumstances not even a first novel could have foreseen.

The second great literary coup of that cold winter week was to be mine. It was not quite a garland *à la Gallimard*, but it was a praise that changed my prose for ever.

My writing had been dormant for over six months. I liked the term 'dormant': it implied a volcano bubbling with words about to burst upon the world. Yet the truth was that I felt extinct; all my Paris experiences just proved that I lacked the key spur of the truly artistic: a dysfunctional family. Boring backgrounds were no place to nurture the neurotic gene, that prime building-block of creativity.

Although scarcely aware of it, I had for some time placed my remaining hopes on a sort of 'creativity thru symbiosis' – a primitive belief system whereby, for example, living next door to Mr Picasso could lead to a Blue Period of one's own, while sharing a toilet with Braque might bring on a facility with cubes. I had also allowed myself to believe that the Latin Quarter's air and water were supplied not by the normal municipal authorities but by the Ministry of Culture. Just the simple act of living in the 5th *arrondissement* would, I told myself, automatically lead to an outbreak of opuses.

It was therefore somewhat ironical – not that I had the self-awareness to notice – that it was the strait-laced, traditional rigours of the French classroom that got my lava flowing. And the applauding critic came not from the counter-culture but the world of pedagogy.

It was a simple enough task, the writing of an essay. Countless schooldays had been filled with the earnest exhibitionism of language being soundly mastered. But to revisit the art of the essay as a quasi-adult, free of constraint and expectations, was to add a laxative to the language. The titles remained as leadenly provocative as ever, but the words could at last lift off.

It was a bleak midweek afternoon, and the least unpromising of the topics was 'A Car Accident'. I knew where the good grades lay, and I was fumbling for an original way of assembling crumpled bonnets, steaming radiators, shattered windscreens and other linguistically challenging car parts into a seamless sentence or two, when I recalled a real accident which I once had the pleasure of witnessing. It was a story of simple but classic lines.

Time and Place: A steep hill, a wet morning, a South London suburb. *Dramatis Personae*: A pensioner in an old jalopy, a young businessman in a new Jaguar. *Plot*: The old man drives downhill at a fast walking pace, a long queue behind him, his old-fashioned indicators managing to signal right and left simultaneously. The businessman overtakes, forces him to a halt, gets out and harangues him on dangerous driving. As he rants, ignoring the pensioner's agitated gesticulations, his parked Jaguar slowly gathers speed, races downhill, fails to take the bend and demolishes the front room of a house. *Genre*: The rare form of Laurel and Hardy and Aesop.

I honed, polished and exaggerated these events into what I hoped was a known literary shape, and handed it on for judgement.

The professor of the course was as quintessentially French as its texts. A Parisian in his early forties, he fizzed with nervous energy and sported expensively chic, lightweight suits. He held few moderate views, and relished the cut and thrust of conceptual debate, with no holds barred on the battlefield of philology. Yet he was both intellectual and sexy, that combination of values regarded as mutually exclusive by the English. I found the daily hour in his company less of a lesson, more of a roller-coaster ride.

Two days passed, two days which were grey and wet and made Paris seem almost provincial. Eventually, at the end of the Friday class, he called me over. He looked at me quizzically through his fashionable steel-rimmed glasses. Then he looked down at my three-page essay, drumming his fingers all the while on the desk. And then he looked up again and sucked in his lips. '*Eh bien*, I have had the pleasure of better French, but this,' and he held the pages up, 'is the funniest essay that I have ever read!'

His words were still doing the rounds of my brain when I left the building, still occupying my thoughts as I splashed through the dark, emptying streets to my 1F40 dinner. I was not just lapping up the plaudits, I was posing probing questions about my genre, wondering about my innermost prose. Was there a humorist trapped inside this unhappy body? Was my style out of touch with my karma? I remembered my sparse inspirational moments, and their short life. Maybe I had the wrong literary role models? Perhaps, after all, I was not meant to be a macho travel-writer? Perhaps I should try to be, say . . . Hemingway with jokes?

It was not a displeasing prospect, and I felt unusually upbeat as I neared my feeding station, the Centre Universitaire Albert Chatelet. This was a bleak, squat glass-and-concrete building, as carbuncular as they come, but it had the bonus of being a short alley's walk from the lost joys of Mouffetard. It enabled me to be a visiting, part-time Bohemian. As I approached its drab entrance steps, my card in my hand, I noticed that a young woman was approaching the steps from the other direction.

A neon light shone briefly down on to a familiar face . . . and I realized with a quickening heart that some kind quirk of fate was about to offer me a third, and final, chance to master the word 'Hi'.

CHAPTER 30

Our feet hit the first step together.

'Hi!' It was a confident 'Hi!', an unforced, outgoing 'Hi!', a friendly, smiling, natural-sounding 'Hi!', which betrayed no hint of nerves or planning. It was a 'Hi!' which made me wish I had managed to speak first.

The accent was American but the teeth came from somewhere else. The wide stretch of her smile – stretched by some secret insecurity – left few molars to the imagination. But hers was no conventional rectangle of dull dentures; her lips (full lips, for the record) curved up and away to expose the type of gleaming white teeth I had last seen clutching a rose in *Carmen*. It was also a mouth full of humour.

'Hi!' I sighed inwardly. As bloody ever, the safety of P to K4.

Our hands pressed on the plate-glass doors together. And together we crossed the crowded threshold. By dextrous adjustments of my pace, we were still accidentally together after climbing two flights of stairs and traversing a foyer. We entered the cafeteria neck and neck.

I had yet to try out any additional words though: cowardice made me keen for my close presence to retain the escape clause of coincidence.

I nudged my tray against hers as we edged our way along the self-service display. The university café echoed to the din of cutlery and colloquy; a large, impersonal eating area, its idea of style was well-lit Formica. Its student food, however, deserved a professorial rosette; the four-course menu options showed a quality and variety sufficient to keep Monsieur Bareste in conversation for a full week. Indeed, even I, who prided myself on being an avant-garde eater, quailed at its more eclectic riches.

'I see neither of us are into brains,' I remarked jocularly as we neared the till.

'Sorry?' A look of bafflement was crossing her face.

I pointed hurriedly. 'Brains.' And added, 'The last food frontier.'

'Ugh! Is that what those were?' She looked more closely at the curiously humanoid contents of calves' skulls. 'How d'you eat them?'

'Rifle and fork!'

'Oh, that's disgusting!' she said. With a broad grin on her face.

There were few free tables, and the laws of logic, for which I transparently held no responsibility, began pointing towards a dinner *à deux*. We found a plate-strewn Formica-top near the bleak expanse of windows, which offered us a rain-streaked view of the concrete bollards in the alley below. We cleared a space and emptied our trays. As we sat down, she showed her teeth again and said 'Hi!' to a tall man in jeans and a white T-shirt at a neighbouring table.

'Who's he?' I asked before I could bite my tongue. It was an all-time speed record in the history of jealousy. I managed, I think, to disguise the paranoid undertow, but it was a prophetic slip. And I was reminded yet again of the insecurity that was the leitmotif of my life.

'I'm not quite sure,' she laughed. 'I seem to be saying "Hi!" to everybody these days. Since I did a journalism course.'

'You're a journalist?'

'No. I've just got a piece of paper saying I've done the course.' She laughed again. 'I'm a bottom-wiper right now. Baby bottoms. Probably a more honourable occupation!'

'Au pair, you mean?' I didn't mention the sighting at the noticeboard. I wanted to seem perceptive.

'Well . . . brat-care's what I call it.'

'Nice family?'

She considered. 'Suppose so. They don't beat me with a

hairbrush or anything. Still, I just visit, I don't live in.' It felt a touch too inquisitorial to ask where she did live. 'But then,' she looked at me, 'how do you define a nice family?'

This seemed an odd remark – and it was awaiting an answer. '. . . Friendly?' I suggested.

'Yes, but isn't it a social institution? With internal dynamics, and power struggles, and conflicting interests? In what sense can it be "nice"? Or "friendly"?'

'Oh, I see what you mean!' I said, my bewilderment total. I had the feeling I had been hit with a Tripos paper in a subject I hadn't studied. 'Yes . . .' I fell into silence, hoping this would pass for thought.

'What's *your* family like?' She put the question with touching curiosity, suddenly very young and intense. I tried to be rigorously honest, yet not disloyal. And eventually I said, 'I don't think of us as a family.' Astonishingly, I had never realized this before. 'Just me; my mother; and my father.'

I could not remember when I had last talked about my family. I certainly could not remember when I had last been asked. The thought of my parents, home alone, with just my postcards for company, was kept in a part of my brain I rarely accessed. Her curiosity stirred unease: the precipitate nature of my departure muddied all my memories of home. I was not sure that my behaviour reflected favourably upon me – even when called a *rite de passage* – and so I spoke to her at unnatural length about the Englishness of the privet hedge, and the social *sine qua non* of our net curtains.

'Sounds like another project for Margaret Mead!' She added the last of her artichoke leaves to an untidy pile and smiled.

'Yeah, I guess!' I smiled back. Who, I wondered, was Margaret Mead?

'I've got some spare family going, you could have some of mine. I found another twenty-two last year!' Not surprisingly, she had my attention. 'I came over for a tour of my roots.' And she went on, 'I'm second-generation huddled masses – my father left Italy in the Thirties. So I had this list of long-lost Guiseppes to look up. The goat-herding side of the family!'

'Anyone still remember your father?'

'In his little hill-top village? Just about everybody! Half of them still burn candles for him. Baffling really – one brother makes it 4,000 miles, the rest don't get further than a hundred yards! It's like they sat in the bar on the square for half a century. Waiting for civilization to arrive.'

I knew the feeling. 'Must have been very emotional, to turn up as you did?'

She nodded. 'And slightly unreal. Like a past out of some dream. Plus endless hospitality I kept feeling I didn't deserve. And lots of wizened old ladies in tears, tugging at rosaries. I felt like a dummy run for the Virgin Mary!'

She laughed at the thought. Indeed, she punctuated her conversation with laughter, not a nervous laugh, but a richly humorous laugh, a laugh that said life was seen in perspective. And that here was a woman with hinterland.

As the clatter of dinner grew muted and the seats around us slowly emptied, I learned that she came from the rural part of Pennsylvania; that the houses in her avenue had white palings and porches; that the train to town had an old-style dining-car and a black conductor in uniform; and that her uncle, although only 5'1", had shaken hands with President Kennedy, and kept a photo of the occasion in three different rooms.

When it came time to leave, fate had one further, final nudge in reserve. Her hotel was on my route home. Not to share the intervening pavement would have been perverse. So I accompanied her. And after fifteen minutes' walking and talking we felt there was still enough chat in us to last a coffee in a café.

Her hotel was one minute from boulevard St Michel, standing on the early part of rue de Vaugirard as it leads from the Sorbonne to the Jardins du Luxembourg. The flasher, brasher cafés of the Latin Quarter did not match the mood I had in mind. Conversation is a delicate flower: a change of location, a change of liquid, a change of social soil, and one's sentences can wither and die; even robust jokes can wilt in the wrong light. So we carried on down past the hotel to the street corner where, opposite the park, Au Petit Suisse had been tucked since 1791.

Its shuttered frontage of drab brown made little concession to fashion, but its galleried interior and its vintage cartoons and its large framed mirrors implied a far from prosaic past. Across one road stood the Théâtre de l'Odéon, across the other road stood the Senate, and I always liked to assume the clientele was a heady mix of actors, artistos and artisans. This was not a mainstream café, with tables in manicured lines, but a cosy, haphazard establishment, which, I told myself, conferred interestingness on its customers.

We climbed upstairs to the small gallery which overhung the bar. From here, through the railings and the rising haze of tobacco, one could gaze down on the regulars below, and treat their animated drinking as a free floor show.

'I hardly ever seem to be in my own room these days!'

'Is that good or bad?'

'It's expensive. But I'm finding my place a bit too cramped for comfort.'

'Sounds familiar! You can touch all four walls without moving, can you?'

'No, it's not that. It just wasn't designed to have a Biafran refugee in it!'

At this point the waiter arrived, prompt to a French fault, and her words were left dangling absurdly in the air, like a conversation that had escaped from another table. We ordered a cappuccino and a tea, and while she struggled to convey her requirement for milk not lemon, I tried to imagine what her role in the Nigerian civil war might be. No doubt Danton and Marat had had similar discussions in the bar when it first opened.

'So how come you've got a refugee in your room?' I asked as soon as the waiter left.

'Good question!' She laughed. 'I sometimes ask myself that!'

'Are you hiding him?'

'Her. "Princess of the Shining Stones." No, I'm not hiding her. I keep urging her to go out more. See the Eiffel Tower from the top. But . . . ! Her parents definitely appear to be missing, and no-one knows whether it's down to genocide or the sorry state of Nigerian mail. So she's not exactly bubbly. She divides her social life between the Poste Restante and the toilet!'

'Oh, I see . . .' I liked her throwaway cynicism, if only because it was unconvincing. 'What was the princess bit?'

'Some tribal title. She comes from what you English would call a good tribe.'

'She rich then?'

'Was. All she's got now is luggage – and it's all in my room.'

'Oh.'

'Don't misunderstand me. She's lovely. Really. Though I sometimes wish she was a bit shorter. She's 6' 1" and takes up an awful lot of the bed. Besides which her bangles make a racket whenever she has a nightmare, which is often.'

I found myself wondering if I would make such sacrifices. At least my house guests had not been that traumatized.

'Has she got any Biafran friends?'

'Not that she's spoken of. Not here.'

'What about other friends?'

'I don't think so. She's quite new to Paris.'

'So how do you know her?'

'I don't.' I looked at her, confused. 'Well, not really. I met her at a bus stop. And I . . . er . . .' She gave a huge, slightly embarrassed grin. 'And I said "Hi!" and . . .' She giggled, and I laughed as well. I felt a brief closeness, the pleasing warmth that comes when the cause of common laughter is understood and unspoken.

Below us, in the well of the bar, the serious drinkers were getting jolly, among them some raconteurs whose windy eloquence suggested that actors were afoot.

'I could have ended up in Nigeria,' I said, 'when I was travelling.'

It was true. It was one of the great 'what ifs' of history. When I had finally arrived at Tamanrasset, bursting with French vocabulary, I had been so mesmerized, so overwhelmed, by the beauty of the desert, that I had resolved to continue on, on across the wildest, bleakest part of the Sahara . . . until I reached the heart of Africa. And thus I would have gone beyond the point of no return, for Africa changes people for ever. In that vastness, that wilderness, the never-ending lure of land yet to be explored would have kept me moving compulsively onward, a brave, lone figure in the infinity of the Dark Continent. Unfortunately, I had forgotten to get the necessary visa. And so I had to come back. But I often wondered – I wonder still – what if . . .

'So how many countries did you go to in all?' she asked, as I modestly outlined my actual travels.

'Seventeen. As far east as Palmyra, as far west as Agadir, as far south as Tamanrasset, as far north as . . . Paris.'

'That sounds a lot.'

'Six different Arab countries and Israel, and ten different Greek islands, and the Black Sea and the Red Sea and the Sea of Galilee and . . .' I gave her a more detailed run-down of my wanderings, spiced with accounts of Albanian border guards and active volcanoes and journeys on camels. She listened for some time. Then, just after I had completed the tale of the Moroccan currency smuggler and his decoy – always a winner in my experience – she spoke again.

'Why do you travel?' she asked.

I found this a curiously naïve enquiry. 'Excitement. Adventure.' I laughed. 'To see the world.'

This didn't seem to be the right answer. 'But being on the move all the time,' she persisted, and here a note of concern entered her voice, '. . . don't you ever find it gets in the way of exploring the self?'

I hesitated and slowly spooned the remains of the cold froth up from my cup while I tried to look thoughtful.

'What I'm saying is, at our age only by rooting ourselves in a personal reality can we make objective judgements on our identity, right?' She leaned forward. 'Don't you think if one's being constantly zapped by random phenomena, one has no yardstick by which to arrive at a true sense of self?'

For the second time that night, my brain went into free fall. Aware that there are limits to the useful deployment of the pause, I issued a holding statement. 'I've not really thought of it in those terms before,' I said.

I sensed that she was disappointed in me. Although I greatly wanted to remedy this, I was hazy about how. I tried to think of something interesting I could usefully say about my sense of self, but I drew a blank.

'Things are very different now, of course,' I said. 'I've stopped travelling.' And I edged the conversation on, towards the safer shores of Paris and the Parisians. It was a fortunate choice. The French were still a rude, hyperactive mystery to her, and she was keen to have them explained. I was the senior resident by nearly six months, and my time in the city had given me a small nest-egg of witty, insightful observations, which I liked to deliver to newcomers.

So I used the occasion to recount, in hyperbolic detail, my definitive story of the French character: the axeman, the Citroen and the people's tribunal. Its ingredients of fiery, theatrical violence and disputatious intellectualism went some way to explaining the French Revolution – and it was also very funny. As I told of the libertarian impulses argued over in the gutter and described the axe wavering in the air, I not only struck a chord in a Democrat heart, but caused a deep, almost nasal, laughter to gurgle helplessly up from her shaking bosom.

I had always told stories, I had always been partial to anecdotage, but this time, as I observed my apparent power to amuse, I kept rehearing the comment of a few hours earlier, kept replaying the judgement in my mind. My faltering claim to a writer's calling had rarely convinced me, had often felt phony. But perhaps I had always ignored the obvious. Perhaps I had simply to commit the jokey bits of me to paper.

The rising smoke wreathing the gallery had reached the fug levels of a jazz club. We had been together for longer than a casual coffee. The time had come to leave. She had studies to complete, I wished to indicate I led a busy life. The short evening had, I judged, been a reasonable success; I had steered clear of *faux pas* and, apart from a systems failure in the abstract thought department, had given the impression of a passably together young man. We stood up to go. As she came round the table towards me, I quickly pulled my old anorak off the back of the chair, flung my woolly scarf casually up and over my shoulder

. . . and accidentally flicked the half-full china milk jug off the table, through the railings, and down twenty feet to the bar below, where it narrowly missed killing two leading actors, showered the prime-time clientele with streaky white blodges of long-life milk, smashed loudly into lethal pieces, and reduced the rest of the happy café to a sudden, shocked silence.

I walked back home along rue de Vaugirard, the padlocked park on my left, and as I did so the black, empty stretches of echoing pavement prompted the very same sadness that Hemingway had written of half a century earlier. This was the route he too was forced to take when afternoon tea with Gertrude Stein lasted beyond the hours of daylight. There were few shops, few signs of life here, only shadowy railings, impersonal buildings and the institutional anonymity of the Senate, its entrance arches guarded by watchful, suspicious sentries of the State. It was an unwanted, lonely detour late at night and it seldom failed to stir an ugly bleakness in my mind. But tonight it was, above all, a walk I resented.

A full year had passed in celibacy, and for all that time I had lived in a lover-friendly community of sweetly decadent charms. Now, when heady with the first faint hint of romance (we had exchanged names upon parting; hers was Theresa) I found myself the hapless tenant of a drab, dispiriting room, in a world deeply hostile to visitors. Within my four rice-paper walls, just to talk was an act of hooliganism, and the sound of even the lowest-octane orgasm would mean instant eviction. So I found it uniquely fickle of fate to have sent into my life a woman whose living arrangements were even more pernicious than mine. I now had the possibility of a partner whose room and bed were shared with a distraught, agoraphobic, female giant with loud bangles, a situation that precluded all known courtship rituals.

As I turned down the silent rue de Fleurus, instinct told me this might be a late-night walk which could well become familiar.

CHAPTER 31

Over the next few weeks we had a lot of hot drinks, and talked a lot in cafés.

From that very first magical Alliance moment when our eyes had met in a shared lightbeam, I had no doubt that I was experiencing the handiwork of Destiny. Destiny, however, appeared to be one of the very few concepts in which Theresa showed no discernible interest. As indeed, were magical moments. All other mysteries of the universe, though, had her keenest attention.

As a consequence of her course in journalism, she not only said 'Hi!' a very great deal, but also 'Why?' and 'How?' and 'Who?' and 'What?' and 'Are you sure?' Only the Internet would have satisfied her. But her conversation was not marked solely by a taste for heavyweight thoughts. She also had the American birthmark of innocence abroad, first made official by Mark Twain, and did not flinch from the most elementary of questions. 'Where is Germany?' she would ask. Or, 'What is the point of the Queen?' I had rarely met anyone so unabashed by fears of foolishness, and I found it disturbingly un-English.

Indeed sometimes, as the days and the drinks went by, and we tried to unravel each other's personalities, it seemed we had scarcely a single trait in common. Where I was inhibited, she was open; where I was cautious, she was spontaneous; where I was deferential, she was a free spirit. The irony, alas, was that until we met I had been much given to describing myself as an open, spontaneous free spirit.

Greater than our differences, though, and more enduring than our disagreements, was the single trait that we did have in common. Terror. The terror of returning home.

'The moment I get off that plane, I'll be Pop's little girl again,' she said ruefully one night in Le Boul'Mich. It was gone twelve, and we were almost the last customers left in its big, brightly-lit salon. 'His precious *bambina*!'

It was the voice of another girl, a girl still trapped by childhood. And I recalled that strange first impression of her, of someone brave yet lost, with a bubbly innocence that only part disguised her struggle to be strong. 'I've got a father who believes in the old-fashioned virtues,' she explained. 'Like patriarchy! And rearing daughters who want to bake apple pies. And like to talk about bridalwear.'

'Not strong points of yours?' I enquired with a smile.

'Nothing about my life is a strong point where my father's concerned!'

'Oh?' I said.

And her teenage years came tumbling out. It was the timeless tale of rebellions and traumas, but greatly compounded by being an only daughter – a bright and wayward only daughter – and having an immigrant father – an Italian and staunchly Catholic immigrant father. Even a course in journalism had been a much fought-over pact with the devil. This was a far cry from the anaemically English and undoctrinaire landscape of my own upbringing. Caught in the crossfire of the American Dream and the Italian heritage, she was kicking and scrabbling and logic-chopping her way to an independent state of mind. But blocking her free-thinking path at each turn were the peasant superstitions and grizzled dogma of her father, whose possessiveness and zeal for purdah were rigorously backed by the Pope. And beyond her autocratic father stood her Republican brother. An exemplary convert to the American Way, the twenty-five-year-old was a God-fearing chauvinist and righteous moralist, whose prestige as an advertising executive had recently enabled him to secure the soap-on-a-rope account.

But other than trauma there was little similarity to be found in our petty post-adolescent crises. Hers was not the fear of disappointing her parents by failure; hers was the fear of threatening her parents by success. Nor had anyone ever classified her as a drifter: most had complained she was too darn bull-headed for the boondocks of Pennsylvania. And neither, strangely, had she fled the country; indeed, she had been sent, reluctant and resistant, to visit the Old World. 'I don't want to go!' she had cried on the tarmac. 'What is there for me in Europe?'

It was to have been a short visit: a few weeks' holiday to steep herself in her roots and her relatives. Perhaps, for her parents, it was a subtle way to narrow her horizons (See Naples and Marry?) or perhaps, for her father, it was nostalgia by proxy. Whatever, it was a miscalculation. The seductive reality of independence took its age-old hold and, on the day of the return ticket, her parents had received that familiar filial equivalent of the Dear John phone call.

Her face tightened at the memory. '"A year", I told my Pop. "I'm not coming back for a year".' I wondered if her father had begged like mine. But before I could speak, she had pulled on her scarf and stood up to leave. The café was long closed and the waiters were stacking the empty chairs. 'I've just got to last till June, that's all.'

We left the café in silence. As we walked the short distance back to her hotel, her words swirled uneasily around my mind, their meaning only slowly settling into shape. And as understanding glimmered, I began to see her anew. This was not a year out to enjoy her freedom. This was a year out to prove her freedom. Young boys go to war and kill other boys to prove that they are men. Theresa was serving her time overseas in the au pair corps, hoping, praying, that the calendar evidence of her willpower would finally, and lastingly, upgrade her from *bambina*.

Her arm in mine, we were each prey to deep private thoughts as we walked along the almost deserted pavements. As we passed the darkened forecourt of the Sorbonne, its three hundred years of student history seemed to bestow a reassuring context upon the angst of young life. In the shadows of rue de Vaugirard, Teri squeezed my arm. 'Not the most mature way to prove I'm an adult, is it?' she said suddenly; and gave a short laugh.

I shrugged, not feeling an expert on maturity.

'Sometimes I think I should just pack up and go home. Hardly a smart career move, knowing how to say "goo-goo, diddums" in a second language. All so as to show I'm a big girl now.'

Three thousand miles from her home, I did not find it easy to understand how somebody so alive, so apparently in control, could still be thrashing around in the thralls of family. But I said nothing. I was hurt that the thought of leaving me had failed to figure in the scheme of things. Admittedly, with only a week or two of mild interfacing between us, I had little more claim on her than a rather regular postman, but to my way of thinking – and I thought as someone with a life-long backlog of testosterone – we could soon have the basic building blocks for an *amour fou*, which was widespread in France.

The large flagstone doorstep of the Hotel de Luxembourg came into view, the traditional site for the end of another evening together. All of a sudden, the infinite time of Paris seemed short: come June, the step would be empty. Teri's words continued to resonate.

We had our hug. And then we had our kiss. It was a regular, but still curiously circumscribed, kiss. Despite the warmth of the passion she brought to everyday life, her physical passion always seemed for some reason to be withheld, muted, as if strained through muslin. I pressed my lips harder.

She pulled away. 'I have to give the kids breakfast tomorrow. I must go.' And she leant on the buzzer, and was gone.

I set off on the trek home, much exercised by the thought that any day could be our last, that any moment the tug of home might triumph. Her warm, oddball presence the far side of a milky tea had become the high spot of my days. She seemed to have both a moral seriousness, for which I blamed the American Constitution, and an irrepressible levity whose tone would have interested the Committee for unAmerican Activities. Her breathless late entrances, and her blithe accounts of serial way-layings by midgets/binmen/opera singers/exiled Russian counts, made her a companion like few others. Indeed, that evening, even as I felt excluded by her words, I was gratified to be chosen as her confidant. The sudden prospect, therefore, of café conversations for one made the future seem a soulless place.

Fortunately, a few days later, her father rang from Pennsylvania, and furiously insisted she return forthwith. This was exactly the provocation required and Teri, in floods of angry tears, proclaimed she would sooner die in Paris. Over the months that followed, her resolution to last the year would waver occasionally, but her father continued to telephone regularly and the crisis was always averted.

The half-drawn brocade curtains, the dust-filled daylight striking the gilt-edged mirror, the hard Louis Quinze chair at right angles to the soft damassin-draped sofa, the creaking conversation between pupil and professor: week after week, the routine had not varied. Then, one mild afternoon, I arrived to find Henri in a suit, and with a collar attached to his shirt.

'I have ordered a taxi.'

He did not say where we were going, but as we juddered down from the apartment in the prewar lift he added, 'I want to learn the vocabulary of death.' An elderly lady in a fur stole, the staple customer of expensive cake shops, was also present in the lift and I did not immediately pursue this remark. As we reached the lobby and I struggled with the highly sprung concertina-gate, I found myself wondering about his childhood.

I had never been in a Paris taxi before. Outside the apartment block a Citroen DS was waiting, the seminal car of the Sixties whose headlights went round corners while the rear passengers machine-gunned the police. The driver gave a subliminal nod, and continued to chew like a man auditioning for a tough Western. We slid silently across the back seat. Only when the car raced off did the day's mission become clear; only then did I learn, from Henri's instructions, that we were headed for Le Cimetière du Père-Lachaise.

I had heard of the famous cemetery, but had never been drawn to a tourist tour of the dead. I knew that Oscar Wilde was buried

301

here, and that heterosexuals were represented by Abelard and Héloïse, but this was the extent of my necrological knowledge. I vaguely thought of the cemetery as the French answer to Poets' Corner, except that – in keeping with their grandiose national view of *La Culture Française* – it was not a corner but forty-four hectares.

'Miles and miles of dead!' said Henri with unusual enthusiasm, twitching his head at the ramparts.

We stopped at the main cemetery entrance, opposite the cemetery hotel, and walked in past the cemetery bookshop. A manicured cemetery boulevard and a sombre Monument aux Morts lay ahead. Here were no shades of Highgate Cemetery, no English romantic nonsense about the wild, brambly forces of nature reclaiming Mother Earth and poetically recycling her corpses. In death as in life, in graves as in gardens, the French prefer their surroundings to be strictly formal. Their cemeteries, like their parks, are worlds where lasting happiness is achieved through firm application of municipal regulations. As we made our way into this prestigious landscape of remembrance, the first sight of note was a large, official sign which, reflecting *le fonctionnaire's* idea of the essentials for a successful after-life, read 'NO WALKING ON THE TOMBS'.

'*Tombe?*' enquired Henri.

'Tomb,' I replied.

'*Catafalque?*' he asked.

'Catafalque,' I said.

'*Sépulture?*'

'Sepulture.'

'Oh.'

He mulled on this as we walked past Colette and Rossini. I had learnt not to initiate conversation; it seemed a stimulus too many for his fevered, reclusive brain, and rarely produced a relevant response. Besides, I was paid for silences.

'*Necropole?*'

'Necropolis.'

He sighed. We were climbing steeply now, and he would occasionally sway with the effort. The outdoor air had brought a colour to his cheeks, but it was somewhere between white and grey. Not for the first time, I wondered if he were dying.

'There's a queue, you know. A long queue.' He paused for breath. 'Everybody wants to be buried here. You must have a reservation. Or be very famous.' He moved on. We turned to our right past Géricault, who had presumably queue-jumped the grave on the strength of the 'Raft of the Medusa.' What type of people booked, I wondered? It seemed the ultimate in snobbery, to worry about the social standing of one's corpse. '*Mausolée?*'

'Mausoleum.' Death, I reflected, was not unlike industrial injury. Etymologically speaking.

The roadway started to gently curve through trees, and I noticed it was called Acacia Avenue, thus confirming my view of heaven as a middle-class construct. Henri promenaded slowly along, pointing out occasional dead people of interest, and his clumsy courtesies suggested I was not here as a jobbing tutor but being rewarded with a treat. Even as he talked to me though, his eyes, unrestrained by social skills, darted about the vast cemetery, as if searching for signs of life amongst its 100,000 dead.

'Do you know de Beaumarchais?'

'Yes. Yes, I do.' I had the Alliance to thank for that.

'*Le Barbier de Seville. Le Mariage de Figaro,*' he said, ignoring my answer. We turned off along a small path for a while, and then he stopped and gestured at an ancient grave. 'Pierre Auguste Caron de Beaumarchais. Began life as the son of a man who built little clocks. Made his way into the royal court. Taught the harp to Louis XV's daughters. Married a wealthy widow. Twice.' He spoke with strange jerks of enthusiasm, like a man with an air-lock in his blood. 'Wrote famous plays. Made a fortune. Lost it all in the Revolution. And had to flee the country.'

We moved on again. I wondered as to the significance of his interest in a comic dramatist. Could it conceivably be that Henri's writing was funny? It did not seem possible to ask.

We wandered without apparent purpose for some time, and emerged upon a flat landscape where the dead were laid to rest in a vast grid system of perfect squares and right angles. Here I found Modigliani buried on an 'Avenue Transversale No. 3'; this seemed an aesthetic misjudgement, for surely it was Mondrian who was perfectly suited to a rectilinear afterlife. Henri gazed at this mottled white world of tombs and crypts and crosses and angels and muttered to himself, 'So many questions.'

At each intersection he would pause, as if lost, and we would change direction once more. He was still asking the occasional word of me, still compiling his foreign thesaurus of mortality, but time and again our two languages merged in death. Then, as I bent to look more closely at a smiling young bride in white, her fading features encased under glass and embedded in a head-stone, Henri said, '*Un cortège.*'

'Cortège,' I replied somewhat apologetically, feeling I was not giving him good value. But when I stood up I saw that he was not asking but pointing, and that a procession of Japanese was following a hearse on foot along Transversale No. 2.

'Japanese!' he cried. 'My first!'

'Your first what . . . ?' But already he was hurrying through the tombs towards them. Uncertain what to do, I followed him. He was fumbling agitatedly in his suit pockets, and I saw him struggle to pull something out. As I drew level I realized that it was a black tie.

The suit, the shirt, the search . . . the day began to make some sense. Henri stepped discreetly into the sombre but unsobbing line of Japanese, still making adjustments to his tie. He adjusted his pace to theirs, and looked quickly around him at the hearse, the flowers, the dress of the mourners. As he did so, he caught sight of the confusion in my face.

'Research,' he said in a quiet voice, and then respectfully bent his head and shuffled slowly with the mourners towards the grave.

I was beginning to sympathize with Teri's father. He had a very headstrong young daughter. 'Look good in granite, that profile!' said Tony wryly at his fifth attempt to capture her.

We had stumbled steadily closer. With a certain coy pride, I had, by degrees, unveiled my world to her. We had knocked back *coups de vin* in Mouff Cinq with Ulrika (Gerard rarely left his atelier these days, compulsively painting and repainting canvases that were never seen) and swapped banter with the familiar crowd of after-hours artists; we had promenaded down rue Mouffetard with the gentle Philippe as our incomprehensible, alcoholic guide; we had eaten breakfast brioches at the market café and watched the latest drop-outs strum their stuff for a fistful of centimes; and I had guided her down the still-dingy passages of my old hotel, and taken tea with its denizens, and told the tales of my life and times at no. 5.

Some nights, for a franc, we would join the basement queue for the Cinematheque; the creation and passion of Henri Langlois, this chaotic archive of world film took no account of cinema's fashions. Silent Russian revolutionary, unsubtitled Indian romantic, baffling Czech symbolism, yawning Chinese epic, we would soak up the genres and guess at the cultures, and for two hours sit side by side in courtship's celebrated dark cocoon of togetherness.

So, all in all, sex seemed the next logical step. Admittedly, to me, sex always seemed the next logical step. Indeed, in my state of mind, even after a visit to the chiropodist's with a maiden aunt, sex would have seemed the next logical step. But, in the Sixties, in a city almost permanently on heat, such trivia as logic were scarcely a necessary precondition. In fact, by all recognized European standards, sex was now officially overdue. It could, I reckoned, reasonably be presented as a cultural imperative.

I had for some time tried to extend the frontiers of the good-night kiss. I had done my beginner's best with the roving hand, the pelvic probe, the pressing chest, all the formulaic ploys of lust of which I had heard, but to no noticeable effect. Loose digits were disentangled, straying legs returned, soft suggestions rejected. Even in the darkened doorway, Teri observed the rules of a non-Parisian propriety for the evening's endgame. Such implacable restraint, such attention to convention, accorded ill with an intellect which charged towards gunfire at the drop of a syllogism. I could only guess at the reasons why. But lurking in the undergrowth of her subconscious, I fancied I could detect the hand of God: always a principal suspect in such cases, His twenty years of soul-searing absolutism in the Italian family bosom had left the unmistakable scorch marks of primitive guilt. And it made me wonder whose fingers were on her buttons.

So far, however, my libido had done little more than limber up, limp in the knowledge that full-blown sex would need new lodgings, and thus foreplay had no future. Fully clothed and scarved on a doorstep was not an ambience to encourage the finer points of romance to burgeon. It was Tony, with his male sensitivity to sexual logistics, who offered me the solution. His bed. 'I'm pushing a mop all night. Leaves a love-nest going spare. Reckon it's worth a try? Free use of the tea bag. And I'll bring you a bun in the morning!' This two-shift system had been pioneered in the autumn by cousin Paula, and had led to many satisfied partners before she moved on to his girlfriend's flat in the Marais. (Paula had since returned to England, having been promised immunity from prosecution and the chance to sit her 'O' Levels without mention in the *News of the World*.) In half-light, the room almost achieved the cosy charm of a cluttered atelier – its latest acquisitions, the several portraits of Teri looking decisively to her left – and from the night cobbles below echoed the voices and footfalls of Paris at its most beguiling. I nodded assent.

It was German Expressionist week at the Cinemathèque and Murnau's 1922 *Nosferatu*, the chilling and definitive version of Dracula, was perhaps not the ideal romantic prelude to a night out. Nor was La Gueuze, a somewhat Teutonic and harshly-lit beer parlour, the most obvious setting for softly edging into intimacy. But I was impatient of delay. I had also never fully grasped – indeed, failed to grasp at all – that mysterious, intuitive process whereby petting escalates ineluctably into passion. The idea of one person being able to trigger a seamless series of animal urges in another, without speech or prior arrangement, seemed as dauntingly impracticable as unaided manned flight. Rather, I felt that my intentions needed advance notice, and accordingly had mentally filed the subject of Sex as a key point for the evening's agenda (Item No. 3 after Matters Arising and Budgetary Problems). In the beer parlour I spoke of our warm, enjoyable acquaintanceship; of how we were several weeks into kissing; of the shortage of suitable courtship space; of Tony's generous offer, and the room's advantages, and its proximity to bakers, and of standard practices among similar couples in the *quartier*. I wanted to stress the importance of urgency, since it was the beginning of the month, when the linen was at its freshest, but my feel for tact deterred me. I also mentioned how much I desired her, though I was concerned this might prejudice the objectivity of my case. And then I left my proposal on the table, as it were.

Teri did not immediately speak, and her mood was unclear. Then, clasping her hands around her half-tankard, she leant slowly forward.

'I think every human being has to work out an OK sense of their relationship to the world, however they define that world to be. And for that to be positive it has to come from a deep-down guts area belief in their own kind of essence . . . so as to give the sort of spiritual feedback that will fire up the urge – some would say the duty – to grow as a person in ways which make their existence meaningful to society . . . and which society then values, and reciprocates. So that life's more than a now moment, more than a dead-end continuum. Because belief in the future is our ultimate validation.'

I decided that was probably a No.

'I hope I'm not hurting your feelings?' And she looked at me with a sweet seriousness.

I shook my head. My feelings were unaffected, but my brain seemed to have suffered a lobotomy. I did not speak for some time. Teri was awaiting a response but I didn't know what I was responding to. Bitterness for those missed years at Oxbridge suddenly returned, with an undulled vigour that staggered me. I felt holed below the intellectual water-line, and long-suppressed panic waves were flooding in.

I tried to laugh. 'So. Is that what you say to all the men?'

Irritation twitched at her face. 'Oh, I see. Just going to stick your head back in the sand, are you?'

'Sorry?'

'You can't buy time for ever. Youth is only cute for so long.'

'What d'you mean, "buy time"? I—'

'—And stop pretending you don't understand.'

'But I don't. I've certainly never been called cute before!'

It was an unwise joke. Angrily she snapped, 'I'm talking about not taking responsibility for yourself. Never wanting to grow up!'

I felt the shafts pass through my defences, and the early-warning hairs on the back of my neck registered a bull's eye. I floundered. 'How—how d'you mean?' I asked, trying not to sound defensive.

'Weren't you listening to anything I said?' I just nodded, fearful of questions. 'You don't know who you are, you don't know where you're going, and you think that's a basis for a relationship?'

'That's not true,' I lied, overwhelmed by the accuracy of her assertions. For the first time in my life, I felt myself tumbling into the numbing black void which attends upon that fateful moment in every affair, when the image we front up for the world is challenged, when the pack of cards we call personality is blown down. 'I'm gaining experience of life . . . of the world.'

'It's called living. We all do it.'

'Well, yes,' I admitted. It seemed to me that the prospects of getting sex back into the conversation were almost nil. 'I guess I'm going through a *rite de passage*,' I added hopefully.

She responded with an exasperated sigh. 'I need to know what you believe in.'

I sensed this was the moment to be profound. But I knew – my lack of a degree told me – that profound was not one of my strong points. I knew I had angst, but it lacked depth. And I feared that introspection was just proof of neurosis. 'Lots of things,' I said.

'Your world is a dream world. An escape world. Somewhere for you to hide – from your fears, and your future, and your friends. And even from yourself.'

I could not bear to hear this. I could not bear her to know this. I lunged to another tack. 'And what about you? Aren't you hiding from anything? What about Catholicism? Are you sure the Pope isn't the real reason you won't sleep with me?'

'Catholicism has nothing to do with this!' she stormed, her anger returned. 'Always the stock answer, that one, isn't it? Put it all down to religion. Nice and glib and obvious. Except that I'm not a Catholic. Not any more. And my thinking's my own. I do my own thing.'

Of course, she was right in her criticism. It did make it harder, not being able to blame the Catholic Church – any church! – for her resistance to me. And yet I did not altogether believe her. There was a touch too much vehemence to her denial. And Catholicism, of all ex-religions, delivers the greatest after-shock. I smugly sensed the long shadow of guilt playing havoc with her loins. But in the midst of the onslaught on my ego, and my intellectual rout, I felt in no position to open a second front with allegations of sexual and religious repression.

I backed off. And instead, I strained once more to come up with even the weeniest *Weltanschauung*, or at least some purpose to my life, something, anything, which might justify my existence – if not to me, at least to her. And so, not for the first time, I made inflated play of writerly aspirations; I spoke of the hours at the table and the pounding at the typewriter; and I let loose the inference that the suffering of my ramshackle life was, in some as yet undefined way, for the service of literature.

'And you wrote these two articles when? Over a year ago?'

'Eleven months.'

'And then you just gave up?'

'Well, yes, but I told you why.'

'Seems a little short on determination. Presumably, there's a second magazine in England?' I flinched at her words, but said nothing. 'And you didn't do anything more about it? Didn't kick any doors down? Or ring up any editors at midnight?'

In her response, I recognized not just a difference of character, but a difference in culture. And her words suddenly brought back the memory of Vernon and his rucksack. As early as Day Two of our friendship, he had pulled from its back pocket a polythene-wrapped copy of a children's TV script and outlined

309

the plot to me, all on the transparently improbable hope that my path might one day cross that of Lew Grade in some hansom-cab rank or hotel urinal. In Teri-the-wannabe-reporter I recognized that same shamelessness, and was both awed and embarrassed.

'Why not?' she persisted.

Why not indeed? This was *the* question, the question that I had so long buried, the question that I had not once dared to ask. Why had I stopped writing? Why had I given in so easily? Why was my life slipping away? Why was I doomed at twenty-one? It had taken her anger, her brash American ways, and maybe her affection for me, to force my post-adolescent black hole into focus. Was it the lack of confidence? Or a lack of motivation? Or lack of contacts? Or just idleness? Or even self-destruction? I feared the answer. Somewhere very deep, somewhere that Teri would have called the subconscious, I feared my failure to act was life's proof that I was indeed the drifter so damningly designated in childhood. And that was one truth I could not bring myself to face. As ever, I prevaricated. 'Oh, I just wanted to get some more material first. Soak up the atmosphere, get a better feel for the place. Thought I might write a book about life in Paris one day!'

'I see. Are you keeping a diary, then?'

'Er, not as such, no.'

'But you're taking notes, that type of thing?'

'Well, more like collecting memorabilia, really . . . you know, Metro tickets, café bills, usual documents of record!'

The fantasy failed. I saw disappointment appear on her face, and a distance came between us. I felt I had slammed a door. I felt that we were finished.

And at that precise moment, as if given the power of life by the fear that these really were the dying seconds of the eleventh hour, all my Grade Five hopes of being a humorist, my new juvenile dreams of joking in prose, my thoughts of becoming an Oscar Wilde version of Hemingway, suddenly coalesced in a clear, almost confident, decision.

'Actually, I'm about to start writing some more pieces,' I

announced, aware that all such declarations now rang with the hollowness of lies. 'But in a completely different style.'

Teri looked at me enquiringly.

'Funny pieces. Funny comical. But not trivial, of course!' I added hurriedly, having been recently introduced to the importance of moral seriousness. 'Saying something.'

Teri leaned back. Beyond our drinking bench was lurid stained glass, striving for an unknown ethnic authenticity, and it cast a cheaply celestial, goldy-yellow glow across her features. 'I don't mind what you write,' she answered gently. 'That's not the point. It's who you are. What I want is for you to believe in yourself.'

There was a silence, and I sensed in her words an unspoken reprieve. I nodded my understanding, and picked up my warm beer.

I looked at her radiating light like a medieval Madonna, and smiled at her. 'Tell you what – I'll believe in myself if you sleep with me,' I said. But I said it in the privacy of my own mind.

The remaining weeks of winter were wet. Our friendship continued its tortured way, marked by existential crises in cafés and ad hoc romance in doorways. Although it was a pleasantly undeniable fact that our affection – as measured by kiss-length – was steadily growing, the bond that truly kept us together was dependency. We clung, one to the other, like unsteady drunks in search of support.

Teri was experiencing the darker side of Paris, the bourgeois world. Her days were spent in the suburbs, traditional home to the slave trade in au pairs. For her, *la vie française* meant a mean and snobbish insularity. Seen as a cheap char, she cleaned everything from attics to bottoms. She was only permitted to be part of the family at lunch-times, when in exchange for teaching English to the children . . . she was allowed to watch them eat. And even hunger was not her greatest indignity. The qualifying hurdle for her post had been the English nationality, and she had found herself obliged to duly reassure the family that she was not from that nasty crass and vulgar country called America.

Less deniable – or so it often seemed to me – was the fact that she hailed from a repressed and prudish land, lurking somewhere between America and the Vatican. I suspected that Henry James would have dispensed infinite sub-clauses upon the un-European asexuality of her clothing: shapeless to the point of androgynous modesty, with barricades of buttons and high-water neck-lines, it suggested membership of a prim Pennsylvanian sorority, founded in the age of Victoria. Admittedly these were the purchases of pre-Paris days, but time and again the lifestyle package of middle America cast its un-liberated shadow over the most daily of doings.

Urinating was one of them.

Few French objects are more iconic than the *pissoir*. Circular in shape, black in colour, made from wrought, understandably rusting, iron, and revealing the head, the feet and the cascading urine of its occupants, it once stood proud in every public place. Able to accommodate up to five penises at a time, it was France's most truly demotic institution; even its stale urine smelt cultural. Had *Dr Who* been a French series, the Tardis would have been a *pissoir*.

I had always enjoyed my brief visits. There was a certain satisfying Frenchness to being a semi-public pisser. It celebrated the frank French attitude to the body – even the verb *pisser* is mainstream, free of smut or giggles – and was a rare classless act. So it was without a second thought that I slipped from Teri's side one wet afternoon, and strolled the few yards to a *pissoir* in bvd St Michel. I relieved myself in the company of a policeman, his kepi in full view, and returned to the window-shopping crowds.

To my surprise, Teri had gone. She was a hundred yards off and still striding. She ignored my calls and, when I caught up with her, she ignored me. We appeared to have had a row of which I had not been informed. As I struggled to get a response, she just kept on walking, eyes front, for block after block, reducing my 'Whys?' and 'Whats?' and 'Waits!' to the cheap importunings of a dirty-postcard salesman. And when she finally did stop, it was to round on me.

'How could you! How could you!'

'How could I what?'

'You don't know? You really don't know?'

'How about a small clue?'

'You bastard!'

'Sorry?'

'You don't care that you humiliated me?'

'Humiliated you? How?'

'How? You go into one of those . . . "things" and you don't know how you humiliated me?'

'No. No idea. Did you want to come in with me?'

'You bastard! You just abandoned me, left me standing there, in full view of everybody, while you . . . while you . . .' Embarrassment seemed to triumph over anger and she let the sentence trail away.

'Whilst I what?' I asked, made provocative by my own irritation. She did not reply and turned away. I took hold of her arm. 'Whilst I what?'

She pulled her arm from me, her cheeks tight with fury. 'It's about manners. Good manners. And respect for others.'

'No, it's not. It's about hypocrisy! And bourgeois prissiness! You just want people to think your friends don't have bladders.'

'I just want friends who aren't degenerates.'

'They do empty their bladders in America, don't they? I mean, I'd have thought that would have been guaranteed under the Constitution, the right of free men to empty their bladders.'

'Not on Main Street!' she retorted. And stormed off into the rain.

That particular row (plus sulk) lasted a good hour or so. Yet it was, in its way, a reassuring row. I had always sensed a certain self-interest in urging her to sexual abandon, and any accusations of repression, however fair, did hint at the timeless ploy of the male predator. But her unnatural reactions to natural functions dispelled any faint fears that Teri's prudery was merely in the eye of the beholder. And this added self-righteousness to my sexual assertions.

Despite the weight of evidence, though, she was so unshrinking a violet, so un-anal a being, that her inhibitions lacked all logic or even plausibility – until viewed through the prism of a church-going family in a land of white palings, until seen from the stance of a flag-waving, God-fearing Norman Rockwell home town. Whilst being raised on the workings of the universe, she was left ignorant in the ways of the world. Around her hearth, they spoke of the Seventy Deadly Sins. I began to sense nurture not nature, and an outer skin of propriety soon to be sloughed off. How soon, and who would help with the sloughing, only time could tell.

Nonetheless, I grew to realize that, in one respect, I was wrong about the Catholicism. Though its malign influence remained, she was as ex a Catholic as anyone who had suffered a catechismal upbringing. But it had left a void, and a need to fill it with a giant philosophical Rawlplug. So now she was searching for new structures, new explanations, new Meanings of Life. This had helped her to produce the earliest recorded examples of psychobabble, but, in essence, that language was just a substitute for older, religious idioms, a flailing, transatlantic attempt to describe the abstract and define the infinite. Without a positive shape to her world, without a sense of purpose to her life, she found existence a pretty thin bag of tricks.

These, however, were the insights of hindsight, and were not to illuminate my state of understanding for several years.

Meanwhile, my own life edged delicately forward. The continuance granted to our relationship, and the quantitative increase in kissing, were in no small measure due to the onset of literature in my vocational game plan.

I had taken to crouching in my room for hours, trying to be funny in writing. And wondering when the Muse of Comedy made her house calls. The trouble with humour, it seemed, was that it disintegrated on the journey from the brain to the page. What began life as a witty thought, ended its days as a tired, crossed-out cliché. Read aloud, even my best jokes assumed the aerodynamics of a pancake.

I also had trouble with form. I was unsure whether to go for the comic epic, or the amusing novella, or the Art Buchwald column, found daily on the back of the *Paris Herald-Tribune*. For a while, even the genre of the completed sentence seemed a touch too challenging. Form, of course, is related to content. And content was another grey area. I found myself constantly torn between a commentary on the human condition (with epigrams) or Great Hitch-Hiking Rides I Have Known. If a blank page is difficult, *carte blanche* is even harder.

Worst of all, my room was the wrong size for writing. Pacing is the key component of creativity, and I was limited to two steps in each direction, and one of those involved hunching. The potential for rhythmic self-absorption was meagre. The other requirement for writers is distraction. All I had were passing clouds, and some days they did not even bother to pass.

And yet, and yet. I slowly began to discover that this new style of writing (if screwing paper into balls can be called writing) was a source of almost sensual pleasure. Squatted at my mini-table, hunting down the *mot juste* and cannibalizing clause after clause, I savoured anew the joy of words. And, as my mind grew ever more occupied by creating laughter from language, there were moments when I felt like a peg which had at last found the right-shaped hole. Some days I would even lose track of time.

One Saturday afternoon, only the fading of the light brought a halt to my earnest scribblings. And I suddenly realized that I had quite forgotten that most Parisian of rites, a rendezvous. I rushed down and out of the building – even banging the sacred lift gates – and ran to make amends. When I arrived, Teri had been waiting by the park entrance for over twenty minutes, a steady downpour pattering on to her plastic rain-hat.

'I'm ever so sorry!' She looked at me, but said nothing. 'I was writing. Trying to finish something off. And I just didn't realize the time. I completely—'

'—Don't apologize!'

I hesitated. 'But I'm ages late.'

'I know. And I'm glad.'

'. . . Glad?' I suspected irony. 'But you're soaked.'

'OK, that's a bit of a bummer. You can beat yourself up over that. But I'm still pleased you're late.'

As so often with her, I was bewildered. 'Why?'

'Come on, let's get out of the rain!'

The park was soon to close, and we hurried along outside the railings, aiming for the nearest bar. Still she offered no explanation, and I felt another metaphysical mystery descending.

'What if I hadn't turned up at all?'

'Oh, even better!' And she laughed, but only to tease. 'I'm just pleased there's something else in your life now. Something more important than me.'

I didn't immediately reply. I had always understood the golden rule of love affairs was to display undying devotion. Devotion with caveats, loved ones coming second, seemed a very iffy way to win a heart. But Teri was looking very loving, and to that end I was prepared to make unpunctuality my life's work. I had yet to learn that independence and intimacy conspire to be the best of bedfellows. That night, on her hotel doorstep, we parted with above-average passion . . . and above-average frustration.

For centuries, couples had parted on doorsteps, under balconies, behind walls, around corners, but this was little consolation in the late, liberated Sixties. Besides, in the age of cars and fridges, one felt entitled to certain standards of personal comfort. Although, occasionally, we snuck in and crept up to the first-floor landing, for a carpeted hug, such acts of furtiveness seemed adolescent.

The hotel owners, however, were gay and, by ill luck, had a barely disguised antipathy to heterosexual bonding. Jean-Pierre was thin and highly strung, and revelled in a camp which predated political correctness, while his lover Ed, a slightly paunchy ex-Marine, beached in Europe by NATO, was given to bouts of pompous authority better suited to a battleship. Both favoured the tantrum style of hotel management, and after 11 p.m. they lost control of their decibels.

The hotel itself was a notch or two above Carcassonne, and had succumbed to wallpaper; when not on tiptoe, I found it had an old-beamed charm. It even possessed a miniature residents' lounge, and sometimes, defeated by weather and poverty, we would slip into adjacent armchairs and watch an evening of bad

316

French TV. Although inimical to privacy – there were other armchairs and other refugees – these times created a curious aura of domesticity, that quiet pleasure in shared inertia; on occasions, in a relationship, even dullness has its soothing place.

Teri had squared a difficult Parisian circle in her choice of accommodation: the hotel was offbeat and yet acknowledged the concept of decor; cheap and yet had bathrooms; clean and yet had atmosphere. I thought of it as ersatz bohemian. The residents were not at the raw, cutting edge of society as in rue Mouffetard. It was essentially a hotel for members of the counter-culture with a monthly allowance; hers was not the only rebellious transatlantic phone call to be heard in the lobby. Moreover, its location was cosily close to the Sorbonne – a one-minute run with text-books – and any art came from lectures. But its appeal was its perversity. Run with the PR of an anti-hotel, its guest list ranged from the Biafran princess in seclusion to a Vietnamese chef in training and a Spanish bullfighter in convalescence. That an ability to settle bills did not appear a priority owed much to the eccentricity of Ed and Jean-Pierre, whose desire to retire to a country cottage was obstructed by distaste for the grubbiness of commerce. No AA stars were ever to be given to an establishment where the proprietors feuded in public and turned away travellers who failed the test of that day's whim.

One wet night, during a particularly protracted nuzzle on the hotel doorstep, Teri and I were dramatically parted by Jean-Pierre in a dressing-gown. Whanging back the entrance door, he pointed accusingly at my feet and shoved me onto the pavement, where he gave vent to an agitated rant. '*Interdit!*' he kept crying, '*interdit!*' At first I thought it was a lecture on morals, but by the third take I realized he was talking about the doorstep.

'*Pas pour l'amour!*' he insisted, brooking no debate. 'That,' he proclaimed with operatic hand gestures, 'is a *State* doorstep!' and he rubbed his slippered feet to and fro, apparently depicting some personal idea of heterosexual activity.

More than a touch nonplussed, I gazed carefully at the worn flagstones, but was hard-pushed to grasp his point.

'*Protégé par la loi!*' he announced, in a voice tinged with hysteria. 'Against damages!'

'Against what?' I caught Teri's eye and felt the giggles rising. The thought of erosive sperm came into my mind.

'*Les vandales, comme vous!*'

'*Comme moi?*' I tried to smile at him, but Teri told me to be a man, so I moved closer to the doorstep.

'*Restez là!*' commanded Jean-Pierre. He raced indoors and returned waving a scroll which he shook in front of us like a terrier with hypertension.

I followed his finger to the text. It was true. This was no ordinary doorstep. This was an historic doorstep. The flagstone on which we had canoodled night after night was officially registered as an ancient *Monument d'Etat*. Teri and I had unwittingly been kissing on a cultural artefact, had been fondling in the footsteps of the famous.

But, though this gave grandeur to a grope, it served only to inflame some sense of nationalist outrage in J-P. Not only were we eroding his doorstep, which apparently bore the scars of three centuries of lust without a permit, but we were foreigners. Foreigners whose nightly passion was, he declaimed, doing permanent damage to French heritage. And it must cease!

Paris being both an old city and the city of *l'amour*, the nightly damage to historic buildings would seem somewhat widespread, and I tried to make a *bon mot* along these lines. It was not successful. He threatened me with the Ministry of Culture, whose penalties for reckless doorstepping appeared draconian. As he started to jab yet again at his eroding flagstone, I realized that, in certain specialist areas, Jean-Pierre was quite unhinged.

Spring came closer, and the rain got warmer. With even doorsteps barred to us, it seemed that physical options were narrowing just when emotions might be deepening. Certainly, if love means confusion, my symptoms were pronounced. My sense of self – that terrain on which Teri had planted the first foreign flag – now felt like a builder's yard, littered with 'work in progress' signs. I had always thought I was at my loveliest when funny and entertaining; the moods which Teri most valued were serious and introspective. When I thought I was being iconoclastic, she said I was being Philistine; when I thought I was being carefree, she accused me of being superficial; and when she laughed at me I had no idea why. At the best of times, we can only guess how the world views us, yet now, when I tried to see myself as others did, the mirror was hopelessly fractured, the image just a fuzzy shadow. I had expected love to be heady and romantic; instead, it was a deconstructionist blur.

And yet, *faute de mieux*, we were still together. Still leaning on each other. Still sheltering from the future . . . And still fully clothed.

One evening, one rare dry evening, our wanderings took us down towards the *quais*. No venue in Paris, no view of Paris, can tug at the heart of a lover so exquisitely as the cobbled, tree-lined *quais*. Lapped by the river, they enclasp the ancient *îles* of Paris, and turn the clock back to a calmer century. I had strolled on them, sat on them, picnicked on them, studied on them, and longed for the day I would court on them. At their westernmost tip, facing the setting sun and the Louvre and the Beaux Arts, is a weeping willow that trails its summer greenery in the river, and when leaning against it, eyes half-closed, one can believe that every romantic dream in life will one day come true.

Teri had nuzzled against me with unusual affection as we ambled through the back alleys, jointly engaged upon a single crêpe of honey. A seemingly perfect confection for lovers, our progress was much slowed by dribbles, and occasionally we would stop to lick each other's lips free of sticky golden stains. In pursuit of errant honey, our tongues had taken to exploring further and deeper than ever before. With an unspoken under-standing, we crossed to the embankment, walked hand in hand past the padlocked book-chests of the *bouquinistes* and aimed amorously towards the islands. The night was still starry, and my mind was on all the hidden niches of the cobbles, all the wooden benches in the shadows. Already I could imagine the moon on the water, I could see the trees hanging low. We started down the steps . . . and then we saw the river.

It was in flood. The weeks of winter rain had roused the romantic Seine into a surging, swirling spate of tumultuous liquid sludge, powering its way to the sea. The *quais* were not even in sight. They lay submerged by feet of floodwater, battered by the debris of the storms. For as far as the eye could see, courtship was cancelled.

We sank despondently down on the cold stone steps, just a foot or two above the vulturous slurp of the water. Miserably, we pressed up against each other for comfort. The padding in our anoraks limited even this opportunity for body contact, and caused a curiously chaste line in cuddles which would have done nothing for the career of Rodin.

Soon, the rain began to fall once more, in ever larger splats. Paris had never looked bleaker. Nor had my prospects for passion. I began to fear it would take a hundred springs for any romance of mine to flower in this city.

The next day a postcard of Chartres cathedral arrived. 'Watercolours going well', it read, and proposed a weekend in the country.

CHAPTER 32

A kilometre beyond the village of Charbonnières, the lane stopped climbing. To the right, a wooded valley dropped steeply away, the occasional clearings streaked by late afternoon shadows. Bare fields stretched across gentle uplands to the left, the furrowed earth waiting for winter to end. The whiff of wood smoke hung in the crisp air.

A delicate pencil sketch had charted the landmarks of our journey: now only the easel and the bales of hay were still to come. A hundred yards on, just short of a copse, stood a primitive cottage, half-barn, half-habitation. A small apple orchard straggled over the rough front lawn, and clumps of mistletoe hung like bee swarms from the bare branches. In the hedgerows, the tangled brambles suggested a summer of dog-roses.

A shot rang out, followed by several more shots. In the field beside the cottage, a loping hare staggered to a standstill, and then slumped leggily to the earth. The noise sent up a dozen woodpigeon, flapping vulnerably into the sky. I looked about me, and three *chasseurs* appeared from the woods, the sun glinting on their rifles.

It was a sun which I had first seen at dawn through a thick white mist. The day had begun light years ago, with a savage hoar-frost across the city. Later, I had watched it slowly melt on the marble nipples in the vast gardens of Versailles, where we had started our journey with culture. For an hour we had wandered like wraiths amidst France's royal past, glimpsing fountains and statuary through the drifting gauze of frosted air.

Neither Teri nor I had been outside the city boundaries since summer – indeed, rarely been together in a double-digit *arrondissement* – and to see each other in unfamiliar surroundings was almost to see each other anew, to find hidden depths of character brought out by open spaces and palaces.

From Versailles, we hitched. Teri was not the *femme fatale* to bring a Facel Vega to a smoking halt, but her presence reassured drivers that my beard signified no criminal intent, and we made good progress down the N10. The countryside was Home Counties, Grade B, but it was French-grown, and that, as always, gave it scenic sex appeal. And, for once in my French travels, I was not en route from disaster to despair, not fleeing from a doss-house, not escaping from a restaurant, not even rebounding from *l'amour*. I was travelling for the pleasure.

Beyond Chartres, the route dribbled away down the D roads, testing our tongues with the rural linguistics of Nogent-le-Rotrou and Authon-du-Perche. Then, with some thirty kilometres still remaining, we reached the region where, said the letter, exact directions would be obtained merely upon mention of . . . '*le barbu Américain*'. It seemed a touching, but vainglorious, belief. In Saint Lubin des Cinq Fonds (a hamlet with more words than houses) we stopped an ancient peasant on a bicycle and he cried, '*Mais oui! Le peintre!*' And sent his regards. Five hours after we left Paris, a bread van dropped us by the small memorial which marked the fork of the only two roads in Charbonnières. We took the right-hand road and slowly climbed up the hill as the sinking sun lost the last of its little heat.

Ahead of us, the hunters picked up their hare and added it to other game in their bag. As our paths crossed in the lane, the three men stopped and jovially showed us their spoils. They were not the tight-lipped, posh-vowelled, upper-class killers of England. Ruddy and rustic, they were after one for the pot, not six dozen for the ego. Dressed in worn brown moleskin, old rifles slung comfortably over their shoulders, this friendly posse were the butcher, baker and candlestick-maker of rural France. We admired their hare and then chatted amicably with them for several minutes while they took aim at the mallards on a nearby pond. We parted without my having raised the subject of my lifelong opposition to blood sports.

There was no gate to the cottage, just a vague person-sized gap in the hedge. The tiny dwelling stood some thirty yards inside, a one-up, one-down in greying stucco edged by flaking brick, pressed against by a wooden lean-to full of hay. Ivy had taken over the side wall, and the solitary chimney leant at the same angle as the mossy roof. On the front grass lay the wires and rocks of a home-made barbecue, built in a corner where apple blossom would soon drift down. The cottage faced south across the valley, with an unbroken view of the sun's daily arc. No other building was in sight, except a concrete water-tower on the muddy horizon beyond the back field.

We walked across the uncut grass and up to the house. Teri rested her hold-all on the step, and I tapped with my knuckles on the top half of the slatted stable door. It was off the latch, and my knocking made it swing slowly back, with the stagiest of creaks.

Teri had not met Jerry before today. Now, he was less than six feet from her, the dying sunlight streaming down onto his easel, where, paintbrush in hand, deep in thought, he was seated upon an ancient wooden commode, with his huge shapeless trousers heaped around his ankles. Beyond him was his subject, Marie-Françoise, reclining naked in a tin hip-bath by a log fire.

I did not dare look at Teri. (She was one of three people present at whom looking did not seem a great idea.) My friends had always caused me a *frisson* of unease when they first met Teri. Propriety and the Puritan work ethic were rarely their defining characteristics. In Teri's presence I feared for their ideological soundness, their spiritual depth. And, by association, I feared for mine. Even so, no previous encounter had so thoroughly threatened Judaeo-Christian civilization.

We stood, smiles fixed, on the doorstep. Jerry swivelled round upon his commode, and on seeing us even *his* happy hippy mindset briefly deserted him. Laid back though he always liked to be, he as yet lacked the absolutist poise of *Le Roi Soleil* for an audience on the john. Only Jerry's taste in outsize lumberjackwear was keeping knowledge of his bodily functions from a wider world, and his situation was causing cracks in his karma. He nodded to us; he gestured a vague welcome with the brush; but otherwise he struggled with his duties as a host.

A bottom bolt held the lower door shut. Realizing the need for an overland journey, Jerry's much-lined face crumpled into sheepishness. He clutched the cumbersome commode with both hands, and tried to manoeuvre it and himself in our direction. His manoeuvrings quickly failed. The commode resisted him, and twisted in a circle. Next, Jerry attempted to hop towards us, clasping the thing as elegantly as he could to his buttocks, with his ankles pressed tight to keep hold of his trousers. But he wobbled, stumbled, and almost fell. He clambered back aboard and contemplated his next move.

Teri started to giggle. At first it was a contained, almost private, giggle. Then she tried to apologize. 'I'm sorry,' she mouthed, through pinched cheeks – and set herself off again. Her giggles turned to laughter. And a wave of relief swept through me. I too was suddenly free to laugh. And my laughter fuelled her laughter. And the sight of Jerry stranded on his toilet fuelled ever more laughter. As a general hysteria gained ground on the doorstep, I noticed Marie-Françoise slip from her bathtub with delicious unhurried calm and wrap a towel around herself. With a barefoot elegance she crossed the stone floor to the door, flicked up the bottom bolt, and affectionately slapped Jerry's head.

'I apologize for him,' she said to Teri. 'He always forgets to introduce people.'

Half an hour later we were all fully clothed and abluted and safely gathered in, and were sitting grouped like an old-fashioned family around the fire. Like the cottage, the furniture was from another century: two horsehair armchairs, of the sort rescued from skips, and a harshly angular pine settle. This had to be dragged from behind the table, and for once the cry 'Draw up a pew!' was more real than metaphorical. The light was beginning to fade sufficiently for the flames to cast flickering shadows, adding atmosphere to the room as we laid back in cosy discomfort, each happily clasping a pewter mug of home-made cider. 'Crushed with my own boots!' claimed Jerry, restored to the brio of old.

Occasionally, the wood smoke would blow back, defeated by the collapsing stonework in the flue and the eccentric angle of the chimneypot. As it drifted past us in pungent grey puffs, Teri sniffed the air pensively. 'I recognize that smell.'

The remark was not lost on Jerry. 'Sounds like the nose of a country girl.'

'Ah guess soh!' She thought some more. 'Apple wood! You're burning apple wood.'

'Jeez! Well done! What a smeller!'

I sniffed hard, and eventually believed I too could detect the evocative aroma of fruit floating around the room.

'Used to smell it in the backyard. Every fall, when Pop had bonfires; with all the wood he'd pruned.'

'You too?' said Jerry. There was a brief pause, and I fancied the air thick with bitter-sweet thoughts of absent fathers. I made no comment of my own, as my childhood had been spent in the presence of a two-bar electric fire.

'D'you grow your own food?' asked Teri, her eye drawn to the plaited onions on a nail.

'No. Not got the land. But I'd like to, some day.'

'He dreams he is a peasant,' said Marie-Françoise, with a teasing smile. She seemed even stiller in the country than in Paris; poised and upright, she sat with her legs effortlessly crossed beneath her, in the launch position for yogic flight, and breathed only *in extremis*.

Jerry seemed pleased at the idea, and went on, 'I'd miss the market though. Worth going just to see the faces. Tony would like the market here. Just his taste in gnarled, twisted bits of body! D'you know Tony?'

'Yes. I've been done,' Teri replied. 'You don't do many portraits?'

'No. Just Marie. Unless you want to be a dot on the landscape . . . ?'

'Oh. Be a long way to drag a tin bath.' She smiled.

A log shifted in the fire, and a flurry of sparks fell onto the flagstoned hearth.

'Is that the valley that was in the paintings?' I asked, nodding towards the twilight beyond the window.

'Mostly. But since the exhibition bombed, I've been experimenting with a few different valleys. I'm into more of an arable period now.' He grinned. I had told Teri about his grins. It was good to see he was as unprecious as ever.

His new paintings, finished and unfinished, were spread haphazardly about the room, some hung, some propped, some half-obscured. The simple distemper of the walls and the primitive backdrop of his living space gave them an intimacy and charm which was lost in the formal world of galleries.

'Any buyers?'

'The landlord sometimes takes one in lieu of rent. But then he once offered to take Marie in lieu of rent, so I don't think he's a bona fide collector.'

'It is not easy to buy Jerry's paintings,' said Marie-Françoise. 'He likes them to go to a good home. Like baby dogs!' She sighed. 'Any new owner has to have a nice face.' Jerry sluiced some cider through his beard and did not respond. 'Sometimes he is a bit of a klutz,' she added affectionately.

Exposure to Jerry had given her a good but odd English. Her effect on him was harder to judge: the elaborate protocols of French society seemed to sink without trace into his Yankee openness. I briefly wondered if Teri and I seemed as improbable a couple.

'What do the locals make of you?' Teri asked him.

'What, mystery artist ravaging one of their women? Oh, they're fine. All smiles and *bonjours*. Complete push-over compared to the time I tried to live in Alabama! There, the town used to hold sweepstakes for the right to lynch me! I lasted two weeks.' He reached for the flagon – it was indeed a flagon – and topped up his cider. 'Only really been one problem here. The hippy bit was fine; the artist bit was fine; even the American bit was fine, so long as I didn't napalm their kids; what they really couldn't handle was me not eating meat. Sign of a serious screwball!' He laughed. 'When Garry and I first moved in, they used to leave us rabbits, against the door, and we had to bury them at the dead of night!'

I had entertained hopes that Marie-Françoise might have converted him to French cuisine, but this, and the sack of rice by the table, suggested otherwise.

For an hour, the flagon continued to circulate like an open-ended aperitif. Warmed by apple juice within and apple wood without, Jerry and I contentedly batted back and forth the latest on our lives; beside me, I sensed an interview-in-depth as Teri charmed a biography out of the usually reticent Marie-Françoise. And then, with the settle seeming almost soft, and the laughter growing loud, we all realized that the room around us was in darkness.

Jerry stumbled up, crossed to the table, and lit the first hurricane lamp of the night. He came back with a heavy cardboard box and dropped it in our midst.

'*La spesheeality de la mayzon!*' he announced. 'Vegetarian couscous!' And he tossed me a swede and a knife.

I remembered my last contact with couscous. Then the surprise had been a Russian and an axe.

This experience had now matured into one of my finest anecdotes, and as each of us settled down with a vegetable and a duty, I duly regaled the company with the story in question. (Ideally I would have liked to reset it in the Wild West, in a saloon bar, with guns firing, and assorted drunken cowpokes and a 'madam' in low-cut slinky stuff and boots.) My pleasure in this Alpine tale was always that it cast me, with effortless subtlety, in such an engaging light: although appearing in my usual role as anti-hero – as befits a man in full flight from a homicidal Cossack – I somehow came over as a swashbuckling anti-hero, with lashings of devil-may-care raffishness. In the normal way of the world, I rarely cast coal into stews, but in the telling it became the action of a cavalierly cool dude. And as for my final exit into a snowy mountain fastness . . . !

Even Teri, who so often cast a corrective forensic eye over my glamorized past, had a small fit of the giggles.

327

'If you've got any thoughts about seasoning the meal tonight,' said Jerry softly, 'perhaps you'd put it to a vote first?'

He had allotted himself the mushrooms, floppy, greyish, suspicious-looking mushrooms, and was peeling them with what appeared to be a nail-file. This was a delicate task for a man with size eleven maulers, and it also suggested a perverse distribution of labour as micro-fingered Marie-Françoise was busy manhandling some of the grossest root vegetables ever to have disfigured the food chain. Watching Jerry at work, I was reminded of those huge animals – the Pyrenean bear sprang to mind – which feed upon the daintiest of berries.

'Bought,' he said, smiling at my anxious study of the mushrooms. 'Not picked.'

'Oh good. That should save on anti-serum.'

'You ought to come in summer!' said Marie-Françoise. 'Jerry is in the fields from dawn. A nightmare! He only picks the ones he likes to draw!'

'The fields round here are carpeted with them,' said Jerry rhapsodically. 'I can fill this up in a few minutes.' He gestured at the old wicker basket by his feet.

It was a wicker basket that stirred some deeply-buried childhood memory of mine. For a moment I could not think why or where from – and then I remembered my bedtime stories and my picture books. This was the basket that Little Red Riding Hood took on her visits to Grandma. This was the basket she carried her sarnies in. The idea of Jerry the Giant striding through the woods with it over his arm seemed strangely appropriate; somehow he too belonged in a fairy tale.

When the massive couscous finally bubbled to its climax – a non-rice meal was a rare honour – we dragged the settle back to the table and improvised the extra dining-chairs. It was a chaotic room for all seasons – dining-room, bathroom, lounge, toilet, kitchen (the ubiquitous Gaz), and studio – yet by the catholic and quixotic nature of its bric-à-brac it managed to defy squalor. Though Jerry was perched on a tea-chest and Marie-Françoise was now wedged in the empty commode, the crockery was hand-crafted in the purest blues and pinks of a primitivist Breton potter. While the brothers brought the disorder of *objets trouvés* to the cottage, reclaiming rural junk like Tate-sponsored Steptoes, Marie-Françoise subjected the Paris flea market to precision-shopping before her country visits, and was steadily feminizing the premises with Art Deco kettles and *fin de siècle* fish-knives.

Jerry lit a second hurricane lamp, and stood unsteadily on the table to reach a huge hook, from which, in less vegetarian times, had once hung a family's salting side of bacon.

'Some people,' I remarked, 'would just switch on the light.'

'Afraid there's a bit of a problem with the electricity.'

'Thought there might be.'

'They've cut it off.'

'Let me guess. Some trivial reason like not paying the bill?'

Jerry nodded, and pointed to the one alcove. 'I've framed it. Looks quite nice.' And then he clambered from the table to his tea-chest.

The lamps cast a nineteenth-century glow over the nineteenth-century setting. The shutters were now closed and full-bodied night was upon us. The tureen steamed with Eastern promise in the middle of the table. The scent of cinnamon wafted from an apple pudding simmering in a second saucepan. And in the hearth, the logs from the orchard quietly roasted in deep scarlet embers. As the wooden ladle circulated, and the vegetables tumbled with soft splashes into the hollowed mounds of grain, we seemed a thousand miles from Paris.

'It's great to see you,' said Jerry, raising his tankard. 'I'm really glad you made it.'

'We nearly didn't!' replied Teri with some feeling.

The other two looked at us, uncertainly.

I gave a sheepish grin. 'She and the French State have had a bad day!'

'Yeah, I've had that problem with America!' said Jerry sympathetically, if abstrusely.

'Yes, but at least you don't think that you're Joan of Arc!' I said, winding Teri up. Eight hours on, I still shuddered at the memory of the incident.

'What, you've had a vision?' laughed Marie-Françoise.

'I have!' I said. 'The paratroopers will be here any minute!' And enigmatically set to work on the couscous.

'What?'

'We're hitching in this tiny village, right,' said Teri, a hint of outrage still detectable, 'miles from anywhere, no-one in sight, and we're passing a police station the size of a phone box – when all of a sudden, these two gendarmes leap out, and demand to know what we're doing. And where we're going. And where we've been. And then, really aggressively, for no reason at all, insist on proof of identity.'

'And what did you do?' asked Marie-Françoise.

'She offered to show them a birthmark for 1,000 francs. And said she thought the Gestapo had gone back to Germany after the war.'

'. . . Aaah,' said Marie-Françoise.

'That could have been a mistake,' said Jerry, nonetheless guffawing with delight.

'Asking *them* for proof of identity was the mistake!' I said.

'You didn't!' said Jerry.

Teri nodded. 'I tried to explain that I'd just overthrown Chartres, but my French got stuck.'

'Thank God!' I said, secretly proud of her.

She had indeed shown an impressive head of steam in the set-to. I had been altogether more English, more moderate, more reasonable, more prepared to hide in the bushes. By good fortune, I was now visaed, another perk of Grade Five, but I always remained wary. In Nice, on the Promenade des Anglais, I had watched the gendarmerie conduct a trawl of hippies. A group of hairy Aussies were having a celebratory Christmas dip, and when they emerged from the sea, nude and dripping wet, every one of them was then arrested – on the grounds they were not carrying identity papers upon their person.

'It really pisses me off!' she said. 'A gun and a badge, it's like super-puberty.'

'Oh, I wish I'd been there!' said Jerry, grinning from big ear to big ear.

'I wish you had too,' I said. 'You could have helped me drag her away.'

'I had the situation under control.'

'Yes. Until you got twenty yards from them and shouted, "*Je viens d'un pays libre, moi!*" and we had to run for it.'

'Oh dear,' said Marie-Françoise, 'if de Gaulle gets to hear that he'll be very cross.'

'If LBJ gets to hear that he'll be very puzzled!' said Jerry.

Marie-Françoise smiled. 'You're lucky you're not sleeping in a cell somewhere tonight.'

To which the obvious response was to ask where exactly we would be sleeping tonight. Because this, without doubt, was the $64,000 question, the question which had occupied all my waking, masturbating hours ever since Jerry's postcard had arrived. I had wondered about it on departing, I had wondered about it en route, I had wondered about it even more on arrival. But I had said nothing then, I said nothing now. I wanted innocence to be my watchword. I wanted no sexual doors foreclosed. I wanted the fates to decide . . . ostensibly, at least.

'I thought there were quite good odds on a morgue,' I said swiftly, and, in high good humour, the conversation moved on.

There is a particular pleasure, a pleasure perhaps touched by vanity, to finding that one's friends like each other. It confirms sound judgement, proclaims good taste, and bestows personal credit for increasing the sum of human happiness. It is also a cause of considerable relief.

All that Teri and Jerry had in common – apparently – was their citizenship; and, an anthropologist might have added, a generous grin. The sole similarity of Teri and Marie-Françoise was their height. But, as the dinner slid steadily down and the lamp wicks burned lower, there came about a camaraderie which far exceeded the protocol of host and guest. Both Jerry and Teri had an exterior which sold the world a false prospectus. Behind the lumberjack look was a gentle, enquiring mind; inside the school-ma'am clothing was a restless digger for truth. Their characters shared a middle ground of unshowy integrity, and each recognized in the other the courage to be unconventional. And to the serene Marie-Françoise, Teri's peals of Latin laughter and gestures unconfined had the age-old attraction of opposites: by the end of the night, the two women were sufficiently bonded to make a date to share the tin bath (albeit motivated by the shortages of water, not the excesses of sex).

To see Teri in company was to be daunted by her openness. And it was an openness which bred openness. Journalism was no accidental career choice.

'"Just a wop! Just a broad! Course I'll rap with her. She don't know shit! And I'll get pussy!" All he got was serious shit and no pussy!' Teri rocked with pleasure at the memory.

'And you got an exclusive?' said Jerry.

'Yeah. "Black Power dude speaks to college rag!"'

'So you did the shafting,' he said, impressed.

'He shafted himself. Innocent teenage girl? From an ethnic minority? She must be dumb. So I'd just ask dumb questions and smile into my notebook. And it'd be scoop time again!'

'What are you going to do when you're middle-aged and white?' Jerry asked her.

'Don't know. Interview you about how you became a famous painter?'

'Not me. Garry. He's the ambitious one.'

'Is it really true you two paint the same?' asked Teri.

'Pretty much. That's why I always say he's a genius!'

I had never asked Jerry directly about the uncanny similarity of their paintings. For some reason, it did not feel an artistic question, but a personal, prying question, an enquiry into the darker recesses of genetics. Yet Teri could ask him, and cause no offence.

'About half of these are his,' said Jerry, nodding at the cluttered walls, now murky with shadow. 'But which half . . . ?' He let the remark hang playfully, teasing rather than evading.

Teri pursued the point, gently. 'But you intuitively share the same view of the world? And the same technique? How is that possible?'

'We're poor – we share the same brush!' He reflected on her

question. 'Sounds odd perhaps, but I've never really thought about it. Just took it for granted.'

'How unusual is it, twin painters?'

'Don't know of any others.' He blew through his teeth while he thought. 'There used to be three brothers, each did self-portraits, and the other two would finish them off. Creepy but fun. The character of the sitter would change in every picture! Because of artistic factors like sexual jealousy and alcohol.'

'Do you and Garry work on each other's paintings?'

'Have done, a couple of times. Nothing major. I put some animals in a meadow of his once, while he was out. He got back and didn't speak to me for the rest of the day!' Jerry's deep-set blue eyes crinkled at the edges. '. . . Mind you, they were giraffes!'

I recalled the secret of their father and the dead brother, and without that knowledge I knew no real understanding of the strange forces which shaped their work would ever be possible. I wondered what Garry might have said, and briefly regretted his absence in Paris, where he too had inexplicably found himself a chic Frenchwoman for weekends. Teri meanwhile had sensed the trail go cold, and delicately dropped her line of enquiry.

The room was now at regulo 3 and, the laughter subsided, we sat for a long moment in contented silence, piercing the last of the goat cheese with toothpicks. The smell of ground coffee floated about us, and the household's two liqueur glasses, brimful of *marc*, were quietly doing their rounds. It was how all good evenings should end. But instead I was seized with apprehension: heavy in the air was the question of bed, and I was loath to trigger the moment of truth.

It was as I sat quietly back, pondering my fate, that I wondered if the answer to another mystery that had troubled me for so many months of my time in Paris, might not also be near to hand. There was an atmosphere of great benignity around the table, of repleteness and sleepiness and friendship. And Jerry was the most benign of all, like a Pyrenean bear with a lifetime's honey, leaning with a drowsy smile against the wall. If his trust in me were ever to be total, now, I believed, was the time.

'Who is the man in the suit, Jerry?'

It was almost as though he had been expecting the question to come. He showed neither unease nor embarrassment. He did not even shift his position on the tea-chest. After a short pause for thought, he glanced at Marie-Françoise. It was immediately clear that she knew the truth. Then he glanced at Teri.

'I've said nothing,' I added.

Teri looked puzzled, understandably, but did not speak.

It was Teri that Jerry addressed, and his words were almost comically uncharacteristic. 'This conversation is off the record,' he said, and he was both joking and serious.

'Damn!' Teri exclaimed. 'Another Pulitzer gone!'

I briefly explained to Teri the little I knew – the warning about an unknown man dressed in a suit; the promise to deny all knowledge of Jerry . . . and the fear that I had seen in Jerry's face. Then I looked again at Jerry, and shrugged my shoulders, as if to offer him the stage. 'So?' I asked. 'Who's after you?'

He paused, that small but irresistible pause of people who know that their words are about to have an effect. And then he answered.

'The FBI.'

'The *FBI*!'

He nodded.

'Jee-sus . . . !' I searched in vain for signs of a leg-pull. '*THE* FBI? We're talking J. Edgar Hoover?'

'Well, not in person. . . . Least I hope not. That could be a real bad start to the day!'

Suddenly, as he spoke, I remembered Helba . . . and the casual East European certainty with which she had said, 'Secret police'. I also remembered that I had laughed. Laughing no more, I said again, 'The FBI is after *you*?'

Once again, he nodded. '. . . And Garry.'

'You're *both* on the run?' My voice seemed to have gone up an octave. Patricide flashed ignobly through my mind. 'Both on the FBI Wanted List?'

'Well, not The Ten Most! . . . Though we are on T-shirts in the States. In fact, in some states I gather we're a bit of an icon.'

334

'Jerry—what the fuck did you do?'

Jerry smiled bashfully. 'Well, we got involved in some anti-Vietnam stuff. You know, demos, marches, and that – pretty much like the rest of America.' I saw Teri grin. Later she said she had thought of her brother, and his belief that napalm should be used for crowd control. 'And then one day Garry and I burnt our draft cards at a big demo in Berkeley . . . and the news guys were filming, and, well, that night we ended up on coast-to-coast TV.' He sensed my puzzlement. 'Because we were twins.'

'Because you were twins?'

'Yeah.' He sighed. 'The only pair of identical-twin draft-dodgers in the history of the Vietnam War. Probably in the history of America.'

'You're identical-twin draft-dodgers?'

'Cool, eh?'

He sipped the *marc* as I struggled to reassess him in the light of his new star status. 'And of course that made great copy.' He smiled at Teri. She had not spoken once, sensitive to this being my friend, my shock. 'And we kinda became celebrities. And the publicity really bugged the FBI, both nostrils. And so they went gunning for us – and thought up a few more charges. Adding up to a total of five years in the pen. So we hightailed it out through Canada. And we've been in hiding ever since.'

Jerry grinned, gently levered Marie-Françoise off the commode and onto his lap, and awaited my reaction. The full implications of identical-twin draft-dodging were still percolating. I thought back to all those weeks when he had been dossing on my floor, just a yard away. 'So when Marie's father came busting through the door that morning . . .'

'I was glad to see him!' said Jerry. 'All that banging, I'd thought it was Interpol. About to add sex and drugs to my list of offences!'

I burst out laughing – and then realized that that debauched night was something else still to explain to Teri. My life was beginning to seem rather glamorous. 'And you didn't tell me all this because . . .' I let the sentence dangle.

'Because it was safer for you if you didn't know,' he said

simply. Knowing Jerry, I felt sure that this, rather than some sordid deceit, was indeed the real reason. I smiled at him. There seemed little more to say. As his strange story slowly sank in, I could see the attraction of life as a gangster's moll, constantly enjoying the thrill of notoriety by association. It would be a hard secret to keep. All the harder because this was the type of exotic underworld existence which I had so long wished to be a member of.

For several moments, no-one spoke. Marie-Françoise snuggled deep into her fugitive's arms, and stroked his great beard into bushy shape. Teri gazed abstractedly at the abstract pattern on her cup, her thoughts unfathomable. And Jerry continued to smile beatifically at the world in general, his sweet pacific nature suggesting that even West Point's finest would struggle to graft the essentials of guerilla-fighting onto his soul.

And for the first time, it came home to me – with overpowering poignancy – that Jerry was yet another exile, and as political an exile as any I had known.

He lifted his legs slowly from their resting-place upon the settle, and placed them on the flagstones. He yawned.

'Well, are you ready to hit the hay?' I hesitated for a second, instinctively glancing towards Teri. 'Thought we'd put you two up in the hayloft next door. Is that OK?'

336

CHAPTER 33

'I have to find a mailbox.'

'. . . A mailbox?' Although I had tried to anticipate all possible responses from Teri, recourse to the postal system had not been among them. 'But it's way past midnight!' Even an allergy to hay would have been more conceivable.

'There are no street lights,' said Jerry.

'It's Flaubert. He's overdue.'

'Oh shit!' I said. We had forgotten to deliver her essay before we left Paris. 'Can't it wait?'

Teri shook her head. 'First post might still just make it.'

'It's in a wall, on the left,' said Marie-Françoise, after we had elaborated. Unlike Jerry, she understood the medieval intransigence of the French educational system. 'About fifty yards after you reach the village.'

I, meanwhile, was dubious that any nineteenth-century novelist, however talented, could be the sole cause for our foray into the frost. But I found Teri's intentions impossible to determine. Were we venturing forth for a detumescent chat or esoteric Pennsylvanian foreplay?

Outside was a moon, of sorts, and we declined the hurricane lamp. The glow from the door guided us across the grass to the lane, and we turned downhill towards the village. We walked slowly and cautiously, sensing the hedgerows by our side. The night was just light enough to see the tarmac, and just dark enough to fear the demons. Teri felt for my hand and clasped it tight. I waited for her to speak, but she said nothing.

Ten eerie minutes later we edged into the village. The village was as dark as the countryside. Not a light was to be seen in any house. Not even a glimmer percolated on to the shuttered street. The terraced rows of low-roofed dwellings merged with the night sky. When we had arrived in the day there had been nobody, when we returned in the night there was nobody. No car, no cat, no dog, no living. Here was the perennial mystery of rural France, the village without people. And the silence was total.

Still Teri did not speak. She seemed content to be a warm presence by my side. The emptiness of the night drew us closer, and we moved on down the street. Twenty, thirty, forty yards we shuffled down into this black maw. The moon drifted behind high clouds and our eyes moved stealthily along the simple stucco walls. I felt as though we were intruders, burglars, invaders, and that discovery of our presence would be beyond all explaining.

'There!' Teri whispered. The faint outline of a metallic mailbox mouth was just visible.

Rarely has a French essay been posted with more relief. Or more mystery. As I stood silently on the pavement, listening to it thud into the empty box, her mission seemed as pregnant in meaning as any mere theme of literature. As to what that meaning might be, only the most skilled in matters of the heart could tell. Had this been an allegorical journey? Was it a metaphorical posting? Could the darkness be symbolic? Then Teri took hold of my hand again, squeezed it gently, and we turned in silence to retrace our steps through the dark, my heart pounding as we walked.

The hurricane lamp was hanging in the hayloft when we returned. A literal lean-to, the wooden outhouse rested against the side wall of the cottage, a rustic ad hocery of planks and beams. The discarded implements of a life on the land cluttered the earthen floor, where they lay as if in hope the nineteenth century might one day come again. A musty, rusty smell of warm decay drenched the air with rural memories. And beyond the retired harrow and the gap-toothed rake was propped an old wooden ladder, climbing up to that story-book hideout of farm cats and children: the den in the hay.

'No *en suite* facilities, then?' said Teri.

'Er, no. It's yer basic one-star hay accommodation, I think.'

'Oh, right.' She gazed impassively across the shadows of the lean-to, looking up at the harvest stored from the summer before, stacked to within a few feet of the sloping roof. 'No bell-boys either?'

I quickly picked up our rucksacks, which Jerry had left beside the ladder, and tossed each of them high into the hay. 'With the compliments of the management, Madame.'

'You're not going to sing "Oklahoma", I hope?'

'Not without a tip.'

Two bed-rolls were also lying at the foot of the ladder, but these had to be wrestled up the rungs, as if in parody of the silk sheets and soft music I had once imagined. As I bundled them onto the bed of bales some ten feet above the ground, I became more concerned about vertigo than virginity. Teri followed me up even less steadily, one hand on the ladder, one hand on the lamp, and casting on every surface the macabre shadows of *film noir*.

'So this is your idea of showing a girl a nice time?' came her voice from below.

I looked around. Her head appeared. A broad grin was on her face.

There was little space on top of the hay. Although, lair-like, it was cosy, the choice was between kneeling, or crouching, or dwarf room-service. I busied myself. Atmospherically back-lit by Teri, I scrabbled among the bales, smoothing and tidying; and tugging the bed-rolls into as erotic a juxtaposition as I could devise.

'What d'you think?' I asked, when my home-making was done.

'I'm just glad there are no chickens,' she said.

I did not find this a very helpful answer. In fact, I had found all her responses too runic by half. So far she had failed to issue me with any guidance, to offer me any kind of clarification, regarding her current disposition to randiness. Here we were, on our knees, face to face, the small hours upon us, the zips of our sleeping bags undone and adjacent, and I still had not been formally advised as to her state of arousal. Legend and literature has it that sexuality operates on a level beyond words; that there is 'an electricity' between lovers; that bodies fuse naturally at a certain temperature. This, alas, was subtlety I was not party to, an erotic domain to which I was never privy. Personally, I would prefer a green light to appear in the middle of the female forehead, flashing the words 'Go! Go! Go!' Practical, reliable, and copper-bottomed in court, it would beat the hell out of leaving sex to the vagaries of inter-hormonal intuition.

'We'd better put the lamp out,' she said.

'Why?' I questioned, eager to pounce on such prudery.

She tossed a handful of hay into the air. 'If I am going to burn in the flames of hell,' she replied, 'I'd prefer it to be after sin, not during it.' And with that, she snuffed out the light.

I remember her breasts most of all. And the exhilarating *tendresse* of her compliance.

Lying in the secrecy of darkness, trembling at the touch of a body, amazed by the softness of flesh, my brain whirred free, like a cog whose chain has slipped. My long-tied hands, scarcely believing their new-found freedom to roam, explored Teri's patient body with all the subtlety of mass trespass. My fingers were ceaselessly on the move, endlessly on the feel, finding which clothes were on her, which clothes were off her . . . here a nipple, there a nipple, everywhere a naughty bit . . . fondling madly, wildly, deeply on an incoherent trawl for thrills. The forbidden, the unknown, the untouched, this night was the ultimate in carnal package tours. Teri's body became but a blur. As I roamed from breasts to buttocks, from lips to labia, I sated myself on a series of sensations, on lust without a plot line; in an era before the G-spot, I was the pioneer of erogenous pointillism. It was exotic, it was erotic, it was hypersensual . . . but my memories of that heady, horny night do not now summon up the joys of love so much as a mental checklist of body parts to examine. 'May I have equal time?' she enquired at one point, irony and tenderness and forbearance commingling in her gentle voice. Alas, witty banter of mine came there none. I had somehow lost the skills of daily discourse; in the darkness of the night my personality seemed suspended, my words ran in ruts, my thoughts in clichés. For if life imitates art, sex imitates pulp fiction. The indulging of original sin does little for original thought, and my mind had shut down. My head was buried deep in the soft, shifting sands of a bosom, my emotions a-wallow in the novelty of nudity. I was on a high, a high and a hard, and it had been a lifetime coming. There was no setting more fitting than a fairy-tale hayloft – nor foreplay more fanciful than tedding the bedding – and all the raunch of Rabelais was added to the romance. Never in the history of rustic rumpy-pumpy had a yokel ever yoked like this before! I was on cloud sixty-nine, and my dreams were coming true. And thus the long first night continued. Until, eventually, with the straw below us, and the stars above us, our sleeping bags were finally as one.

. . . And yet, as with all nostalgia, my memories are founded on both rock and sand. True, a roll in the hay *is* life's most pleasing imagery of carefree sex. And, yes, that night *was* full of forbidden delights and secret pleasures. And, certainly, that barn *was* the lost barn of all our childhoods. But, dry straw is a much overrated substance, particularly when pressed against bare flesh. It scratches, it itches, it prickles, it gets up bum holes, it makes nasty rasping noises and can all too easily come between a man and his orgasm; its dust makes you cough, it leaves indentations on your private parts, and it can remain in your underwear for years. In short, it makes horsehair seem like silk – and sex seem like press-ups on sandpaper. In non-macho moments of honesty, one would have to admit that the 'oohs' and 'aahs' of that gold-starred night were as often to do with agony as with ecstasy – and that some of the most tender caresses of all were to relieve hay damage.

There was, moreover, one other shortcoming to those memorable hours, and even a suite in the Ritz would have altered nothing. The night had begun as the last word in romance. It ended as the last word but one. Teri, though tender and loving and definitely melting, would, in the end, only cede access to 99 per cent of her territory. There remained a lingering concordat which gave the Pope first call on her virginity. This was, of course, an arrangement she would deny, a commitment she would dispute, but God or no, the hurdle of her hymen was still *in situ*.

Though the situation was, she added with a disarming smile, under 'constant review'. Once she was sure that I was a deserving cause . . .

CHAPTER 34

Once again, it was springtime in Paris. And everywhere the trees of Paris were turning green again. And the pavement cafés on the squares and the boulevards were crowded again. And the young lovers were strolling arm in arm through the parks again. But this year I was no outsider, no onlooker, no stranger to the lyrical mood. This year, albeit the wrong year, albeit twelve months behind schedule, I too was at last in love in Paris in the spring.

There was a new pattern to my days. I buffed my French in the mornings, and in the afternoons, as the sun grew seductively warmer, I would sit alone on the balcony of Teri's hotel room – and write. The narrow sloping street was quiet then with the torpor of siesta, the all-hours family grocery briefly lowering its shutters for a lie-down, the knots of once-noisy students drifting past for a slow *citron pressé* or a seat in the park. With the sun on my face, and the murmurous sounds of the city just a pleasing blur to my ears, I would place my heels on the low wrought-iron railings, and methodically, conscientiously, set to work on my pads of feint-lined A4. Situated in voyeuristic isolation on the first floor, with the life of the street below and the view of the park beyond, I had tracked down that most mythical land of literature: the perfect writing position. Here, I could think and write and pace undisturbed, for Teri was always out at this hour, tending to the vowels and bowels of the next generation of the bourgeoisie; even her royal-blooded room-mate, now restored to smiles and sanity by news of her missing parents, was rarely to be found in on fine days.

I had been drawn to the story of the scorpion. After many false starts, in many foreign countries, my flame of creativity had settled upon Israel . . . Upon my time on the kibbutz . . . Upon my days in the bananas . . . Upon my hours with Nicole. The idea had everything: exotic location, international cast, a threat of war, beautiful dusky women, and a wide variety of fruit. More tricky was the text. I was after a touch of anti-hero, but a hint of idealism; the savvy of the well-travelled, but the wide eyes of the innocent; the inhibition of the English and the poetry of the Irish; the charm of Casanova, but the luck of Quasimodo. Plus jokes. Preferably one per line.

Nonetheless, slowly the article coagulated into shape. Sometimes the process would require more extensive pacing than the balcony could offer, and I would transfer my thinking to the Jardins du Luxembourg. Barely a hundred yards away, with space enough for one to be either public or private, to play *boules* or read poetry, this was a park I had grown to love. Its glory days were as royal gardens, but the panache of perruqued promenaders was not lost: as soon as the early summer sun was felt, all the class walkers and talkers of Paris appeared, strolling volubly up and down the wide, worn boulevards of gravel as if guests at an outdoor salon. At the heart of the park, beyond the shade of the trim rows of trees, was a grand sunken concourse, centred on a circular model-boat pond, adorned by the fastidious symmetry of lawns and flowers, and rimmed by a neo-classical stone balustrade; from up here, like spectators at an amphitheatre, one could gaze down upon the celebration of spring. A Parisian spring. I never tired of this setting. The dusty white of the ground and the broad sweep of the views created a dazzling Lowryesque landscape, but one where the brightly coloured matchstick figures moved against a background of plinths and statues and pillars – only the absence of parasols placed the scene in the twentieth century.

Here I had the perfect park for pacing, for writerly thinking, for artistic breathing. I was especially drawn to scuffing slowly back and forth through the long, criss-crossing lines of chestnut trees, in whose shadows I frequently flushed out an elusive adjective. Nor was I the only one to muse through the dust with a furrowed brow and a pad. It seemed some days that the trees had been expressly planted to provide a path for blocked writers. 'Just slipping out for a quick verb,' was no doubt a familiar cry in the literary salon of Gertrude Stein.

And so, with the aid of the balcony and the park, I chiselled away until, eventually, my piece had its full complement of adjectives and verbs. Then, once the last joke was lowered into place, I typed up the two-and-a-half page manuscript in my own room, two fingers at a time and hoping the slave-labour neighbours from the Third World had not been given the day off for a lie-in. But, though its completion gave me great satisfaction, the opus did not bring unalloyed singing and dancing. There remained the small problem of publication. In the publishing world of the Thirties, there were many proving grounds for the essay. Then, the essay was a genre. Magazines such as the *Transatlantic Review* queued up to train the likes of Hemingway, and cross his palm with a few bottles' worth of silver. Whereas I, an exile of the Sixties, could think of no editorial desks onto which fifteen hundred of my honed words would drop with any hope of favour.

Then, several days later, as I sat browsing idly through the periodicals in the American Centre, always a favourite refuge when I felt the want of a sofa, it slowly dawned that I was, technically, now a specialist writer. An alleged writer of humour. I only knew of one English magazine which was interested in humour. Which indeed specialized in humour. Which was famous for humour. Was, in fact, probably Britain's most famous magazine. Perhaps the world's most famous magazine. *Punch*.

'*Punch*?' said Teri, and paused over her student dinner. She was impressed. Not for her any fusty associations of dentists and waiting-rooms. To her, an American, *Punch* was the acme of all things witty. 'You're going to send it to *Punch*?'

'Why not? I can afford the stamp.' I told her my specialist-writer theory.

'Sounds good. What d'you think they'll say?'

'"Fuck off!" But with great wit.' We both laughed.

'And if humour isn't your speciality?'

'That's OK. I'm multi-faceted.'

'You are?'

'Yes. I have specialist knowledge of citrus fruit. I'll send it to *Banana Weekly*.'

'Wow, I just love British ambition!' she said, smiling broadly, and speared another wedge of carrot râpée.

The following day I sent the article off, in a large brown envelope and with rather more sticky tape than was perhaps essential.

I had put blinkers on my mind. Whenever I had thought of our love-to-be, it was love in a timeless, nameless, placeless place. Whenever I had pondered on us and togetherness, the grid reference for this coming contentment had the fuzzy imprecision of heaven. And whenever I had dreamed these dreams of happiness, all they seemingly required to attain reality was the simple and small fact of manuscript pages, the very minor act of a little light art. The implications of involvement, the logistics of love, were realities never faced, were practicalities never contemplated. But my failure to look forward was no naïve insouciance, no carefree bravado. It was denial. For me, the future was not just a closed book. It was a banned book.

The deadline of Teri's departure was but weeks away. Like a condemned man focusing on chequers with his prison guards, I rarely alluded to this looming date. Rather, I allowed the heady drug of love in Paris in the spring to keep me on a high, to be my tab of E as together we took to pottering through those parts of the city still on our list of unseen sights. Yet even then my peace of mind was intermittent. For Teri's love, though now definitely evidenced by warmth, still seemed curbed by caveats. How much she loved me I did not know. I did not know because she did not know . . . or did not say. The days were nervous days. Little was defined, little was aired, little was admitted. We spoke of our mutual feelings like clients advised by their lawyers to say nothing incriminating. Loose talk costs loves – and we each knew that two futures were at a crossroads.

I was not of an age to comprehend it then, but our love – for now at last it had joint membership – was, in essence, that most vulnerable, most doomed, of romantic genres, the holiday affair; its nature had merely been disguised by three months of student life, and by the illusory permanence of 'residence'. Second only to the wartime fling, the holiday affair is love against the odds. Begun for short-term gain, indulged for short-term pleasure, it is never designed for the long haul of living. It is lust in limbo, in a leisure land for encounters without consequences, and in this place love makes no plans. But with reason, for such plans, in such settings, will need both luck and armour-plate. Lives must be uprooted, cultures distorted, careers rebuilt and families abandoned if the hormones are truly to triumph. Holiday lovers do best just to gaze at the moon, and not wish upon it.

And yet, and yet. As the spring days went balmily by, the waiting buffers at the end of the line cast an ever-darker shadow, her waiting parents an ever-deeper gloom. The stakes of any commitment were dauntingly high: we came not just from different cultures, but different continents, our gulf not just history but geography. Had we been older, maturer, securer, we might even have had a yen for the bittersweet of parting. But we were young, open to dreams and without the dull perspective of sense. As always, our muddled adolescent mix of honest love and selfish fear made no judgement sound or safe, but, inexorably, in the more pragmatic corners of the brain, the thought of life together gained a silent ascendancy over the prospect of life apart . . . of life alone, again. And then, slowly, one by one, I heard the old taboo words from my past – my suppressed, abandoned past – start to surface in her thoughts.

'University?' I repeated.

She was lying on a grassy slope beside the lake in the Bois du Boulogne. Sunny Sundays here, with a picnic and ice-cream, were a habit inherited from the Italians, though we rarely achieved their mad frivolity. 'Why not?' she replied.

'Oh, I'd need to get more exams.'

'Well, get them.'

'No, it's too late.'

'It's not too late. You can go back to school at any age in the States.'

'Yes, but . . . but then I wouldn't get to start work till I was over twenty-five.'

'Oh, I see. I never realized you were in a rush to start work.'

I did not reply – what reply was there? – and Teri, seemingly content with this thrust, did not pursue the subject. But the subject pursued me, all lunch long, for still I found my missing university years as humiliating to explain away as a stretch in the Scrubs. Indeed, when regaling Teri with my past, I had always implied it was I who had rejected academia, and made failure sound like choice.

In the afternoon, as we strolled along the woodland walks, I managed to forget such thoughts, for the Bois du Boulogne, though haven for many perversions, was too full of birdsong for morbid regrets. Here was the nearest Paris came to the English idea of a park, with trees allowed to grow at random, paths which curved, grass instead of gravel, and – nature at its most subversive – undergrowth. Here we could allow ourselves to succumb to escapism, here one could let the blinkers back on the mind.

Several days passed, and we went to les Halles for the evening. And for a chunk of the night. Such a choice was not accidental: we were squeezing the last pips of time out of every passing day, every passing night. It was well gone two when at last we set off for home. Our route through the empty echoing streets was painfully familiar: it took us across the very bridge where once in the same small hours I had seen the long sad line of middle-aged voyeurs . . . and had so despaired for my future self. By some malign coincidence Teri too paused to gaze down into the shadowy waters. And then I remembered the dark night of the Seine in spate. As I leant quietly on the parapet beside her, it seemed that nowhere in Paris would ever be free of some past association, some poignant memory.

'Don't you ever worry where you'll be, what'll you be doing, five years from now?' she asked, after a long silence.

I felt a familiar, sickening chill at her words. Then, whilst I was struggling to summon up the sound of confidence, she spoke again.

'You won't have a future if you don't have an education.'

'You sound like my mother.'

'At times I feel like your mother.'

'Oh. So, it's not the Pope you're worried about, it's incest!'

The joke was not a great success. But for once it was ignored. She was not to be deflected. 'It's still not too late to try for university.'

'That again?'

'That again.'

I could not express the dread this created. To return home, three years on and three years worse off, to square one, to tedium and Englishness, and with just the mouldy carrot of years of studious betterment ahead, was a prospect too awful for the bohemian mind to contemplate. 'Yes, well I think I'll stick to the university of life, thank you.'

'Oh, they do degrees in clichés, do they?'

I smarted. 'Lots of people don't have degrees.'

'All your friends do, though. Wasn't that what you said? Oxford and Cambridge? You sounded a bit impressed to me.' Not for the first time, nice Teri's ability to play hard ball caught me unawares.

'Yes, well . . . It's only a month to Finals, and then my friends'll be finished. All gone. By the time I got to university, I'd be surrounded by kids half my age. Fresh from swotting, with spots. Great way to spend three years!'

'Yes, but your age, you'd get more out of it.'

'I'd get more out of writing.'

'Oh, selling well, is it?'

I bit my tongue. 'OK, but going to university isn't going to help that.'

'Maybe, maybe not, but at least it might help *you*.'

'Oh yeah? And how's that?'

Teri suddenly stood upright, and turned her face to mine. 'Because you wouldn't have to be so fucking negative all the

349

time, that's why. You might just possibly have some confidence in yourself. You might even stop feeling inferior for the rest of your life.' And with that she strode off across the bridge.

I felt panic. Panic at rejecting her concern, compounded by guilt at dashing her hopes . . . and humiliation at deserving her onslaught. I had no more glib answers to give, no more sophistry to square our circles. Life had finally trapped me. On the one hand, to leave Paris was unthinkable, on the other hand, to stay in Paris was unworkable. The whole world, it seemed, was rocks and hard places.

I hurried after her, if only to attempt an apology. I knew from experience that her temper lasted a minimum of four blocks, and I walked alongside her in silence for some time. She seemed to know so much of the truth that it left little to say. But to spend our last days in acrimony would sour a lifetime of memories.

Part of the dread that gripped me, that was so hard to convey to her, was the thought of starting over, of beginning life four years too late. No normal race was ever won from so far behind. It was perhaps a very English dread, its origins that corrosive concern for status which so inhibits the Anglo-Saxon mind. And, after failing to misspend my youth in such ostentatious Parisian poverty, I found it catatonically depressing to imagine the long years of adult penury that must precede the most modest of BA Hons. When Teri's pace began to slow and I sensed her anger was subsiding, I tried gently to reassure her that I was not being a negative no-hoper, that rationality lay behind my thinking. As we walked through the silent streets, I tried to explain the harsh financial facts, to make real the snags and pitfalls, to make sympathetic my limited horizons, and to make plain the impracticality of her ideas.

And still she said nothing.

'You see, I simply couldn't afford it.'

There was a long pause. '. . . I could support you . . . if you wanted me to.'

I stopped. I stood in the middle of the deserted rue de Buci, and stared at her nervous young face. With those few simple unromantic words I knew that she had just ceded the last 1 per cent of her territory.

We walked the streets of Paris for the rest of that night. The ending in my soft-focus daydreams had always been that we lived happily ever after, but despite the imprecision of dreams, despite their unreality, I had somehow allowed myself the assumption that we had lived happily ever after in Paris; to learn that if we had a future it was in a brave new world elsewhere, was finally, irrevocably, to inject the virus of realism into the body romantic. Now, the grown-ups' world of choices and priorities, of decisions and actions, of errors and consequences, all too suddenly came centre-brain. Most pressing of all, the question of Hamlet dimensions: to stay or to go? And if to go, when to go, if to move, how to move, if to study, what to study, if to resettle, where to resettle? On to the new clean-slate agenda came tumbling two lives in free fall. There was even talk of zip codes.

If I had been a reader of Teen Romance magazines, I would have recognized all my dilemmas; if I had subscribed to Mills and Boon, I would have known all the answers. And if I had had the Parisian's innate understanding of love in the spring, my genes would have told me the age-old truth that pain is part of the package. But I thought my tortured sensibilities were unique and original, not universal and immemorial, and felt myself the first to have faced a chilling world of chaos, a personal Year Zero.

We walked on through the dawn, Left Bank and Right Bank, boulevards and alleys, struggling to find the formula which shaped life to fit love. If the two of us were to depart Paris in harness – and 'if' was still the sheet-anchor of our discussions – we had few funds, and even fewer safe havens. Indeed, these could be summed up in one word: parents. And parents too could be summed up in one word: problems. I had left home with no warning; to return home with no warning and a woman was not the recommended route to happy families. Then there would be jobs to be sought, money to be earned, exams to be taken . . . and the dead, dread hand of suburbia to be resisted. Plus a Home Office arm to be twisted: a nodding acquaintance with the Fourth Estate, and the yellowed clippings of a Pennsylvanian scoop, were no guarantee of a work permit. There was brief thought of my joining the huddled masses, of stretching my exile across the Atlantic. Being the land of opportunity, America abounded in institutions of easy learning: at those upstate, backwater dishers-out of degrees, my English accent would, Teri said, most probably count as an A level. But, even if such tawdriness did not deter, the cost of the air fare did. By the end of the night, we had gone round in as many circles as *arrondissements*, and the jury was still out on our future.

During the days that followed, and as the deadline for Teri's departure drew closer, I felt debilitated by indecisiveness. My great fear was of failure, and of failure magnified by the presence of Teri. Back home, as a man of no means, in a place of no interest, I feared an affair of no hope; I had yet to grasp that the purpose of a partner was to provide support, not be a passive spectator of pratfalls. Thus, where once I had hoped to be ennobled by the lofty emotions of love, to be inspired to grandiloquent gestures, I was crudely weighing the fears of going against the fears of staying.

My daily routine took me three times a week to visit Monsieur Bareste, and twice a week to visit Henri. As had always been my habit, I tailored the route to my mood of the day and my latest taste in aesthetics. This was the hour when I spent quality time with myself. So now each afternoon, as I walked through my favourite streets in the warm spring sun, I tried to bring Paris into focus. I tried to ignore the siren songs of the city, and browbeat my thoughts into some kind of objectivity. And I began to realize that, though I never tired of the beauty of Paris, my days had indeed grown routine, that novelty was giving way to normality, and that gradually the sense of *déjà vu* was drifting like a filter across my life.

No matter how charming the company of dear Josef Bareste, 150 hours on the subject of menus, even the calorifically charismatic menus of a top person's restaurant, left the brain short of nourishment. And, though I had come to share M. Bareste's regard for Breughel, I felt that my sixteenth-century knowledge of low life in the Low Countries had peaked some time ago. Consequently, our lessons now moved in the predictable grooves of a much-played 78.

Henri, however, still retained sufficient of the sphinx to defy prediction. Two weeks earlier, we had celebrated spring with a trip to a local park; his purpose, though, had not been to enjoy the sun, but to recite the Latin names of an entire flowerbed. He liked, he said, dead languages. But his character did not attract the living and our rapport had developed little beyond a halting, repetitive formality. For me, any remaining interest lay in the creepiness of his St Germain apartment, and the impending launch of his novel.

It had often been my habit to stroll down onto the islands after our hour of ossified conversation, but now, in my new mood of heart-searching, I found myself drawn back to where all my nostalgia began: place de la Contrescarpe. As I climbed steeply up rue du Cardinal-Lemoine, passing one more time the home of Hemingway, I was aware that my visits had lately grown less frequent. By living and loving elsewhere my ties had subtly weakened.

I walked past where the mad axeman and the libertarians had once exchanged concepts and sat down at the small pavement café on the corner of the square. I ordered a *pastis*, a recent addition to my repertoire, and leant back on the enamelled white chair to watch the world go by. It was here, a spring ago, a life-time ago, that M. Molmar had won the climactic battle of words, and stalked off in victory, not ever deigning to acknowledge me again. No-one had seen him now for months. Whether he had departed to the hosannas of the poetry world, as the new Byron of the age, or whether he had failed to meet the rent, was a mystery never likely to be solved.

As I watched the comings and goings in the square, with the late afternoon sun slipping towards the rooftops, I realized just how few were the faces I now recognized. This was a *quartier* of transients, and to be absent was to become rapidly a stranger.

Sitting, sipping, feeling a sense of distance, I called to mind all those I once knew who had now gone, both in the hotel and out. It was a long list of names from such a short passage of time. Yet all that remained of them were memories . . . none had left a trace of their days in the street. Except Gerard, of course – 500 square feet of medieval hunting mural was hard to miss.

Perhaps, if the truth be told, and if the maths were rigorous, I had just three friends left on Mouffetard. And indeed in Paris.

I had felt myself in sentimental bondage to Sherry since her red rose. We had shared troubled times and tears, and hers were the first ovaries I had circumnavigated. Yet her days too were marked by fading hopes. Running low on funds – a very minor legacy from an Alaskan aunt – and baffled by how to carbon-date European men, she now entertained dreams of moving on, of seeking the happy-ever-after land of Meaningful Relationships.

All that would then be left in the old hotel was the great survivor, Tony, who had so long ago been the first to knock at my door, offering third-hand tea and tableaux. He, though, would never be one for the close kinship of friends. Away from his work it was rare to hear him talk more than ten minutes at a stretch. And in my heart I knew that what interested him most in me was the possibility I might one day remove my beard and give him access to my bone structure.

And then there was Ulrika, with whom the story had started. We still met, sometimes with Teri, sometimes without. She had dreamt of life with an artist; now she shared a studio with a depressive. She was still as beautiful as ever (give or take the millimetre) but there was a seriousness to her that was new. Her detached irony had grown stronger, her recourse to poetry more frequent. In the past, she had been protective of her writing, but recently, in want of an opinion, she had shown me her latest poems.

I had not been prepared for their darkness, for their bleak view of life. I felt I had seen the unlit side of her soul, and caught off guard had said, 'It's like an angel pissing on the world from the clouds!' It was meant to be flip. It was certainly not Lit. Crit. But she took these words for disparagement, and she never forgot them, and perhaps never forgave me. Nonetheless, though I was sorry to have hurt her, I was not sorry to have seen her poems. Because, for the first time, I had proof of the discontent and the unfulfilment she felt – and of the loneliness she had so long denied. And at that moment I had understood that I was wrong to envy her . . . and knew then that there would always be a distance between us. Without understanding why, I felt liberated by this knowledge, and released from the remains of my long undeclared passion.

A shaking of silver interrupted my reveries. The waiter was eager to finish his shift, and I realized that this side of the square, always the last to receive the sun, was now in deep shadow. I paid for my drink and, longing for the day I could afford to drink *pastis* not diluted to ninety-nine parts water, I stood up to go.

'*Non, non, restez là, monsieur!*' the waiter cried, mistaking me for the pathologically apologetic English tourist. But I was ready to go. I wanted to walk slowly down rue Mouffetard, sniffing the air and listening to the sounds that were once so familiar. My mood had changed, had shifted in some way that I could not define.

Before leaving the square, I lingered briefly by the boulangerie, where I had become bilingual in buns. This time I settled for *un gâteau à pommes*. Then taking to the middle of the street, as was the way of natives, I started unhurriedly down the hill. As I passed the corner I found myself recalling how, on my very first day, I had seen a man with a performing monkey standing here: watching them from Tony's room, I felt that I had come to live in some exotic Eastern bazaar. On the opposite side of the road, the hotel itself was, despite its internal tarting-up, still as doggedly dour a brown as ever. Defiantly uninviting with its grille and its grime, the old exterior stayed reassuringly true to the French tradition of the anti-hotel. I continued on, without pausing. Next I went past the local greengrocer's, where Dave used to wait patiently for the fruit to go bad. A few yards on, I came to the minimart where once, under the malign influence of Colin and his 'Property Is Theft' T-shirt, I had liberated a small brown comb, at the cost of several panic attacks and a day's diarrhoea. A short distance further, I reached the

Laundromat, where those with freshly washed clothes were currently being encouraged to go to Magritte. A pace more, and I saw that the gallery, née bike shop, was still in business, though nudes had now replaced landscapes. Little, however, had changed the streetscape: as rue Mouffetard curled gently down, the same plaster was still flaking off, the same walls were still crumbling down, the same washing was still strung out, and the same sense of history in stasis was still potent.

What had changed, however, were my feelings. As I struggled to analyse my mood and my memories, I could not escape the disturbing truth that when I now thought of Sherry and Tony and Ulrika and Gerard, the mental image they most evoked was solitude. Solitude and lives in limbo. From my old friends I no longer gained the feelings of *joie de vivre*, or of free spirits, or of brave new worlds. Instead, I felt haunted by their sense of isolation, their loss of hope. And I remembered once more the old men of Grenoble, fighting over their crusts of bread.

When I reached the market, the trading was done for the day. The shutters were down, the hawkers were home, the street was empty, the Espagnol with five flutes had gone. The only noise was from the sanitation unit, its men sluicing the greasy cobbles with thick jets of water. If I was seeking a symbol, I had found it.

I turned away and started back to the Latin Quarter.

An hour earlier that day, a decision had seemed impossible to achieve, the arguments hopelessly, evenly balanced. But, like a ro-ro ferry on an even keel, once there had been a slight tilt to one side, all the loose thoughts in my brain flooded to throw their weight in the same direction – and suddenly the most delicately balanced decision of my life became the most obvious conclusion in the world.

I wanted to be alone no more. I was ready to return to England.

CHAPTER 35

The clouds around the sun had turned purple as it set, and the colour had spread like a giant bruise across the sky. The sky was at its widest and deepest above the Luxembourg Gardens, and from where we sat, on the cramped pavement outside Au Petit Suisse, we had a view *sans pareil* of the slow, spectacular sunset, as it sank behind the beigey-gold of the Senate and the clean green of the trees. This was a sky raging against the dying of the light: this was Paris searing itself on the memory.

'Great place to die,' said Teri, breaking a long silence.

'We could come back for that.'

'Who knows, you might have a plot at Père-Lachaise by then.'

The single row of pavement tables had still to fill with takers. On the streets, a few people hurried by, not yet in couples, not yet organized for the evening to come. In a nearby restaurant, a waiter in a red waistcoat moved an unlit candle nearer to the window, and then moved it back again.

'What will you tell your father?' I asked.

'Lies.'

'Oh, that's a relief.'

'It's what fathers expect.'

'What will you tell him about me?'

'That you're called Bartolomeo.'

'What, and living in England?'

'Okay, so I'll busk that one.'

She slowly rolled the plastic ashtray marked Ricard to and fro across the table. Neither of us had answers, for anything.

'Seriously, what d'you reckon he'll do?'

'Oh, he'll be very Italian about it. Lot of breast-beating, lot of speeches about family honour, lot of appeals to God.' She leaned back against the wall and smiled. 'And then he'll hire a Mafia hit-man and have your brains blown out.'

'Ha–ha. What about your brother?'

'Yeah, he'd do it if the money was right.'

'. . . Aaah! So his sympathy's out of the question?'

'Everybody's sympathy is out of the question. They'll probably convince even the dog I'm a bad person!' She laughed again. She seemed neither bitter nor distressed, but almost maternally tolerant of their narrowness.

Our drinks arrived. Each cup was delivered with a crispness close to military precision. '*Un thé. Un chocolat. M'sieurdame.*' Another order executed, another table done. All that was lacking was the clicking of heels. But yet, as always, I loved it: loved the style, loved the panache, loved the self-regard. This was how they served hot chocolate in the real world. And already, somehow, I knew that such tiny moments, such cultural trivia, contained the seed-corn of a lifetime's nostalgia. And that already a matrix of these memories was forming for the comfort of long suburban nights. I even felt sentimental towards my unchic *chocolat*, the poor man's drink whose taste outlasted tepidity, whose services dated from the Battle of Borodino.

'More to the point,' she said, a touch less laid-back, 'what'll *your* father do?'

'Offer you a reward, I expect. For safe return of a son.'

'Oh. So what should I say? "I've brought your black sheep back, Mr Pilton"?'

'It's times like this I wish they'd had other children. I'm not just the black sheep. I'm the whole bloody flock.'

Teri said nothing, and I sensed in her a need for reassurance. 'Dad'll be fine. He'll make you very welcome.' And he would.

He would be curious about her, as he was curious about all things. And he would talk to her as an equal.

'What about your mother?'

'Just tell her you're a virgin. That'll cover the essentials.'

'Oh good,' said Teri, and sipped her tea.

She did not know it, but I had almost come to dread her tea drinking. As usual, she had ordered tea with milk, and as usual, the waiter had been baffled. To the French stomach, it was a beverage without logic, an alien foolishness. Consequently, her order had always to be argued for, syllable by ill-accented syllable. But Teri never gave up, never forgot her American birthright to consumer satisfaction, and so there was scarcely a café I had not squirmed in. At such times, I felt the most compelling case for our move to England was its cultural affinity with milky tea.

And yet, this being the messiness of love, it was the very fact that she had such bottle, such chutzpah, which most drew me to her. Which most made me proud to be loved by her.

A silence descended on our sipping, a silence full of the presence of the future.

'I guess we're being quite unconventional in one sense,' I suggested.

'Which sense is that?'

'Elopement's supposed to be *away* from parents. We're eloping *to* mine!'

'Not to get married, though!' said Teri quickly, like one who had just heard the patter of small print.

'Oh, no, definitely not!'

'How *are* you going to explain me? I mean, what are you going to explain me *as*?'

I too had wondered this. Neither asylum-seeker nor runaway were parent-friendly terms. (And, I suspected, fathers of such children were bonded in fraternity – and sympathetic to re-patriation.) But to call us anything in the spectrum of sweethearts made us sound foolish and headstrong. I shrugged. 'I could say you're my au pair!'

Teri gave it exaggerated consideration. 'Well, emotionally you are still in the late stages of potty-training.'

'Or I could tell them you've come to learn the language. That should take six months.'

'It's just written humour that's your speciality, right?'

I grinned ruefully at her, and attempted to think constructively. Once more we sat in silence, side by side in the fading light. Neither of us found it easy to focus our minds. The evening air was soft and warm and made the reality of a new life seem far away.

'I could try and get work as a stringer. I've got a friend on *Time* magazine.'

'Ah, now that would impress my mum and dad. The South London voice of *Time* magazine. Reporting from their box-room.'

Teri giggled, her best warm throaty giggle. 'Are there many international scoops in your street?'

'Well, let's see . . . there's the Russian agent at no. 27, with the extra-large reception aerial . . . and the black man from Kenya, believed to be a Mau–Mau terrorist, at no. 56 . . . and Mrs Goering in the shed at no. 78 . . .'

Soon after this, we gave up on career plans for the day.

Instead, we sipped our way through a round of alcohol and thought deep thoughts and gazed out towards the dusk and the gardens. For the first time in my life, I wished that I had an artist's eye. I wanted to commit to memory every detail of the scene. I wanted to memorize it all, from the gilded tips on the park railings to the avant-garde posters outside the Théâtre de l'Odeon, from the chandeliers starting to glow in the high Senate windows to our small and rickety metal table on the pavement. I wanted to be sure that the memories of this evening would stay with me until I grew old and grey.

'Yes,' I sighed, taking her hand, 'this is the meaning of true romance.'

'Oh dear!' she said. 'Are you about to compare my eyes to limpid pools?'

I hesitated. 'I was working up to it. Thought I'd have a go at a bit of charm.'

She shook her head. 'It won't suit you. Besides . . .' She smiled. '. . . If you'd had charm, I would never have been interested in you.'

'Oh,' I said, baffled, and wondering whether to be hurt. 'That's rather a bind.'

'Not really,' she replied. And she squeezed my hand, which still held hers. And there we sat, in silence, hands enclasped, soppy smiles on our faces: the perfect picture of contentment, the embodiment of *l'amour Parisienne*.

The last of the colour had all but faded from the sky. The last of the stragglers were drifting from the park. Exhorting them on their way were the garden gendarmerie, who stood, keys in hand, waiting to clang the gates shut for the night.

That same night we decided to depart Paris for London at the end of the following week.

The following day *les événements de mai '68* began.

CHAPTER 36

The taste of tear gas clung in the air of boulevard St Germain des Prés. It was late afternoon and no car was to be seen: the four-lane highway was crowded with pedestrians, milling uncertainly, apprehensively. Each new rumour that the riot police were regrouping caused a spasmic ripple of panic. For the second successive day, violent running battles had spread like flash floods through the streets of the Latin Quarter.

A few yards from me, a French hippy, exotically dressed and beaded and with a beret full of flower-power badges, leapt up onto a wooden bench.

'Man achieves nothing by the use of violence!' he cried to the crowds. 'Nothing! Except more violence! And more hatred!' Those nearest turned to watch him. 'Violence is the wrong way! The bourgeois way. Love is the only way!' He had a loud, clear voice, and soon others were drawn into the ambit of his audience. 'Don't fight! Give a flower to your enemy! Show him you are human!' The young hippy produced a bunch of flowers from a canvas bag slung over his shoulder and waved them in the air. The growing audience started to smile as they warmed to his gentle eccentricity. 'We are all human! We all want to be loved! We all have feelings!' A murmur of agreement greeted his words. He paused, his eyes drawn to the middle distance. 'That gendarme there—' He gestured at a lone policeman who was standing, observing, on the pavement at the back of the crowd. '—he has feelings too!' The policeman – a local man, no riot

362

squad import – looked awkward, unhappy to be the focus for such attention. 'He just wants to be loved.'

The crowd laughed good-humouredly. The policeman smiled, pleased by this recognition of his needs. 'Here, give him a flower!' The hippy tossed a lily into the crowd. It was passed back, with cheers, to the lone policeman, who stood clutching it rather sweetly, and exchanging good wishes with those around him.

'What fucking bollocks! Are you mad? We give this bastard flowers and then he and his fascist mates smash our brains out!' Onto the bench had leapt one of the riots' hard men, an anarchist dressed in black leather, and clasping a motorbike helmet. 'One hundred yards from here, in rue St Jacques, dozens of our comrades are lying covered in blood!' A gasp of shock rose from the crowd.

'The cops didn't give *them* flowers!' A murmur of anger was heard. 'The cops gave *them* rifle-butts to the head!' The sense of outrage was now tangible. 'Did the cops ever ask our comrades if *they* were human?' he cried rhetorically. 'Did *he*?' And the anarchist agitator pointed dramatically at the lone policeman who, still clutching his lily, once again reluctantly found himself the centre of attention.

'No!' cried a number of the crowd in catechismal response. 'No!'

Another yelled, 'The bastard!'

'You answer violence with violence!' cried the anarchist. 'Not with love!' Roars of support came from all around. 'Violence is the way! The revolutionary way!' And with that the crowd, transformed by righteous fury, turned upon their new-found enemy. Before he could raise his baton, before he could even run, the policeman was knocked to the ground, and boots and fists hammered into him. Within a minute he was unconscious, and blood was streaming across the pavement. The mob – for now it was a mob – ripped the rest of the flowers from the canvas bag and thrust them down his throat as he lay gagging. But then, with the timing of the cavalry, the sound of sirens was heard.

And the crowd rushed off to battle stations new. As suddenly as the action had begun, it ended.

Events were soon to make it exceedingly clear that this Paris rioting was not the one-off, set-piece battle so favoured by the organizers of English radicalism. This was no Grosvenor Square ticket-only demonstration, as advertised by the appropriate organs of the press. This was raw, spontaneous anger from the cobble-throwing descendants of the French Revolution. And they had a cause.

It was little more than a minute's walk from Teri's hotel to the Sorbonne. Except that one could no longer reach the Sorbonne. The Sorbonne was sealed off. By riot police. For only the second time in its 700-year history – according to *Le Monde*, journal of record and riots – the Sorbonne was closed. The first time was by the Nazis.

There was a sinister physicality to the closure. Rank upon rank of the paramilitary CRS, the feared and grim-faced servants of State security, were drawn up across the statued forecourt of the ancient university. Standing just yards from the pavement of fun-loving boulevard St Michel, these lines of craggy men in dark-blue uniform, black boots and visored helmets, armed with shields and guns and sticks the size of cattle prods, transmitted the alien chill of an occupying power.

What had begun as the disciplining of eight student activists had now escalated, via some doctrinal fisticuffs in the street and a ministerial over-reaction at a desk, into the establishment of French education's first armed fortress. *Langue et civilization* was now a redoubt, ringed by paddy wagons. Yet, upon reflection, I was not surprised. I had seen what happened when a piano had posed a threat to law and order, and given that two vanloads of police had been deemed necessary to suppress a pianist and a female nudist, it seemed not unreasonable that the entire French military – short perhaps of the nuclear *force de frappe* – should be used to contain nonconformist conduct in more academic circles.

The problem, however, as with Vietnam, was disengagement.

This twenty-four-hour-a-day phalanx of Robocops, clad – as one journalist put it – in Martian plastic, was rapidly becoming the object of pilgrimage for every soi-distant student in the city, all of them bearing a supply of libertarian invective and, in some cases, spit. (And, perhaps even more humiliating for these men's men, trained to defend the State by skull- and bollock-crushing but now as inertly ceremonial as the British Horse Guards, was their inclusion in the latest tourist itinerary: fresh from the Eiffel Tower and the falderols of Montmartre, coachloads of sightseers would glide gawpingly by, their Instamatics clicking as they captured for the folks back home a close-up of the hated Neanderthals of gay Paree.) Each day, like a contagion, more and more dark anonymous uniforms congregated in quiet streets close by, bulky and hostile, silently intent on intimidation. And each day the buildings of the city echoed to more running battles, more flying cobbles, more howling sirens. Each day the journey to the Latin Quarter grew a little more hazardous. And each day my memories of the city grew a little more ugly.

As Teri worked out her week's notice, I continued the last of my lessons. But no longer were they begun with a dreamy preambling through the park. The chestnut tree walk and the model-boat pond were now barred to the population of Paris. The dust remained unscuffed and the sunlit amphitheatre empty, for the promenaders and spectators were kept from their pleasures by padlocks. And at each great padlocked gate stood the black-booted Klingons, in pairs. The innocent pleasures of spring had been suspended by the State for – in that all-purpose phrase of hand-me-down despotism – 'reasons of security'.

On one of my last afternoons, I set off as usual for Henri's. I turned down the heavily shuttered rue de Fleurus, deep in bourgeois quiet and five storeys of shadow. Ahead of me I could see the park trees and the closed gates and the new guardians. As always, I resented the coming detour: even in daytime the perimeter walk had a dull, dusty anonymity which lowered my spirits. I paused on the kerb to let a taxi pass. Across the road were the two CRS men, standing silently side by side, like sentries. Except that they stood with their legs apart, giving their presence a swagger even when stationary. Coming towards them along the park railings was a tall, slim man in his twenties, wearing Levis and an open-necked shirt. He was reading a paper as he walked, his eyes cast down. As he passed by the gates, the larger of the two riot police suddenly swung an arm through the air and smashed his long baton across the young man's skull. As the victim crumpled to the ground, the attacker immediately reverted to his original impassive posture.

Long seconds passed. None of the three moved. Then the barely conscious victim dragged himself on to his knees. Blood was guttering down his face, and his shirt was starting to stain. He vomited helplessly onto the pavement. Still kneeling, he looked up at the two CRS men in bewilderment. They each stared straight ahead, unblinking, motionless, absurdly innocent. Like the monkeys who see no evil. The young man staggered to his feet, moaning incoherently with pain. He clutched his newspaper to his leaking skull, and then, recognizing the impracticality of any complaints procedure, he stumbled away down the quiet bourgeois street.

There were no seasons in the half-dark salon, and the air temperature kept to the constant coolness of marble. Indeed, as I took my usual seat on the Regency sofa, amongst the square-backed Sheratons and the horizontal-armed Hepplethwaites and the Italian lacquered secretaire – each a family heirloom, none a vulgar purchase – I felt myself enter a world where not only temperature was unchanging, but time itself. I accepted my usual coffee in its bone-china cup, with the two *amaretti* on the bone-china side plate, and I made my usual enquiries as to my pupil's well-being during the previous few days.

'Do many Englishmen believe in God?'

Despite my tuition, Henri's small talk had not improved. I tried to consider the question objectively.

'In England,' I said, 'God is for people with good manners. It's like Henley. And Ascot.' We had covered class in earlier talks, and he had seemed to respond to the concept of a land of emotionally crippled people. 'The middle class like the idea of heaven, provided it's reasonably exclusive.'

366

He mulled the answer. 'So doctrine is not important to the English?'

'It's a sign of bad taste, using the brain to be clever.'

He mulled again, a little puzzled. His inability to winnow either irony or cynicism placed a heavy responsibility on any conversationalist, and in these last days of lessons I had found myself growing demob-happy in my assertions.

'And absolute truths? What about absolute truths?' he asked.

Thus, in this strangely fundamentalist vein, the conversation edged onward. What most interested me was the trigger for his train of thought, but this was no question to be posed by an employee. Behind his enquiries seemed to be some wish to define the nature of a national psyche. By fits and starts, he spoke of the power of abstract thought, of obscure French philosophers, and the premature age they had died at. I chipped in with a Rousseau or two, but was made to feel mainstream. His allusions were to the likes of Montesquieu and Baron d'Holbach, and as he sat waxen-faced in his Madame Tussauds of furniture, dominated by the dark oils of the March to Moscow, I at times felt my hold on reality was slipping slowly away. We had been together in gloom – physical and metaphysical – for some thirty minutes when the shouting began.

At first it was just a distant roar. A background roar, almost a roar of traffic. But the roar grew closer, and louder. And then I recognized the noise not of cars, but of voices. And not just five voices, or ten voices, but a hundred voices, a thousand voices. A thousand voices shouting in unison . . . and in anger . . . and in the street outside.

Henri led the stately rush to the balcony doors and fumbled back the sticking bolts. Then with unnatural speed he pulled open the chenille curtains – and for the first time in all my many visits, the natural light of day shone into every corner of the room. As the gilt-edged mirrors glittered in the new-found sun, the revelatory rays lit up the fading fabric of a time-worn salon. And the mystique of history was dissipated beyond recall. The ending of the reign of discreet shadows showed cracks in the cornice and repairs to the armoire and stitches to the Regency

367

stripe. To have let there be light was the *lèse-majesté* of exposing a dowager duchess in her corsetry.

We opened the doors and stepped out onto the second-floor balcony, blinking in the sudden sunlight. 'CRS-SS! CRS-SS! CRS-SS! CRS-SS! **CRS-SS! CRS-SS! CRS-SS!**' The roar filled the warm spring air. A chaotic crush of people on the march was pouring down boulevard St Germain. There were red flags of Leninism, black flags of anarchy; there were banners from faculties and posters from lycées and agitprop slogans from les Beaux Arts; there were hard men in helmets, pretty girls in dresses, and John Does in jeans. The demonstrators were young, they were animated, they were united. This was the Sorbonne-in-exile, this was the Sorbonne on the streets, this was youth *enragé*. From above, it was a scene of colour and tumult, of camaraderie and emotion and energy. It was a rare raw moment of action, rich in startlingly fresh images. . . . And yet, somehow, it was strangely familiar. And then I remembered. I remembered where I had seen it all before. I had seen it in the one-franc films of Eisenstein at the Cinemathèque. 'CRS-SS! CRS-SS! CRS-SS! **CRS-SS! CRS-SS! CRS-SS!**' The roar echoed down the street like an angry carnival cry, bouncing off the bourgeois walls with the venom of a verbal grenade.

But then, as the column came closer, my eye was distracted by a movement on the balcony next to ours. And into view shuffled two elderly men in suits. The taller was hunched, venerable and over eighty. The younger was bald but almost dapper, with a buttonhole and a silver-topped cane. Not since my first day had I caught any glimpse of Henri's uncle and grandfather. I had, however, always been aware of their presence: a door just closing, a distant cough, a pair of shoes squeaking on a polished floorboard. Often I would hear them in the study adjacent, their voices an indistinct and disembodied murmur, like the snuffling of domestic rodents behind the wainscoting. And now they too had been brought blinking into the light by the events of the world outside.

The two old men gazed aghast upon the surging crowd, and t'sked with force in French. Henri's grandfather shook his patrician head in sombre disbelief – his demeanour that of George VI emerging onto the Palace balcony to discover the Germans were goose-stepping up his Mall – and took a tight hold of the rococo railings. His sexagenarian companion seemed almost as shocked by the students' dress sense as their slogans, and fell to focusing on their unserried ranks with a pair of opera-glasses. Each man in turn would point to some fresh facet of the barbarian hordes – a raised fist, an offensive banner – and would shudder in quiet disgust. Theirs was a private world with neither television nor newspapers, and one sensed a thousand canons of convention being broken in the melée below.

And from this melée now rose taunts of revolution and tumbrils as the student vanguard sighted the bourgeoisie upon the balconies above. Jeers and catcalls jarred the air. And the cry '*J'accuse!*' was hurled at all the well-heeled watchers. As I stood in my cavalry twills on the wrong side of enemy lines – and wondered what effect a wave would have – I ruefully reflected on the unjust volatility of class warfare. Two full years of underdog credentials to my name, and now, by a fluke of geography, I was brutally harangued for representing the forces of reaction. The stoicism of Sidney Carton I found quite baffling.

Meanwhile on the neighbouring balcony, recognizing the body of the march was soon to be upon them, the two old men had decided to retreat. Passing the opera-glasses from hand to hand, they took a slow last look at the uproar in their once quiet part of town, a slow last look at the lamentable indiscipline of youth, a slow last look at the fluttering flags of treason, and then they turned to shuffle back into their book-lined, map-filled sanctuary. And as the frail grandfather disappeared from my sight for ever, I heard him sigh with elegiac regret, '*Ah, si Napoléon était là . . .*'

The words drifted away on the spring breeze. His old companion, steadying himself with his stick, nodded in sad concurrence. '*Ah, oui,*' he said with infinite softness. '*Si Napoléon était là . . .*'

And the shutters closed behind them.

When I emerged from the apartment half an hour later – after a lesson which never quite recovered from its intermission – the crowds had dispersed. But they had dispersed like an oil spillage is dispersed. The heavy-duty demonstrators had not gone away but stuck together in small groups, coagulating on street corners throughout the Latin Quarter – and the less committed, the curious, the hangers-on, were still drifting, apparently aimlessly – and now formed a light coating on the surface of the town. Meanwhile, in café after café, the locked-out students were huddled together talking, not boulevard chitchat, not light-weight banter, but intense, unsmiling exchanges. It was everywhere the same: though the marching was over, there was unfinished business in the air. I strolled circumspectly through the streets to meet Teri for an early dinner and the tension was palpable. Tucked silently down side alleys were the ominous grey vans, by the dozen. And behind their wire-grilled windows, their reinforced bodywork, their protected headlamps, their bulletproof glass, sat the rows of CRS. Brimming with rage, and primed to explode without warning.

Teri was often late. She had yet to find a way to walk past people without asking them a question. Her lateness, however, was easy to forgive. She rarely arrived without a set of answers that suggested she had just met the world's ten most improbable people. It was a miracle that she had survived childhood. So I was not worried when she was late for dinner.

But when an hour had passed I began to suspect trouble. And when she had not shown up after a second hour – the hour that university kitchens closed – I knew for sure there was trouble. I made my way back down from the first floor – wondering whether I would later feel ashamed that I had eaten without her – and began to fear the worst. Uncertain what to do or where to go, I lingered a few moments more on the steps outside.

And then I heard the helter-skelter of her rambler's feet. I turned. She was running down rue du Pot-de-Fer towards me. I waved and dashed across to meet her.

'I'm sorry I'm late!' She gave me a hug and a big kiss.

'Are you all right?' She nodded breathlessly. Her face was

flushed, her hair chaotic, and she seemed more than a little excited. 'Where've you been?' I asked.

'Jail.'

We found a no-frills restaurant not yet closed near the School of Industrial Chemistry. A neighbourhood restaurant, in a neighbourhood of bleakly institutional buildings, it had long communal tables covered in oilcloth and a bustling *patronne* who recited the dishes on offer. She seemed unsurprised by my own request for wine only, and briskly laid out a rectangle of white paper just for Teri, who at once set to work on the bread.

'It wasn't my fault,' she said between bites.

'Of course not.' I grinned at her. 'I remember how it wasn't your fault when those nice country policemen took offence at being called Gestapo.'

'That was different. This lot were plain-clothes,' she protested. 'I had no way of knowing who they were.'

'I see.' I smiled. 'What did you do? Ask them to help you throw a cobble?'

'I didn't do anything!'

A few days ago I might have been sceptical. Teri's idea of innocence usually caused more trouble than most people's proven guilt. But after the mindless beating I had seen outside the park gates that afternoon, I was now uncomfortably aware that such a triviality as an arrest needed no reason. Indeed, after all the random violence of the last few days, I was becoming uncomfortably aware that many an old naïve belief of mine was now threatened by contact with life.

'So?'

'I was in rue de Seine. And this guy came up to me. A regular sleazeball.' She paused. 'Now, of course, I didn't know that over here plain-clothes cops have their badges attached to their trouser belts. And this guy starts pointing, and fiddling, and trying to show me something. And, well . . .' For the first time since I had known her, I sensed she was admitting to foolishness. '. . . Well, I incorrectly thought he was masturbating.'

I was midway through a mouthful of wine, and for several

seconds I could not stop coughing. 'What did you do? Ex-communicate him?'

'I ignored him.' She smiled. 'As any properly brought-up young girl from Pennsylvania would do. And then I walked away.' She hesitated. 'Which, with hindsight, was probably a mistake.'

'He arrested you for walking away?'

'Er, no. No, he arrested me because when he said, "I'm a policeman" I shook his hand and said, "And I'm Marie-Antoinette".'

I gawped at her in disbelief.

And then she added, 'That's when the other three jumped me.'

'The other three! What other three?'

'It wasn't my fault. They were plain-clothes as well.'

'Oh. Not your day. Did you upset them too?'

'Well, I sort of kicked them. Accidentally.'

'Kicked them . . . ?'

'Well, they threw me on the ground and sat on me.'

'That should be worth the Croix de Guerre. Who won?'

She smiled, a coy but irrepressible smile. 'I got a couple of bites in.'

'I see . . .' I was having trouble with my sympathetic, caring look. 'And this is what you meant by "not doing anything"?'

'Well, not under the American Constitution,' she said, a touch petulantly.

'Yes, that should be a very useful defence in France.'

'Oh, I'm not being charged,' she replied.

'You're not?'

'No. They cuffed me; and chucked me in the paddy wagon; and took me down the precinct; and kept me in a cell; and generally tried to make me feel like a piece of shit. But basically it was just a routine identity check.'

I knew what had really happened. She had kept asking every-body so many questions – questions about her rights, about the French legal system, about ringing the Ambassador, about what it was like to be a policeman, what they enjoyed most about the job, what was their most interesting case, would they like to do an interview for an American university magazine – that they had declared the arrest a draw and asked her to leave.

'One thing puzzles me,' I said. 'What sort of police badge is it that looks like a penis?'

Her potato soup arrived, the first of three large courses, and her hunger left me time for my own thoughts. Or perhaps thoughts was putting it too grandly. What churned round inside me were as yet emotions, the larval stage of thoughts, and I had come to no clear conclusions. For several days I had felt disturbed. For the first time in my life I had seen violence. And somewhere deep down a belief that reason could always prevail had suffered a direct and bloody hit. (It was perhaps a childlike belief, a self-deluding belief, which in other, less pampered, worlds would have been extinct by puberty, but it had until now offered me comfort.) And with the sight of violence had come impotence, the only apparent remedy more violence. And impotence meant guilt. Yet such was the compelling sense of drama on the streets that I was drawn back again and again as a spectator. Or was the term voyeur? For in *les événements* I found an excitement which filled me with dubious pleasures – and which I pursued with deep ambivalence.

I was just reflecting that this might, in its modest way, be the same conflict of emotions as stirred by war, when a breathless man in a linen jacket burst through the door and, over the frenzied jangling of the bead curtain, announced that war had in fact begun. Three blocks away.

True to the spirit of journalism Teri turned down the meat and cheese courses and we rushed off in the direction of the war front. I recognized the dark, echoing backstreets we were running through: it was here I had sometimes wandered in those lonely early hours when gripped by existential crises of the soul and shortages of sex. The high concrete walls were ill-lit and decades-deep in peeling fly-blown posters, a vision of desolation peculiarly French. This was *film noir* territory, an anonymous landscape wallpapered with poignant testimony to the ephemerality of causes.

Panting, we turned into the top end of rue Gay-Lussac. As we did so, a car blew up. I had never seen a car blow up before. It seemed to lift off the ground in surprise, and then fell back in flames, a car no more. After the whooshing explosion of petrol came a strange tinkling of glass fluttering gently to earth. Through the oily black smoke and the blinding tear gas we saw the street was littered with burnt-out cars, their skeletons skewed in makeshift barricades across the roadway. Underfoot was a debris of kerbstones and cobbles crowbarred into action as missiles. The streets around were a mass of running figures, the air thick with screams and cries of hate and the sound of ambulance sirens. The fiercest fighting was barely a hundred yards away, where, enveloped in the choking murk of the tear gas, the rioters had wet scarves tied bandit-style over their faces and were hurling every last piece of rubble, even railings, at the enemy lines of the CRS. Behind the action, an assembly line of students was filling milk bottles with petrol and, as time and again the police launched frenzied clubbing sorties into the crowds, these fire-bombs would curl through the night sky and crash in no-man's land, lighting up the carnage in a lurid glare.

We watched this scene for a long, awestruck moment. It was Teri who spoke first.

'I don't think this is your normal, regulation-size riot.' She paused. 'I think this might be the start of a revolution.'

'What, 1792, but with petrol?'

'Something like that.' We stood in silence as we thought. 'Be a shame to miss it.'

I nodded. And we put Norbury in the pending file.

It was halter-top weather, tourist weather, but under the fierce blue of the afternoon sky there was only one sight in Paris that simply had to be seen. I squeezed myself up on to a crowded window-ledge, and squinted down the wide street through the trees. The pavements were packed as if for summer sales, but no-one was scrummaging, no-one was moving. All of boulevard Saint Michel was waiting, anticipating, preparing to be part of history.

'*Les voilà!*' came the cry at last. '*Les voilà!*' And a great roar went up.

And then I saw them. Arms linked across the entire width of the boulevard, twenty deep, thirty deep, advancing like a giant human bulldozer, came the first ranks of the greatest assembly of French citizens that Paris had seen since World War Two, since de Gaulle, now the enemy, had victoriously swept down the Champs-Elysées. This was no *ad hoc*, madcap, adolescent demo, but the full and serious-minded might of the trade union movement of France. This was their response to the call for a twenty-four-hour general strike and a march across Paris. It was perhaps a reluctant call to arms – the CGT (the TUC *français*, a carthorse trained in Moscow) was not so much in the vanguard of revolutionary action as in the guard's van – but events were spiralling out of their control, and it was no longer just students who were *enragés*.

This was a march with traditional banners, this was a march that dug deep into the bedrock of the citizenry, this was a march that said solidarity. It had begun at La Bastille, as bloody a symbolism as was to be found in the annals of France, and already had cheerfully terrorized three miles of the Rive Droite with its chanting. Now on home territory, this vast multi-coloured tide of shirt-sleeved shock troops moved slowly up the boulevard with the bonhomie of a post-prandial stroll. As the marchers started to pass by, waving and smiling, their numbers were constantly swelled by spectators, each eager for a role in destiny, and the huge demonstration rolled spasmodically onwards like a snake swallowing all in its path.

Amidst the throng, I glimpsed face after face that I knew: stall-holders in the market, drinkers in the Mouff, strangers in the street. Even the postman was there. But I remained on my window-ledge. In part, it was puritan fastidiousness: an English reserve, a distaste for mass emotions, a distrust of public knee-jerks; in part, it was ideological fastidiousness: the affairs of France were hardly within my bailiwick. And in part it was caution. I was once more a foreigner without a valid visa. And all of a sudden it had become open season on foreigners.

The apprehending of Teri was no accident, no isolated incident. Rather, it was in full accordance with that well-known rule of government which states that any crisis in any country is always caused by foreigners. (Indeed, this is probably the pre-eminent rule of government; the only surprise is that no government has as yet established a Ministry of Scapegoats.) For days, the Gaullist media had been dutifully and direly warning of 'foreign forces', 'foreign influences', 'foreign plots'. It appeared that it was some years since a French student had enrolled at a French university, and that French was a language no longer heard in the Latin Quarter. And now, foreigners being apparently a virus spread by the wind, the wider population was in mortal danger. I found it a novel experience to be the enemy within, and started to become suspicious of my every move.

But the French students had found the antidote to such primitive propaganda. Wit. And the loudest cheers of the day were in response to the banner which bore the slogan: '*NOUS SOMMES TOUS DES ETRANGERS!*'. It was a phrase fast becoming famous, and I doubted even the most blinkered of bourgeoisie could still swallow the leaden-footed government line. Unfortunately, though, the baton-happy CRS felt no need to actually believe in the rightness of their battering, and I remained alone on my ledge, glad that Teri had a sick-note for the day.

And all the while the throng passed endlessly on. I saw a professor from the Alliance, a waiter from Ledoyen, the ticket-taker from the Cinemathèque. I saw couples who walked their dogs in the park, I saw a man who sold *gaufres* by the Metro, I saw a woman who solicited down rue Mouffetard. I even saw a contingent from a former French class. As I watched the multitudes march by, it was like a roll-call of all my days in Paris, like a line of my memories strung like beads along the boulevard.

On and on the uprising flowed. People playing trumpets, people walking dogs, people carrying children, people pushing wheelchairs: this was as much festival as march. It seemed that in time all Paris would go past. A quarter of an hour went by, and on the far side of the crowd I saw the unmistakable outline of Jerry and Garry, up from the country to bring their peace and love to the occasion. I waved, but they did not see me, perched two yards above the tumult. I recognized their risk, and wondered again at my caution. Was I fence-sitting on my window-ledge? Did I still not know what I believed in? Would I march for *anything*? Another quarter of an hour went by. And then, in the middle of a long row of *copains*, stepping with the jerky pride which was his hallmark, I saw Gerard.

It was months since I had seen him. As I watched him move, my mind went back to the sunny Sunday almost exactly a year ago when, his black beard jutting, he strode so angrily across place de la Contrescarpe, to the strains of Joplin and the wild applause of the packed square. On that surreal day, his cause – his lost cause – had been a honky-tonk piano and the rights of a maverick musician. I remembered well his bafflement that commonsense (*'le fairplay'* as he had said to me in a rare stab at English) should not be the rule of life. His purpose here today was, I suspected, to defend a similarly uncomplicated view of fairness and decency, of right and wrong.

And beside Gerard, her arm linked happily in his, was Ulrika. From this distance her missing millimetre was of no consequence and her sunlit beauty was quite dazzling. She had forsaken her buttock-hugging jeans for the afternoon march and was wearing a simple blue and white cotton frock, its only adornment her tumbling ruff of blonde hair. Then, as I gazed down at her, she looked across the sea of banners and spotted me. She smiled and waved and indicated me to Gerard, and beckoned me to join them. Then Gerard too smiled and waved, and they both beckoned me to join them.

I could resist no longer. I abandoned my window-ledge and my policy of non-intervention. And threw my illegal foreign weight behind the revolution.

The march still had a mile to go. Ulrika slipped her spare arm through mine and, bonded together like Jules et Jim and that other enigmatic smiler, Jeanne Moreau, the three of us edged our way on, on through the increasingly excited crush. I pressed by mouth to Ulrika's ear, the only way now to be heard.

'You managed to get him out the studio then!'

She nodded.

'Is he painting again?'

She made a *comme ci, comme ça* face.

'He looks happier.'

She smiled, and mouthed, 'He is.'

'Has he found a new style?'

She in turn pressed her mouth to my ear. 'Come to tea in a couple of days.'

And then communication became impossible. The cheering and the chanting of the crowd drowned all except the business of politics. For this was Wembley, with the home team playing the government. The monstrous demonstration was entering its last lap, along the avenue de l'Observatoire, and there was no balcony, no parapet, no lamp standard, no bus shelter, no rubbish bin, which did not have a clapping, shouting, stamping, whistling, wildly exultant supporter. In sight now was our destination, our venue for the ringing oratory to come, the unlovely but large place Denfert-Rochereau. Long a favoured arena for rousing the rabble and raising the consciousness, its appeal lay not in its aesthetics – no columns with Nelson, no famous fountains, and a very poor species of lion – but in its choice of over half a dozen exit routes should discretion become the better part of being batoned to a pulp.

Slowly, inexorably, we were pummelled and funnelled into what passed as spare space in the square. And there, in the crush and the chaos, we waited. The immensity of the gathering would not have disgraced Judgement Day. And all the while that we waited for a new Danton to stir our souls and fire our bellies, we were inched and edged and nudged and shoved ever deeper into the maw of the masses. In a matter of minutes, I lost touch with the other two, swept out of sight by the grinding pack-ice of bodies. And still the crowds poured in. And still everyone waited.

'*Comrades!*' Onto one of the lions had leapt an official. '*Comrades!*' boomed the PA system. '*Comrades!*' Finally a sort of silence fell over the vast audience. The speaker paused dramatically. 'We must continue! We must go on! We cannot stop! Our comrades are still . . .' His voice almost broke with emotion. '. . . are still leaving La Bastille!' A collective gasp rose from the crowd, stunned by the implication of his words. And then, trembling at the enormity of the truth, he cried out, '*IL Y A UN MILLION DERRIÈRE NOUS!*' And a roar that knew no end went up, a roar that would not have disgraced VE day.

I will never forget the emotion of that moment. In that moment all was possible. In that moment we could have seized the Elysée Palace, we could have stormed the citadels of power, we could have overthrown the Fifth Republic, we could have destroyed de Gaulle. We could have taken control of France.

Unfortunately no-one had brought a list of suitable buildings to seize. Or the address of a citadel to storm. Or even the phone number of anyone famous. For while strong on abstract thoughts, the French are weak on practical details. Almost immediately a dispute broke out on the podium over what to do next. And where it would be a good idea to go to. And who should be in charge of it. And what the semiotics of the situation now were.

In the face of such factionalism, I too was unsure what to do. Reluctant to end on anti-climax, I hung about, waiting for a *groupuscule* to form – it being a useful rule of the French left that if you miss one sect, another will be along in five minutes.

And so it proved. Within minutes, a breakaway group decided to march on the Eiffel Tower. The exact political advantage to conquering a collection of steel girders (even ones with a high-speed lift) was not immediately apparent but, as it seemed to come under the heading of direct action, no-one minded. And as it meant a walk through parts of Paris with which I was unfamiliar (the 14*ème* and 15*ème*) I too was happy. Which was how I found myself at the head of the 10,000-strong post-Bolshevik libertarian Makhnovites . . . whose principal manifesto position was to scare the shit out of anyone living in an expensive apartment block.

We had barely gone a hundred yards into the bourgeois heartland when the old red and black flags came out again, and before I knew it we were shouting orchestrated abuse at the sort

of people like my landlords, and Henri's uncle and grandfather
. . . and tutor. Not that the abuse was unreciprocated. Being in
an *arrondissement* unused to any form of non-Gaullism, or
indeed to anyone with facial hair, the rerun of the Russian
Revolution by thousands of anarchists direct from Central
Casting caused a level of invective that was quite shocking. And
several of our number were hit by pot-plants. Flung from some
of the most genteel balconies it has ever been my privilege to
walk under.

The scene grew steadily dodgier. Attention quickly focused
on a tricolour flying provocatively from a thirty-foot flagpole at
the entrance to a particularly snotty mansion block. The French
national flag being synonymous with fascism, racism, col-
onialism, capitalism, barbarism and an unjust exam system, the
crowd immediately decided, nem. con., to replace it with
the more fashionable red flag. The movement's spokesmen on
radical dialectics (and photo opportunities) also insisted it was a
more revolutionary act to achieve this by climbing the flagpole
rather than by simply lowering the flag. Described to me later as
an example of the Situationist theory of 'spectacle', the dis-
appointingly philistine residents saw it more in terms of
vandalism, and a violent bottle exchange broke out. Then, as
hand-to-hand fighting developed amongst the tulips, the post-
Bolshevik gymnast up the flagpole was overcome with an
anti-Statist urge to set the tricolour on fire. Whereupon a variety
of objects, including a black-and-white television set, were
hurled onto the heads of the crowd from the balconies above –
an anti-consumerist act not, I felt, doctrinally appreciated to the
full by the *groupuscule* in receipt below. Somewhere around this
point, the decision was taken to uproot the flagpole, and test its
merits as a battering-ram. Also somewhere around this point, I
took the decision to leave. The Seventies were to see the rise of
the floating voter: I feel I was probably that little-known
precursor, the floating rioter. When rocks were in the air I found
I had allegiance to nobody.

Feeling a little sickened and a lot disillusioned, I turned down
a quiet side avenue. On the next corner I saw a boulangerie. It

had been a long day's march and I decided to treat myself. In moments of crisis I often had recourse to a chocolate nun.

In the boulangerie there was a huddle of ladies, talking not buying. Of a certain age and a certain class they all had *épatement* etched on their bourgeois faces, and resembled not so much a queue of customers as a concierge convention. The events of the day had clearly done damage to their systems. In shocked and confidential tones, they each were offering detailed accounts of the mighty march, full horrors of the city under siege, and the insurrectionary plans of the mad million now roaming free. In the matter of the revolting masses, nothing had escaped their attention.

A silence fell as I stepped up to the counter.

'*Monsieur?*' said the young girl assistant.

As I glanced below the glass at the *religieuses à chocolat* on show – some can be dissatisfyingly dumpy, some can have too light a dusting of the icing – I heard a half-hushed voice resume the revelations.

'*Vous savez,*' she said knowingly, '*ils sont tous des étrangers.*'

By the dawn of the following day the Sorbonne was liberated. Its cordon sanitaire of bovver-boys in blue had vanished, goose-stepping sulkily into the night. The march, the strike and the nationwide demonstrations had caused the government to blink first.

I joined the happy holiday hoopla. In the ancient precincts of the Sorbonne, the imagination had, as promised on the posters, taken power. Since the heady early hours the militants had been partying. Across the august busts of the good and the great and the boring were now draped the flags of revolution: the red, the black and the Vietcong: the severe stone plinths were plastered with the iconography of bedroom walls: the T-shirt trinity of Trotsky, Castro and Che Guevara; and the engraved classical maxims were fast being flyposted with agitpropisms and glori-ously offensive graphics – rushed out hourly from the new 'Atelier Populaire' of the Beaux Arts. It had been a night of politically orgasmic carousing. Bodies lay sprawled all about in happy exhaustion, high on wine and dancing and the after-effects of tear gas. A cluster of silver balloons bobbed implausibly from the stone hand of a medieval dignitary. Soft strains of 'We Shall Overcome' drifted sentimentally yet hauntingly through the air. Empty wine bottles clunked across the ground in idle convoy. A handful of drowsy dope-smokers gazed benignly on the scene. And centre stage, at the very heart of the historic courtyard, like an apparition from a Fellini dream, stood a familiar and battered . . . honky-tonk piano. It had triumphed at last over the law.

Glad confident morning had, it seemed, come again. In the air and on every street corner one had the sense of a defining moment, a feeling that the tectonic plates of history were on the move once more. Throughout the Left Bank, groups were gathering like bee swarms, blocking the boulevards with ardent debates – the young and the old, the rich and the poor, the bourgeoisie and the students. That the State might fall, seemed not a matter for fear or for outrage: instead, being French, there was a pride that their nation, as in 1792, had led the world in intellectual ferment. 'In Berkeley, they just grow beards, and think they've invented fucking. The French change the societal structures,' pronounced a middle-aged *fonctionnaire* with a briefcase and circumspectly spotted tie. For on the crowded pavements the talk was everywhere of the issues; an eager middle class was queuing up to grasp Marcuse and Situationism, and learn the latest dialectics from their juniors. Such unlikely bonding with the ragged-trousered radicals owed much to the savagery of the CRS – even gendarmes were complaining of police brutality – and this had provoked an almost parental protectiveness in the *quartier*. Occasionally though, as I listened to the well-heeled and the full-bellied offering sympathy sound-bites to student critiques on the evil 'isms' of capital, I sensed I heard echoes of Vichy, of the middle classes' infinite sensitivity to the weather-vane of ideology . . . and then I realized it was no longer some idle fantasy that the Fifth Republic might indeed fall to home-grown Red Guards. But mostly I was reminded of the mad axeman and the parking tribunal.

'Yes, but are fridges ethical?' I heard a Jesus look-alike cry to a seminarial crowd in place de la Sorbonne.

'It's not the fridge that's the issue,' someone retorted. 'It's one's attitude to the fridge.'

'No. It's *society*'s attitude to the fridge that matters,' responded a third. 'And that's determined by capitalist ideology.'

'A fridge isn't a product of ideology!' said a fourth. 'It's a consequence of civilization.'

'The Ancient Greeks never had fridges,' offered a voice from the back.

'Everything's a product of ideology,' said a man with a crash-helmet.

'Commodities are the opium of the masses,' said his girlfriend.

'Look, the social usefulness of a fridge is a given,' interrupted her neighbour. 'It's the acquisition of objects for *status* which debases society. Which is immoral. Unethical.'

'What's ethical about rotting food?' asked a practical-looking woman in a blue dress.

'The fridge is just a fucking symbol!' snapped the first speaker. 'Of a rotting society! Corrupted by the stench of consumerism!'

I remembered similar discussions from the sixth form. I had not understood those either.

For the rest of that day and the next, I wandered the police-free streets, eavesdropping on revolution in progress. Distrustful joy was the public mood of the moment: like a man who has shoulder-charged a door and found it open, the student move-ment was suspicious of the door's motives. And, as ever, divided on how to decorate the vacant room.

The Sorbonne had become the centre of the world's atten-tion. Not since the storming of the Winter Palace had a change of tenancy so threatened the established order in continental Europe. The Sorbonne *libéré* was now the Sorbonne *occupé*, HQ of the student generals (not that they believed in generals) (or indeed in HQs), and had become a People's (*la parole à tous*) Parliament where every day was Open Day. An exam-free zone for all ages, it was the ultimate experiment in liberty, a hothouse for the revolution's mantra, *Tout Est Possible*. For a week the Sorbonne had dominated international news with shots of its barred doors, the footage of armed custodians raising Juvenal's classic fears; now the television screens showed its amphitheatres packed day and night, the scenes of wild utopianism raising NATO's worst nightmares.

Despite my affiliation to the Sorbonne – and already even to possess a card was suspect revisionism – I had never in fact been inside. On around the third day I decided to pay a visit.

The courtyard now resembled a medieval fair, overflowing with ideological hucksters. Every faction and sub-faction and break-away splinter had its own stall, its own leaflet, its own world view. And at least three adherents. But factionalism was not the only gauntlet to run. The age of the political pamphleteer had returned to the land, and equally agitating were the new Tom Paines. At every step was another student with another bulletin, hot from the front, fresh from the Roneo, high from the rhetoric, with the consequence that scuffed underfoot was the most polysyllabic litter in Europe.

I sweated my way through the froth of the revolution and up to the Sorbonne entrance. On the columns supporting a carved paean to Cardinal Richelieu were now plastered the posters of Marx, Lenin and Mao. On the main door was a poster announcing the future.

The revolution which is beginning will call in question
not only capitalist society but industrial society. The
consumer society is bound for a violent death. Social
alienation must vanish from history. We are
inventing a new and original world. Imagination is
seizing power.

Although clearly an improvement on the manifestoes of most British election campaigns, I felt these were policies yet to be fully costed, and could well presage a tax increase for the middle classes.

Crowds were everywhere, struggling up and down every stone staircase, opening every hallowed door, claiming their birthright in every amphitheatre. The Sorbonne was now an 'Autonomous Popular University', and had an occupation committee and a Commission of Cultural Agitation, with the result that there was a lot of shoving.

As I too opened the closed doors and gawped like a guilty burglar at inner sanctums, I rapidly gained the sense of an archaic institution, of knowledge geared to the needs of a bygone age. It was a world exemplified by the word 'amphitheatre'. Even in the satellite era many Sorbonne students still had to learn – or rather retain by rote – while packed in tiers in wooden indoor Delphis; they gazed down from the gods (small g) upon the professor (big G) and the knowledge wafted up. And those were the lucky students. So great was the increase in university numbers – the result a weeding-out rate second only to myxomatosis – that the others learnt by overflow, by listening to the *ex cathedra* lectures on loudspeakers. And the subject they learnt was alienation.

'Take Your Desires for Realities' read the new rubric on the old walls. 'It is Forbidden to Forbid.' I bobbled along on the tide of history as it swept down the venerable corridors and eventually arrived at the single most critical hub of activity: the 'ampi', the central amphitheatre, where the voice of the people was in permanent session. Here the Muse of political philosophy took no sleep. Here the great issues were argued day and night, the student orators declaiming in shifts – no doubt as a symbolic gesture to factory workers, with whom bonding was a mystical experience much sought after by the middle-class pamphleteers.

I was eager to see the epicentre of France's political earthquake. I had always found the nature of power a baffling concept, as hard to grasp as air. Where does power come from? How do you recognize it? What makes it work? As I squeezed into the great 'ampi' I half-expected to see some H. G. Wells machine, some shiny object quietly humming, and to be able to say that over there is the centre of power. But instead what I saw was an antique coliseum, steeply raked and slightly shabby, with a motley mass over 5,000 strong listening intently to a gaunt and middle-aged man in a shapeless jumper denouncing examinations as the rite of initiation into capitalist society. This was clearly a key topic since wild bursts of applause kept punctuating his semantics.

I squashed on to the end of a row. I was now part of the Constitutional Assembly remaking French society.

As I sat and listened I was struck both by the boisterousness of the audience and the respect they afforded the speakers. It was like being part of a football crowd discussing philosophy. Unfortunately, I had missed the tumultuous debate on whether or not to plaster over Puvis de Chavannes's fresco 'Ancient Greece unveiling herself before archaeology' (narrowly defeated), and attention had moved on to the equally vexed but more modern question of qualifications and the unelected hierarchies who controlled knowledge. (I summarize in a crude tabloid form, of course.) There soon emerged from the (predominantly young) assembly an overwhelming consensus that the weakness of the exams system lay in being controlled by those who set them. Rather than by those who sat them. (Here they had my vote.) Indeed, it seemed that many of the ills of society could be traced to the fact that teaching was run by teachers and accordingly it was agreed that the courses, the curricula and the appointment of professors should be subject to student approval. In fact, that everything should be subject to student approval – if not student control. This led on to the reorganization of the world in general.

As the hours passed and I watched impassioned fingers jab the air and listened to plans to democratize the peasantry and the workers – enabling them to live a life of luxury and sainthood – my own thoughts began to stray to the past, and to the politics of the people I had known in France. And I realized that, extraordinary though these *événements* were, in retrospect they appeared to have that old cliché, historic inevitability. Discontent and dislocation ran like a vein of pus through the lives I had so briefly crossed. It had begun with Alain in a sub-zero hut below Mont Blanc, fleeing France to find a world where he could be good, and possessing – irony of ironies – a Sorbonne philosophy degree; it had continued through the long line of exiles – WRP house painter on the run from the *flics*, Estonian gouache painter on the run from the KGB, US water-colour painters on the run from the FBI; it had flared in the tin-tacky room of Tony as he yearned of marble equality; it had lurked in the swish world of Dr Poli as he hankered after the *mots* of Maoism; it lay hidden behind the thin doors of the Third World as they slept exhausted on their seventh floors . . . and it never left the doss-houses where the ballet dancers died of fallen arches.

I, though, was now harbouring (and guiltily suppressing) my first doubts about revolution, the end-user certificate of the counter-culture. I preferred cobbles to stay on the ground, and I preferred words not to float in the air. I found 'the poetry of the streets' as dubious as the solidarity of the masses. And I found long idealistic speeches effective only in the creation of piles. I was beginning to feel that I wanted my bohemianism to stay in the cafés, where it would do no harm and not be taken seriously.

When I drifted back to reality (or should I say to 'my desires'?) the debate had indeed moved on – seamlessly if mysteriously – to the central role of poetry in the working-class struggle. And a bearded man of about seventy had stood up and announced he had penned a few verses to the brave youth of the hour. The only Gallic relative of Mr McGonagall, he recited them to shifting feet for some ten minutes. A burst of unnaturally loud applause, to appreciate his efforts and encourage their cessation, greeted a far from final stanza. Whereupon he announced that these seminal documents of the revolution were available for purchase at a very reasonable 1F50 a copy, and began to move among the front rows. An audible dialectic confusion arose among the audience, and democracy started to falter. I chose this moment to slip quietly out.

I made it back to the ground floor and, picking my way across television cables, explored a little further, looking for the more traditional insurrectionary features, like a list of the day's heads to be cut off. I had just reached the flagstoned calm of a cloister when I hit a queue – and realized it was for one of several improvised snack bars. Being intramural, and on a prize pitch, these were clearly accredited suppliers of food to the revolution, and so I treated myself to a non-exploitative cheese roll. I was just pushing it into my mouth when a blinding light was shone into my eyes.

'Svedish television,' said a voice.

I screwed my eyes up and was able to make out a tall, earnest Swede.

'We are the evening news. We are filming the voices of the revolution.'

I nodded gravely.

'The Svedish people wish to learn of the dreams and the aspirations of the students fighting for social justice in France.'

'Right on!' I said.

He held up a microphone. 'You will explain the Svedish nation about your dreams, yes?'

'What, me? . . . Oh . . . um . . .' I had by now quite a few views on French society and the French character, and the opportunity to disseminate them on a more global scale came as a rather attractive proposition. I found myself filling with a nervous self-importance. 'Yeah, I guess so,' I replied. I quickly checked my beard for crumbs.

Sven – at least, he looked like a Sven – gave a thumbs-up to his three-man crew, spoke to camera in Swedish for a couple of moments, and then, as the light swung blindingly back into my eyes, he turned and asked me, 'What made you and your comrades decide to occupy the Sorbonne? And what are your intentions for France?' He handed me the microphone.

I cleared my throat, and tried to look statesmanlike. 'Yes, I decided to occupy the Sorbonne because . . .' And then it dawned on me that this broadcast – indeed all broadcasts – were very probably being monitored by the French government. 'Because . . .' And by Interpol. And by the FBI, and the CIA, and Scotland Yard. 'Because . . .' And by my father. 'Because,' I said, and smiled feebly, 'of the cheap cheese rolls.'

CHAPTER 37

At the end of the third week in May, Teri withdrew her labour, trying to help bring the country to its knees by hitting the bourgeoisie where it hurt most: baby bottoms. Her action was partly to show solidarity with the spreading general strike, but mainly because the transport strike now made it impossible to travel across the city. Or indeed leave it. Paris now had no buses, no trains, no Metro, and one by one the other props of life were crumbling. At last we had the time to spend almost whole days as a couple.

'Great! All we need now is money!' said Teri.

'Haven't you read the papers? New minimum demand is for everybody to be a millionaire. With retirement age at twelve.'

'Does it mention free food?'

I shook my head.

'Typical bloody sell-out!'

It was ten in the morning, and we were standing on the flagstone step of Hotel de Luxembourg, poised for a lazy day of togetherness. 'Still, at least we've got all the time in the world now.'

'Yes.' Teri paused. 'Have you noticed everything's shut?'

'. . . We could try some of that walking again.'

And off we set.

As so often the entertainment was on the streets. Spring was about to cede to summer. The blossom was at its fullest, its pinkest, its most perfect, and the trees brought scented Technicolor to the boulevards. For nature, it was just one more season in the round of seasons. But the other aesthetics of the city, the human aesthetics, were daily being transformed as never before. By graffiti, by graphics, by posters, by wall newspapers, by every known cyclostyle of agitation.

The ORTF – the BBC of France – had degenerated dutifully into a de Gaulle's Diary: the police were pussy-cats, every citizen was foursquare behind the Fifth Republic, the Sorbonne was closed for redecoration, the tear gas was Scotch mist. So, in counterblast, the young ersatz Zolas wrote luridly of the blood in the gutters, the screams from the dungeons, the testicles shredded to tatters. On the roughest of paper, in the scrawliest of capitals, they railed daily, twice-daily, hourly it seemed, against the dark night of the truncheon and the jackboot. It was as though the world of the samizdat had collided with the world of the penny dreadful.

Truly triumphant, though, was the world of the poster. Vicious and Brechtian, offensive and didactic, the avalanche of drawings from the radicalized Beaux Arts sprayed their subversive spleen onto every street corner. Contemptuously flyposted over every sign proclaiming the illegality of flyposting, their lethal mix of ridicule and bile and wit unerringly chainsawed through the pillars of the State. Each picture worth a thousand diatribes, the populace grew daily more familiar with the sight of skulls in police helmets, barbed wire across the television screen, a bottle of poison as the press ('Do Not Swallow'), the profile of de Gaulle as a workshop vice crushing the workers.

But even more prolific were the graffiti. In keeping with the land of la Rochefoucauld, these were not eff-offs to the world but fresh maxims for the masses, a new street art, applied liberally – and literally – by the broad brush strokes of revolution. Surreal, utopian, obscure, anarchic, romantic, eccentric, prophetic and simply mad, these outpourings of minds allegedly unlocked by liberation were the new decor of every public place. When we walked along the ravaged rue Gay-Lussac the wall read, 'Under the cobbles, there's a beach'; when we passed the Panthéon, giant curly white letters said, 'Death is necessarily a counter-revolution'; when we crossed the road at the entrance to the Lycée Henri IV, shaky capitals announced, 'We are reassured. 2+2 no longer make 4'; and when we went to gawp at the burnt-out Bourse – and tremble at the imminence of civil war – some Right Bank bolshevik with fancy loops had written, 'The economy is suffering, let it die'. Elsewhere, though, our textual exegesis was tested to destruction by the likes of 'Boredom sweats', 'Be salty' and 'I dream of being a happy idiot'.

'Are you sure you didn't write that?' asked Teri.

Yet it was at an antiquarian bookshop, tucked in fusty obscurity some fifty yards further on, that she and I found the best slogan of all. Except it was not a slogan. It was a promulgation. And it dated from the previous revolution. In big, bold, old-fashioned typography reminiscent of the *Daily Telegraph*, the poster heading simply read, 'ANY MEMBER OF THE BOUR-GEOISIE FOUND ON THE STREETS OF PARIS WILL BE SHOT ON SIGHT'. And the poster was now, with the plangent irony of history, for sale at a price only the bourgeoisie could afford. Nowhere – so far – had *les événements* achieved words of such robustly chilling authority. Closest in rigour was the vaguely poetic declaration I had seen outside a bank: 'Mankind will not live free until the last capitalist has been hanged with the entrails of the last bureaucrat'. Yet even that managed to sound a bit like the paddy of someone objecting to overdraft charges.

Nonetheless, the tension in the streets continued to rise. One sensed the State waiting for the students to overreach themselves, to hang themselves not with entrails but with too much rope. Already, though, the adult intelligentsia were trying their hand at revolutionary acts. The fashion was for occupation. Radical doctors, radical actors, radical architects, even radical businessmen – the oddest oxymoron in politics – had taken to seizing their headquarters (or whatever building was to hand) and demanding the end of the world, as currently constituted. Even our very own Cinémathèque was now at the service of the revolution, its founding father, Henri Langlois, throwing his lot and his legend behind the students. And just down the road from Teri, Jean-Louis Barrault's famous Théâtre de France – whose actors I had so nearly wiped out with a milk jug – had not only taken over their Odéon Theatre, but had declared the sumptuous chandeliered premises to be open house, the new show to be by the people, for the people. 'Since the National Assembly has become a bourgeois theatre, all bourgeois theatres should become national assemblies.' More glitzy, ritzy and ecumenical than the rival Sorbonne performance, this vast philosophy chat show, where the last word was seldom heard before daybreak, quickly became the hottest scene in town, throbbing with heavy thinkers out for the night with their latest doxy.

'We should go. I hear they do a nice line in concepts,' I said. 'Five francs for one, or fifty francs the dozen.'

A month earlier I would not have risked the joke. But then, a month earlier Teri would not have laughed. We were daily growing closer.

'Yes. Might even be worth making a speech or two — we could end up in history textbooks one day!' She grinned. ' "The ideas that changed France"!'

'Oh, I think this revolution's making the ideas up as it goes along.'

And so for night after night we too joined the in-crowds. Here, before a packed house of populists, the old Left literati and the high-octane activists swopped *zeitgeists* in the stalls. And by choosing seats in the Circle, we were able to watch the top celebrities from the world of egalitarianism. We even saw Jean-Paul Sartre himself, the prince of existential darkness, as he struggled to the stage through a crowd of fans, and offered, like a gnomic gnome, his critique of the revolution so far.

But such a notorious forum for free speech, albeit the Blue Peter idea of Trotskyism, soon offended the right. The feared forces of *L'Occident* — skinheads with hair — already resented the left's capture of bourgeois citadels; to see such places nightly packed with egregious socialist intellectuals was doubly galling for a group whose idea of meaningful conversation was an exchange of rocks. Their growing presence began to fill the evening air with menace. Then the chat shows drew death threats, which can spoil an evening out, and ushers with baseball bats had to frisk against fascism. Our hundred-yard walk to the theatre was no longer a serene stroll.

However, just for once during *les événements*, it was to prove the turn of the right to be creative. One evening, our chins pressed upon the velveted parapet of the Circle, Teri and I were listening to a long, rambling dissertation against the fad of washing. As its text, it took the slogan 'Cleanliness is the luxury of the poor, be dirty', which had been sprayed, with geopolitical appropriateness, on a toilet door in the Odéon. The speaker was Californian, and his Haight-Ashbury message (which seemed to be that soap was a weapon of the counter-revolution) was somewhat lost on the historically more abstract French. Nonetheless, the idea was being given the usual due and earnest respect by the audience. Until, that is, the cry of 'Fuck off, cunt!' was heard to echo from high above. There followed a brief and uneasy silence whilst the auditorium waited for a further exposition of this point, and then it began to snow. A dense, dusty-brown snow.

The snow fell in waves, lit up in myriad points as it floated through the chandeliers. It eddied to and fro, swirling amidst the Belle Epoque splendour like a surrealist blizzard. It came in constant flurries, settling on the gilt and the plush like the onset of indoor winter. Mysterious and soundless, guided by gravity, it fell without meaning or reason.

Then, as we watched it drift lower, Teri gave a sudden sniff. An instant later, I felt an itching in my nostrils, sensed a snuffling in the air. And all at once I realized what dark deed had been done.

With a *coup de théâtre* worthy of Artaud, packet upon packet of neo-Nazi sneezing powder was being hurled from the gods in vast spiralling clouds. The right wing had at last discovered an answer to intellectuals – and, like an avalanche of dirty dandruff, that answer was steadily, inexorably, descending upon their heads. I watched, and waited, and wisely suppressed a grin. Then the powder began to land, in wave after anti-nasal wave, and the voice of the people started to splutter. For a moment there was bewilderment, the mouth no longer the dominant orifice. Then the alarm and the panic began. Suddenly, in a wild bedlam of Atishoos! a thousand revolutionaries sneezed uncontrollably, explosively, seismically . . . and the forum was brought to its nose.

We rarely went back to the Odéon after that, for fear lest one night the beanfeast become a bunfight, to the death. I found myself wondering whether Jean-Jacques had really made it to the Congo, or whether he was in some Right Bank bar requesting fragmentation grenades by mail order. For, despite the famous fevered freedom of this spring, dangers were now looming on all fronts. Even the sweet seasonal pleasures of romance and young love had lost their charms. The Jardins du Luxembourg, purpose-built for the lovesick to wander in, still remained under lock and key, the State eager to ensure that the puppet theatre and the crêpe stand did not fall into the hands of subversives; the blossom-filled boulevards could at any moment become battlegrounds, the fissiparous factions of left and right needing no provocation to be virtuously violent; even the cafés were war zones, since night after night the sight of people having a quiet cappuccino so upset the forces of law and order that they felt obliged to pistol-whip all available customers.

One warm cloudless afternoon, I found Teri waiting for me outside Ledoyen, where my sixty minutes of paid English was now ritualized to the point of liturgy.

'Bit of Tuileries?' she enquired.

I nodded, and took her arm. She too had come to value the pleasures of my favourite walk, and would occasionally arrive to share the journey with me.

We made a long hour of it, taking advantage of the tourist shortage to wander round and round the Rodins.

When we reached the Latin Quarter, neither of us was in the mood for a pavement café. Instead, we decided to cobble together a *casse-croûte* and lounge on her balcony in the sun. Her flatmate was nowhere to be seen, and we declared her olives communal. The family grocers opposite was still shuttered for siesta, and a familiar torpor was in the air. Teri rummaged in a plastic bag beside the basin as I opened the balcony doors.

'Cheese?'

'What's the choice?'

'Two days old or four.'

I envied Teri her room. It was a large room, a double room, and even stretched to an oak beam and a fitted carpet. There was a softness to its features, made almost homely by the warm shafts of afternoon sunlight.

Teri was wearing a plain pink T-shirt and, as she bent, the weight of her breasts pressed hard against the cotton. I stroked her neck, running my fingers over the faint signs of an early tan. She straightened her body, and leant against me. The intensity of the last few days had brought us closer together, our emotions tested by the troubles around us, my sense of self proving steadily stronger. I hugged her to me, and kissed her gently. There was a sexuality to her response that I had not registered before. I tested the water.

'I saw a new slogan this morning.' I paused. 'Really profound. I think it could change my life.'

'Oh yeah?' Teri smiled, waiting for the punch line.

'Seriously. Just the sort of philosophy I've been looking for.' And, trying not to grin, I quoted, ' "The more I make love, the more I make the revolution. The more I make the revolution, the more I make love." '

'Oh,' she said, without a flicker of reaction. Then she smiled again, but slowly. 'Not as good as the one I saw.'

'Oh, what was that?'

She looked unwaveringly into my eyes. ' "Live intensely, have orgasms without restraint." '

And she put her arms around my neck, and in seconds we had tumbled to the floor.

There is a special wildness to impromptu sex, an implicit lust that is lacked by night-time and sheets. Never before had I sensed such emotions, in myself or in Teri. We rolled to and fro across the floor as we tore at buttons and zips and in seconds we were naked – or as naked as we needed. We kissed and fondled and licked and sucked with a sexual single-mindedness that was

395

awesomely new. For weeks I had felt the corset of her Catholic tenets loosing its final stays. Now, as she sat astride me with the sunlight upon her breasts, rocking erotically back and forth on my erection, I was suddenly certain that the hymen was in sight. Without a word said, with just a grin passed, she slowly rolled off me and onto her back – and lay waiting, oblivious to any fifth-floor voyeurs across the street. Her knees up, her legs open, I knew that this was the moment, this was the end of virginity. My heart palpitating, I lowered myself onto her. My head started to throb with a dizzying noise as she gently but oh so surely helped me into her. As I kissed her harder and harder, she became wilder and wilder, and the noise in my head grew louder and louder. The passion turned to abandon, the sweat started to pour, and in my dementia I could hear voices, I could hear shouting, I could hear screaming. Then as the long, long awaited moment of ecstasy finally began, and the first forceful thrusts finally started, there was a loud explosion . . . and a tear gas bomb rolled across the carpet. I stared at it in disbelief. Even I had not expected the Pope to take such direct action.

Rarely had coitus been so rudely interruptus. We scrambled panic-stricken across the floor and the grenade hissed slowly by. It trundled over where Teri's crutch had just been resting and came to a halt in the 36B cup of her bra.

'Kick it!'

'You kick it!'

'You've got the sock on!'

It started to smoke. We cowered in the corner, useless and suddenly ludicrous in our nakedness. Outside, the roar of a riot filled the narrow street.

Desperately, I looked for a solution. We had just seconds of breathing time left. And already the brassière damage was serious.

'A pillow?' cried Teri.

'No, no!' I shouted, and raced across the room to the lunch. It was my only hope. Taking up the stance of a no. 11, I thwacked the tear gas bomb with the baguette.

It started to roll back towards the balcony, threatening every second to burst into acrid life. I hit it twice, three times – and then the baguette broke. But Teri came up behind me, now wearing her sensible walking shoes – and nothing else – and dribbled the grenade on to the balcony, causing the only moment of light relief in the riot. With a deft flick of her instep she kicked it through the railings and it fell fuming onto the crowded pavements below.

'De l'eau! De l'eau!'

Everywhere the same scream went up. The canyon-like street was packed with students stampeding from boulevard St Michel – only to be fatally trapped at both ends by the CRS. Four, five tear gas grenades had already been fired, and the street was a pea-soup of choking fumes, every eye rubbed red-raw, every door hammered on for help. But there was no escape, the police were advancing, and the panic was spreading.

Teri grabbed her T-shirt and rushed to the bathroom on the landing. She ran back in with a bucket and a bowl, and time and again we filled them up from the basin and raced to the balcony and emptied them over the terrified people below. Several times the police aimed their grenade launchers at us, and each time we darted back for cover.

'De l'eau! De l'eau!' went up the constant cry. On balcony after balcony the residents were hurling down water in every conceivable container, in glasses, in soup plates, in soaking flannels. Below us, students were vomiting and fainting and desperately trying to scale the drainpipes, reaching vainly for outstretched hands. But by now the police were wading in with their night-sticks, cracking every bone in reach. The fighting was hand-to-hand, the blood was staining the pavements. We watched helplessly from above as the bodies, some kicking, some screaming, some slumped unconscious, were dragged away by nightmare men in gas masks and hurled into rows of waiting paddy wagons.

The terrible scene seemed to go on for ever, but when it finished it was still only five o'clock, and a beautiful spring afternoon was still warming the streets of Paris. But I had lost my erection and we abandoned sex for the day.

Shaking with emotion, we tidied up the bedroom, now drenched with the odour of battle. Teri sighed wearily and laid her arm around my neck. 'There was another slogan I didn't tell you about,' she said with a teasing smile.

'Go on,' I said warily.

'On rue de Buci. It said, "I find my orgasms among the paving stones."' And with a big grin she fell back exhausted on the bed.

It was late evening when I left Teri and her flatmate. I had intended to go straight home as usual. It was dark and I was weary. But I had not gone fifty yards before I sensed something was amiss. There was no obvious sign of trouble, no-one running, no-one shouting, no-one hurling bits of the local architecture. But the cobble-packed weeks of *les événements* had taught me that a riot has a footprint. That while the hard core fight it out, the faint-hearts and the affronted quickly flee, only to regroup a few blocks distant, and stand in little anxious huddles. This night, little anxious huddles were standing on every corner.

Except they were not talking. They were listening. Because every anxious huddle was grouped around a transistor. Indeed, almost every pedestrian – and the night seemed strangely full of pedestrians – was walking with a radio clasped to one ear. And all were tuned to Europe One.

Perhaps the unlikeliest folk heroes of the revolution were the reporters of Europe One and Radio Luxembourg. With ORTF regarding truth as an anti-government position, the mantle of honest journalism had fallen onto the antennae of smaller, independent stations. Dodging the missiles and revving through the streets in logo-loud radio cars – jazzy-coloured Citroen Estates crammed with cumbersome recording gear – their news crews were in the fray, on the ball, and up to the minute. So much so that they were more in danger of arrest than the rioters. Most renowned, though – and most listened to of all – were their running riot commentaries, their blow-by-blow accounts of each fresh fracas.

'*Qu'est-ce que ce passe?*' I asked a huddle.

'*C'est affreux!*' said one.

'*C'est la pagaille là-bas!*' said another.

I followed the jerk of the head, and retraced my steps up rue de Vaugirard and on past Teri's hotel. As I got nearer to boulevard St Michel I could hear the familiar roar of the mob and taste the familiar tang of the tear gas. And soon I could see the familiar sight of neckerchiefed figures darting through the bilious murk. But when I walked onto the roadway opposite the Sorbonne and looked downhill to the heart of the action, there was nothing familiar in the horrors of the scene.

This was an escalation beyond all others, this was the Second Coming of the Communards. A great barricade blocked the boulevard – and it was ablaze. But this was not just a barricade of cars and rubble, though every car possible was being frenziedly dragged and bounced to feed the burning barrier. This was a barricade of trees. Systematically, one by one, the great plane trees of the avenue were being hacked down and crashed into service as kindling for the revolution. On the far side of the smoke and the flames, the CRS – the para finally removed from military – were ferociously edging forward, their shields fending off fusillades of firebombs, their launchers firing salvo after salvo of tear gas. But each time they made headway, another barricade was built, another tree was butchered. And as the grim battle inched up the hill, the buildings on either side were looted and firebombed. My favourite cinema went up in flames, my favourite bookshop was trashed, my favourite evening stroll was gutted. And as each plate-glass shop window shattered to the onslaught of boots – its detested consumer durables mysteriously much in demand – another wild burst of cheering broke out, and another victory dance was done on the shard-strewn pavements. This was the destruction that the Reich had only dreamed of.

Sickened by such sights, I was about to turn and go. But all at once my eye was caught by the silhouette of a lone figure in the swirling smoke on the barricades, his outline lit every now and then by the raging flames around him. His fist was raised in exultation, and he leapt ceaselessly back and forward, urging the mob on, on to ever greater acts of mayhem. There was a charismatic zealotry to him, an almost demonic manner – and a vague familiarity. From somewhere I knew him, but when and why . . . ? For a second time, I squinted through the tear gas and the smoke, and strained vainly to remember. His face was masked by a scarf, but it was his gestures, angry and imperious, that were triggering some faint memory, some forgotten history. I moved a little closer, fearful at the danger but drawn by the mystery. Then, as yet another building succumbed to the carnage, I remembered a breakfast long ago. And I recognized the fur-lined leather driving jacket. It was Augustus. The politically preposterous, self-deluding little rich boy Augustus, now at last seeing the realization of his dreams for architecture. And proving, in the ubiquitous graffiti of the revolution, that desires could indeed be realities, that, truly, everything was possible.

I turned away, my eyes streaming from the constant tear gas. And in that moment, as I stood amidst that nihilism, and gazed upon that orgy of destruction, Paris ceased to be the city of my dreams. All the romance of its hedonism, the thrill of its free thinking, the joy of its bohemianism, went ugly and sour as a deep, disturbing shame swept through me. I felt a giant stain spreading through the beauty of my memories and I wanted to be a million miles away. I felt tainted by hatred and brutishness and wanted no part of it. I wanted to deny its reality. I wanted to go home.

Suddenly, all around me, people started to run. At first, there seemed no reason. But as the running escalated into panic, I realized the reason was the radios. All eyes were turning south, turning away from the barricades and up boulevard St Michel towards the Jardins du Luxembourg and beyond. Yet still there seemed nothing to be seen, nothing to be heard, nothing to be feared.

And then I felt the rumble.

And slowly, stealthily, sinisterly, column upon column of grey, unlit armoured cars emerged from the distant shadows. They were numberless, anonymous, impregnable, and their unforgiving advance vibrated every cobble in the *quartier*. They were coming from the ring road, coming from the boulevard du

Montparnasse, coming from the boulevard du Port-Royal. They were coming as had been planned for over a century. They were coming down the boulevards of Paris just as Haussmann had intended – to crush civil insurrection in the city.

It was the textbook pincer movement, and I was about to be trapped by it. For a moment, I was almost mesmerized by the drama, and simply stood and watched while the grim wire-meshed crates of steel rolled ever closer. Inside, their lethal cargoes were poised, and waiting – as one famous poet put it that night – 'like mastiffs'. Suddenly, it began. Without warning, a thousand armed men, primed to give no quarter, were sprung from their traps and burst upon the street, racing forward in a phalanx like 'a thick wedge of mercury up a glass tube'.

I turned and bolted for my life down rue de Vaugirard. I had but seconds to outrun the flailing clubs and boots, seconds to escape the terror of the paddy wagon and the police cell. As I desperately made my bid to reach the drab safety of home, I knew that this night had seen the end of innocence.

Jean-Pierre was even more tetchy than usual as his whole hotel packed into the small nondescript lounge to watch his television. The future of France was not for foreigners, he kept muttering. He was, of course, ignored, and the old worn sofas had started to fill up soon after four o'clock, nobody wishing to miss a broadcast that could change the course of history. In the city outside, the sunlit streets were almost empty, the cafés crammed only with viewers.

This was de Gaulle's second attempt to rally the nation, and likely to be his last. His first address to the people had been remembered only for the phrase '*chie-en-lit*', an obscure historical expression apparently meaning 'shit in bed' (and a distant cousin of the dandelion, *pissenlit*). The President had intended this to describe the rioters (or just possibly the entire population except himself) but instead had unfortunately prompted the now legendary poster '*Le chie-en-lit, c'est lui!*', depicting him in a rather unfavourable light on almost every street in Paris. *Le Monde*, meanwhile, with its commendable sense of priorities, had interrupted its riot coverage to publish a long, scholarly article examining the etymology and previous literary usage of this little-known archaism. It all tended to create the image of an old man out of touch.

Since the bloody night of the barricades, there had been days of silence from the President, climaxing in rumours of a mysterious and dramatic flight to his army chiefs, allegedly to check whose side they were on. Now all of France was waiting to learn his future and their own. (Not to mention the fate of their fridges.) From student crisis to social crisis, to economic crisis, to political crisis, it had been the most hyperactive four weeks since 1792. And now the nation wanted to know whether its postal address was to be the Western bloc or the Eastern bloc . . . or the independent republic of Shangri-la.

It was a small television set, probably 12", and still only black and white. There was something innately ludicrous about a 6'5" Head of State being squashed into so puny and monochrome a space – especially since he claimed to be the incarnation of France – and one felt a man of such unbending grandeur could only be effective when orating from some great height. Like clouds. So it was with both populist derision and political disdain that the packed lounge awaited his last throw of the dice.

He did not smile. As the camera moved in on the veteran warrior, he sat with a gravitas so great that he scarcely seemed human. His immense old head absolutely still, he gazed unblinkingly out like a demi-god inspecting the soul of France. And then he spoke.

'*Français! Françaises!*' Never had I heard these simple words invested with such moving majesty, every syllable of the sound ringing with orotund formality.

The jokes died away.

Then ensued a stunning staccato sequence of brutal yet rhythmically perfect sentences, each beginning with I, each blazing with resolve, each defying the world – and each spoken with a classical eloquence. The phrases escalated in passion, each phatic *ne* and *pas* punching home his resistance to revolution, but with the passion in thrall to the prose. Not ever had I found so sublime a pleasure in the sound of spoken French. The words and the message marched to their climax and then, the room in total silence, the clock scarcely at 4.32, he declared with deathly slowness, the imperious syllables falling like hammer blows, '*Eh bien, non! Je Ne Me Re-Tir-Er-Ai Pas!*'

And in that moment I knew it was all over.

Although he spoke for two more minutes – about Parliament, about the army, about the calling of elections – the tingle in my spine already told me that *les événements* would be but a footnote in history.

And within an hour the triumphant bourgeoisie were gathering in their millions in the Champs-Elysées.

CHAPTER 38

Four hours remained before the afternoon train.

I looked around me one more time. I had at last discovered the only advantage to living in a cupboard. The likelihood of leaving anything larger than a microbe behind was nil. And here even the microbes had been removed before my arrival.

All the cumulative detritus of my last two-and-a-half years now stood packed and boxed in front of me. All the loose ends of my private life had also been tied. More or less. I had just one last wish to grant myself before the taxi came. To sit a final time in a pavement café, and watch the world go by.

I shut my door silently – as had now become second nature – and walked slowly down the long bleak corridor.

It had been an emotional few days. One never knew whether the farewells of travel were for ever. I had been deeply touched by Monsieur Bareste. Throughout the weeks of mayhem he had discreetly intimated that his assistance – financial or diplomatic – would not be lacking in the event of 'misfortune'. And then, as my departure became a certainty, he offered me the one great gift at his disposal: to be waited on by his colleagues in a luxury restaurant. And, as a further token of his affection, the occasion was *en famille: M. et Mme Bareste et fille*. Thus, with great appropriateness, our final, farewell conversation was held in the company of his favourite subject, his beloved 'Claudette', a sweet and charming bride-to-be.

It was a unique meal. The reputation of my pupil preceded us: Josef Bareste's forty years at top tables had made his

404

presence an honour, his approval an accolade. We were guests to be cosseted. For the first time in my life the waiters were more nervous of me than I was of them. Yet the joy of the lunch was not just the six-course meal and the five-star service and the massed ranks of silver cutlery. For the one and only time in Paris I was part of a family outing – part of that warm world of convivial bourgeois gatherings that I had so often glimpsed through the frosted glass of unknown restaurants. There seemed no finer finishing touch to a friendship which, for so long, had kept the wolf of England from the garret door.

Afternoon tea with Ulrika had been a more ambiguous occasion. Her news was not of Gerard. It was of another. I was uncertain whether I should be happy or sad – not least because I was uncertain whether she was happy or sad. For she was pregnant. The change from jeans to frocks was no fashion fad. The news of fatherhood had cheered Gerard for a while, but the more pressing problems of pigments and palettes had soon drawn him back into the gloom. 'D'you think a kid'll mind having an artist's moll for a mother?' was all Ulrika said, with her usual sweet-sad, hard-to-read smile. I stroked her long blonde hair, and kissed her cheek. I remembered how we had each arrived, rootless and aimless and lost. Now I was moving on, and going home. Deep down I think I knew that she would never leave Paris.

I pressed the button for the lift, and far below I heard the machinery clank into action.

But perhaps the sadder memory had been the last sight of Sherry, as she stood waving farewell outside the *merde*-brown entrance to Hotel de Carcassonne. Her small, sustaining legacy had now been exhausted, but her search for a psychotherapeutic meaning to life was still not over – nor was her quest for a man beyond the age of acne. The all-American optimism remained in position like a protective crust over a sunk soufflé, and we took care to talk not of the future but of the past. There had been a time when I had hoped to offer her my love, but by this, our final meeting, I knew that she was right, that she had needs beyond my understanding. On parting, the only gift of value I could offer her was Teri's vacant post as bottom-wiper to the bourgeoisie. Which she accepted.

The lift gave a familiar rattling shiver as it arrived. It stopped its usual six inches from the floor, as if to make yet again the point that it was too old for this type of work, and should be retired. Nonetheless, I had always taken pains to use the lift, mainly out of a suspicion that this annoyed the concierge, whose demeanour seemed to suggest that seventh-floor persons were socially better suited to stairs.

As the lift juddered slowly down – encouraging the constant hope it was vibrating her knitting – I could only think of one real regret at my departure. I would now never mingle with the gilded literati who dwelt in the world of book-launch parties. As vivid as yesterday was my memory of the velvet jackets, the backless dresses and the giant granite fish whose gold-leaf glinted in the coloured spotlights: I could still hear the cheerful laughter and the clink of wine glasses as I huddled alone in the rain in the flooded doorway opposite. But Henri's publishers had judged the sight of *jeunesse dorée* would not come cheap in plate-glass if they flaunted their vol-au-vents at the height of *les événements*. So late June was now the new date, the venue but doors from 12 rue de l'Odéon, where Ulysses had long ago been launched upon an apoplectic world. And sadly, to add pique to regret, the verbally Pinteresque Henri would let drop no hint as to the nature of his *oeuvre*. Thus the truth about his great first novel, and the mystery of his genius, was to remain an unsolved puzzle until my dying day.

The lift reached the ground, more or less, and, rejoicing in my new freedom to ignore all handwritten house rules, I vigorously assisted its gates to clang shut. Immediately Madame(oiselle) appeared. Indeed, with an almost preternatural sensitivity, she seemed to appear *before* I had clanged the gates shut.

The concierge already knew of my planned departure – no doubt multiple red rings adorned the date on her calendar – and I observed her eyes register my lack of luggage.

'*A midi, mademoiselle,*' I said. '. . . *Si je ne change pas d'avis.*' My smile was inch-perfect.

She nodded the minimum nod, and held out her hand.

'*Une lettre, monsieur.*'

The nation's mail had, for weeks, lain in piles the size of slag heaps, testimony – according to the press – to the innate wickedness of postmen. Now that the general strike had ended, settled by negotiators skilled in Monopoly, a vast avalanche of post was engulfing the country. The letter in Madame's hand represented my personal avalanche.

'*Merci, madame.*' I took the letter from her without displaying a blink of interest, it being my policy never to give her the emotional thrill of watching me open my mail. This policy was immediately abandoned when I saw the word PUNCH franked across the top of the envelope.

With all the casualness at my command, I ripped it open. The letter was short. It was from the doyen of all *Punch* writers, J.B. Boothroyd, and it read:

> A lot of us here at *Punch* are very old, with failing eyesight. It would therefore help your chances no end if you could see your way to buying a new typewriter ribbon. However, what you have written seems to be quite funny and we have agreed to publish it.
> Yours sincerely,
> Basil Boothroyd

I let out an enormous whoop, and punched the air (in a manner to be patented by footballers in later years) and did a dance for joy on the marble floor. I turned to Madame. Had it been a Hollywood film, I would no doubt have kissed her and thrown her in the air three times. But instead I just looked at her, and shouted, '*Je suis écrivain!*' And rushed out of the building.

I wanted to shout '*Je suis écrivain!*' all along the street, but settled for some fast walking and a bit of light skipping. In any case, being Paris, the real surprise would have been someone shouting '*Je ne suis pas écrivain!*' But I still felt dizzy with excitement. I even felt my posture was different, that I now had a writerliness that was visible from a hundred yards. And I felt so, so happy.

Not until I reached the Jardins du Luxembourg did I start to be normal again, and to think calmly about what had occurred. For ten minutes I just walked up and down the lines of chestnut trees, the scene of so many writer's blocks, and tried to fully grasp what I had achieved. For perhaps the first time, despite my hype to Teri, I was beginning to believe that I did have a future.

And as I walked through the patchwork pools of sunlight I was at first much tempted to surrender to nostalgia. 'To fall in love in spring, to be a writer by summer.' It seemed that Paris had indeed worked its magic. Those early dreams really had come true. (Though they had cut it fine.) And yet the more I reflected on my life in Paris, the more I was assailed by scepticism. Nothing had happened according to the grand plan, nothing had corresponded to the myth. I had been inspired to write not by the buzz of café life, nor by the beauty of the *quais*. Instead, I had been kick-started by a middle-aged bespectacled professor in the chalk dust of an old-fashioned classroom. And even the article I had sold had not been of raffish Paris adventure, but of sweat and scorpions in a banana hell-hole. Moreover, I had fallen in love with no chic French bombshell, no slinky *femme fatale*. Instead, I had been swept off my feet by a slightly dumpy, rather provincial and definitely repressed American from the boondocks. Our first conversation had not been by candlelight but on Formica-tops, not in a romantic dive within sound of cobbles, but in a concrete carbuncle overlooking an alley with bollards. And our affair in the city of love had, thanks to my sterile eyrie in the *sixième*, possessed as little lyricism as the lights-out regime at a single-sex boarding school. Somehow my life had bypassed the legend.

And as I pondered such ironies I realized that I was suppressing perhaps the most poignant irony of all, the irony which proved that maybe I had indeed become a writer. It had taken the sad memory of my failure with Nicole to provide the literary spur for what I had written. With cruel perversity, it had taken my failure with Nicole to provide my success with Teri.

I strolled slowly across the sunken concourse, where the stone urns were once again being sketched, and the foreign au pairs were once again pushing prams, and the model yachts were once again floating on the pond.

But as I emerged from the park, I heard again the sounds of destruction – only this time the streets were full of workmen. Everywhere in the *Quartier Latin* the cobbles were being replaced with tarmac. *Les événements* ended, the demands of security were now triumphing over the needs of aesthetics. The government was taking its revenge, and the pickaxes were continuing where the rioters had left off. And the beauty of Paris was about to change for ever. It was indeed time to leave. The end of an era really had arrived.

I made my way to a café which overlooked the gardens, a mid-morning favourite, always full of both French and tourists. Eager though I was to tell my news to Teri, I wanted just a few more moments alone with my new persona. And I wanted to sit and drink one last time as a resident of Paris, albeit illegal, and exude that smug superiority of a local, languidly observing the day unfold.

I settled in a corner seat with a view of the fountains, and ordered a *citron pressé*. As I watched the fashionable young girls and the map-clutching tourists go by, a Parisian family – thirty-something parents and two youngsters – came and sat at the next table. They were out for a treat – a typical French family scene. Their mother, beautiful, immaculate and sexy, fussed with their milk-shakes and their hot *saucissons*. Their father, elegant roll-neck sweater and slacks, was absorbed in a book from the moment that he sat. There is a publishing house in Paris which, with wonderful disdain for modern marketing, has no garish covers on its books. Just a plain white front, acknowledging the joy of reading. Despite the squawks and laughter of his family, the father never once looked up. I waited patiently to see what he was reading, and when his coffee came, I at last had a view of the title. It said simply, '*Aux Abîmes du Désespoir*'. *In the Depths of Despair.* And in that moment I knew why I would always miss Paris.

EPILOGUE

Madame, doyenne of the Hotel Carcassonne, finally died aged ninety, and the hotel is no more. Serious people with long-lease flats now go their separate ways behind the *merde*-brown door.

Jerry married Marie-Françoise, and they opened a health-food restaurant in Copenhagen. Jerry never painted again. They revisited Paris in the Seventies and then the trail goes cold. Whether the FBI are still after Jerry, and whether he is still on the run, I do not know.

Gerard and Ulrika had a baby girl, and then they separated. Gerard destroyed all his old paintings, worth thousands of francs, became a recluse, and then re-emerged as an abstract artist. The pictures were stunning geometrical works dominated by black, but rather than sell them, Gerard decided to wait for recognition by a millionaire collector. He now lives alone in a council high-rise studio, packed wall to ceiling with a quarter of a century's unsold paintings. Ulrika has spent her working life in a bank.

Tony apparently returned to England, still poor, still uncompromising, still without any marble to work on. Many years later, I met Fran, his ex-girlfriend, serving in a Communist bookshop. She said he had become bitter and twisted.

Paula, his young runaway cousin from Liverpool, decided to become a film star, and spent several years as a cinema usherette. Her only role was as a walk-on part in the nude for an Andy Warhol play. She left for Hollywood, set up as speech therapist to the stars, and was responsible for many B movie actors believing Liverpudlian was the Queen's English. She resolved her sexual ambivalence by spending long weekends in San Francisco's only bisexual bath-house, setting new house records for stamina.

Colin, the ne'er-do-well who absconded from the hotel with Eleanor, the careworn and well-connected American girl, subsequently married her. They moved to England, qualified in law, and became my solicitors. For some years, Colin's knowledge of the underworld and Marxism was invaluable to the National Council for Civil Liberties.

Sherry eventually returned to California, and had her life changed by EST. Although this still did not provide her with a man of the right age, it enabled her to talk a great deal more inarticulately about the problem.

Monsieur Bareste and I remained in touch. I was much honoured to be invited to Claudette's wedding in the spring of '69, but by then I was a poor student with no London waiter to subsidize me, and could not afford the fare. He retired in 1975 and is still going strong in his eighties, nourished by the warm sun of the Riviera.

And Teri? After a few months in England it was agreed, for all the painful reasons of youth, that she should return to Pennsylvania for twelve months – and that the following fall we would meet again in London, a year older, a year wiser, and decide our future. Nine months later, in the week that I was accepted for university, and on the day the Americans landed upon the moon, I received a postcard from the Grand Canyon. It was from Teri, and said that she was on her way to California with an Iranian Maoist. And would not be coming back to Europe.

A quarter of a century passed. And then, a few days before I was to leave once again for Paris, to go down memory lane in search of a book, the phone rang. And an American voice, as unchanged and full of life as ever, said, 'Hi! I'm coming back to Europe. I want to see Paris again.' She paused. 'Would you meet me outside my old hotel . . . ?'

And I knew that the fates had not finished with us.

I'M A STRANGER HERE MYSELF
by Deric Longden

In 1990, spurred on by the success of his writing and his marriage to the writer Aileen Armitage, Deric Longden made a momentous move to a foreign country. Huddersfield, in Yorkshire, with its distinctive manners and customs and its wealth of remarkable characters, would surely provide him with all the material he needed for his planned book, one of the great classics of travel literature. But two years later, when he sat down to write it, the major events of everyday life kept intruding: the demands of a houseful of cats, the problem of getting the cooker repaired, the memories evoked by sorting through old clothes in the wardrobe . . .

Still, *I'm a Stranger Here Myself* is a travel book of a kind, where the most hilarious adventures can happen between the kitchen and the bathroom, and where a morning's shopping can provide enough anecdotes to last a lifetime. Once again Deric Longden demonstrates his genius for taking the most ordinary materials of life and transforming them with his own special brand of gentle, inspired humour.

'Give this man a black cloud and he'll find its funny silver lining sooner than you can say bestseller . . . As hilarious and compassionate as its predecessors'
Good Housekeeping

0 552 14050 3

THE HOUSE OF BLUE LIGHTS
A Summer on the Gulf of Mexico
Joe Roberts

One hazy southern summer, *en route* to New Orleans, Joe
Roberts lodged at the House of Blue Lights, a ramshackle
beach house just off Highway 87, facing out to the Gulf of
Mexico and Galveston Island. Here he met Mary Alice, his
hostess, a former stripper who would recount how she once
danced for Elvis and who now kept open house for all the
neighbours, There was Sparling, who slept under the house
because Mary Alice had promised his estranged girlfriend
Ronnie Sue that she wouldn't take him in; Princess, fifteen
years old and pregnant; Lucky Paradise, the geriatric country
singer; and Miss Kinsolver, a frail ghostly woman who rarely
left her derelict trailer.

Once established at the House of Blue Lights, Joe Roberts
found it hard to leave, He became immersed in the
fascinating local history: the fearsome Karankawa Indians
whose homeland was at Galveston Bay and, more recently,
the ill-fated visit of Oscar Wilde, and the great storm of 1900
when 3,600 homes were destroyed and 6,000 people
drowned in one tempestuous night.

Joe Roberts captures with zest and honesty the voices and
stories and the lazy rhythms of life in this dreamiest of
American backwaters.

0 552 99579 7

BLACK SWAN

NOTES FROM A SMALL ISLAND
Bill Bryson

'NOT A BOOK THAT SHOULD BE READ IN PUBLIC, FOR FEAR OF EMITTING LOUD SNORTS'
The Times

After nearly two decades in Britain, Bill Bryson took the decision to move back to the States for a while, to let his kids experience life in another country, to give his wife the chance to shop until 10 p.m. seven nights a week, and, most of all, because he had read that 3.7 million Americans believed that they had been abducted by aliens at one time or another, and it was thus clear to him that his people needed him.

But before leaving his much-loved home in North Yorkshire, Bryson insisted on taking one last trip around Britain, a sort of valedictory tour of the green and kindly island that had so long been his home. His aim was to take stock of the nation's public face and private parts (as it were), and to analyse what precisely it was he loved so much about a country that had produced Marmite, a military hero whose dying wish was to be kissed by a fellow named Hardy, place names like Farleigh Wallop, Titsey and Shellow Bowells, people who said 'Mustn't grumble', and *Gardeners' Question Time*.

'SPLENDID . . . WHAT'S ENJOYABLE IS THAT THERE'S AS MUCH OF BRYSON IN HERE AS THERE IS OF BRITAIN'
Sunday Telegraph

'ALWAYS STRIKES A BALANCE BETWEEN ENTERTAINMENT AND INFORMATION . . . HIS BOOK IS SUFFUSED WITH THE SHEER JOY OF BEING ALIVE'
Sunday Express

0 552 99600 9

BLACK SWAN

A SELECTED LIST OF FINE WRITING
AVAILABLE FROM CORGI AND BLACK SWAN

99600 9	NOTES FROM A SMALL ISLAND	*Bill Bryson*	£6.99
99572 X	STRANGE ANGELS	*Andy Bull*	£5.99
99707 2	ONE ROOM IN A CASTLE	*Karen Connelly*	£5.99
99479 0	PERFUME FROM PROVENCE	*Lady Fortescue*	£6.99
99557 6	SUNSET HOUSE	*Lady Fortescue*	£6.99
99558 4	THERE'S ROSEMARY, THERE'S RUE	*Lady Fortescue*	£6.99
12833 3	THE HOUSE BY THE DVINA	*Eugenie Fraser*	£6.99
13937 8	THE FIRST FIFTY – MUNRO-BAGGING WITHOUT A BEARD	*Muriel Gray*	£8.99
14185 2	FINDING PEGGY: A GLASGOW CHILDHOOD	*Meg Henderson*	£5.99
99364 6	VIDEO NIGHT IN KATHMANDU	*Pico Iyer*	£6.99
99637 8	MISS McKIRDY'S DAUGHTERS WILL NOW DANCE THE HIGHLAND FLING	*Barbara Kinghorn*	£6.99
14181 X	IRONING JOHN	*James Leith*	£4.99
13944 0	DIANA'S STORY	*Deric Longden*	£3.99
13943 2	LOST FOR WORDS	*Deric Longden*	£4.99
13822 3	THE CAT WHO CAME IN FROM THE COLD	*Deric Longden*	£4.99
14050 3	I'M A STRANGER HERE MYSELF	*Deric Longden*	£4.99
13946 7	NICOLA	*Nicola Owen*	£4.99
14322 7	THE MAZE	*Lucy Rees*	£6.99
99579 7	THE HOUSE OF BLUE LIGHTS	*Joe Roberts*	£6.99
99658 0	THE BOTTLEBRUSH TREE	*Hugh Seymour-Davies*	£6.99
99601 7	JOGGING ROUND MAJORCA	*Gordon West*	£5.99
99666 1	BY BUS TO THE SAHARA	*Gordon West*	£5.99
99366 2	THE ELECTRIC KOOL AID ACID TEST	*Tom Wolfe*	£7.99